PERFORMANCE-BASED STUDENT ASSESSMENT: CHALLENGES AND POSSIBILITIES

PERFORMANCE-BASED STUDENT ASSESSMENT: CHALLENGES AND POSSIBILITIES

Ninety-fifth Yearbook of the
National Society for the Study of Education

PART I

Edited by

JOAN BOYKOFF BARON AND DENNIE PALMER WOLF

Editor for the Society

KENNETH J. REHAGE

Distributed by THE UNIVERSITY OF CHICAGO PRESS • CHICAGO, ILLINOIS

The National Society for the Study of Education

Founded in 1901 as successor to the National Herbart Society, the National Society for the Study of Education has provided a means by which the results of serious study of educational issues could become a basis for informed discussion of those issues. The Society's two-volume Yearbooks, now in their ninety-fifth year of publication, reflect the thoughtful attention given to a wide range of educational problems during those years. Each year the Society's publications contain contributions to the literature of education from scholars and practitioners who are doing significant work in their respective fields.

An elected Board of Directors reviews proposals for Yearbooks, selects the proposals that seem suitable for a Yearbook, and appoints an editor, or editors, to oversee the preparation of manuscripts for the projected volume.

The Society's publications are distributed each year without charge to members in the United States, Canada, and elsewhere throughout the world. The Society welcomes as members all individuals who desire to receive its publications. Information about current dues and a listing of its publications that are still in print may be found in the back pages of this volume.

This volume, *Performance-Based Student Assessment: Challenges and Possibilities*, is Part I of the Ninety-fifth Yearbook of the Society. Part II, published at the same time, is entitled *Technology and the Future of Schooling*.

Library of Congress Catalog Number: 95-071783
ISSN: 0077-5762

Published 1996 by
THE NATIONAL SOCIETY FOR THE STUDY OF EDUCATION

5835 Kimbark Avenue, Chicago, Illinois 60637
© 1996 by the National Society for the Study of Education

First Printing

Printed in the United States of America

v

Acknowledgments

As is the case with all Yearbooks of the National Society for the Study of Education, this volume is the product of the work of many authors, to each of whom the Society is greatly indebted. This volume, originally planned for publication in 1994, has been delayed by circumstances beyond our control. We are especially grateful to the authors who have kindly updated their chapters by making changes and additions needed because of the delay.

Performance-Based Student Assessment is a welcome addition to the growing literature on this topic. It is a balanced account of the current status of this development in the field of assessment. Commitment to the ideas that undergird the notion of performance-based assessment is clearly evident in each chapter. But that has not prevented the authors from acknowledging the major problems that must be confronted if this approach is to be widely accepted.

Joan Boykoff Baron and Dennie Palmer Wolf, the editors of this Yearbook, are responsible for the initial planning of the volume. Both have been deeply involved in work on performance-based assessment. Their wide knowledge of what is going on in the field enabled them to invite contributions not only from individuals who write about the topic but also from professionals at the national, state, and local levels who have themselves been involved in one way or another in the development of "authentic assessments." The Society is grateful to them for the wisdom reflected in the planning of this project and for their assistance in bringing it to completion.

Professor Margaret Early of the University of Florida has read every manuscript for this volume with great care, as she has done for all our recent Yearbooks. Her perceptive comments and her helpful suggestions have been of extraordinary assistance. We are most grateful to her.

Jenny Volpe, assistant in the NSSE office, has prepared the name index and has helped with the reading of proof.

KENNETH J. REHAGE
Editor for the Society

Editors' Preface

In the closing years of this century we are debating—and quite possibly recalibrating—our sense of public obligation. Everywhere, we are engaged in rethinking our most familiar systems for distributing wealth, access, and hope in American life: health care, welfare, affirmative action, and certainly public education. We have in front of us two dueling visions: Are we to become a fiercely American nation driven by an even franker free market enterprise where entry and belonging are a matter of elbowing your way in? Or, conversely, are we to be a culture where a basic safety net of services allows large numbers of diverse Americans opportunities to be healthy, to work, and to gain the education which will make them productive and wise citizens?

In order to win the necessary hearts and minds (as well as the votes, dollars, jobs, and programs that ensue), we translate these different visions into competing narratives. Nowhere is this clearer than in the sphere of public education. On the one hand, there is the story crystallized over a decade ago in *A Nation at Risk*. That narrative was—and remains—dire. American schools have lost their way. Despite a significant investment of dollars and effort, the schools no longer produce students who rank high in international competition. The only viable solution lies with the tools of free enterprise and increasingly local control. The proposal is that privatization in the form of charter schools and voucher systems will restore our educational vitality.

Facing off with this dire narrative is a second, and radically different, account. It argues that American education has always been distinguished by the struggle for common schools—free public education providing all children with intellectual and social mobility. This is a story that stretches as far back as Horace Mann and threads its way through the Warren court's decision in *Brown v. Board of Education*, the Elementary and Secondary Education Act, and current efforts to create high standards for American students. As a story, its point is that, as conditions change, we constantly have to reinvent what will keep schools and their effects common.

But for either of these narratives to carry the day, its adherents have to be able to translate their story into the daily mechanisms and the larger systems that will make their vision of public education a functioning reality. Significantly, in both the dire and the hopeful accounts of American public education, diversified forms of student assessment, coupled with high public standards, have been nominated as a major force. No matter who is telling the narrative, there is an urgent demand to create assessments which will inform us about what American students "know and are able to do" in contexts that are far more demanding and authentic than the long-dominant, curriculum-independent multiple-choice tests that have been the staple assessment practices in this country since World War I. For those who fear American schools are broken and desperate places, more demanding assessments hold out the promise of establishing tough metrics and consequences for individuals, schools, and quite possibly teachers and administrators. Contrastingly, for those who hope to keep alive the promise of common schools, new forms of student assessment could be treated as public announcements of higher expectations. In the wake of that announcement, it would be possible to raise fundamental questions about who has the opportunity to learn to those standards.

Given this prominent role as a tool for change, the field of student assessment has become the focus of much heat and light. Districts, states, and even national systems are suddenly experimenting with open-ended performance tasks and portfolio-based assessments. But unlike nations such as Great Britain or Holland, with long established traditions of open-ended exams scored by multiple judges, this move to performance-based assessment challenges everything from our operating definitions of "knowing" to the technical measurement issues that open-ended tasks involving human judges raise. In many respects, this volume is a record of what is now a decade-long, but far from settled, exploration.

The first section of the volume highlights the fundamentals on which any lasting change in student assessment will have to rest. To begin, Wolf and Reardon argue that any such system demands a radical change in the epistemology that informs much of classroom teaching. Specifically, they argue for practices founded on the belief that it is possible to learn how to learn and on a developmental view of achievement in which support and effort make high achievement widely possible. Gordon and Bonilla-Bowman extend this discussion of learning by describing how American classrooms must exchange a divisive focus on difference for a more productive discussion of human diversity which, in turn, must be reflected both in classroom practices as well as in larger public systems of assessment. To this discussion of learning, Darling-Hammond and Ancess add the importance of regarding both adult practitioners and educational organizations like schools as learners. Without building the capacity of both educators and their organizations, no substantial change in assessment systems can occur. The closing chapters in this section both point out that such local efforts to rethink learning require significant protection. In a realistic vein, Linn and Baker point out that no reconceptualization of learning and its assessment can go forward without a simultaneous effort to develop measurement techniques which are consonant with varied and extended performances at the same time that they are technically responsible and interpretable by a wide public. Finally, Smith and Levin describe how mechanisms like national content standards can provide the coherent framework which can help to align teaching, student assessment, and professional training for teachers. The recurring point is that without such basic shifts, changes in student assessment systems are likely to be cosmetic and vulnerable.

Unlike a decade ago, we are no longer confined to arguing about what new systems of student assessment ought to or might be. We have acquired a history that could inform future efforts—if we are careful to capture its lessons. This is precisely the point of the second section of this volume. To begin, in their history of districtwide writing portfolio programs in Pittsburgh, LeMahieu and Eresh make a strong case that successful implementation requires creating a community of judgment. Such communities require sustained development, the discussion of opportunity to learn, and time for the qualitative appraisal of student work. Moving to the state level, the next chapters all carry a common lesson about the necessity of change efforts building on one another. Honig and Alexander report on California's pioneering efforts to design a student assessment system incorporating performance tasks and portfolios. They record how the California system taught those that followed about the enormous importance of rethinking curriculum and teacher education. At the same time, the chapter uses the California experience with ensuing conflicts over the content and conduct of assessments to argue for the absolute necessity of continuously building public understanding and endorsement of changes in student assessment. Baron uses a series of examples drawn from the experience of the Connecticut State Department of Education to demonstrate that developing thoughtful models of new assessments initially is facilitated by a low-stakes environment supportive of innovation, away and apart from the immediate demands of the political arena and the full weight of technical responsibilities. In that context, it becomes possible gradually to move to higher-stakes settings without sacrificing the validity of new assessments. Echoing this theme, Mills writes from the perspective of a commissioner of education who oversaw not only the initiation but also the technical struggles of the portfolio program in Vermont. That case demonstrates the considerable importance of creating an educational and political setting in which stakeholders come to understand that creating innovative, fair, and technically respectable systems of student assessment is no different from students' work—to achieve quality it must go through a number of drafts. Finally, Gong and Reidy use the recent experiences in Kentucky to warn us that while the technical quality of new assessments must be strong, we cannot afford to let those concerns bury our commitment to using assessments to broadcast new visions of student learning. With equal force, they emphasize the necessity of building a public discourse about assessment reform that can enroll a wide spectrum of educators and families.

In the third section of the volume, authors address the question of whether new forms of student assessment are feasible at a national level. In their introductory chapter, Romer and Fitzgerald underscore that at the level of national politics—among governors and legislators—there is a broad-based national consensus on the importance of such an effort. Each of the following chapters describes actual attempts to move in this direction. Describing the most recent efforts of the New Standards project, Daro argues that our best hope lies in creating a voluntary, rather than a compulsory, system based on portfolios of student work which will respect local specificity at the same time that it employs commonly held national standards. Using the recent history of the College Board, Stewart and Johanek demonstrate how that nationwide system of examinations has gradually shifted from a program designed to measure students' aptitudes using the technology of multiple-choice testing to a program for reporting on student achievement that uses increasingly diversified approaches to assessment. In addition, the authors use the Board's new programs (EQUITY 2000 and Pacesetter) to point out the necessity of insuring equal access to learning as a necessary concomitant to any more demanding system of assessment. In closing, Haertel and Mullis use the history of the National Assessment of Educational Progress (NAEP) to make several important points. First, they remind us that even at the national level we have a twenty-year history of incremental change on which to build. At the same time, they point out that at the national level innovative assessments may not provide the fairest or stablest measures of student learning, since if large numbers of students are not familiar with new forms of assessment, only a few will have the experience to perform well.

Looking across the full sweep of chapters, the challenges of sustained development and systemic design are everywhere. Clearly, we can never meet the intellectual, technical and political challenges carried by diversifying student assessment unless we have the time, the resources, and the civic permission to draft our way toward an increasingly fair and productive approach. In addition, the changes cannot fall with their entire weight on the shoulders of any single level of education. Certainly any assessment system has obligations to be valid, fair, and reliable. But, in addition, we ought to think about the particular contributions each level of assessment is best suited to make.

Perhaps it is up to low-stakes classroom and local efforts to provide the most innovative and instructionally relevant models of student assessments. At the state level, where large and diverse constituencies are involved, the pressing issue becomes one of constructing widespread public endorsement of new forms of assessment that gracefully cross political lines. The challenge of state-level assessment systems is to attend both to accountability and instructional improvement. Such systems must strive to shield and motivate local experiment while creating assessment systems that encourage and assure widespread access to challenging curriculum and diversified forms of learning and help to build the necessary capacities of teachers and administrators. Finally, states must be continually vigilant in working toward establishing coherence among the various state-level initiatives so that a clear and common message is sent and heard. At the national level, whether through NAEP, New Standards, or the College Board, the challenge of assessment designers is to create efficient forms of assessment that nevertheless also serve as catalysts for the development of best practice. This challenge is intensified as the stakes increase. If tests are going to serve as gate-keepers, it is particularly important that they are created with commitments to access, capacity, and coherence in mind and that they stimulate rather than stifle experimentation at the local and state levels. In closing, we must keep in mind that none of these levels exists in a vacuum. Changes in national assessments perturb state assessments, which in turn influence local assessments. Designing new assessment systems that meet the demands currently being placed upon them will require new levels of collaboration and cooperation.

JOAN BOYKOFF BARON
DENNIE PALMER WOLF
February, 1996

Table of Contents

TABLE OF CONTENTS

Section Three
Possibilities at the National Level

Section One
TOWARD ACCESS, CAPACITY, PSYCHOMETRIC SOUNDNESS, AND COHERENCE

CHAPTER I

Access to Excellence Through New Forms of Student Assessment

DENNIE PALMER WOLF AND SEAN F. REARDON

Introduction: A Dream of Common Schools

From the time that Horace Mann fought for common schools in Massachusetts towns, American education has been organized and motivated by a vision of *public* education.[1] Early on, the definition of "common" was straightforward enough: it simply meant publicly funded education for free male students. With passage of the Fourteenth Amendment, that comfortable meaning of common was substantially revised to mean public dollars for the grammar school education of all children, both free and freed alike. A long and segregated century later, Thurgood Marshall reshaped the meaning of common for a second time. Arguing before the Warren Court in *Brown vs. Board of Education*, Marshall denied the logic of "separate, but equal," proposing instead that equality meant access to a common community of peers, adults, and experiences, not merely the raw provision of buildings, desks, books, and teachers. However, exactly as Marshall taught that we had outlived the selfishness of *Plessy vs. Ferguson*, we are learning that we have reached the limits of what Marshall himself could ask for, and what the Court could enforce as common. The strictures of shared

Dennie Palmer Wolf is a Senior Research Associate at the Harvard Graduate School of Education, where she is the Director of Performance Assessment Collaboratives for Education (PACE), a national school reform project for urban middle schools. Sean Reardon is a doctoral candidate at the Harvard Graduate School of Education.

1

facilities and equal spending, while important, have proved insufficient. Poor and minority children still lag behind their peers in the mastery of just those skills—writing, problem solving, drawing inferences from texts—that are the passport out of the ruthless bottom half of an increasingly bimodally distributed economy.[2] For just one example, between 1990 and 1992 the gap in mathematics performance widened between Hispanic and white students in grade 8, and between black and white students in grades 4 and 8.[3] Unless we want a nation divided against itself, then the shared and matched facilities of common schools have to give way to universal access to the course offerings, standards, and forms of assessment that have long remained the private preserve and restricted cultural capital of economic and intellectual elites.[4] Even more radically and urgently, common schools must come to mean common accomplishments: equivalent forms of readiness for thinking, working, and participation after the compulsory limits of high school.

This renewed definition of "common" already threads through the public rhetoric of education reform. It was called for in President Bush's "America 2000," the report of the National Council on Education Standards and Testing to Congress in 1992,[5] and the Clinton administration's *Goals 2000: Educate America*. The Senate Committee on Labor and Human Resources, in its report on *Goals 2000*, boldly stated that "America's economic future increasingly depends on the education and training of its workforce. . . . Building a world class workforce starts first with building a world class education system."[6] The ensuing legislation was even plainer; it said that "the Congress finds that all students can learn to high standards and must realize their potential if the United States is to prosper."[7]

In response, we have formulated a very particular wager for reinventing common schools. First, we have placed our faith in specific technologies including world-class standards, challenging performance assessments, public reporting, and a new and/or different system of rewards and sanctions for schools and/or students. Second, we assume that once in place, these strategies will drive both higher general levels of student achievement and increasingly equitable access to worthwhile educational activities like writing, problem solving, and scientific experimentation, eventually closing off the gap that currently separates the performances of high- and low-status students. Finally, we are betting that we can insulate these efforts from the ravages of political and educational debate long enough to produce results and to master the technical difficulties such as the measurement issues raised by performance assessments. (See chapters 4 and 10, this volume.)

In this chapter, we question this wager as it is currently formulated. In essence, we have rushed to leverage change via standards and student assessments by largely ignoring questions of classroom practices or community understanding. There are reasons why we have seen the harsh overturning of a number of bold and generous attempts to rethink teaching, learning, and assessment in California, Colorado, and Kentucky. The changes required in the claim "all children can learn to high standards" are wholesale. If we want this level of change, not just passing tinkering, we will have to think systemically, harnessing every conceivable level and endeavor into a coherent system that carries the same message in all its parts. Here we argue that classroom-level realizations of work up to high standards by all students are an indispensable component of any coherent system of concerted school change. If the relative stasis of school reform over the past twenty years has a lesson, it is about the error of privileging policy over practice and concentrating on reorganizations at the cost of rethinking teaching and learning. There can be no changed vision of common schools until we learn three critical lessons and how to return the implications of those lessons to classrooms and schools. First, we have to confront our own history and the habits it has encouraged, among them the long-running habit of pitting equity against excellence, and the almost reflexive definition of intelligence as fixed and tied to such unchangeable factors as race, class, and gender. Second, we have to learn how to share what has long been hoarded: the small and constant details of achievement—demanding assignments, provocative questions, thoughtful responses, stiff demands, and high expectations. Third, we have to rethink student assessment in ways that reach far beyond exchanging multiple-choice items for performance tasks or portfolios. We have much to construct, long prior to high-stakes accountability measures. At the most basic level we have to create embedded tasks that grow directly out of what has been taught and which consequently carry crystal clear signals that effort can make a difference. And, using data from those tasks, we have to enable teachers to develop common languages for describing difficulties and strengths in work drawn from the full diversity of their classrooms: students who are gifted, troubled, migrant, limited in English proficiency, mainstreamed, and average.

In her novel, *Their Eyes Were Watching God*, Zora Neale Hurston reflects on phrases we come to use all too easily. She remarks on how the people in the small town of Eatonville come to speak of their mayor and her husband, Joe Sparks:

There was no doubt that the town respected him and even admired him in a way. But any man who walks in the way of power and property is bound to meet hate. So when speakers stood up when the occasion demanded and said "Our beloved Mayor," it was one of those statements that everybody says but nobody actually believes, like "God is everywhere." It was just a handle to wind up the tongue with.[8]

Declaring that "all students can learn to high standards" could mark another and an important evolution in the meaning of common schools. However, the work of realizing that promise will be much harder— particularly if we mean to push past broad policy decisions to daily practices and if we mean for those practices to reach deep into schools that rarely register reforms. But unless we make those choices, we will have, as Hurston puts it, only "a handle to wind up the tongue with."

Reworking a Troubled Legacy: Equity and Excellence as Alternatives on the National Educational Agenda

Our habit of pitting equity against excellence and our persistent belief that intellect is fixed and ineducable are two nearly intransigent features of American education that have recurrently endangered our ability to revitalize the vision of common schools. As far back as 1910, when public high schools were first opening, Charles Eliot, then president of Harvard, rejected the notion that those schools should be separated into academic and vocational tracks:

Thoughtful students of psychology of adolescence will refuse to believe that the American public school intends to have its children sorted before their teens into clerks, watchmakers, lithographers, telegraph operators, masons, teamsters, farm laborers, and so forth, and treated differently in their schools according to those prophecies of their appropriate careers. Who will make these prophecies?[9]

But throughout the next decade as high schools became overcrowded, large numbers of untrained teachers were hired to fill the ranks, the selfish views of social Darwinism took hold, and industry pressed for workers, rather than students. By 1918, the notion of a common intellectual footing for all students lost its hold. The National Education Association drafted the *Cardinal Principles of Secondary Education*. That document argued that all the majority of young adults needed was instruction in health, citizenship, worthy use of leisure, and a mastery of basic processes (e.g., literacy and arithmetic skills). Yes, there would be the equity of a guaranteed high school education; however, for all but a few college-bound students, the business of schools was training, not thinking.

It has proven difficult to shake this initial opposition between equity and excellence. Even in the period beginning with the *Brown* decision and ending in the early 1970s, when there was a tremendous push toward expanding civil rights, we allowed our concern to focus largely on improving the simplest kind of access to educational institutions for minorities and the poor.[10] Characteristically, equity cases centered largely on issues of equal access or the even distribution of easily quantifiable inputs: racial balance in schools, matched facilities, equivalent levels of teacher preparation, and equal funding. Unfortunately, where we turned our attention to teaching and learning, we developed educational programs that stressed repairing "cultural deprivation" rather than securing "access to knowledge."[11]

In the 1970s and 1980s we reformulated the perceived tug of war between equity and quality once again and dramatically. *A Nation at Risk* (1983) offered a dire account of the decay of public education where the obligation to excellence had been lost.[12] It promised shrinking numbers of skilled workers, a growing population of undereducated young adults, and a shameful loss of world status. Thus, even the most recent calls for excellence were built on the premise of the failure of public education. In particular, the implication was that we had paid too much attention to equalizing opportunity—a choice that had sentenced us to lowest common denominator achievement. This formulation remains alive and well. Many advocates of national standards argue that the surest form of equity is to set public standards for excellence. The argument is that there is no need to set standards that lay out what schools must do to provide students with adequate opportunities to learn. Standards about that kind of obligation only thrust a stick into the accelerating wheel of excellence.[13]

Where does this opposition between equity and excellence get its tenacity? Underlying any educational system is a set of beliefs about intelligence. Largely from the theory of intelligence, and its associated testing, we have inherited quite a problematic, even a destructive, view of the nature and distribution of intelligence among individuals and groups. In this view, (1) intelligence is a single unidimensional entity; (2) it is utterly fixed—effort and education make no lasting difference; and (3) since individuals and groups can effectively be ranked and sorted along this single dimension, it provides a basis for deciding who deserves what quality of education. Thus, today as much as a century ago, American education is conducted in the terms that Lewis Terman laid out at the beginning of this century:

Preliminary investigations indicate that an I.Q. below 70 rarely permits anything better than unskilled labor; that the range of 70-80 is preeminently that of semiskilled labor; from 80-100 that of the skilled or ordinary clerical labor; from 100-110 or 115 that of the semiprofessional pursuits; and that above all these are the grades of intelligence which permit one to enter the professions or the large fields of business. Intelligence tests can tell us whether a child's native brightness corresponds more nearly to the median (or one or another of these classes). This information will be of great value in planning the education of a particular child and also in planning the differentiated curriculum.[14]

This view has led to a fundamental confusion of ability and achievement that has made for a long-running circularity in arguments about intellect: essentially social groups with less access to school-based knowledge have been viewed as intellectually deficient and thus undeserving of demanding educational opportunity.[15] Even though subject to diverse research critiques[16] and counter-demonstrations (e.g., Headstart programs in the United States and Asian examples of an effort-based conception of education)[17] the belief is dogged. It reappears with particular virulence when definitions of worth shift. For example, Herrnstein and Murray's *The Bell Curve*, which argues that race explains differential intelligence in Caucasian and minority populations, appeared just as employment opportunities were shifting away from large numbers of industrial workers to much smaller cadres of highly skilled information workers. Thus, this history is anything but ancient. It lives on in reading groups, the contrast between general math and Algebra 1, the tests and cut scores we use to decide who is gifted, the choice about whose paper gets comments and whose is simply corrected, the borrowed and xeroxed materials in many second language classrooms.

Given this long-running and powerful history, standards and assessments are not fulcrum enough for serious school reform. They have to be a part of a coherent system suffused by the conviction that high achievement is widely attainable. To illustrate just how far-reaching this work has to be, we will look at observations emerging from Project PACE (Performance Assessment Collaboratives for Education), a network of urban middle schools. PACE began as a project designed to investigate the feasibility and effects of performance assessment for at-risk urban students. However, early in the project two things became stunningly clear. First, unless there were significant opportunities to learn important ideas and strategies, performance assessment was, at best, beside the point. Second, simply waiting for the trickle-down effects of higher standards and new assessments would guarantee at least another generation of urban students without access to understanding. Consequently, the project added an intensive program of curriculum development aimed at creating demanding and engaging courses of study that did not sacrifice fundamental skills. At the same time, teachers, administrators, and researchers built a deliberately lateral set of professional exchanges in which they acted as one another's critical friends working to provide all students with significant opportunities to learn. The final result is a national network of urban middle schools where large numbers of adults (teachers, principals, counselors) are engaged in figuring out how students can forge identities as learners[18] and build a history of serious academic success. Though sites certainly vary in the emphasis and extent of their programs, their work carries common messages for designing new forms of student assessment. First, long before there can be valid and fair student assessments, we have to create curriculum and teaching which (1) replace belief in fixed intelligence with a developmental and evolving view of achievement, and (2) make the process of thinking public and therefore attainable. Second, prior to expecting that new forms of student assessment will be reliable we have to (1) open up the discussion of what makes work good; (2) make it possible for teachers to develop common languages for describing the strengths and difficulties they discern in diverse student work; and (3) embed assessment in the curriculum so that it makes sense for students to expend ongoing effort and to show what they understand. These changes are not just liberal niceties. On the one hand, they significantly affect whether teachers and students decide to invest in their work. On the other hand, only if they are in place will a robust system of public accounting built on performance ever become a reality.

From Fixed Intelligence to Developing Achievement

Most assessments of student performance are organized to look at how a range of fourth (or eighth or tenth graders) perform relative to one another and to other fourth graders in the nation or world. We pay virtually no attention to investigating how that individual (or group) has changed over time. Interestingly, the introduction of content and performance standards have done little, if anything, to affect our indifference to development. While any number of disciplinary organizations and states have described what fourth graders "must know and be able to do," there is very little thinking about how a kindergartner becomes that much desired nine-year-old. We have never learned what Ralph Tyler tried to teach us: to know how well fourth graders have learned we need to know what those students knew as third graders, what they can do as fourth graders, and how much of that learning lasts into fifth grade.[19]

In PACE schools, an interest in development, or change over time, prevails. This apparently simple difference turns out to give much of teaching and learning quite a different cast. At the level of individual assignments, students are not hostage to the past, they often continue to revise a piece throughout the semester or year, as their understanding of a topic or process changes. In one language arts classroom, for example, students begin a problem-solving essay early in the fall and revise it at least four times within the academic year, as their command of essay form, their repertoire of models, and their skills as human problem solvers grow. Elsewhere, in a science class, all students must turn in at least three pieces of high-standard work (e.g., above a level 4 on a 6-point rubric) each semester. To do so they revise, consult with peers, stay after school with the teacher and look at models from earlier years until they attain that level of performance. At still a third school, entering sixth grade students receive a list of what their final eighth grade portfolio must contain, and throughout their career at school they steadily replace pieces as they have more substantial samples demonstrating their mastery of mathematics, social studies, or research, etc.

There are equally large ramifications for how teachers think about and conduct their work. In this developmental frame, any given year's curriculum has to become "a steadily rising escalator" as one teacher put it.[20] In place of a series of changing subjects, we see two other quite distinctive approaches to sequencing learning. In the first approach, a teacher engages students in a deliberately linked sequence of experiences which eventually add up to a larger whole. For instance, working in the area of language arts, one teacher wanted her students to become skilled nonfiction writers capable of engaging in the lively type of essay writing often known as "immersion journalism."[21] Such writing demands the use of multiple sources, interviewing, observational skills, and perhaps most challenging of all for a young writer, the ability to select and sequence information so as to make a point. Knowing that she was setting a difficult task, one teacher created a carefully sequenced set of experiences:

You can't just say, "Write me an interesting essay." They just look at you. So you have to build a scaffolding of the kind that lets them work gradually on different parts of a building. Say I want them to be able to take a perspective and make a point, then way long ahead of time, we read folktales that have a moral. We read fairy tales and then re-write them from the perspective of a different character. We look at pieces that other people have written and pick out all the ways in which they use language to get their point across. If I want them to be able to use their interviews, then we have to look at dialogue in fiction and ask good questions. Then, when they finally go to write the piece, they have all the tools they need. You can say, "It needs a stronger point of view," and they know what you mean.[22]

In the best of these settings, students, long used to memorizing for the test and then forgetting, can begin to think of themselves as having a learning history in which they accrue information. This is evident when this student reflects on how he will adapt his earlier acquired interviewing skills to the new task of writing a folktale:

Earlier, Mr. Jenkins taught us how to interview people so they would tell you not just "yes" and "no," but about their lives. Now, we are going to interview somebody and make a folktale about them. I wanted to interview someone who plays baseball. I wanted some questions that would get me one word answers, because that's going to give me lots of room to exaggerate. I don't want to know too much with a folktale. See, so if I ask "What kind of a pitch did he throw you?" and the guy says, "A double," that is the beginning and the end of it. Then I can write: "The pitcher was the oldest and the toughest in any league, any time, anywhere. He threw the batter a 300 mile an hour curve, and when it connected, the ball went from Delaware clear to the West Coast." But if it was a biography that would be different. There you need something truthful, but good. So there, when you already knew it was a double, you don't ask that. You maybe ask, "So I hear that the ball he threw you was a curve, a double. Tell me what happened." And then the guy will say, "Well, the pitcher, Nolan Ryan, threw a very rounded curveball, which I hit off the wall for a double and ran my quickest into first base and on into second by sliding. My toe just made it before the umpire called out 'Safe'." And that would be it.[23]

In a second approach, teachers have designed their courses, not as a serial ordering of topics (e.g., heat, light, friction, etc. or short story, novel, poem), but as an ordered sequence of increasingly demanding opportunities to accomplish a task that is key to a particular field of study (e.g., writing an essay, piecing together historical evidence, or conducting an experiment). For instance, one science teacher has created a series of carefully constructed consumer product testing laboratories

to introduce sixth graders to scientific experimentation including forming questions, designing measures, collecting data, and drawing conclusions. Each lab builds carefully on the ones before, adding concepts
(e.g., mass, density, mean, median), loosening the structure of the data
set, and asking wider-ranging questions. Every student keeps a lab
notebook that functions as a combination data bank and a scientific
autobiography. As they fill these pages, students develop a sense of
their own growth. For instance, in a lab where students were investigating which brand of Easter candy was the best value, students established a range of dimensions of value: amount of chocolate per piece;
lowest fat per piece; density; lowest cost per piece. When asked how
they would decide on "best," if no single brand or type was tops in all
the categories, a small group of students quickly explained:

Oh, that's easy. See, back here (turning in their notebooks to an earlier lab) we
already had that problem with the chocolate chip cookies. We wanted to know
which brand was the best, so we had all these different factors like number of
chips per cookie, area of the cookie, stuff like that. But there was no one win-
ner. So we gave points to the most and least important features, like number of
chips was worth more than area. Then we added them up to give a total score.
This problem is a lot the same, so we will probably use a strategy like that.[24]

As a part of teaching this way, and of participating in a network
with other professionals, teachers also build their expectations of
themselves. Nowhere is this clearer than when they expend this same
kind of developmental thought on their own work, reflecting on the
alterations in their curriculum and teaching from year to year. A sixth
grade teacher comments:

I gave a social studies assignment last year that I was very proud of. It came at
the beginning of the year right when I wanted them to be thinking about what
a culture is. We discussed the features that all cultures had: religion, art, ways
of surviving like food and shelter, etc. Based on that list I asked my students to
invent a culture. I thought I was asking them to be creative and to apply their
knowledge—I mean, I gave myself lots of points in the "higher order" column. But students treated it exactly as I had laid it out—as pure fantasy. I got
hunters with swimming pools. There was no way it was an exploration of the
workings of an ancient culture in a specific time and place. This year, I did it
again, but very differently. This time I gave them each a specific geography,
along with its climate and natural resources. They had to think through what
kind of life such a place would support and what technologies a people living
in that region might have invented or come in contact with. So they had to
research neighboring regions. Then, and only then, on the basis of all that

they knew, could they invent the culture, but every step of the way it had to be based on what they had learned. When I listened to students working, I was pleased. At first they didn't understand. If their region was where modern Spain is, they would write that their country had this much rain because Spain has this much rain. But I kept telling them, no, the point was to build on the information, to figure out what early life in that region might have been like. One kid finally understood and he gasped, "Oh you mean use it, not just *be* it."[25]

The central point is that students and teachers both benefit from a developmental frame for their work. The structure of a steadily more demanding curriculum allows a wider range of students to move forward. Mastery is actually taught, not merely called for. Similarly, once a working group of teachers agrees to look at annual revisions of their earlier work, they have the opportunity to reflect on adult learning and the institutional factors that support or impede such learning. That discussion drives home, at a personal and professional level, the fundamental difference between raw aptitude and hard-earned achievement.

Performances of Thought and Attainable Excellence

If understanding is to develop in all rather than a few students, then everyone in a classroom must have equal and abundant opportunity to learn.[26] This is easy to simulate: purchase mathematics manipulatives, assign a problem of the week, and institute mathematics portfolios. But it is a considerably longer and harder process to teach a heterogeneous group of seventh graders to be accurate and avid problem solvers.[27] There are two major challenges. The first is making thinking visible. The second is making excellence attainable.

If we are genuinely interested in equalizing achievement, then even the kinds of developmental opportunities just described only make learning a *possibility*, not an *actuality*. Learning requires seeing that the latch trips and a door flies open. Many of the students who do well in school have someone who sees that this happens—a parent, grandparent, or older sibling who actively mediates a student's learning. It is not enough for this person to ask whether the student has homework, whether it is done, and if it has been checked. They have to be able to explain the point of an assignment, proofread and comment, suggest resources, reword the task, offer entry points, and explain why it matters.[28] That person is all the more powerful if he or she has access to the way academic learning works, to knowledge of the subject matters, and to a keen sense for what passes in school as compared to home culture.[29] To acknowledge the power of this kind of mediation is to point out the danger of defining a high-standards curriculum simply as the *presence* of certain books, activities, and assignments. Those are opportunities on display, not for use. They will not be used unless someone x-rays or unpacks them for students, especially in urban classrooms where growing numbers of students raise themselves or come from families whose own histories have not provided the luxury of schooling.

Consider what this effort looks like in a seventh grade social studies class, where a teacher is working with students who have been trained simply to answer questions at the end of the chapter by flipping to the relevant paragraph and copying. Instead, she wants them to be able to explain what it is "to have a theory" and "support it with evidence." She puts two visual images up on the overhead projector, one of a hunting scene from a cave painting, the other taken from an early Egyptian mural. She asks her students to think about what might have changed as early tribal cultures became settled civilizations, telling them to prove their ideas using only what they see. The leap is big, perhaps too hard. So she helps them, asking questions and thinking along with them. First, she asks them to notice everything they can about the images. As they call out their observations, she helps them build an organized list of what they see, with like items clustered together. Next, she asks what is similar and different in the two images, still insisting that students provide evidence for any claim they make:

Hunters and Farmers

Same	Different
Both used tools	One hunting, one planting
Both had animals	One has more people
Both used sharp tools/instruments	Many different tools
Both not wealthy	Animals for food and work
Both use water	Using water to plant
Animal food	Meat and vegetables
All men	
Both providing food for themselves	

Based on this discussion, the teacher pushes students to forge some inferences about the major differences between cultures organized around hunting and gathering and cultures that settled down. As students reach for these broad generalizations, their teacher diagrams their logical relationship:[30]

stay in one place   land/water/seeds

Settled Civilizations

build structures   plant for food

These efforts to perform thought aloud have an important complement in teachers' efforts to make achievement attainable. Nowhere is this as clear as when teachers offer their students a look at the anatomy of good work. Interestingly, no matter what the subject or grade, many of these portraits break faith with simple unidimensional accounts of excellence. Typically, these classroom discussions focus on the multidimensional nature of any serious performance. This is evident in the way another seventh grade social studies teacher discusses the culminating assignment in a study of Mayan civilization: a myth about the collapse of Palenque that might have been handed down from generation to generation.[31] Central to this discussion is a brainstorming session in which students and teacher generate the dimensions along which the myths, the illustrations, and students' use of peer editing will be evaluated. This is what they decide on for the text of the myth:

Excerpt from Mayan Myth Evaluation

Myth - 11 points each   •
___ Describes why Mayan center collapsed
___ Gives clues to how an archaeologist would figure out what
     happened to the Mayans
___ Has 3-5 significant events from Mayan brainstorm list (i.e.,
     class-generated features of Mayan culture)
___ Has 3-5 show, not tell, sensory detail words
___ Has 3 similes or metaphors
___ Has a beginning, middle, and end
___ Correct usage of grammar and sentence structure
___ Thoughtful care put into the story

While some might argue that such detail is prescriptive, teachers working in this way reply that such frank detail is an act of equity:

It publishes what counts rather than leaving a kid's performance vulnerable to whose family has been through high school, or can be at home in the evening, or who has been read to, or who has consistently had teachers with high expectations.[32]

Moreover, teachers argue that this dimensional approach has significant effects on student work, changing the quality of first drafts, the purposefulness of revisions, and ultimately the quality of finished work of which the following excerpt is an example.

The Collapse of Palenque (excerpt)

Once there was a radiant and opulent city named Palenque that was built between a great river and massive mountains. It is like looking from a cloud onto earth because from the dazzling city you can see a delta region and an immense lowland plain. Plantations of cacao grow in the delta. The beans make chocolate, the most prized crop of the ancient Maya. The chocolate is so smooth, sweet, and irresistible.

Beyond Having Standards: Owning and Negotiating Quality

Just the presence of standards in classrooms is not transformative—particularly if those standards are externally mandated. It is all too easy for students and teachers to make the same treaty they do in dealing with algorithms, complex scientific processes, or time sequences in world history: "Memorize it for now."[33] The early work in PACE sites was no exception. Subject matter standards, exhibitions, and portfolios were all subject to misconceptions and rote applications. In several sites, students were asked to form year-end, cross-disciplinary portfolios containing evidence of such broad-based capacities as creativity, collaboration, and problem solving. In virtually every portfolio creativity was represented by a poem and problem solving by a mathematics test. When asked, students explained that creativity was when you express your feelings, which could be in a poem, or perhaps a story or drawing. For problem solving, only mathematics was appropriate since that was the only class where teachers assigned problems. Or when asked to write a letter of introduction to their portfolio, students simply strung together sentences using key words from the content standards posted in their classrooms:

Dear Reader—Welcome to my reading portfolio. You will find many things in it. My reading log shows that I have read over thirty books this year. The other pieces show you that I read actively like when I read a mystery all in one day. My vocabulary and spelling tests show that I can communicate my understandings to others. . . .[34]

If the standards or new forms of assessment, like portfolios, are to be tools for redistributing opportunities to learn, then they can't have that inert, imposed quality. They have to be entered, used, and translated into students' own language. For example, in response to the new mathematics standards one teacher began assigning her class weekly "math stumpers."[35] These assignments required that students not only get the answer, but that they be able to prove it. Initially, her students had little ability to explain and defend their approaches. No amount of rattling off the standards or scoring responses as 1s or 2s made any difference. In class, the teacher asked students to generate a scoring system describing weak, average, and strong proofs. An early draft of that scoring system read:

> 0 - No attempt
> 1 - Wrong, no proof, little effort
> 2 - Right answer, no proof
> 3 - Right, but proof needs more
> 4 - Right and good

The draft made it clear that students owned only two relatively unhelpful dimensions (right vs. wrong, and less proof vs. more proof) when, in fact, the set of proofs ranged widely in their quality on a number of other criteria such as clarity, precise use of mathematical language, and strong use of analogies. Consequently, several days later, the teacher selected additional examples and projected them, saying she didn't think that "right and good" made it at all clear *exactly* what made a proof effective. She issued them the challenge of proving what a good proof was. Over time, students compiled the following list of features and examples to back them up:

> Underline the important words (first, next, then; add, divide)
> Restating important facts of problem
> Use number words that order
> Use words that say what to do (add, divide, etc.)
> Use words that are exact: places, time
> Every step needs to be explained
> Keep track of the chain of events
> Give examples
> Tell strategy used
> Answer has to fit the problem

As the semester progressed, the teacher issued a second challenge: turn the list into a rubric that could be used to score or judge the quality of anyone's mathematics proof. In answer, students edited out redundancies, selected the most important items, and found mathematical language for their thoughts, turning out this to-the-point rubric:

Sequencing of thoughts and processes
Use of math vocabulary
Use of math examples
Use of various tools
Strategies cited
Corrections when necessary
Accurate conclusions

Only at this juncture did the rubric become the agreed-upon way of assessing subsequent proofs, for guiding the revision of unsuccessful attempts, and for choosing examples of strong proofs to include in their mathematics portfolios.

Standards must also function as a constant reminder to negotiate, not just announce, what counts as quality to students.[36] One of the most important and recurrent discussions in PACE classrooms centers around the struggle to open up the difference between correct and courageous or distinctive work. In a sixth grade science class, students were to figure out how to make Easter egg dye the most intense.[37] One student's notebook contained a carefully detailed description of mixing the dyes, which ignored a number of key decisions such as how to control the variables at work in the experiment:

Procedure:
1. Empty dye from package
2. Separate the packages
3. Tear open red package and pour into cup.
4. Add 15 ml water to cup
5. Add 15 ml of vinegar to cup to get a 1:1 ratio
6. Use q-tip to stir the solution.
7. Remove 1 egg from carton.
8. Use q-tip to paint the entire egg with the dye.
10. Tear open blue dye
11. Add 15 ml of water to a different cup.

(This continued iteratively until she had described the process for four containers.)

Circulating through the room, the teacher paused to scan these elaborate directions. She noticed that this painstaking detail may have kept the student from thinking through exactly those parts of her procedure that will permit her to get viable results (e.g., controlling the variables). She spoke to the student, trying to tease apart the difference between careful measuring and mixing and powerful science:

T: It is important to be careful here. But not so careful that all you are doing is the housekeeping. You can write it once and then say repeat it three times. What I really want to know is what your idea is about what will make the colors brightest and how are you going to show that so people will believe it?

S: Because they'll see it's done very carefully. It's all exact.

T: Exact is part of it. But what if yellow is just always a pale color? How can I compare that to this bright turquoise blue here?

As teachers begin assigning and responding to new forms of student work, the need to examine and discuss the nature of the excellence they are striving after is as important for them as it is for students. Teachers are encountering the effects of first languages and dialects, class, and culture that barely show up in the homogenized formats of workbooks and short-answer test questions. For instance, when a sixth grade student was asked to write an essay—not a short paragraph—about her city neighborhood, she wrote a loosely organized first draft, using her neighborhood dialect.[38] In her next draft she and her teacher struggled to get her ideas clear and organized. That done, her third draft exposed a sharp sense of image and personal experience. But as she readied her work for publication in a class newspaper, both she and her teacher concentrated on rewriting the piece in the language of school: standard English. This progression is shown in the following excerpts from the four drafts:

Draft 1: Last night some got shot in the lag he ws gust walk down the hill.

Draft 2: I am going to tall you what happen to my uncle.in Sept of 92 it was the 9 day of that mouth he was taking some on home him and his friend. after they took him hom they (were?) at a red light a bad car rode up next to them and shot 14teen shot's and my uncle get shot in the hand. the next day he die at 12:05 that noon. That is why I ask people why they stand in the street.

Draft 3: People fight all the time's. I think at night and I say how come it can't be like it was before when the old people were sick

not young people. This past 2 year we had all this young teen
ager's dieing. I thut that it could been someone in my family but it
was my best uncle in the would that I loved so much hadto die just
stand on the corner. That is way I can't see why teen ager's stand
on the corn'er and get (unreadable) where the book is. That is why
our mother's care about us if they did not care would be on the
street's. that is not all there is a baseball fleed up the street. I be
crying think well I die one day be for my time. this is all I have to
say right now. Stay in those book's. we need them.

Draft 4: I thought that no one in my family would ever die. but
someone did my best uncle. It hurt so much I cried every day . . .
Kids need to put their head back into the books and stop trying to
be so cool. Some of the parents don't even care. We think that they
are being strick but they are just trying to keep us off the streets.

Reflecting on these revisions, the classroom teacher comments:

It is always like being pulled two ways, to honor student voice while trying to
help them see that Standard English is a skill/language that they need to master. We read a book called *Yellow Bird and Me* and I stress how the author has
her characters using the "street English" from the Bronx. We honor this and
try hard to read it as it is written not correcting it. But I do get comments
from some colleagues when I don't correct or teach grammar enough . . .
What they don't realize is that change isn't going to happen overnight, or
from doing isolated grammar exercises. These kids have two languages, maybe
we need to address it as in an ESL classroom.

At one level, this would seem to be a fairly usual piece of writing and
revision. However, much of its power lies in what happens long after it
was originally written and commented on. Later, in a portfolio reading, when those drafts are shared with other teachers, an important,
too rarely explored conversation forms. A second teacher asks if the
revision went too far: Did the young writer edit out the force of voice
and experience so evident when she wrote about her uncle's death? In
the process, had the student lost the edge and immediacy in her writing and the force of details? However, still another teacher, reading
the several pieces, remarked to her fellow reader: "You have to be
careful. Don't colonize her. What you find interesting, other people
could see as wrong. It could hold her down."[39] The language is strong,
but these teachers are mapping new territory. They want to figure out
how they can thread a path between offering students the conventions

which will make them immediately recognizable as learners and, at the same time, preserve the integrity and distinctiveness of their voices. They want not to have to choose between these outcomes, but inventing that possibility requires one another's presence and strong points of view.[40] Like their students, these teachers are negotiating, not merely accepting, standards. Without that kind of understanding it is unlikely that we can ever build toward assessment and accountability systems capable of reliably reading the work of diverse students.

Assessment as an Opportunity to Learn: Embedded Assessments and the Creation of a Common Language

Ironically, the fierce hold that multiple-choice standardized assessment exerted over the curriculum, focusing it narrowly on only certain information and easily correctable formats, is the source for our understanding of just how powerful new forms of assessment might be in leveraging school reforms. But not unless we confront two other problematic legacies of our long history of multiple-choice testing and teaching. The first is meaninglessness. Because tests have so long been curriculum-independent, we have destroyed both students' and teachers' sense that any prior effort or specific learning really matters. The second legacy concerns the constriction of teachers' professional judgment.

Far too much of the current discussion about changes in assessment focuses on the single shift from multiple choice to open-ended items. Another shift which is at least as critical is the change from curriculum-independent to curriculum-embedded assessment. In many school settings the abundant lack of connection between what children work on and what they are tested on promotes a keen indifference to investing in the assessment. It feels disembodied, students sense being unprepared, and there are few, if any, learning-related consequences for doing well. It is not unusual for students to make random patterns of dots on their answer sheets and for teachers to ignore the results (except where they bring shame and anger.) We clearly need a system of assessment that is curriculum-dependent. Such assessments reconnect effort, teaching, assessment, and results. For a number of young urban students who doubt they live in a fair or justly consequential world, this connection is absolutely important.

In PACE schools, many teachers have taken the notion of curriculum-dependent assessment quite far. In particular, they have collaborated widely on designs for what is often called curriculum-embedded assessment, where the culminating product or performance at the close of a unit *is* the test. A strong example comes from a school in Delaware, a state actively moving toward an assessment system based on performance tasks. Based on its recently formulated language arts frameworks, the state developed an on-demand task entitled "Tell Me a Story," in which students are to develop both an oral and a written version of a story that derives from the community in which they live. At a school that is the regional in-take center for bilingual students, teachers collaborated with folklorists and artists to provide a substantial and sustained introduction to this task for both English- and Spanish-speaking students. For six weeks prior to taking the final assessment, students built the relevant skills. Working with a regional folklorist, they learned how to interview (the earlier example of the student preparing his baseball interviews comes from this site.) They discussed how objects and narratives carry the flavor of a community or culture. They read sample folktales from both languages. They worked with an illustrator and a musician, thinking about how illustrations and music could enhance the written and oral versions of their tales. In the end they created both audio-taped and illustrated book versions of their tales, which they presented to a public audience at the Latin-American Community Center. With this varied and sustained instructional history in place, it was clear to the students that the on-demand task was an opportunity to display their recently acquired understanding. They knew that they had been building the relevant skills and that a fully engaged, rather than merely an obedient, performance was the point. Correspondingly, teachers and administrators are interested in the results. They will compare students' speaking and writing prior to instruction, during the folktales project, and in the task. The results will inform state-level discussions of the importance of including embedded assessments in the comprehensive assessment system as a way to think about the consequences of improving opportunity to learn. Such work could also fuel the equitable design of performance assessments for dual language students. But there is a larger point as well. Embedded assessments are, in fact, instructional: they carry crystal clear messages about what it means to display an understanding of the material or strategies being studied.

In the wake of a school curriculum that has shrunk to reflect the content and format of multiple-choice testing, many teachers' diagnostic powers have shrunk to percent of correct answers and the most general sort of admonitions such as "Excellent" or "See me." If we acknowledge the power of precise and thoughtful response in shaping first draft performances into stronger revisions,[41] this atrophy of the response to student work amounts to nothing less than an abdication of a major source of instructional power, as well as the slackening of vital professional knowledge. In fact, the consistent difficulty of reaching respectable levels of agreement in state and national assessments of student portfolios in the absence of a high proportion of common, anchoring pieces may be symptomatic of this loss.[42] This fragility of judgments compares poorly with the more robust ratings obtained in settings like Advanced Placement readings where teachers have considerable command of their subject matters and long-term involvement in moderated scoring.[43] In sum, until we invest in the development of teachers' capacity for making professional judgments, it is difficult to imagine building a system of performance assessment where the reliability and validity of scores runs any deeper than agreement on highly standardized anchor pieces produced under common conditions at specified grade levels. While that kind of agreement would be an important technical accomplishment, it offers little promise that teachers would have and use a common language and shared standards of performance when they return to the heterogeneity of their classrooms. Since that common language is a key ingredient in equalizing opportunity to learn, we cannot, in the long run, afford such artificial and bounded forms of agreement.

As a network of professionals, PACE teachers and researchers are attempting to build a conceptual and practical basis for these much-needed common languages. Within individual classrooms, teachers have turned their attention from checking or correcting, to responding to student work. One teacher explains:

I still collect homework or daily assignments. But I don't spend my time correcting paper after paper after paper. We do that quickly at the start of class. Once a week or so, I read through the work looking only for a few things: is there someone who doesn't understand? Is someone way underperforming, just tossing what the kids call "bus work" onto my desk? Has someone made a leap of understanding or an unusual burst of effort? I put the bulk of my time into responding to student work. Every week, I take three or four students' work on a current project. I ask: what is he or she going after? What difficulties? What successes? Then I write back a response. The point is to make it possible for the student to do more the next time around. If you are used to writing "√+" or "84/75", it is very very hard work. Suddenly you have to look at the work as a piece of mathematics or history, not just an assignment. You're looking for quality, not obedience.[44]

But individual judgments are inevitably idiosyncratic: partial, parochial, or colored by long interaction with a student. They need the light and air of public discussion. Consequently, as an integral part of their collegial activity, PACE teachers share their diagnostic judgments. Typically, they bring samples of what they see as perplexing or strong student work to a shared discussion. The work is posted on huge sheets of chart paper, teachers examine it, writing up their judgments of its strengths and difficulties, then they discuss the overlaps and divergences in their opinions. The point is quite different from what occurs in benchmarking sessions or scoring conferences. The object is not to arrive at one reliable score. It is first of all to develop a common set of dimensions for diagnosing and responding to student work. Second, teachers are building their skills in looking at work that is challenging to assess, for instance, they are thinking through how to read a dual-language student's mathematics work as independent of her current level of English usage. They are also establishing a common language to use where matters of taste, belief, and culture enter into reactions. (See chapter 2, this volume.) The earlier exchange over the multiple drafts of the student's essay on her neighborhood provides an excellent sample of what occurs in such sessions. This proposed *systematization* of professional judgment is an urgent, but largely ignored, foundation for any kind of responsible public accountability, and certainly for any system of student assessment with consequences for learners, their families, teachers, or schools.[45] And we are not without models. Excellent examples of such common languages for making judgments include those developed by the National Council of Teachers of Mathematics to describe the ingredients in their concept of mathematical power and the work on proficiency developed by the foreign language teachers. The NCTM language helps teachers to understand that mathematics involves more than calculation, for it entails the development of number sense, a command of probability and statistics, the ability to communicate mathematical understanding, etc. The proficiency work exemplifies a fine model of a common language for the dimensions of a performance, by suggesting that such performances inevitably are a combination of fluency, accuracy, and communicative power in the situation.

Ideally, these common languages become widely shared tools for evaluating the success of students and of the educational programs we offer them. For example, in one PACE site, the faculty has agreed that across the three years of middle school, students will do sustained projects in each of the NCTM strands (e.g., algebra, probability and statistics, number sense). In the summer, curriculum committees meet to decide which of these strands will be the focus for each of the four quarters for the coming year. For instance, in the academic year 1994–95 the four strands emphasized were: number sense (quarter 1); number theory (quarter 2), measurement (quarter 3), and algebra (quarter 4). Based on this decision, the faculty wrote performance assessments focused on major concepts within each strand. In each case, faculty wrote both a pretest and a posttest. Each quarter began with teachers administering the pretest and discussing the results with students. Samples of their initial work follow.[46] For example, in quarter 2, the pretest for the number systems and number theory strand (NCTM standard #6) was as follows:

Eggs in a Basket

If the eggs in a basket are removed two at a time, one egg will remain. If the eggs are removed three at a time, two eggs will remain. If the eggs are removed four at a time, three eggs will remain. If they are removed five at a time, four eggs will remain. If they are removed six at a time, five eggs will remain. If they are taken out seven at a time, however, no eggs will be left over. Find the *smallest* number of eggs that could be in the basket.

You must show how you got your solution and need to remember that your paper will be scored on how powerfully you communicate appropriate mathematical reasoning. Feel free to use words, charts or tables, diagrams, formulas or generalizations, etc. to make your processes and solution clear.

Following this pretest, teachers each teach a project or unit of their own design addressing the relevant areas of mathematics. At the close of the quarter, teachers administer a posttest on the central concept. For instance, in the case of number systems and theory, the posttest was as follows:

Community Service Clean-Up Competition

Recently, some students participated in a community service clean-up project sponsored by the recreation center. Prizes were donated for the event and students who participated were assigned to teams. To make the competition fair, the organizers insisted that every team have exactly the same number of team members.

When they tried to make teams of two, one student was left over. When they tried to put three on a team, two students were left over. When they tried to make teams of four, three students were left over. However, when they put students in teams of five members each they realized that no one would be left over. What is the *smallest* number of students who could have participated?

You must show how you got your solution and need to remember that your paper will be scored on how powerfully you communicate appropriate mathematical reasoning. Feel free to use words, charts or tables, diagrams, formulas or generalizations, etc. to make your processes and solution clear.

Originally teachers took a professional day to score the performances schoolwide and discuss the results. The effort was exhausting. In revision, teachers now score just across classrooms (i.e., a sixth grade teacher will score papers from seventh and eighth grade classrooms and vice versa.) That exchange provides the basis for professional conversations about which student papers fail, meet, or exceed the expected standard. Teachers collect benchmark papers for each of these score points and use that collection as the basis of discussion with students. Subsequently, students have the opportunity to revise their performances to meet or exceed the performance standard their teachers have set. This kind of schoolwide exchange can help individual teachers realize what they are neglecting and whether their students have done the amount and kind of work that would permit them to perform well. Where the information is used, not just collected and forgotten, it can be extremely helpful to a mathematics faculty invested and brave enough to be interested in asking the question, "How well are we doing by our students?"

Conclusion: Toward More Than
"A Handle to Wind Up the Tongue With"

There is a huge difference between declaration and realization. What can effectively be set out regarding standards, assessments, and consequences at the policy and planning level is tested by whether it can take root in classroom practice and schools' choices. In this chapter, using initial data from a network of urban middle schools, we have provided an estimate of the far-reaching shifts in belief and practice that will have to occur. We gauge that no fewer than three major enterprises will be involved: (1) overturning tenacious misconceptions

about intelligence; (2) equalizing opportunity to learn; and (3) designing curriculum-dependent performance assessments which will afford
the development of deep-running diagnostic capacities in large numbers of teachers.

While we have argued avidly for paying attention to whether and
how this work plays out at the classroom level, it is absolutely clear
that it will require shelter, acknowledgment, and support. This must
begin at the level of individual schools. Schools could be much more
hospitable to creating and sustaining settings in which performance
assessment could take root. One of the major ways would be to reor-
ganize into developmental spans (grades K-2, 3-5, 6-8, 9-10, 11-grad-
uation). This would provide periods of developmental time in which
teachers, families, and students can move toward clearly defined
benchmark achievements. School counseling must fall in line: creating
sustained conversations with students and with the adults in their lives
about progress toward these benchmarks and the available resources
for reaching them. Similarly, schools must concentrate their curricula;
the present splintering across subject matters fractures attention and
prohibits depth. For example, a course like "American Studies," which
combines history, social science, and literature, can flourish without
doing damage to subject-matter learning or skills. The same is true of
mathematics taught in the context of science. For large numbers of
students to do high quality work demands time on task, and these
kinds of cross-disciplinary efforts may be one way to get that valuable
time even under present union contracts. But eventually school time
(day, week, and year) has to be reorganized. We have to move away
from forty minute modules to more sustained blocks of time which
permit science experiments, play rehearsals, interviews, and follow-up
discussions. We have to consider alliances with community service,
apprenticeships, and cultural organizations so that students have the
experiences of applying and transporting their knowledge.

But school-level endorsement is not enough. There will also have
to be a wider policy environment that is hospitable and protective. To
date, district, state, and national policy support for new standards and
student assessments has come largely in terms of regulation: the prom-
ulgation of standards; recertification based on professional development points; mandated portfolio assessment, or state-level systems of
sanctions and—occasionally—rewards. While these policies send
important signals, from the point of view of changing classroom or
school-level practice, they are, at best, long-distance help and, at
worst, blunt instruments which drive false compliance. The work of

PACE reviewed here—along with that of the Comer schools, the Coalition of Essential Schools, Project Zero's ATLAS initiative, as well as other efforts—underscores the importance of two quite different areas for policy initiatives: (1) the redesign of professional opportunities for teachers, and (2) a change in the tempo at which we expect new forms of student assessment to mature into measures to be used for accountability purposes.

Historically, much of teacher education has aimed at providing methods and techniques, rather than subject-matter knowledge or the grounding to enter into discussion of complex issues like standard setting or measurement.[47] But if, in the new common schools we envision, teachers will be responding to student work, debating quality, and thinking through issues of cultural diversity in student performances, then we need expertise at school sites. Old inoculation models of professional development will not do. In their place, we need support for both laterally organized and sustained capacity building. In laterally organized opportunities, teachers work shoulder-to-shoulder as colleagues, both seeking and offering expertise. Subject-matter organizations offer one model. The urban network supported in PACE is a second model. But for this kind of lateral work to flourish, we have to rethink the career ladders available to teachers. In many school districts, the only way an experienced teacher can advance is to leave the classroom to become an administrator. This strips many schools of what should be their council of elders: skilled and experienced teachers whose wisdom would permit them to chair and to guide the challenging and sometimes charged discussion of setting high standards for all children. (This is especially serious in a period when restructuring efforts have left many districts bereft of subject area supervisors). One immediate solution is to create a cadre of master teachers who could mentor the implementation of standards-driven education, splitting their days between teaching and mentoring (possibly using the National Board of Professional Teaching Standards certification process). Hovering in the background, but not to be ignored, is the wage-labor nature of teaching contracts. Whether it is an eleven month year, or a longer school day, we have to find time for teachers to think, plan, and collaborate in a way that will not break districts or states financially. We cannot pursue these reforms without expertise.

Another lesson is about tempo. Performance assessment thrives in settings where it is an extension of underlying beliefs about achievement as opposed to aptitude, the importance of educating and assessing complex performances, a trust in—even a preference for—human judgment, and a patience with the complicated and evolving nature of high-quality work. Thus, it thrives in nations which have long histories of essays and oral examinations for university entrance; in clinical fields like social work or medicine where diagnosis is the recognized aim of assessment; and in fields like the arts where the discussion of quality is understood to be a necessary, if contentious, source of invigoration. We are just now attempting to grow those beliefs in students, teachers, families, and the psychometric community. Without those beliefs being widely held, it will prove extremely difficult to sustain large-scale assessment and accountability systems founded on the examination of complex student performances. In California, Colorado, and most recently, Kentucky, we have witnessed promising and generous systems of standards and assessments become the target of both technical criticism and political invective. The danger is that we will burn up the chance for major changes in expectations and assessments by asking too much too soon, by hustling performance assessment into the heat and light of high-stakes testing prematurely. The cases of successful development are all on the other side of the ledger. For example, the Advanced Placement examinations have evolved over several decades.[48] The state of Connecticut developed its most adventurous (and eventually reliable) assessments in mathematics and science under low-stakes conditions. (See chapter 8, this volume). Vermont's portfolio initiative took shape in a state that had never had a state-wide assessment program based on standardized testing. Moreover, the actual assessment was preceded by careful community work in using the long-honored format of the New England town meeting. (See chapter 9, this volume.) The high reliabilities and equitable functioning evident in Pittsburgh's writing portfolio initiative were the result of sustained discussions across a deliberate cross-section of the city's teachers and outside readers. (See chapter 6, this volume).

In a serious effort to make assessments like portfolios as valid and reliable as they ought to be for use in public systems of accountability, it has been increasingly necessary either to specify the types of contents of the portfolio quite explicitly (as in Kentucky) or to embed common tasks in the portfolios. In addition, it has become expedient to concentrate on holistic rather than dimensional scoring. While these are reasonable technical solutions, they may not be particularly motivating decisions. Many teachers endorse the use of portfolios because they reflect the individuality of students and allow for considerable professional autonomy on the part of teachers. In addition, as discussed earlier, the use of dimensional scoring systems provides both teachers and students with an articulated sense of how high-quality performances are achieved. The systemic danger is that as the options for variety and instructionally relevant information diminish, portfolio assessment becomes more and more of an externally imposed chore. Increasingly, when portfolios are "due," there is a last-minute scramble to produce the required pieces, with the result that teachers only model and collect the required pieces. As these pieces cease to grow out of instruction, the power of performance assessment to reflect back on classroom practice diminishes. Moreover, if student work homogenizes, then many of the most critical issues in teaching and assessment are driven underground.

Given their emphasis on local variation, school-level reforms in standards and assessment suggest that as we continue to develop approaches to measurement and regulation that are more hospitable to performance assessment, perhaps we ought to suspend the high-stakes, reliability-driven path. First we ought to concentrate on the development of common languages for describing student performance and their use in productive, low-stakes, instructionally relevant settings which acknowledge the individuality of students, the autonomy of teachers, the fundamental dimensionality of complex performances, and the range of communities to whom such assessments must make sense.

This is not a call to abandon our public obligation to make reasoned and fair judgments about student performance. Instead, teachers ought to acquire and apply these common languages, working in deliberately low-stakes environments such as parent conferences or school report nights. Judgments ought to be refined in those situations which call for maximum diagnostic wisdom: the development of individualized education plans for special education students or the informal assessment of students acquiring English. Teachers ought to be able to agree on a student's strengths and weaknesses, even when the body of work varies, and when a student's cultural and linguistic history may make assessment more demanding. In particular, they should be able to make consistent judgments about where and when special support is needed, whether that is tutoring for a struggling student or more challenging opportunities for a student who is otherwise bored. In addition, teachers' clinical judgment ought to be exercised in a second domain. Wherever school reviews or accreditations take place, samples of student performances (ideally, portfolios of the full range of students in attendance) should have a prominent place when it comes to evaluating the level and the equity of the opportunities available to students. If performance assessments and the judgments attached to them were to figure strongly in both these diagnostic and evaluative contexts, they would have a significant function, one deserving of resources and support. We have to acknowledge that we have nearly a century of strongly reinforced training in an entirely different tradition of assessment. In that tradition performance was a simple aggregate of the number of items correct, there was little debate about correct answers, and there was little reason to engage teachers in any discussion of large-scale assessment. The proposed work on consistent judgments and common languages, while clearly not the same as the reliability required for high-stakes public accountability, is, after all, a necessary foundation for eventually achieving that reliability.[49]

New forms of student assessment, coupled with clear standards, could help to build a new vision of common schools where equity comes in terms of achievement, not in the arithmetic of matched facilities and spending. But if new forms of assessment are to work in that way, they require serious gestation. We have to rework our views of intelligence, curb our tendency to hoard excellence, and reexamine our oldest measurement habits. This will not happen fast, but it ought to happen steadily.

The writing of this chapter, as well as the research that underlies it, was supported with grants from the Rockefeller, Annie E. Casey, and Richardson Foundations. We would like to thank Karen Bachofer, Joan Boykoff Baron, Linda Carstens, Ruben Carriedo, Edmund Gordon, and Warren Simmons, as well as the teachers and students in PACE schools for helping us to understand how deliberate, rather than assumed, our approach to equity must be.

Notes

1. Lawrence Cremin, *The Transformation of the School: Progressivism in American Education* (New York: Vintage Books, 1961); idem, *Traditions in American Education* (New York: Basic Books, 1977).

2. Lawrence Stedman, "The Condition of Education: Why School Reformers Are on the Right Track," *Phi Delta Kappan* 75, no. 3 (1993): 215-225.

3. National Goals Panel, *The National Education Goals Report: Building a Nation of Learners* (Washington, D.C.: U.S. Government Printing Office, 1994).

4. John I. Goodlad and Pamela Keating, eds., *Access to Knowledge* (New York: The College Board, 1990).

5. National Council on Education Standards and Testing, *Raising Standards for American Education* (Washington, D.C.: U.S. Government Printing Office, 1992).

6. U.S. Senate, Committee on Labor and Human Resources, *Report on Goals 2000* (Washington, D.C.: U.S. Government Printing Office, 1993), p. 6.

7. U.S. Senate, S. B. 1150, 301 (1), (1993).

8. Zora Neale Hurston, *Their Eyes Were Watching God* (1937; Urbana, Ill.: University of Illinois Press, 1991), p. 77.

9. Charles Eliot, as quoted in Herbert M. Kliebard, *The Struggle for the American Curriculum* (Boston: Routledge & Kegan Paul, 1986), p. 15.

10. Gary Orfield and Sean F. Reardon, "Separate and Unequal Schools: Political Change and the Shrinking Agenda of Urban School Reform" (Paper presented at the Annual Meeting of the American Political Science Association, Chicago, 1992); idem, "Race, Poverty, and Inequality," in Susan M. Liss and William L. Taylor, eds., *New Opportunities: Civil Rights at a Crossroads* (Washington, D.C.: Citizens' Commission on Civil Rights, 1993).

11. Goodlad and Keating, eds., *Access to Knowledge.*

12. National Commission on Excellence in Education, *A Nation at Risk: The Imperative for Educational Reform* (Washington, D.C.: U.S. Department of Education, 1983).

13. National Council on Education Standards and Testing, *Raising Standards for American Education.* See also, chapter 11, this volume.

14. Lewis Terman, *The Measurement of Intelligence* (1916; New York: Arno Press, 1975), p. 27.

15. Richard J. Herrnstein and Charles A. Murray, *The Bell Curve: Intelligence and Class Structure in American Life* (New York: Free Press, 1994); Charles A. Murray, *Losing Ground: American Social Policy, 1850-1980* (New York: Basic Books, 1994).

16. Ann L. Brown, "Motivation to Learn and Understand: On Taking Charge of One's Own Learning," *Cognition and Instruction* 5 (1988): 311-321; Howard Gardner, *Frames of Mind* (Basic Books, 1983); Robert J. Sternberg and Richard K. Wagner, *Practical Intelligence* (New York: Cambridge University Press, 1985).

17. Harold W. Stevenson and James W. Stigler, *The Learning Gap: Why Our Schools Are Failing and What We Can Learn from Japanese and Chinese Education* (New York: Summit Books, 1992).

18. Ann Davison, "Students' Formation of Learner Identities" (Unpublished paper, Cambridge, Mass.: Project PACE, 1995).

19. George Madaus and Daniel Stufflebeam, *Educational Evaluation: Classic Work of Ralph W. Tyler* (Boston, Mass.: Kluwer Press, 1989).

20. Dennie P. Wolf, Research field notes from PACE sites, 1994-95 (Cambridge, Mass.: Harvard University, 1995).

21. Lee Gutkind, "Immersion Journalism: A Seminar for PACE Teachers," Harvard University, December 2-4, 1994.

22. Kelley Peacock-Wright, Classroom work and interviews (Cambridge, Mass., Project PACE, 1995).

23. Wolf, Research field notes from PACE sites.

24. Ibid.

25. Chris Hargrave, Classroom work and interviews, Cambridge, Mass., Project PACE, 1995.

26. Andrew C. Porter, "School Delivery Standards," *Educational Researcher* 22, no. 5 (1993): 24-30; idem, "National Standards and School Improvement in the 1990s: Issues and Promise," *American Journal of Education* 102, no. 4 (1994): 421-449.

27. David Cohen, "A Revolution in One Classroom: The Case of Mrs. Oublier," *Educational Evaluation and Policy Analysis* 12, no. 3 (Fall, 1990): 311-329; Richard Elmore and Milbrey McLaughlin, *Steady Work: Policy, Practice, and the Reform of American Education,* R-3574, NIE/RC (Santa Monica, Calif.: Rand Corporation, 1988).

28. Donald Schön, *The Reflective Practitioner: How Professionals Think in Action* (New York: Basic Books, 1983).

29. Dennie P. Wolf, "Essay Writing" (Unpublished manuscript, Harvard University, 1988).

30. Tammy Swales-Metzler, Interview and classroom materials, Rochester, N.Y., June 1995.

31. Marguerite Costello, Interview and sample classroom materials, San Francisco, Calif., April 1995.

32. Ibid.

33. Cohen, "A Revolution in One Classroom"; Linda M. McNeil, *Contradictions of Control: School Structure and School Knowledge* (New York: Routledge, 1988).

34. Wolf, Research field notes from PACE sites.

35. Cynthia Robinson and Kay Shambaugh, Classroom work and interviews, Project PACE, 1995.

36. Elliot Eisner, *The Enlightened Eye* (New York: Macmillan, 1991).

37. Wolf, Research field notes from PACE sites.

38. Angela Joseph, interview, Pittsburgh, Penn., March 1994.

39. Wolf, Research field notes from PACE sites.

40. Judith Warren Little, "Teachers as Colleagues," in Ann Lieberman, ed., *Schools as Collaborative Cultures: Creating the Future Now* (New York: Falmer Press, 1993); Brian T. Lord, *Subject Area Collaboratives, Teacher Professionalism, and Staff Development* (Newton, Mass.: Educational Development Center, 1992).

41. Joan Boykoff Baron, "Assessment as an Opportunity to Learn" (Unpublished manuscript, Connecticut State Department of Education, Hartford, Conn., 1994); Carl Haywood and David Tzuriel, *Interactive Assessment* (New York: Springer Verlag 1992); Dennis Palmer Wolf, "Assessment as an Episode of Learning," in Randy Bennett and William C. Ward, eds., *Construction vs. Choice in Cognitive Measurement* (Hillsdale, N.J.: Erlbaum, 1992).

42. Daniel M. Koretz, *The Reliability of Scores from the 1992 Vermont Portfolio Assessment Program*, Interim Report (Washington, D.C.: RAND Institute on Education and Training, December 4, 1992).

43. Robert J. Mislevy, "Evidence and Inference in Educational Measurements," *Psychometrika* 59 (1994): 439-483; C. M. Myford and Robert J. Mislevy, "Monitoring and Improving a Portfolio Assessment System," Research Report 94-05 (Princeton, N.J.: Center for Performance Assessment, Educational Testing Service, 1995).

44. Wolf, Research field notes from PACE sites.

45. Edmund W. Gordon, *Evaluation Report on Project PACE to the Rockefeller Foundation* (New York: Rockefeller Foundation, 1995). See also, chapter 6, this volume.

46. Anita Hills and Becky Breedlove, Classroom work and interviews, Project PACE, 1995.

47. Larry Cuban, *How Teachers Taught* (New York: Longman, 1984).

48. Myford and Mislevy, "Monitoring and Improving a Portfolio Assessment System."

49. Dennie Palmer Wolf, "Curriculum and Assessment Standards," in Robert Orrill, ed., *The Future of Education: Perspectives on National Standards in America* (New York: College Board, 1994), pp. 85-105.

CHAPTER II

Can Performance-Based Assessments Contribute to the Achievement of Educational Equity?

EDMUND W. GORDON AND CAROL BONILLA-BOWMAN

Teaching, Learning, and Assessment in a Psychosocial Political Context

The intersect between the teaching, learning, and assessment processes in education presents us with an interesting paradox. We are beginning to recognize that some well-established principles and practices in both instruction and educational measurement are dysfunctional to what we regard as necessary for the achievement of optimal levels of teaching, learning, and intellective productivity. Some of the established professional practices in education and many of the traditional methods of educational assessment may actually get in the way of the purposes for which they exist. In teaching, too many of us continue to be caught up in the didactic paradigm, where demonstration and transfer of knowledge and skills are the dominant modalities. Yet modern cognitive science represents learning as a process by which learners selectively experience elements of their own and novel worlds, conceptualize and assimilate symbols and relationships around problems that they understand, and ultimately construct or at least interpret knowledge and its meanings in ways that are their own. The end toward which such cognitive development is directed is the honing of the ability to interpret critically, to understand from more than a single perspective, and to apply one's intellect to the solution of novel as well as practical life problems. With pedagogy so conceived, our conceptions of teaching, learning, and assessment are undergoing change.

In the field of assessment, it has been narrowly assumed that since teaching and learning concern the transfer and assimilation of knowledge and skills, the assessment process should sample the pool of that acquired

Edmund W. Gordon is the John M. Musser Professor of Psychology, Emeritus, at Yale University. He currently serves as Distinguished Professor of Psychology at City University of New York, where he is director of the Institute for Research on the African Diaspora in the Americas and the Caribbean, and professor of Educational Psychology at the CUNY Graduate Center. Carol Bonilla-Bowman is a doctoral student in applied linguistics at Teachers College, Columbia University.

knowledge and skills. This logic seems to be based on the assumption that if one can produce, on demand, evidence of having mastered such assimilated knowledge and skills, one not only knows but can use the knowledge and skill whenever it is required. This basic conceptual model for assessment ignores the fact that the traditional assessment process is also heavily dependent upon the ability of the person being tested to recall and symbolically represent knowledge, and to select iconic representations of skills, on demand in decontextualized situations. Resnick and others who have compared intellective work in school and out of school have concluded that while the assumptions may be correct and may operate for some learners, there are vast differences between the ways in which mental work is experienced in school and in real-life settings.[1] In real life one actually engages in performances that contribute to the solution of real problems, rather than producing, on demand and in artificial situations, symbolic samples of one's repertoire of developed abilities. In real life one works with others to solve problems and often complements one's own knowledge and skills with those of others. And even more likely is the collective production of new knowledge and technique in response to experience with real problems that have special meaning to the persons encountering them. When we put these differences together with the relatively low correlations between scores on standardized tests and performance in real life, we recognize that there is some dissonance between what we typically do in educational assessment and the processes of optimal intellective functioning, between test taking and actual performance in life. Thus much of what we have done traditionally in instruction and educational measurement is increasingly viewed as being nonsynchronous with optimal conditions for learning and sustained mental productivity.

It is, perhaps, the changing nature of the populations served by mass education and the changing criteria for what it means to be an educated person that have forced greater attention to this paradox. When the population was more homogeneous and society could absorb its school failures in a workforce that performed few conceptually demanding tasks, the fact that schooling did not work for some of our members seemed less important. As the proportion of folks for whom school did not work increased, and as we became aware that even persons for whom schools once were adequate are not being enabled to function at intellective levels appropriate to changing societal demands, the potential crisis became more obvious. Teachers and schools became the targets of closer examination. Concern for how both of them can be held more accountable began to gain the focus of public attention.

Since what teachers and schools produce is thought to be the achievements of their students, and since it is these achievements which were increasingly viewed as inadequate, attention also came to be focused on educational tests and the processes by which we make judgments about the outcomes of schooling. It is this closer scrutiny which seems to have revealed to serious observers the contradiction between what we do in teaching and assessment, on the one hand, and optimally what should be happening in learning on the other.

Perhaps it is in the field of educational assessment where the problem of obfuscated purpose is most painfully clear. From the beginning of the testing movement Binet called attention to the importance of doing something about the dysfunctional mental behaviors of persons who did not do well on formal tests of intelligence.[2] Davis and Eells et al. called attention to the culturally truncating effect on demonstrated abilities of standard approaches to assessment.[3] Meeker and Gordon advanced models for the qualitative analysis of standardized test data to address problems of academic development as opposed to sorting and predicting.[4] Models grounded in criterion-referenced and performance-based assessment have been around for twenty to thirty years. Yet these concerns, ideas, and technologies are not well represented in the available products of the testing industry. As educational opportunities have become more widespread, modern assessment measures, for asserted reasons of efficiency and objectivity, continue to probe for truncated indicators of developed abilities, to focus on the measurement of status to the neglect of process, and to privilege sorting, predicting, and selecting over informing educational intervention.

It is understandable that those who do not agree on the purposes for assessment will disagree on the form of assessment. Different philosophical and educational beliefs undergird opposing positions in assessment debates. Among the many currents of popular educational philosophy, two tend to dominate the landscape. The first of these views educational achievement as an egalitarian force in our society, a social Darwinist argument. They believe that in a system that offers all children the opportunity to learn, those most able will rise to the top, regardless of their origin. A curriculum that develops the intellectual abilities valued by the dominant society will empower students to succeed in the educational arena and thus equip them to compete successfully in the economic sphere. It focuses upon the student as an individual, out of context of both ethnicity and class.

The second current views the task of education as that of preparing individuals for the labor needs of the society, socializing persons to the needs of the economic structure. Society is viewed as a caste-like hierarchy, and while lip service may be paid to the equity issue, the focus is on maintenance of the status quo. A person's intellective capacity may be seen as a fixed and inherited quantity which the educational experience is incapable of changing. The stimulus for educational change comes not from a wish to improve education per se, but from changes in the demands of industry.

As these two currents merge, concepts and bases of educational assessment are undergoing critical examination. The dialogue addresses both what students should know and know how to do, and how we go about their assessment. Reform of assessment from a labor-oriented stance generally questions the validity of standardized tests because the kinds of academic assumptions upon which the criteria for success are based do not correspond to what they would like incoming employees to know how to do. The changing character of work, due especially to technological developments, is redefining what is useful knowledge. Reform that hopes to further the opportunities for all students to develop their intellective capacity to its fullest potential, though practically aligned with many of the labor concerns, has a more autonomous vision of an educated populace. It is also more concerned with the sorting of students, because if we are not simply turning students out the way they came in, we need some way of identifying those who deserve to receive society's goods. These two strands of criticism, born from different ideological bases and with very different goals, now find themselves in an uncomfortable marriage in initiatives to reform both assessment and educational practice.

The movement toward performance assessment attempts to bridge these two paradigms. However, enabling rich educational experiences for all kinds of learners may simply be incompatible with the sorting function of assessment and education, which is continually redesigned in ways that continue to exclude those who have been historically underserved. What may be necessary is not only a retooling of how we assess, but also coming to some common ground on why we assess.

It is our increased awareness of this implicit paradox that appears to have made long-recognized weaknesses in the technologies of educational measurement almost as prominent on the education agenda as is concern with the quality of educational achievement itself. Academic departments of education, education professionals, the psychometric community, public and private schools, and the public at large are in considerable ferment all across the nation concerning needed reforms in education, accountability for the quality of education, equitable outcomes of education, and the most effective ways to measure those outcomes. It is in this professional and political context that we examine curriculum-embedded, performance-based assessment and the educational portfolio as its most prominent and widely practiced model.

Curriculum-Embedded Performance Assessment

The stimulus of labor-oriented reform, pressure for a more equitable distribution of opportunity to learn, technological innovation, as well as the explosion in the knowledge base, have created the context in which new pedagogies and assessment methodologies are essential. Curriculum-embedded performance assessment is responsive to these conditions in that it assumes a system in which teaching, assessing, record keeping, criticizing, evaluating, exhibiting, and reflecting all serve to enable and enhance learning. Its practice assumes little or no separation between teaching, learning, and assessment and treats them as continuously interacting components, utilizing instructional materials to provide opportunities for assessment and assessment procedures as instruments for instruction. Such organization eliminates the competition for time between the demands of the instructional process and the assessment process. Additionally, curriculum-embedded performance assessment is heavily dependent upon students' engagement in and performance of real tasks and projects, as opposed to engagement in symbolically and iconically representative behaviors or memory exercises.

FUNCTIONS OF PORTFOLIOS

In a system of teaching and learning so configured, documentation of, reflection upon, and accessibility of the records of these educational experiences are crucial. The portfolio has been introduced to serve these functions. It is, in its most basic form, a system for keeping records. It may consist of accumulated teaching and learning materials which are used as a part of the implementation of curriculum and instruction. The portfolio is an assessment device. It is the stimulant for, and vehicle of, student and teacher reflection. It is an instrument of evaluation and accountability. It is an instrument of self-presentation.

The portfolio systematizes the collection of information concerning: (a) the teaching and learning experiences of students; (b) selected products of these teaching and learning experiences; (c) samples of on-demand and sustained performances; and (d) reflections of students, teachers, and parents upon these experiences, performances, and products. As collections of evidence of learning, portfolios can provide both the vehicle for the conduct of teaching and learning transactions and the modality for the management of student information and student products. In classrooms where portfolios are used they:

1. are vehicles for the development and conduct of teaching and learning transactions, the mediation of curriculum experiences, the structuring of student projects, and the stimulation and guidance of reflection;

2. contain evidence of educational processes and outcomes, including on-demand products and performances, short-term and sustained performances, projects, self-conceived work as well as work that is the result of teacher-created prompts;

3. capture both the affective and cognitive dimensions of teaching and learning transactions and their implicit socialization processes; and

4. enable more comprehensive and equitable approaches to the documentation and assessment of educational inputs and outcomes.

Despite the critical nature of these several aspects of a "portfolio culture," perhaps the portfolio's paramount function is to enable teaching, learning, and assessment as integrated processes and reflection upon these processes. The relationship between authentic reflectivity and the production of quality work is the nexus of the development of a worthwhile portfolio system. One of the potential values of the portfolio is its capacity to enable the individual student to internalize criteria and develop personal standards. Portfolio work can provide the opportunity for teachers and students to have a public dialogue about what constitutes good work. In class, students and teachers brainstorm around the task of defining criteria for choosing the best work for their portfolios. Students are encouraged, either by the teacher or by recognized criteria for portfolio entries, to reflect on the processes by which the work was produced as well as on the work itself. In many cases, the unfolding understanding and incorporation of standards illustrated by the students' self-assessment and reflection brings students to a personal working definition of excellence. Where portfolios have been adopted on a large scale, discussion of standards tied to actual student work can become community-wide, helping to develop public attitudes and values in relation to education.

Teachers and schools reflect eclectic combinations of these functional elements. While some stress the function of cumulative records of students' experiences, performances, and achievements, others may see portfolios primarily as tools of reflection for both teachers and students. The cumulative record function may be realized by an articulated portfolio system with portfolio records on file in a central office as part of a comprehensive assessment system, while the reflective function may be served when classroom portfolios are used for organization and storage of students' work. However, a highly organized system of documentation is only as valuable as the quality of the efforts represented in the individual portfolios.

Tensions are created when these functions are juxtaposed. Tensions arise between systems valuing the measurement of growth and those valuing the comparison of students' achieved status on a given dimension with an external standard or with a multiple-student standardized norm. The format of a portfolio and the materials it holds that serve one function may not serve the other well. Much of the current work on the development of portfolio systems is directed at models that serve both functions concurrently. Many portfolio systems have been developed for the purpose of monitoring educational achievement. Much of this work gives insufficient attention to: (a) the potential for portfolios to reflect the diversity of experiences and products, and (b) the difficulty in using portfolio-type data in comparative evaluation and in creating uniformly calibrated standards.

STUDENT BEHAVIORS IN PORTFOLIO CULTURES

In what ways may portfolio assessment be said to be associated with changes in the academic experiences, learning behaviors, and academic achievements of students? Because of the relatively short length of time that students have been working with portfolios, it may be premature to attempt to judge the success of the portfolio process on the basis of improved academic performance. However, many of the students we have observed who are involved in the creation of portfolios display behaviors that are less common among students in more traditional school settings. Among these behaviors are higher levels of engagement in learning tasks, more focused deployment of their energies, a high degree of persistence in the completion of learning tasks, and the frequent use of reflection and self-evaluation. Although these students' perceptions of the purposes and uses of portfolios vary widely, one must be impressed by the consistency with which such behaviors are observed in portfolio cultures. Those students with the most developed understanding of the functions of portfolios are articulate in expressing their understanding of the concepts and goals of curriculum-embedded assessment as reflected in the use of portfolios. The following summative judgments have been made from our clinical observations conducted at about a dozen sites where portfolios are in use.

1. *Many portfolio students show interesting levels of metacognitive awareness.* They are quite sophisticated in reflecting on their own work and converse with ease when they are encouraged to talk about their thinking processes. They exhibit an understanding of how their minds work, how they learn best, in what contexts they learn best, and what content they learn best. For instance, one student articulates an understanding of two metacognitive concepts: perspective and context. She thinks people reading her portfolio would see her as "very creative and imaginative, see that I can put myself in other people's places very well, and would just enjoy what I wrote." She learns best "by actually doing stuff. It's hard if a person just hands me a sheet; it's easier if I have it in context so I understand it a little better." She attempts to explain her ideas, at first stopping before the words "in context," then returning to it a second time with the affect of someone using a term for the first time. Students express a variety of learning style preferences. Many say that they learn best in groups or from hands-on projects. A few extremely independent students say they learn best when they are free to go about it in their own way.

In our interviews with students who were not exposed to the portfolio culture, those few students who were cognizant of their personal criteria for good work and their own preferred learning styles appeared to be most successful academically. Most of our comparison students were without this self-knowledge or metacognitive competence and were unable to articulate strategies for improving the quality of their work. They were also less likely to come up with criteria for judging the quality of academic work independent of the teacher's judgment.

2. *Students who work with portfolios appear to make frequent use of reflection and revision.* Many display a sensitivity to purpose, process, and substance in their own conception of development of a good piece of writing. A learning product will typically go through many drafts before a product satisfactory to the student is achieved. These students generally take the major responsibility for thinking about, reflecting upon, and editing their work before the initial submission to the teacher. They describe good work as a combination of good thinking and hard work, as well as expressing an awareness that a piece of

work is never really finished. In critiques of their weaker work, students suggest changes that should be made in future revisions. Some reflections reveal students' original thinking about their own work, while others are more superficial.

3. *Students utilize many modalities of learning.* They learn from and teach each other in cooperative groups, seek help aggressively and from a wide variety of resources, and recognize a positive correlation between the amount of collaboration and the quality of the final product. For example, when asked to use a bar graph to rate different aspects of their work, including their ability to find the kind of help they need, one student correlated her weaknesses in her project with little effort in searching out peer and teacher help. Other students feel more productive working on their own. One says, "I can't think things over in a group—too much pressure."

4. *Students articulate a connection between the use of portfolios and teachers who have a better understanding of the students' work.* Students remark that teachers' access to samples of students' work over time helps teachers to know them better. They also observe their teachers in the process of development, and they appreciate richer and more engaging tasks that are both more interesting and provide better evidence for the evaluation of their efforts.

5. *Portfolio students experience much of their assessment as instruction.* Many students comment that traditional tests only demonstrate that "you got the right answer," as opposed to the understanding of a concept as indicated by the ability to apply it. One student remarks that "standardized tests don't help you to learn, you never know what you got wrong or right." Another student comments that tests are less important because "you only take them once, there's no chance to make it better." Some students feel that both standardized tests and portfolios are important, while others feel that standardized tests are more important. One second language student says that "a test is a big deal, but a portfolio is more important. You learn more from portfolio [work]; tests are just review." Students demonstrate a good understanding of how a portfolio represents their abilities and their learning characteristics. They feel that it is helpful for them and for others to look back and see where they are strong and where they need work. As one student says, "My portfolio is me without a face!"

6. *Many of the students relate schoolwork to their life outside the school.* One eighth grade minority student from a large inner-city school expresses the optimistic and practical viewpoint that "portfolios will help you be successful in life. They could help you get a job because

you could show someone what you can do. School has a lot to do with success in the future. It helps you get the proper things that you need to succeed in your future life."

7. *Students talk about the strengthening of the ties between home and school.* One student speaks about the teaching and learning fairs held at his school, where student projects are presented at different centers to other students and to parents. He says his mother is aware of what he does because he sits down with her, and they go over what levels he "messed up at." He talks about overcoming her skepticism about an assignment that involved writing a report about an imaginary country. "My mother didn't like this project. I kept explaining to her until she agreed. She thought it wasn't important—it wasn't like traditional school work." He convinces his mother by explaining to her that his project involved "thinking skills, problem-solving skills, research skills, and learning about different places in the world." In other schools, families are brought into the discussion through parent review sheets that must be completed before a piece of work can become a part of a student's portfolio. Students are very positive about their parents' reaction to their work and say their families are proud of their portfolios.

8. *For portfolio students criteria and standards are explicit and are recognized as instrumental to their learning.* At many of the sites observed students are regularly involved as evaluators of their own work. In some schools the criteria are generated by teachers; in others they are generated by teachers and students together. At one school, every portfolio selection must have an evaluation sheet from a teacher, another student, and a member of the student's family. In other schools, criteria on which a piece of work will be judged are included in the assignment information. Characteristics that students use to describe good work include something they worked hard at, that involved several drafts, that had a content that engaged them, or that they felt they had expressed well, and that earned a good grade. One student remarks, "Before I didn't really know the difference between a good and bad piece. Now I see what's good about a good piece and know what to put in a bad piece to improve it."

Equity and Assessment: A Diversity of Voices

Performance assessment is facing several challenges concerning the instruction and assessment of students of diverse characteristics. Traditional efforts to measure nonstandard characteristics of students have been moving toward varying degrees of documentation through work samples. The task requires both teachers and assessors who are capable of viewing and valuing from a variety of perspectives.

In interviews of students and study of their work we observed ample evidence of *diversity of learning styles*. Many students, among them the more academically confident, expressed their preference for small group work. A minority of students preferred a more traditional learning situation. As one student expressed it, she wanted her teacher to "teach and teach and tell me what I need to know."

We looked for evidence that teachers were using portfolios to gather information concerning individual learning styles and adapting instruction accordingly. One mathematics teacher, who is also a visual artist and a musician, was sensitive to the multiple applications of mathematics that incorporate art and music in the development of tasks in innovative ways. One task focused on designing a long-playing record (lp) and record cover. The project involved applying mathematical knowledge such as the formula for the area of a circle, inventing titles of the songs, and writing one song about caring and responsibility which was transcribed onto the face of the record. Another project involved creating a collage from pictures in magazines, but each was cut into corresponding shapes to form a tessellation. An important aspect of this program was the understanding that if students were unsatisfied with their grade they could redo their projects paying attention to the criticisms in the evaluation. In another school a good portion of the mathematics curriculum is focused on measurements taken by students in field experiences at an outdoor camp. Student groups are responsible for the development and execution of a biological field study involving both analysis and presentation of field data. Teachers focus on creating engaging and challenging authentic tasks that involve students on many levels. An important aspect of the high level of engagement present in these students is student choice. The drawback of this approach is that students may continually choose to do that at which they excel, and continue to leave undeveloped their weaker areas. Some teachers are beginning to use portfolio review to identify students' areas of weakness and to plan curriculum accordingly.

Concerns from teachers and parents in regard to *diversity in the developed abilities of students* are both critical and affirming. Minority teachers and parents have voiced concern that portfolios may serve the needs of those who excel academically, but fail those most needy in terms of instruction. However, the experience that minority parents expressed has been overall positive. One African-American parent observed that for her son, who had some learning problems related to writing, the portfolio-based class gave him the extra attention and sense of accomplishment that kept him from falling behind.

The comments of special education teachers have been mostly positive. They have been active in the development of portfolio assessment, remarking that the concrete experience of seeing a collection of their work over time served an important purpose for students who were not able to hold that much in their memory. In one special education class, the students participated in a schoolwide portfolio evaluation task focused on the integration of social studies, mathematics, and language arts through an imaginary trip around the world. Students were given a budget, tickets, calculated distances, studied about and wrote a diary about the places that they visited. Many of the special education students successfully completed this project, with the help of both their teacher and other students from the mainstream who receive community service credit to work with the class.

In schools in which there were large populations of both European-American and African-American students, tensions focused on policies concerning ability grouping. At one school that is more traditionally organized, conversations with teachers and parents revealed that racial tensions in the school were an underlying and sometimes unconfronted issue. Homogeneous grouping by ability has been the mechanism that this particular school and district have used to attract and retain children of the middle class. The school offers a two-tiered educational program with a cultural/racial demarcation line crossed by a number of middle-class minority students. In our observations it appeared that the lower "tracks" were mainly populated by African-American students. All of the students who were involved in discipline problems and were brought to the office during our brief stay were African-American students. We spoke with several of the most academically successful African-American students, as well as with their teachers and parents. The parents were cognizant that the extended opportunities available to their children were not available to other African-American students with fewer academic advantages.

The pressure for equitable opportunity, as well as current research on effective learning environments that supports heterogeneous grouping, have led some schools to implement heterogeneous grouping in selected components of their programs. Many of the teachers report enhanced learning for their lowest achieving students without sacrifice of the learning opportunities for their most successful students. However, many parents, teachers, and principals in a variety of such schools express some difficulties with untracked classes. Parents complain that the slower students hold back the more advanced students. Teachers are not prepared, either methodologically or politically, to deal with a diversity of abilities within a single class. Administrators must deal with both the political and instructional aspects of this issue.

Teachers involved increasingly in work with heterogeneous cooperative learning groups voice concern about the ways in which the students' products may best be represented in the portfolio. Some sites have students include photos and self-evaluations of their presentations. Several sites have an extensive system of publishing the work of the entire class in small booklets, which then become part of each student's portfolio. While they propose that the less able student benefits from the support of the group and interaction with students with more academic resources, teachers also worry that the less able students get little chance to develop their individual skills. In the evaluation of the group work, a student who is not engaged may slip by repeatedly because of the support of his peers.

Culture and language diversity can amplify the effect of differences in both developed ability and learning style. A student's cultural background may limit the way in which she interacts with adults so that her teacher feels she is not paying attention or participating appropriately in the classroom. As there is great variation between members of identified groups, individual learning styles vary in the range of divergence from the culture of the classroom.

Educators of language minority students are wary of two major potential difficulties in the adoption of portfolio assessment: (1) the greater reliance on the student's own use of language than occurs in standardized tests; and (2) the introduction of teacher bias in assessing portfolios—a bias that is mitigated in standardized testing. The claim that performance assessment will more accurately assess a student's real learning is not reassuring. If performance assessment is indeed more accurate, its use will more clearly illustrate how the educational system has failed those students who have traditionally had less opportunity to learn because of the inequitable distribution of opportunity that is associated with economic class. Linguistic minorities face another obstacle in that much of the educational experience that is available to them is inaccessible because of the linguistic incompatibility between the language of instruction and the students' language of communication.

Bilingual educators have a legitimate concern that the implementation of a new assessment system, without a simultaneous shift in the conceptual framework that defines educators' attitudes toward language minority students, will not radically change the outcomes for these students. Our review of collected student portfolios reinforced our observations that even content teachers tend to prioritize the teaching of English over the teaching of conceptual content. One of the bilingual portfolio readers noted differences between teachers' remarks on the papers of bilingual and monolingual students. Comments on the monolingual English speakers' work ignored errors in usage and spelling and dealt with the concepts and thought processes of the student, while the remarks on the bilingual students' papers tended to focus primarily on language rather than content. One of the primary reasons for the lack of success of many educational interventions focused on bilingual/bicultural students has been the isolation of the linguistic from the cultural and socioeconomic realities of students' lives. Research by Hakuta,[5] among others, which indicates that linguistic diversity is detrimental to student learning in proportion to the status differential between linguistic groups, dictates consideration of these factors. Minority language students will again be shortchanged by the educational community if we succeed in amplifying curriculum to bridge the gap between home and school cultures, but permit monocultural and monolingual biases and perspectives to pervade our standards and rubrics.

The unsatisfactory level of achievement of bilingual/bicultural students can also be attributed to the inappropriateness of many of the treatments. The tendency to ascribe common characteristics to individuals within diverse groups ignores the fact that differences in culture, nationality, and literacy are often as vast *within* language groups as they are *between* language groups.[6] Educational policy often prioritizes less educationally crucial characteristics, such as English proficiency, which is more easily observed and measured, over characteristics such as academic preparation. The philosophy that education should be a common prescription for all, or even for all language minorities, fails most spectacularly where diversity is greatest.

Language diversity issues in the African-American community focus on the role and status of non-Standard English in the classroom. Low achievement of students who speak non-Standard English is not generally recognized as a problem relating to bidialectalism, and is more often looked at as simply speaking "bad" English. Approaches and methodologies that have proved successful with bilingual students are not often part of the repertoire of teachers of these students.

In his review of the research on intellective development in bilingual students, Cummins states "the research findings clearly refute the assumption that bilingualism per se is the cause of minority students' academic difficulties. Rather it is the failure to develop students' first language for conceptual and analytic thought that contributes to 'cognitive confusion.' "[7] The development of educationally and linguistically sound programs for bilingual and bidialectal students lags behind the knowledge base, most notably in the area of support for the development of proficiency in and maintenance of students' native languages. While many teachers have been resourceful and innovative in finding solutions to the challenges of the education of language minority students, lack of communication between teachers of bilingual and bidialectal students isolates these innovative practices in the individual classroom.

Can portfolios authentically represent the academic achievement of diverse populations of students? Our readings of existing student portfolios show little evidence or representation of students' home cultures. Very little work in the students' home language was observed. Because many of the classes for students with limited proficiency in English we observed were conducted at a low cognitive level, evidence of conceptual growth and understanding was not abundantly available. Where students were given rich and challenging tasks, the ability to make judgments about students' conceptual understanding was enhanced because of the availability of information beyond simply the ability of the student to understand English. As teachers become more able to analyze the work of their bilingual students for content mastery rather than English mastery exclusively, portfolios could become an invaluable tool for the evaluation of their students.

The Issue of Standards

What does the dialogue around "higher standards" or "new standards" mean for the underprepared student? Lisa Delpit relates an incident within a college faculty regarding the writing of a talented Native American student who had reached her senior year at a state university without having developed the technical writing skills to meet basic standards for graduation.[8] The faculty members had divided reactions: some believed that the student should never have been admitted, while others insisted that she was displaying a different but culturally appropriate writing style.[9] The choice cannot be between denial of opportunity or acceptance of lower standards. Failure to hold students of color to a common standard because of an acknowledgment of the inferior quality of their previous schooling is crippling, though perhaps not as destructive as exclusion from the opportunity for correction because of the failure to meet arbitrary standards. Obviously, the solution of this problem lies in the direction of more appropriate pedagogical intervention.

Appropriate pedagogical intervention does not mean the mindless adoption, in an inappropriate context, of what would otherwise appear to be a good idea. We visited a school with a particularly heterogeneous population. Thirty-nine native languages were spoken and the majority of the students at this school were in ESL (English as a second language) programs. Teachers despaired that their students would ever be able to meet district outcome targets. The district offers a program modeled on a successful accelerated learning program, whose goal is to bring students up to grade level by accelerating their progress through the work in which they are deficient. One aspect of the model which is being implemented is a low student-to-teacher ratio that makes one-to-one tutoring possible when needed. Not surprisingly, the district could not afford to lower its student-to-teacher ratio and has implemented the program within regular classrooms. Under these conditions the prognosis for success is not good. It is important that innovative programs be developed that focus on raised expectations for students of diverse linguistic and cultural backgrounds. However, it is critical that they be coupled with the conditions and resources that will allow for those expectations to be met.

Will the use of performance assessments enable broader access to educational opportunities for culturally and linguistically diverse students? Many concerned members of various minority communities are taking a critical look at what performance assessment may offer their children. Delpit is quite critical of some of the applications of process-oriented theory to the teaching of writing to children of color, a standard feature of curriculum-embedded performance assessment. At the heart of her criticism is her assertion that an understanding of the rules of power is essential if African-American and poor students are to gain access to power. She proposes five aspects of power that frame education. The last two of these relate directly to our discussion:

1. If you are not already a participant in the culture of power, being told explicitly the rules of that culture makes acquiring power easier.

2. Those with power are frequently least aware of—or least willing to acknowledge—its existence.[10]

It is these two tenets that "explicate . . . the schism between liberal educational movements and that of non-white, non-middle-class teachers and communities."[11] Children outside the "culture of power" do not come to school with an internalized code that corresponds to what they will be required to do in school, as do many children of the middle class. For that reason, explicit instruction, as opposed to a process-oriented approach, may better serve the needs of these students. Parents of children of color want to ensure that "the school provide them with discourse patterns, interactional styles, and spoken and written language codes that will allow them success in the larger society."[12] Making those standards and the conditions for achieving them explicit may be essential to enabling such competence in these students.

Educational advocates for students of color as well as their parents become quickly aware that "pretending that gatekeeping points don't exist is to ensure that many students will not pass them."[13] In a meeting of parents and educators, it was the only African-American present who brought up this concern. "These kids are way out there in self-esteem and higher-level thinking skills, but they can't spell. Is that something I should be worried about or not?" Parents and educators of children of color are adamant that their children must be prepared to succeed in the world that is, which includes "gatekeeper" type assessments, and that failure to do so may result in loss of opportunity to demonstrate the abilities they do have. While spelling may not be a powerful criterion for members of the dominant culture, for other cultures it may be part of the admission ticket.

The ultimate goal of education is not passive adoption of the "codes of power" by students of color. Instead, "they must be encouraged to understand the value of the code they already possess as well as to understand the power realities of this country."[14] A system which values only the extrinsic codes of power assaults students' sense of self, while adherence strictly to intrinsic codes limits students' abilities to function within the larger culture. What portfolio culture has to offer this discussion in its best iterations is a chance for students and educators, together, to craft understandings of and connections between both these intrinsic and extrinsic codes.

The tensions of this discussion must find a place in the consideration of both criteria and standards for performance by the whole educational community. The categories (criteria) upon which we focus in making judgments of quality (standards), vary between individuals within cultures as well as between cultures. (We are using the term criteria here to refer to the "what" of education and standards to refer to the "how well.") Just as standards of beauty vary from culture to culture, so do the criteria and standards for intellective processes considered essential to the well-adjusted individual. It is important to consider seriously the question, Is the focus of education acculturation on the priorities and practices of the hegemonic culture, or is it on a set of practices specifically selected to develop excellent intellective capacities that are transcultural?

Attributes of excellence vary according to our perspectives. Those standards are as different as is the work produced by students. Each piece of considered work by students must first meet the authors' intrinsic standards that are influenced by the various markers of their individuality, i.e., age, culture, gender, language, social and economic status, and temperament. Extrinsic values relating to a piece of writing are equally important for students to understand. Intrinsic and extrinsic value systems are not interchangeable. They are different ways of viewing life as well as writing. They interact to produce what most people would consider quality work of originality and value. In the application of that sense of standard we must be inclusive of many cultural possibilities. In that sense, standards can be "high" without being exclusive.

The tension between the intrinsic and the extrinsic is illustrated by two contrasting reactions to a sixth-grade boy's essay about his opinion of the origins of human beings. One passage in his essay relates that when Adam and Eve disobeyed God and ate the apple offered by the devil, they were punished by "having children and having to go to work." While one reader reacted to this paper as poorly written, lacking a scientific knowledge base and evidence of intellectual reflection, the other reader was pulled into a journey of shared experience, sharing the author's interpretation of his intimate family relationships in relation to the cultural and religious foundations for his thinking. The boy was Latino, the first reader was monolingual English, and the second reader was bilingual/bicultural though not a native speaker of Spanish. The value and meaning of the writing does not exist somewhere on the page. It exists in the mind of the reader, which may be fertile and receptive to the message of the author or hostile and rejecting. The anticipation of the author's message often comes not from what is written on the page, but from shared experiences. One is more likely to have had shared experiences if both the reader and the author share a common culture. As teachers and evaluators, we have the limitation of our own experiences to consider when we approach student work.

This discussion poses several challenges for the application of performance assessment in classrooms. Schools tend to adopt criteria that focus on a single dimension of teaching and learning, with some schools leaning heavily to the side of extrinsic values while others focus on intrinsic values. Those focusing on extrinsic values develop a fair amount of technical writing ability in their students, but the students' work reflects that sense of outer direction. Their portfolio work is characterized by a focus on directive rubrics and questionnaires that leave little room for validation of the students' exploration of their intrinsic and individualistic codes. Those schools whose orientation is toward the development and validation of intrinsic codes tend toward the development of rich, innovative, developmentally appropriate curriculum and less toward technical excellence. In one school we observed, where instruction and tasks are rich and exciting, the portfolio does not reflect that richness. The portfolios there are used mainly to house a collection of those kinds of required essays that reflect disembodied extrinsic standards and values that are peripheral to the real learning going on in the classroom. At another school, the portfolio is so large and inclusive that, by the completion of the eighth grade, a strong pair of arms is required to carry it. Students store their work as well as their smaller projects accumulated during their three years of middle school in a large plastic blanket box. While the items in the portfolios represent a vast range of quality in the individual student's work, they do represent well the richness of the curriculum. The cornucopia illustrates the capacity of a school that has restructured organizationally, methodologically, and curriculum-wise to maximize its ability to engage students in high-level intellectual tasks that are developmentally appropriate and which, to some degree, mold a set of intrinsic standards of academic behavior and work.

NOTES

1. Lauren Resnick, "Learning in School and Out," *Educational Researcher* 16, no. 9: 13-20.

2. Alfred Binet and Theodore Simon, *Development of Intelligence in Children (The Binet-Simon Scale)*, translated from articles in *L'Anee Psycologique* from 1905, 1908, 1911 by Elizabeth S. Kite (Baltimore: Williams and Wilkins, 1916).

3. Kenneth Eells, Allison Davis, Robert J. Havighurst, Virgil E. Herrick, and Ralph W. Tyler, *Intelligence and Cultural Differences* (Chicago: University of Chicago Press, 1951).

4. Mary Meeker and Robert Meeker, "Strategies for Assessing Intellectual Patterns in Black, Anglo, and Mexican-American Boys or Any Other Children: Implications for Education," *Journal of School Psychology* 2, no. 4 (1973): 341-350; Edmund W. Gordon, "Toward a Qualitative Approach to Assessment," in College Entrance Examination Board, *Report of the Commission on Tests II. Briefs* (New York: College Entrance Examination Board, 1970), pp. 42-46.

5. Kenji Hakuta, *Mirror of Language: The Debate on Bilingualism* (New York: Basic Books, 1986).

6. Edmund W. Gordon, *Human Diversity and Pedagogy* (New Haven, Conn.: Center in Research on Education, Culture, and Ethnicity, Institution for Social and Policy Studies, Yale University, 1988).

7. James Cummins, *Bilingualism and Special Education: Issues in Assessment and Pedagogy* (Clevedon, England: Multilingual Matters, 1984), p. 108.

8. Lisa D. Delpit, "The Silenced Dialogues: Power and Pedagogy in Educating Other People's Children," *Harvard Educational Review* 58, no. 3 (1988): 280-298.

9. Ibid., p. 291.

10. Ibid., p. 282.

11. Ibid.

12. Ibid., p. 285.

13. Ibid., p. 292.

14. Ibid., p. 293.

CHAPTER III

Authentic Assessment and School Development

LINDA DARLING-HAMMOND AND JACQUELINE ANCESS

In recent years, the school reform movement has engendered widespread efforts to transform the ways in which students' work and learning are assessed. Much of the rationale for these initiatives is based on growing evidence that traditional norm-referenced, multiple-choice tests fail to measure complex cognitive and performance abilities. Furthermore, when used for decision making, these tests encourage instruction where the emphasis is on decontextualized, rote-oriented tasks that impose low cognitive demands rather than on meaningful learning. Thus, efforts to raise standards of learning and performance must rest in part on efforts to transform assessment practices.

In addition, efforts to ensure that *all* students learn in meaningful ways that result in high levels of performance require that teachers know as much about students and their learning as they do about subject matter. However, teachers' understandings of students' strengths, needs, and approaches to learning are not well supported by external testing programs that send secret, secured tests into the school, and whisk them out again for machine scoring that produces numerical results many months later. Authentic assessment strategies can provide much more useful classroom information as they engage teachers in evaluating how and what students know and can do in real-life performance situations. These kinds of assessment strategies create the possibility that teachers will not only develop curriculum aimed at challenging performance skills but that they will also be able to use the resulting rich information about students' learning and performance

Linda Darling-Hammond is the William F. Russell Professor in the Foundations of Education at Teachers College, Columbia University, where she also is Co-Director of the National Center for Restructuring Education, Schools, and Teaching (NCREST). Jacqueline Ancess is also associated with NCREST, where she is a Senior Research Associate.

This chapter has been adapted, with permission, from the authors' *Authentic Assessment and School Development*, a publication of NCREST (National Center for Restructuring Education, Schools, and Teaching) at Teachers College, Columbia University.

to shape their teaching in ways that can prove more effective for individual students.

Finally, when schools wrestle with their own standard setting, the collective struggle to define directions, to evaluate progress, and to "map backward" into new curriculum and teaching possibilities can create an engine for schoolwide change that is absent when assessment is entirely externalized. If authentic forms of student assessment are shaped and implemented by members of the whole school community, they can enable the kinds of teacher, parent, and student learning that are needed to support the classroom and schoolwide changes required for student success.[1]

It is for this reason that the locus of assessment development and implementation is as important as the nature of the assessment tools and strategies. Assessments that are externally developed and scored are unlikely to transform the knowledge and understandings of teachers—and of school organizations—even if they are more performance-based than are current tests. This is because teachers' learning about the deeper structures of curriculum, the nature and nuances of students' thinking, and the connections between teaching efforts and student performances derives substantially from firsthand, constructivist encounters with assessment development and the subsequent evaluation of students' work. Assessment reforms can increase students' success by increasing organizational learning if they change not only the kinds of tasks students are asked to engage in but also the kinds of inquiry schools and teachers are called upon to undertake as they bring assessment into the heart of the teaching and learning process.

Using data from a set of case studies of schools currently involved in assessment development,[2] we describe in this chapter how the development of authentic assessment practices within schools can create a dynamic process of staff development and school development. This dynamic is set in motion as teachers struggle to articulate their goals and standards, look for and create common ground in their views of subjects and students, reflect on their practice, and attend to learners and learning in new ways. The personal and organizational growth that occurs in this process depends on the intense engagement of staff in collaboratively defining, redefining, testing, and activating their own constructed and contextualized understanding of what is worth knowing and how it can be assessed.

In the course of this analysis, we also rely on the growing bodies of research on teacher learning and organizational change and development. From these vantage points, we evaluate the extent to which various current policy options for encouraging authentic assessment in schools are likely to create the conditions for professional growth and improvement of practice needed to sustain long-run improvements in the quality of education for children.

The Current Movement toward Authentic Assessment

Over the past decade, an increasing number of policymakers, educators, and researchers have sought to overcome the now acknowledged problems of traditional standardized testing by developing alternative assessment practices that look directly at students' work and their performances. These alternatives are frequently called "authentic" assessments because they engage students in "real world" tasks rather than in multiple-choice tests, and evaluate them according to criteria that are important for actual performance in the world outside the school.[3] Such assessments include oral presentations or performances along with collections of students' written products and their solutions to problems, experiments, debates, constructions and models, videotapes of performances and other learning occasions, and results of scientific and other inquiries.[4] They also include teachers' observations and inventories of individual students' work and behavior as well as of cooperative group work.[5]

Over the last several years, interest in these alternatives has grown from the classroom-based efforts of individual teachers to district and statewide efforts to overhaul entire testing programs so that they become more performance-based. Major national testing programs, such as the National Assessment of Educational Progress and the College Board's Scholastic Assessment Tests, are also undergoing important changes. These programs are being redesigned so that they will increasingly engage students in performance tasks requiring written and oral constructed responses in lieu of multiple-choice questions focused on discrete facts or decontextualized bits of knowledge.

The current movement to change American traditions of student assessment in large-scale and systemic ways has several motivations. One is based on the recognition that assessment, especially when it is used for decision-making purposes, exerts powerful influences on curriculum and instruction. It can "drive" instruction in ways that mimic not only the content but also the format and cognitive demands of tests.[6] If assessment exerts these influences, many argue, it should be carefully shaped to send signals that are consistent with the kinds of learning desired and with the approaches to curriculum and instruction that will support those kinds of learning.[7]

A second, and somewhat related, motive for systemic approaches to assessment reform is the belief that if assessment can exert powerful influences on behavior, it can be used to change school organizational behavior as well as classroom work. The idea of using assessment as a lever for school change is not a new one. Many accountability tools in the 1970s and 1980s tried to link policy decisions to test scores.[8] Unfortunately, these efforts frequently had unhappy results for teaching and learning generally, and for schools' treatment of low-scoring students in particular. Research on these initiatives has found that test-based decision making pushed instruction toward lower-order cognitive skills and created incentives for pushing low scorers into special education, consigning them to educationally unproductive remedial classes, holding them back in the grades, and encouraging them to drop out.[9]

In addition, district and state incentives tied to test scores have undermined efforts to create and sustain more inclusive and integrated student populations, as the incentive schemes punish schools for accepting and keeping students with special needs and reward them for keeping such students out of their programs through selective admissions and transfer policies. Those with clout and means "improve" education by manipulating the population of students they serve.[10] Schools serving disadvantaged students find it increasingly hard to recruit and retain experienced and highly qualified staff when the threat of punishments for low scores hangs over them. Thus, the unequal distribution of educational opportunity is exacerbated rather than ameliorated by such policies.

Nonetheless, a variety of proposals have recently been put forth that involve the use of mandated performance-based assessments as external levers for school change.[11] Even those who do not endorse such proposals share the view that assessment can promote change. Other proposals, raised from a different philosophical vantage point and envisioning different uses of assessment, suggest the use of alternative classroom-embedded assessments as internal supports for school-based inquiry.[12]

A third reason for assessment reform addresses concerns about equity and access to educational opportunity. Over many decades, assessment results have frequently been used to define not only teaching, but also students' opportunities to learn. As a tool for tracking students into different courses, levels, and kinds of instructional programs, testing has been a primary means for limiting or expanding students' life choices and their avenues for demonstrating competence. Increasingly, these uses of tests are recognized as having the unintended consequence of limiting students' access to further learning opportunities.[13]

Some current proposals for performance-based assessment view these different kinds of tests as serving the same screening and tracking purposes as do the more traditional tests. The presumption is that new and more authentic assessments would both motivate and sort students more effectively. Others see a primary goal of assessment reform as transforming the purposes and uses of testing as well as its form and content. They argue for shifting from the use of assessment as a sorting device to its use as a tool for identifying student strengths and needs so that teachers can adapt instruction more successfully.[14]

Approaches to Assessment Reform

These various motivations and viewpoints shape the kinds of proposals for assessment reform that are currently being proffered and acted on by schools, districts, and states across the country. Strategies for assessing learning through exhibitions, portfolios, projects, and careful observations of children have been invented and shared among grass-roots school reform initiatives stimulated by such organizations as the Coalition of Essential Schools, Project Zero, the North Dakota Study Group, the Prospect Center, and other networks of progressive schools. These approaches to assessment development have aimed at strengthening teaching and learning at the school level by engaging students in more meaningful, integrative, and challenging work and by helping teachers to reflect on their practice. "Bottom up" initiatives embed assessment within the teaching and learning context and place teachers at the center of the assessment development process. They view authentic assessment as generated and used by members of the school community for shaping and supporting curriculum and teaching in accord with the school's own standards. Local standard setting is viewed as fundamental to the process of change, enabling the debate and discourse that produce commitment and ownership of community ideals.[15]

State and local district initiatives vary in their views of the uses of assessment results and of the role of school and teacher participation in the development and use of assessments. At one end of the continuum is a state like Kentucky, where performance-based assessments are to be developed externally and used at every grade level above third grade not only to rate children but also to allocate rewards and sanctions to schools. Ignoring the instability of student populations and the perverse consequences engendered by similar incentive schemes during the 1980s, the Kentucky plan will use specified percentage changes in students' test score performances as the basis for automatically rewarding some schools and punishing others. Because the planned system intends to continue the tradition of development and management of most testing by agencies external to the school— and the uses of such tests for individual and organizational decision making—the costs of developing Kentucky's state assessment system are now estimated at nearly $100 million, not including implementation costs.[16] (See chapter 10, this volume.)

Many other states, such as New York, Pennsylvania, Vermont, Connecticut, and California, are taking a different approach. These states envision carefully targeted state assessments at a few key developmental points that will provide data for informing policymakers about program successes and needs, areas where assistance and investment are needed, and assessment models for local schools. Meanwhile locally implemented assessment systems—including portfolios, projects, performance tasks, and structured teacher observations of learning—will provide the multiple forms of evidence about student learning needed to make sound judgments about instruction. In these models, assessment is used as a learning tool for schools and teachers rather than as a sledgehammer for change.

These different approaches to developing and using performance-based assessments reflect different theories of organizational change and different views of educational purposes. One view seeks to induce change through extrinsic rewards and sanctions for both schools and students on the assumption that the fundamental problem is a lack of will to change on the part of educators. The other view seeks to induce change by building knowledge among school practitioners and parents about alternative methods and by stimulating organizational rethinking through opportunities to work together on the design of teaching and schooling and to experiment with new approaches. This view assumes that the fundamental problem is a lack of knowledge about the possibilities for teaching and learning, combined with lack of organizational capacity for change. This organizational inertia results from regulatory constraints, inadequate knowledge about possibilities and processes for organizational change, insufficient local authority for autonomous decision making, and lack of incentives for taking risks.

Similarly, there are two competing views of the uses of assessment which relate to differing views of educational purpose. When education is seen as a vehicle for sorting students by common standards for future educational opportunities and projected roles in life, assessment is seen as an efficient means to track and select students. Reliable scoring on standardized tasks with external oversight is important for this goal. When education is seen as a means for developing all of the diverse strength and talents students bring with them—and others they develop in school—and for opening up as many opportunities as possible to as many students as possible, assessment is viewed as a means for identifying and supporting those talents and multiple ways of knowing. Diverse and wide-ranging tasks that use many different performance modes and that involve students in choosing ways to demonstrate their competence become important for this goal.[17] Substantial teacher and student involvement in and control over assessment strategies and uses are critical in this instance.

We endorse this latter perspective. In our view, the goals of assessment must be to serve accountability that is *learner-centered*—that is, focused on providing the most challenging and supportive education possible for every student, taking full account of his or her special talents and ways of knowing. As Gordon puts it:

The task is to find assessment probes which . . . reflect the life space and values of the learner. . . . Thus options and choices become a critical feature in any assessment system created to be responsive to equity, just as processual description and diagnosis become central purposes.[18]

In this way, assessment should help schools provide education that is both *responsible*, that is, informed by professional knowledge of good practice, and *responsive*, that is, appropriate to individual students' needs. Assessment systems, in turn, should support rather than just measure learning.

Using Assessment for Learner-Centered Accountability

The fundamental conditions for responsible and responsive practice include teacher knowledge, school capacity for improvement and problem solving, flexibility in meeting the actual needs of real people, shared ethical commitments among staff, and appropriate policy structures that encourage rather than punish inclusive education.[19] An emphasis on controlling school and classroom work through externally applied assessment schemes makes it difficult to produce this kind of responsible and responsive practice. Peter Senge explains why organizational controls operating through extrinsic rewards and sanctions undermine the development of learning organizations:

(M)aking continual learning a way of organizational life . . . can only be achieved by breaking with the traditional authoritarian, command and control hierarchy where the top thinks and the local acts, to merge thinking and acting at all levels. This represents a profound re-orientation in the concerns of management—a shift from a predominant concern with controlling to a predominant concern with learning.[20]

Learning, he goes on to explain, builds on intrinsic motivation—people's innate curiosity and desire to improve their work, which is encouraged when they have the opportunity to discover, experiment, observe the results of their actions, and continually refine their approach. The engine for continual improvement that is created through this process is removed when goal setting, planning, and evaluation are conducted outside the organization or by those at the top of a bureaucratic hierarchy. The opportunity for improvement exists when the hands-on work of simultaneous thinking and creating is spread throughout the organization and is motivated by shared goals and vision. In addition, this intrinsic motivation for change and learning is impeded by an emphasis on competitive performance, in which there are winners and losers and in which the taking of risks—a requirement for deep learning—carries with it the probability of punishment.[21]

These understandings have been developed and applied in the restructuring of business and industry.[22] While managing business differs in important ways from managing schools, through twenty years of research we have learned over and over again that successful school change is not a process of implementing decisions or programs developed externally. Instead, it is achieved by engaging school practitioners and their communities in evaluating their work and goals, trying out and adapting ideas, developing a shared vision and direction, and participating in the ongoing decisions that bring it to life.[23]

Actually, the lesson is much older. The Eight Year Study, conducted by the Progressive Education Association in the 1930s, illustrates the significance of participatory decision making about matters of real substance. During those years, a group of thirty experimental schools individually created "break the mold" forms of education.

Three hundred colleges and universities agreed to accept students from these schools based on alternative assessments—teacher recommendations and student work products—rather than traditional test scores and Carnegie units. The study demonstrated, from its evaluation of nearly 1500 matched pairs of students from experimental and nonexperimental schools, that on virtually any dimension of student development and performance—from academic honors to civic and social responsibility, based on the judgments of professors, teachers, or others—the students from experimental schools outperformed those from traditional schools.[24]

Most important, the study found that the more successful schools were characterized not by the particular innovation they had adopted but by their willingness to search and struggle for valid objectives, for new strategies, and for new forms of assessment.[25] It was the *process* of collective struggle that produced the vitality, the shared vision, and the conviction that allowed these schools to redesign education in fundamentally important and different ways. If the processes and outcomes of education are already defined by those outside of schools, there is nothing left to talk about. The removal of local responsibility for thinking things through then deprives schools and community members of the opportunity to engage in the empowering and enlivening dialogue needed for making change.

The lessons learned in those schools and today's restructuring businesses are being rediscovered in current efforts to restructure schools. Jane David describes the restructuring districts she studied as encouraging inquiry and risk taking:

Teachers and principals are asked to experiment and to continuously assess the effects of their experiments. . . . District leaders encourage school staff to learn from their successes and their mistakes. School staffs are urged to experiment without fear of punishment for failures. These districts are moving from the known to the unknown, so risks are an essential part of progress. All the districts face the challenge of getting teachers and principals to imagine new ways of organizing their roles and their work. They recognize that risk taking requires knowledge of what to do and how to judge it as well as support and flexibility.[26]

Thus, when a safe environment for innovation has been created, responsible risk taking is strengthened by opportunities for evaluating results. Engaging teachers in assessment is a critical aspect of the evaluation process that can help transform schools from procedural bureaucracies to learning organizations.

Authentic Assessment and the Development
of Learning Organizations

Illustrations of the research findings described above are emerging in case studies of schools involved in the development of authentic forms of student assessment. In each school we and our colleagues have studied, it is striking how the assessment development activities stimulate both professional development for teachers and organizational development for the school as a whole. The examples describe how their engagement in using authentic assessment strategies helps teachers think more deeply about their teaching and their students while increasing their knowledge of alternative approaches to teaching, learning, and assessment. The case studies also demonstrate how the development of authentic assessment strategies helps organize, motivate, and sustain organizational rethinking and restructuring as teachers work together across subjects and grades. As they collaboratively create assessment tools, standards, and measures, they are also empowered—by greater understanding and by new collegial opportunities—to reshape teaching practices so that students will succeed.

PROFESSIONAL DEVELOPMENT

Teachers' learning is a recurring theme in studies of schools engaged in authentic assessment. Over and over again, teachers explain how their understanding of learning generally, and of the learning approaches and styles of individual students, is enhanced by opportunities to look at student work deliberatively and collectively with other teachers, sometimes parents, and frequently the students themselves. Looking at students' learning through new lenses, against collectively developed standards and toward shared schoolwide goals, helps them to reflect on what the work demonstrates about students' understanding, their learning strengths and needs, and the nature of classroom work itself. In many cases, engagement in these assessment strategies helps teachers develop a curricular vision for their teaching as well as a focus on how to connect learners to those learning goals.

At Central Park East Secondary School (CPESS) in New York City's East Harlem, staff have developed a system of graduation by exhibition. In order for students to graduate from CPESS, they must complete fourteen portfolios in various subject areas and present and defend them to a graduation committee, which decides upon their readiness for graduation. In the course of developing their portfolios over two years, CPESS students engage in scientific and historical investigations, debates, literary criticism, internships in work settings, inquiry into social and moral dilemmas, and much more. They demonstrate their knowledge through research papers, projects, essays, works of art, videotaped performances, and written and oral examinations. Each student's graduation committee includes teachers from different disciplinary backgrounds and grade levels, an external reviewer, and another student, bringing a range of perspectives to bear upon the evaluation.

The public and collaborative nature of the CPESS portfolio assessment process is a learning experience for all involved, as it activates continual inquiry into the goals and standards of the school in a manner made more compelling because it focuses on the actual work of students. The process also "stimulates deep thinking about goals for teaching and learning [as committee members weigh] the student's responsibility for his or her work and the school's responsibility for struggling to find ways to help him or her succeed."[27]

As teachers collaboratively confront students' work and one another's judgments, they raise critical questions about students' achievement and their own practice. When evaluating student work, how do they encourage historically discouraged learners while simultaneously upholding a standard of excellence? Which support structures for student achievement need to be adjusted and how? How can teachers in all the grades refine their teaching to support student success?

CPESS staff have used these questions as incentives for professional development as well as guides to collective action. Faculty meetings and retreats have focused on rethinking curriculum and on revising the school schedule and organization to provide greater supports for students. Staff have sought to understand and integrate the lessons of other schools' efforts; have studied and adapted practices such as the Vermont standards for mathematics and writing portfolios; have examined their curricula in light of efforts like the National Council of Teachers of Mathematics standards; have involved authentic assessment experts, colleagues, and college faculty in critiquing their work; and have reshaped both their teaching and their assessment practices in an iterative process.

Engaging in the development, use, review, and revision of assessments has appreciably changed the ways teachers think and work. While lower grade teachers are emphasizing research, writing, and project work in their courses, upper grade teachers are focusing on how to stimulate and support meaningful learning that will reflect the high standards embodied in the portfolio. Edwina Branch, a science and mathematics teacher in the Senior Institute (eleventh and twelfth grades), explains the difference authentic assessment has made in her pedagogy. When she taught the New York State Regents physics course, she was preoccupied with covering factual content to prepare her students for the multiple-choice Regents examination. By contrast, the portfolio assessment at CPESS has refocused her attention on the structure of the discipline of science and on the interrelationship between mathematics and science. Can students design an experiment that can be replicated? Can they use mathematical tools appropriately in reporting and drawing inferences? Are they able to critique the results of an experiment from a scientific perspective embodying the norms and values of the scientific community? These are the kinds of questions that now drive her pedagogy and that of her colleagues.

Similar questions and responses have emerged during the development of the Senior Project at Hodgson Vocational-Technical High School in suburban Delaware. The teachers' engagement in creating a cross-disciplinary exhibition for graduation has been a significant impetus for professional development that has begun to change teaching practice, curriculum, and the organization of the school. The Hodgson Senior Project integrates academic and vocational education as it requires students to select a topic from their occupational major, conduct academic research on the topic, produce a product in shop as well as a research paper, and do a public presentation and defense. Examples of Senior Projects during the second year (1991-92) of operation include: "The Architecture of the Sistine Chapel and Its Effects on Other Churches," "Fiber Optics," "Drainage Systems," and "AIDS and the Dental Office."

When teachers found students unprepared for the demands of the Senior Project, they began to evaluate how to change their curriculum and teaching so that students would be more able to succeed. The faculty steering committee planned the professional development for school in-service days to address the needs that had begun to emerge from the Senior Project. At one such recent event, faculty developed and ran their own series of workshops around some of the core issues that had surfaced: integrating mathematics into other curriculum areas; creating vocational subject clusters; core team planning; and inclusion of special education students in courses. While the staff has called upon and profited from the advice of many experts, Mary An Scarbrough, chair of Hodgson's English Department, remarked, "the best things we've done are those things we've done ourselves."[28]

In similar fashion, faculty at the Urban Academy (UA), a New York City alternative high school for students who have been alienated or unsuccessful at other schools, developed a set of proficiency requirements for graduation. The assessments reflect the school's emphasis on inquiry learning and include portfolios, exhibitions, papers, and student presentations in science, literature, contemporary problems, social science/history, mathematics, community service, arts and culture, contribution to the school community, and a piece the student has chosen as an example of outstanding work.

As the faculty sought to develop assessment strategies that would be both instructive and evaluative and would foster skills that are critical to students' postsecondary success, they became more aware of their students' need to learn the skills of school success, skills such as perseverance, time-management, responsibility, organization, and assignment analysis (breaking down into bite-size chunks exactly what a class assignment is asking the student to do). As a result of their heightened awareness, teachers have focused on developing a pedagogy that nurtures the development of these skills. When students enroll in community college courses, as most do, they are accompanied by Urban Academy teacher, Avram Barlowe, who sits in on the course and meets with the professor to discuss students' responses and assignments. Back at UA, Barlowe helps students analyze the assignments, organize realistic time-lines to get the work done, and develop strategies for producing quality work. Such mediated teaching ultimately helps students mediate their own learning and increases their chances for success, especially when they have graduated from UA and go on to less nurturing environments. The success of this venture in mediated learning has led UA to restructure its own approach, attaching such mediating labs to certain of its own courses. On a formal basis, teachers attend one another's classes and then, in separate class meetings, teach the skills students need in order to do class assignments. The Urban Academy has institutionalized this kind of critical learning opportunity by integrating it into the structure of the school. As a result, the chances of students internalizing the skills for school success are greatly increased.[29]

Teachers' learning about how to support student learning has also occurred as interdisciplinary teams of teachers have developed authentic assessment strategies at New York's International High School, where the entire population is made up of immigrants with limited proficiency in English. These assessments have become the primary instrument for judging the effectiveness of both their students' progress and their own instruction. Students' portfolios and products are evaluated by the students themselves, their peers, and their teachers. These multiple perspectives on students' work, along with student evaluations of teacher-developed courses, provide teachers with a steady stream of feedback about their curriculum and insights about individual students. This system of assessment makes teaching an act of professional development because teachers analyze students' responses and use them in the development of their pedagogy. The press to cover the content has been supplanted by the press to support students in successful learning.

The organizational structure of these interdisciplinary teams also heightens opportunities for teacher growth because as teachers uncover problems, they are able to respond to them collectively and to make changes as needed. As a result, teams such as those that teach the interdisciplinary *Motion* course combining physics, mathematics, language arts, and physical education) have evolved highly calibrated and customized systems of instruction, assessment, and management that have increased students' chances for success. Since the inception of *Motion* over two years ago, no student has failed the rigorous program. Students who have completed *Motion* increase the number of leadership roles they take in the school. Newer teams use the *Motion* team as a model as they struggle toward developing and refining their own authentic assessments. The tightly braided integration of assessment and learning combined with the collaborative nature of teaching gives these teams the potential to be self-monitoring learning organizations whose daily practice incorporates learner-centered accountability.

As teachers learn about how students approach tasks, what helps them learn most effectively, and what assessment tasks challenge and support the kinds of learning desired, they find themselves transforming both their teaching and their assessment strategies. The more information teachers obtain, the more capacity they have to reform their pedagogy, and the more opportunities they create for student success. *Motion* teacher David Hirschy explained the correspondence between improved pedagogy and improved student outcomes: "As the questions [in the portfolio] got better, the portfolios got better. Reading the portfolios is often a validation of what we're doing, and it gives us insights as to what (the students) are really doing."[30]

It is this insight into what students are really doing, thinking, and learning that is one of the greatest contributions of authentic assessment to teacher development. This insight is greatly encouraged by opportunities for teachers to evaluate and document students' work in ways that help the teachers attend to what students can do, how they approach their work, and what types of teaching approaches seem to support what kinds of learning. In the parlance of many currently proposed performance assessment schemes, this kind of insight might be supported by participation in "scoring" activities; however, the kind of teacher participation needed for full attention to student learning must extend beyond evaluations of discrete pieces of work against a common grid or rubric. A focus on distinct tasks scored against necessarily narrowed and standardized criteria can be periodically helpful, but a more comprehensive view of teaching, learning, and the diverse capacities of students is needed to ensure that teachers have the understandings they need to help students learn. This learner-centered information can be derived only from extensive involvement in looking at children and their work from many different vantage points.

Teachers involved in using tools like the Primary Language Record (PLR) and other literacy development profiles find their observations of children engaged in authentic learning and performance situations to be more revealing and comprehensive.[31] The PLR is a system for assessing young children's language and literacy development in the primary grades by using multiple sources of information from multiple perspectives to evolve a rich, expansive, and complex portrait of young learners and their development. Sources of information include student/teacher literacy conferences, parent and teacher conferences about children's literacy learning at home, students' reading logs and writing samples, teachers' observations of students in literacy encounters—reading, writing, listening, and speaking—and running records, including miscue analyses, that provide an individual portrait of developing readers.

At Brooklyn's P.S. 261, use of the Primary Language Record transformed professional development from the workshop model of information transmission to a dialogue and inquiry model of collegial knowledge building.[32] Teachers report that using the PLR improves their precision as observers and helps them adapt their instruction. ' Bilingual K-2 teacher Lucy Lopez put it this way:

Using the PLR has helped me to focus on the kids more—to see what they say and about what. It has helped me to understand them, to understand their language in different situations, to focus more on how they communicate, to see their needs and their strengths.[33]

Teacher Mark Buswinka finds that his guided observations of students' responses and behavior evoke his curiosity and his "teacherly" investigative impulse along with his creativity to invent strategies specifically targeted to their learning styles. Rather than viewing the differences as aberrations to be corrected, he sees them as a foundation for his work like a sculptor who delights in coming to know intimately the unique properties and textures of a new medium so as to richly and wholly engage it for all of its potential. The PLR has increased his sensitivity to and acceptance of students whose efforts to achieve literacy are unconventional.

Pre-kindergarten teacher Alina Alvarez describes how the PLR provides a conceptual map of children's literacy development which supports teaching that is both grounded in a knowledge base about literacy development and responsive to individual children's needs:

The Primary Language Record has supported my view of children and of learning by encouraging observation of students' reading, writing, speaking, and listening in the context of classroom activities. It offers me a framework in which I can pull together and organize these observations. This provides me with concrete information about each student's learning process which then guides my teaching in a way that standardized test scores and preconceived developmental checklists simply cannot do.[34]

Through classroom use of the PLR and accompanying collegial discussions, teachers report they are finding that students' problems do not make for problem students but rather for problem-solving opportunities. The PLR provides them with a framework both for collecting information about student learning and for using it to create instructional approaches that will increase students' opportunities for success. Because the assessment process includes structures that involve all of the child's teachers across subjects and grade levels, it provides a vehicle for professional communication. Because this communication is focused on concrete indicators of children's work and accomplishments, it deepens and enriches professional discourse and the development of shared norms and standards for teaching and learning.[35]

It is important to note that in all of these schools the process of assessment development is ongoing, and the assessment system is continually evolving. This is not a short-term project that a faculty engages in and then moves on to another. It is difficult and demanding conceptual and practical work that requires comparison against external standards and experience in implementation as bases for rethinking and revision. It is also educative work that inspires new teaching strategies that then make new assessment strategies possible. In all of the schools described above, there are several stimuli for continually improving the assessment process and for ensuring that the standards being set will stand up in what CPESS director Deborah Meier calls the "court of the world."

One strategy is the use of external reviewers. At CPESS, for example, professors from local colleges have been invited to evaluate student portfolios to assess the work against that of freshmen in their universities. On these occasions with external reviewers and on other in-service professional development days, CPESS faculty have engaged in exercises to look at how they are rating students' work and whether they are deriving similar scores based on common interpretations of the criteria.

In addition, faculty in all of the above-mentioned secondary schools engage in assessment development and scoring as a collective activity in which they must test and argue their ideas and views against others' perspectives. This collective process maintains a critical eye on the work and its meaning from several vantage points—the nature of the task as seen by teachers from different grade levels and/or disciplines, the experience of the student as perceived by close advisors and other staff, and the procedures for evaluation as perceived by staff and, frequently, by students and parents as well—thus creating a reflective and continuously inventive process.

Finally, all of these schools belong to networks that support teacher and school learning and sharing of ideas. These include the New York Assessment Network, which sponsors study groups on the Primary Language Record and other assessment strategies, and the Center for Collaborative Education, which represents New York City members of the Coalition of Essential Schools and sponsors a variety of professional development (and assessment development) opportunities for faculty of those schools. The schools also ensure that their faculty have opportunities to participate in national networks dealing with school restructuring and authentic assessment, like the North Dakota Study Group and the Coalition of Essential Schools, as well as professional organizations like the National Council of Teachers of Mathematics and the National Council of Teachers of English. A continual flow of professional learning into these schools ensures that practices are scrutinized against new ideas and perspectives.

ORGANIZATIONAL RETHINKING AND RESTRUCTURING

As teachers work together across subjects and grades to develop assessments and practices that enable their students to succeed, authentic assessment development helps organize, motivate, and sustain organizational rethinking and restructuring. Assessment strategies such as the Primary Language Record and the portfolios and projects used by the schools discussed earlier stimulate changes in the roles of parents, students, and teachers, thus creating new partnerships for learning. They also stimulate changes in traditional school structures that typically isolate teachers, compartmentalize knowledge, and depersonalize students' interactions with adults.

New roles for parents, students, and teachers. Changes in parental roles are a critical component of school restructuring. When authentic assessment is an ongoing part of daily life in classrooms, it can also reach into students' homes and create new bases for parent/school interactions. The PLR, for example, legitimizes the role of parents as a source of educational as well as social information about the child since parents are interviewed about their observations of their children as language users. This information is incorporated into the children's language records. As parents become engaged in reporting on the language and literacy development of their children, they are educated about the process of language development and about the unique developmental processes of their own children. Parents are thus better able to understand and support both their individual child's learning efforts and the school's efforts to advance their child's language and literacy development.

The teacher/student literacy conferences that are a component of the PLR also cast students in the role of co-constructors of the teachers' knowledge base about the child. Like other forms of authentic assessment that involve learners in evaluating what they know and how they learned it, the PLR legitimizes students as valuable sources of information and feedback about their own development as language users and their own learning styles. Both teachers and students are empowered to develop and demonstrate competence by an approach that rejects the notion that students must learn only by virtue of formulaic instruction delivered through packaged programs and decontextualized tests. Personalization and customization become new norms because approaches building on student learning styles and strengths bring greater success, especially to vulnerable students.

Similarly, the assessments at International High School cast students in the key role of formal evaluators of their own learning, their peers' learning, and the effectiveness of their teachers' courses. Teachers use the feedback on their courses to revise their teaching and curriculum. Additionally, the *Motion* team at International legitimizes the role of students as curriculum developers by including student-made activities in the curriculum and portfolio requirements for all of the students.

The assessments at CPESS, International High School, Urban Academy, and Hodgson Vocational Technical High School expand the teacher's role to include advisor, facilitator, coach, and mentor. As International High School teacher David Hirschy describes it, because assessment focuses on intellectual development, the role of teacher as dispenser of information is transformed to that of "wizened guide," that is, teachers as facilitators of inquiry who "restate or recontextualize [students' questions] and direct [the students] to resume their struggle in search of solutions."[36] Because content is a vehicle for the development of powerful intellectual skills, mastery of content is no longer merely a function of memorization, but of well-developed reasoning abilities that enable students to support diverse points of view with evidence, to find and to synthesize various sources of information as a basis for solving serious intellectual problems. These new teacher roles are accompanied by new kinds of student learning that increase the probability for long-run student success. Learning is no longer a one-shot deal. Students learn that lasting accomplishments involve an intense process of conceptualizing, constructing, evaluating, refining, and reconstructing their ideas and products; of writing and rewriting; of striving and refining. They learn that, as Grant Wiggins explains, "the work is not done until it is done right."[37] Students learn that good work, excellent work, must be crafted, requires time, and has the input of expert others. Students learn perseverance; they learn that they can improve; and they learn that success requires work and struggle. These assessments redefine learning and achievement. They also create the possibilities for more lasting learning. As a newly immigrated student at International High School described it:

The portfolio is important because you build, you put everything together, all your experiences during the cycle in the class. . . . You look at the work and you are able to see what you did and how you did it. When you do the [traditional] tests, you study, you learn by heart, next day you pass the test, that's it—out of your head. You will forget about it, I guarantee.[38]

New possibilities for structuring schools. When teachers are engaged in collaborative assessment development, the practice of teaching extends beyond classroom walls and classroom-related work to broader school concerns. The regular meetings generated and required by the collective development and scoring of assessments enable teachers to contribute to one another's knowledge and a schoolwide understanding of individual students, teaching practice, and the structure of the school as it facilitates or inhibits its goals.

Spurred by their ongoing conversations and assessment design initiatives, the Hodgson faculty has begun to restructure itself to promote the kinds of teaching, learning, and assessment represented by the Senior Project. A technical writing course was added in the senior year to help students learn how to write research papers. Research projects were added in lower-grades courses as well. After the first year, a few teachers created interdisciplinary courses and project-based curricula emphasizing active learning in areas like social studies and English. Motivated by the climate of change and a desire to see his students engaged in mathematics, a veteran mathematics teacher transformed the standard mathematics curriculum to one rooted in problem solving and requiring the use of manipulatives. Math teachers began to spend a period a week in shop classes to integrate instruction. By the third year, the school faculty had created a plan to conduct most of their work in interdisciplinary team teaching clusters using experiential and project-based approaches and including special education classes. The forms and uses of authentic assessment are evolving throughout the school. Because teachers are the co-constructors of their own systems for improving teaching and assessment, their collective inquiry is leading the school down a self-paved road for educational redesign.

At Central Park East Secondary School, staffing patterns are arranged and student advisory classes are structured to enable personalized attention to the development of students' demanding portfolios. At International, as the faculty learned of students' success in self-contained clusters such as *Motion*, increasing numbers of teachers became interested in forming their own clusters. The principal, Eric Nadelstern, adopted the interdisciplinary, self-contained cluster as his goal for long-term, whole-school restructuring, and teachers have initiated new teams and courses.

As faculty work together through the evaluations of portfolios and projects, they are wrestling with articulating their individual standards for what constitutes good work and useful learning, and they are developing shared standards that drive an overall school development and improvement process. CPESS school founder Deborah Meier notes that the process of working through portfolio requirements, standards, and evaluations leads to improvement of teaching across the entire school. By tackling the question of graduation standards with authentic examples of student work as the focus of conversations, "we've created a school that's more collective in its practice."[39]

The ways in which the use of portfolio strategies and approaches like the Primary Language Record have helped teachers learn from one another and establish collective norms of practice have been replicated at many other schools engaged in similar processes of child observation and documentation.[40] The outcomes of the Descriptive Review process, developed at the Prospect Center and adapted in many schools as a way for teachers to look collectively at the work and learning of individual children, are similarly generative of schoolwide rethinking.[41] As teacher Rhoda Kanevsky explains:

(T)he assessment we use determines the way we see children and make educational decisions. . . . Because the Descriptive Review is a collaborative process, it can contribute to the current efforts to restructure schools. The Descriptive Review process allows teachers to hear individual voices and to pursue collaborative inquiry. As teachers draw upon their experiences and knowledge, they begin to envision new roles for themselves and new structures for schools. They are also creating a body of knowledge about teaching and learning that starts with looking at a particular child in depth and ends with new insights and understandings about children and classrooms in general.

Teachers must have opportunities to participate in an educational community; to examine what they care about and what is important for children; to have ongoing, thoughtful conversations about teaching and learning in order to plan meaningful restructuring.[42]

In these schools and many others, assessment development has become an opportunity for teachers to become both problem framers and problem solvers, taking hold of the destiny of their school and collectively steering its course to enhance student success. Their willingness to submit themselves to a rigorous process of inquiry evaluated by the outcomes of their students makes them reflective decision makers about how and what students learn, what strategies and supports are necessary for high levels of learning, and what changes are needed for these things to occur.

In all of the schools we have studied, authentic assessment practices have encouraged faculties to rethink traditional allocations of time and traditional organizational structures. Because the work demanded of students is more intense and challenging than passive forms of learning, all of the high schools discussed have developed flexible time frames for classes featuring longer blocks of time than forty-five minutes. Interdisciplinary clusters of courses enable more integrative forms of teaching with longer periods of time for extensive project and research work. Teaching teams have more control over the use of time within blocks, so that they can regroup for different learning and teaching goals, to provide small- and large-group instruction as needed and to team teach.

Interdisciplinary teams that manage the allocation of time for their own students and teachers use the resulting scheduling flexibility to attend to student needs and to establish regular opportunities for collaborative teacher planning and communication. Several of the high schools have creatively "squirreled" time for regular meetings by establishing external learning opportunities for students through community-service programs, internships, and courses on college campuses. Others have created time for collegial work by rearranging course schedules, adding time to each school day to allow an early dismissal or special "club" time for students one day a week (during which teachers work together), or rearranging school staffing patterns to "buy" more teacher time for shared planning.

Other changes include reallocation of staff so that virtually all adults are working directly with students on academic tasks. In contrast to typical American school staffing patterns in which only half of professional staff work closely with students as classroom teachers,[43] these schools are organized for more personalized and intensive adult-student relationships. When schools are reconfigured into smaller self-contained learning clusters, the need for nonteaching personnel such as deans, assistant principals, guidance counselors, and special program staff diminishes. Instead, these roles are assumed by teachers who take responsibility for a greater range of functions for fewer total students with whom they work more intensely through newly developed structures such as advisories and teams.

Authentic assessment development and practice have helped these schools reframe the reform debate by changing the fundamental question of restructuring from "How can we achieve our goals within the current structures?" to "What kind of structures do we need to establish in order to achieve our goals?" These schools have seen their structures as porous, flexible, and changeable in service of their goals. Structures become servants to school goals rather than school goals remaining servants to school structures. These schools have toppled the hierarchy of regularities—the immutable "master schedule" (indeed the "master" of possibilities within most high schools), the standard-ized time frames for classes, the rigid role definitions, and the frag-mented instructional program, that have been obstacles to serious learning and higher levels of performance.[44]

The process of authentic assessment development can fuel this dynamic. It can become the method by which the school community obtains the information about whether its parts are working indepen-dently and in tandem to achieve its goals. Authentic assessment devel-opment can encourage student-centered accountability by focusing a school simultaneously on student outcomes and the processes by which it seeks to achieve those outcomes. By providing information and insights on the connections between means and ends, the process of collectively developing and using authentic assessments can help all the members of the school community become part of a synergistic, learning-centered organization. The power of such schoolwide norms and practices in support of student success is illustrated by the gradua-tion and college admission rates of central city students at CPESS, Urban Academy, and International High School, which reach 90 per-cent or more for students who would otherwise be expected to have at least a 50 percent probability of dropping out and virtually no chance of going on to college.[45]

Though it might be argued that these schools are so unusual that their experience is not applicable to "regular" public schools that oper-ate in leaner, less willing settings, there is evidence that this kind of organizational learning is possible in many schools under a wide range of circumstances. While the schools we have described have the advan-tage of being connected to networks like the Coalition of Essential Schools, a number were "regular" and, in some cases, not noticeably extraordinary schools before they began the work we have documented. Those that are part of the New York City school system continue to be poorly funded, operating—like all New York City schools—on budgets that fall below the state average and have been reduced in each of the last several years due to city and state fiscal crises.

Though we do not yet have a sufficient body of practice or re-search to evaluate how such school-based assessment initiatives might play out under various conditions, there is evidence that "regular" schools that are motivated to undertake assessment reforms undergo substantial learning as a result. While these practices do require extra-ordinary efforts—including the securing of state waivers, continuing negotiations with district offices around curriculum directives, and creative rethinking of traditional modes of staffing and organization (which often require progressive agreements with both district offices and unions)—they also take root when nurtured by these external influences. In 1991, for example, over fifty elementary schools launched work with the Primary Language Record and other alternative forms of assessment under the auspices of the New York Assessment Network, which is a collaborative effort of the New York City Board of Education's Office for Research and Evaluation, the Fund for New York City Public Education, and the Center for Collaborative Education. A group of faculty from these schools joined together to study multiple forms of evidence for documenting and evaluating children's early literacy development. All members of the group experienced the kinds of professional growth we have described above.[46]

Implications for Authentic Assessment Policy

If authentic assessment is to realize its potential as a tool for school change, policies must enable assessments to be used as a vehicle for student, teacher, and school development. Like students, teachers also learn by constructing knowledge based on their experiences, conceptions, and opportunities for firsthand inquiry. They must be deeply engaged in hands-on developmental work if they are to construct new understandings of the teaching-learning process and new possibilities for their own practices in the classroom and in the school. They must come to understand the kinds of higher-order learning and integrated performance goals of current school reforms from the inside out if they are to successfully develop practices that will support these goals. They must create partnerships with parents and students in working toward the achievement of jointly held goals if the will to change is to overcome the inertia of familiar patterns.

This suggests a policy paradigm which provides top-down support for bottom-up reform rather than top-down directives for school-level implementation. As discussed earlier, different policy proposals envision different uses for performance-based assessments. Some state programs plan to change the nature of existing standardized tests but not the locus of control of test items, scoring, and uses of results. Tests will still be used primarily for ranking students and schools and controlling instruction from outside the school. Similarly, some proposals for national testing envision instruments such as those developed by the National Assessment of Educational Progress (NAEP) being used to rank schools, districts, and states on measures that use more performance-oriented tasks, but these instruments would enter and leave schools on "testing days" just as current assessments do. Due to their intended uses, the tests will need to be carefully controlled and managed to ensure scoring reliability and security. This means local teachers, parents, and students can have little voice in choices of tasks and assessment opportunities or the means of configuring them; that those assessments that count will still be occasional and threatening rather than continuous and developmental; that the strategies for assessment will be limited to what can be managed with external development and reliable scoring at "reasonable" costs; and that the learning available to school people will be limited to that which can occur at several removes from hands-on participation.

If performance-based assessments are used in the same fashion as current externally developed and mandated tests are used, they are likely to highlight differences in students' learning even more keenly, but they will be unlikely to help teachers revamp their teaching or schools rethink their ways of operating. If tests arrive in secured packets and leave in parcels for external scoring, teachers will have only a superficial understanding of what the assessments are trying to measure or achieve. If assessments are occasional externally controlled events used primarily for aggregated measures of student achievement levels, they are unlikely to be constructed in ways that provide rich information about how students learn and how they approach different kinds of tasks and opportunities. Consequently, teachers will have little opportunity to use the results to understand the complex nuances of student learning in ways that support more successful instruction, and little information on which to act in trying to rethink their daily practices. They will have no new grist for ongoing conversations with parents and with their peers about the insights and dilemmas raised through an ongoing, integrated, collaborative process of teaching, learning, and assessment. Furthermore, if the results are used to allocate rewards and sanctions for students, teachers, and/or schools, the assessments will inspire fear and continual gameplaying to manipulate student populations, but they will be unlikely to open up the kinds of honest inquiry and serious innovation needed to stimulate new learning and transform practices in fundamental ways.

Other states have begun to envision new systems of local and state participation in assessment development and use that acknowledge the importance of involving teachers, parents, and students in the processes of assessment development and implementation. While state assessments would provide comparable data on student performances on a periodic sampling basis, these would include data from longer-term projects and portfolios as well as controlled-performance tasks. In addition, investments in the development of local assessment systems would support schools in developing continuous, multifaceted records of achievement and information about students in authentic performance situations. Recently proposed local portfolio systems in Pennsylvania and New York that are intended to augment redesigned state assessment systems are examples of this approach. The New York plan, developed by the New York Council on Curriculum and Assessment, includes the following components:

- state-developed statements of student learning goals that are further explained in curriculum frameworks organized around desired learning goals;

- a state system of assessments for program evaluation purposes, using state-of-the-art performance assessment methods on a sampling basis (and providing district level data for each district on a regular periodic basis);

- a state assessment "bank" of prototypes for performance tasks, exhibitions, portfolio and project ideas, and systems for structured teacher observations of students;

- a local system of assessments for individual student assessment, targeted at the state learning goals, enriched by the state assessment bank, and using multiple sources of evidence—including performance tests or tasks, portfolios of student work (from which some of the state program assessments may be drawn for predetermined, on-demand tasks), and teacher observations of student learning;

- a Regents portfolio for graduation by exhibition, developed by local schools and districts to meet state standards and to be approved, along with the rest of the local assessment system, by an Assessment Quality Assurance Panel.[47]

In the New York proposal, accountability for ensuring the quality and appropriateness of local assessments would be managed through a state approval process for evaluating assessment systems, while teacher and school learning are supported by an ongoing, developmental school quality review process.[48] Both California and New York are currently piloting such practitioner-led school-review processes modeled, in part, after long-standing practices of Her Majesty's Inspectorate in Great Britain. Meanwhile, the widening use of the Primary Language Record in California Chapter 1 schools and New York City schools provides another example of school-based assessment supported by state-level and district-level technical assistance.

These initiatives use assessment as a vehicle for student development and adaptive teaching rather than as a tool for sorting, screening, and selecting students out of educational opportunities. They also aim for assessment that informs teacher and school learning so that the possibilities of multiple pathways to student success are enhanced. These kinds of initiatives acknowledge the need to experiment with diverse methods for assessment that can support Gardner's conception of "individually configured excellence"[49]—efforts that will tap the multiple intelligences and potentials of students obscured by traditional testing practices.

Assessment initiatives that embed authentic assessment in the ongoing processes of teaching and curriculum development share the view offered by Glaser that schools must move from a selective mode, "characterized by minimal variation in the conditions for learning" in which "a narrow range of instructional options and a limited number of paths to success are available" to an adaptive mode in which "conceptions of learning and modes of teaching are adjusted to individuals—their backgrounds, talents, interests, and the nature of their past performances and experiences."[50] Fundamental agreement with this view leads to a rejection of the traditional uses of testing, even performance-based testing, as an externally controlled tool for the allocation of educational opportunities, rewards, or sanctions. As students are offered wider opportunities for learning and the assessment of their achievement becomes an integral part of learning and teaching, tests are required that provide multidimensional views of performance.

As an alternative to past uses of standardized testing, Glaser proposes the following criteria for evaluating how new assessments should be designed and used:

1. *Access to educational opportunity*. Assessments should be designated to survey possibilities for student growth, rather than to designate students as ready or not ready to profit from standard instruction.

2. *Consequential validity*. Assessments should be interpreted and evaluated on the basis of their instructional effects, i.e., their effectiveness in leading teachers to spend time on classroom activities conducive to valuable learning goals and responsive to individual student learning styles and needs.

3. *Transparency and openness*. Knowledge and skills should be measured so that the processes and products of learning are openly displayed.

The criteria of performance must be transparent rather than secret so that they can motivate and direct learning.

4. *Self-assessment.* Because assessment and instruction will be integrally related, instructional situations should provide coaching and practice in ways that help students to set incremental standards by which they can judge their own achievement, and develop self-direction for attaining higher performance levels.

5. *Socially situated assessment.* Assessment situations in which the student participates in group activity should increase. In this context, not only performance, but also the facility with which a student adapts to help and guidance can be assessed.

6. *Extended tasks and contextualized skills.* Assessment should be more representative of meaningful tasks and subject-matter goals. Assessment opportunities will themselves provide worthwhile learning experiences that illustrate the relevance and utility of the knowledge and skills that are being acquired.

7. *Scope and comprehensiveness.* Assessment will attend to a greater range of learning and performance processes, allowing analysis of what students can do in terms of the cognitive demands and performance skills posed by tasks, in addition to their content.[51]

These guidelines suggest strategies for creating assessment systems that serve the daily, intimate processes of teaching and learning. Though a continuing role for external assessments that provide information for policymakers and guideposts for district and school analysis is legitimate, the broader vision of school restructuring demands a much more prominent and highly developed role for school-based assessment initiatives as well.

As the case studies and other research reported in this chapter suggest, collective development and use of authentic assessments—bringing the assessment function inside the school rather than leaving it to outside experts or agencies—provides a catalyst for changing many fundamental expectations about how schools operate. Schools deeply engaged in developing and using assessments become learning organizations, initiating changes from bureaucratic, individualized, and specialized forms of organization to collaborative and synergistic forms; from subject-centered to learner-centered approaches for evaluating and planning work; from hierarchical transmission of directives and information to horizontal information links and learning networks; from competitive rewards and incentives to cooperative, shared incentives for helping students—and colleagues—succeed; from patterns of isolation to opportunities for communication; from adversarial relations between administrators and teachers—and teachers and students—to mutual advocacy aimed at progress toward shared, community-developed goals.

Properly introduced, authentic assessment strategies can help schools become educational communities committed to self-determined common core values and goals. When this happens, all members of the community become learners struggling to construct knowledge that they can individually and collectively use to achieve their goals. The development and practice of authentic assessment casts teachers in the role of problem framers and problem solvers who use their classroom and school experiences to build an empirical knowledge base to inform their practice and strengthen their effectiveness. In this way, authentic assessment increases the capacity of schools to engage in a recursive process of self-reflection, self-critique, self-correction, and self-renewal. As schools thus become learning organizations, they increase their capacity to ensure that all of their students learn.

NOTES

1. Joseph P. McDonald, Eileen Barton, Sidney Smith, Dorothy Turner, and Marian Finney, *How to Redesign a School: Planning Backwards from Exhibitions* (Alexandria, Va: Association for Supervision and Curriculum Development, 1992).

2. The case studies were conducted by the authors and colleagues at the National Center for Restructuring Education, Schools, and Teaching at Teachers College, Columbia University.

3. Grant Wiggins, "Teaching to the (Authentic) Test," *Educational Leadership* 46, no. 7 (April 1989): 41-47.

4. Douglas A. Archbald and Fred M. Newmann, *Beyond Standardized Testing: Assessing Authentic Academic Achievement in the Secondary School* (Reston, Va: National Association of Secondary School Principals, 1988).

5. National Association for the Education of Young Children. "NAEYC Position Statement on Developmentally Appropriate Practice in the Primary Grades: Serving 5 through 8 Year Olds," *Young Children* 43 (January 1988): 64-84.

6. Linda Darling-Hammond and Arthur E. Wise, "Beyond Standardization: State Standards and School Improvement," *Elementary School Journal* 85, no. 3 (1985): 315-336. George Madaus, Mary Maxwell West, Maryellen C. Harmon, Richard G. Lomax, and Katherine A. Viator, *The Influence of Testing on Teaching Math and Science in Grades 4-12* (Chestnut Hill, Mass.: Boston College Center for the Study of Testing, Evaluation, and Educational Policy, 1992).

7. Jennifer A. O'Day and Marshall S. Smith, "Systemic School Reform and Educational Opportunity," in *Designing Coherent Education Policy: Improving the System*, edited by Susan Fuhrman (San Francisco: Jossey-Bass, 1993).

8. Arthur E. Wise, *Legislated Learning* (Berkeley, Calif.: University of California Press, 1979); George F. Madaus, "Public Policy and the Testing Profession—You've

Never Had It So Good?" *Educational Measurement: Issues and Practice* 4 (April 1985): 5-11; Robert L. Linn, "Accountability: The Comparison of Educational Systems and the Quality of Test Results," *Educational Policy* 1, no. 2 (1987): 181-198.

9. Lorrie A. Shephard and Mary Lee Smith, "Escalating Academic Demand in Kindergarten: Counterproductive Policies," *Elementary School Journal* 89, no. 2 (1988): 135-145; Daniel Koretz, "Arriving in Lake Wobegon: Are Standardized Tests Exaggerating Achievement and Distorting Instruction?" *American Educator* 12, no. 2 (1988): 8-15, 46-52; Frank Smith et al., *High School Admission and the Improvement of Schooling* (New York, N.Y.: New York City Board of Education, 1986); Linda Darling-Hammond, "The Implications of Testing Policy for Quality and Equality," *Phi Delta Kappan* 73 (November 1991): 220-225; idem, "Educational Indicators and Enlightened Policy," *Educational Policy* 6, no. 3 (1992): 235-265; Richard L. Allington and Anne McGill-Franzen, "Unintended Effects of Educational Reform in New York," *Educational Policy* 6, no. 4 (1992): 397-414.

10. Smith et al., *High School Admission and the Improvement of Schooling*.

11. David Hornbeck, "The True Road to Equity," *Education Week*, 6 May 1992; Commission on Chapter 1, *High Performance Schools: No Exceptions, No Excuses* (Washington, D.C.: The Commission, 1992); O'Day and Smith, "Systemic School Reform and Educational Opportunity."

12. Linda Darling-Hammond and Carol Ascher, *Accountability in Big City Schools* (New York: National Center for Restructuring Education, Schools and Teaching and the Institute for Urban and Minority Education, Teachers College, Columbia University, 1990); Dennie Palmer Wolf and Joan Boykoff Baron, "A Realization of a National Performance-Based Assessment System," in *Promises and Perils of New Assessments*, edited by David Stevenson (Englewood Cliffs, N.J.: Erlbaum, forthcoming).

13. Darling-Hammond, "The Implications of Testing Policy for Quality and Equality"; Jeannie Oakes, *Keeping Track: How Schools Structure Inequality* (New Haven: Yale University Press, 1985); Robert Glaser, *Testing and Assessment: O Tempora! O Mores!* (Pittsburgh: Learning Research and Development Center, University of Pittsburgh, 1990).

14. Robert Glaser, "The Future of Testing: A Research Agenda for Cognitive Psychology and Psychometrics," *American Psychologist* 36, no. 9 (1981): 923-936; idem, *Testing and Assessment: O Tempora! O Mores!*

15. Theodore Sizer, "No Pain, No Gain," *Educational Leadership* 48, no. 8 (1991): 32-34; idem, *Horace's School: Redesigning the American High School* (Boston: Houghton Mifflin, 1992).

16. A. Wheelock, "School Accountability Policies: Implications for Policy Making in Massachusetts," 1992 (Mimeograph).

17. Mindy Kornhaber and Howard Gardner, *Varieties of Student Excellence* (New York: National Center for Restructuring Education, Schools, and Teaching, Teachers College, Columbia University, 1993); Edmund Gordon, "Implications of Diversity in Human Characteristics for Authentic Assessment," nd (Mimeograph).

18. Gordon, "Implications of Diversity in Human Characteristics for Authentic Assessment."

19. Linda Darling-Hammond and Jon Snyder, "Reframing Accountability: Creating Learner-Centered Schools," in *The Changing Contexts of Teaching*, edited by Ann Lieberman, Ninety-first Yearbook of the National Society for the Study of Education (Chicago: University of Chicago Press, 1992), pp. 11-36.

20. Peter Senge, "Building Learning Organizations," *Journal for Quality and Participation* 15, no. 2 (1992): 30-38.

21. Ibid. See also, Peter Senge, "The Leader's New Work: Building Learning Organizations," *Sloan Management Review* 7, no. 1 (1990): 7-23.

22. See, for example, Peter F. Drucker, *The Frontiers of Management* (New York: Harper and Row, 1986) and Thomas J. Peters and Robert H. Waterman, Jr., *In Search of Excellence* (New York: Warner Books, 1982).

23. Michael Fullan, *The New Meaning of Educational Change* (New York: Teachers College Press, 1992); Seymour Sarason, The *Predictable Failure of Educational Reform* (San Francisco: Jossey-Bass, 1990); Paul Berman and Milbrey W. McLaughlin, *Federal Programs Supporting Educational Change: Vol. 7, Factors Affecting Implementation and Continuation* (Santa Monica, Calif.: RAND Corporation, 1977).

24. Eugene Smith and Ralph W. Tyler, *Appraising and Recording Student Progress* (New York: Harper and Brothers, 1942).

25. Dean Chamberlin, Enid Chamberlin, Ned Drought, and William Scott, *Did They Succeed in College?* (New York: Harper and Brothers, 1942), p. 182.

26. Jane David, "Restructuring in Progress: Lessons from Pioneering Districts," in *Restructuring Schools: The Next Generation of Educational Reform*, edited by Richard Elmore (San Francisco: Jossey-Bass, 1990), pp. 226-227.

27. Linda Darling-Hammond, Jacqueline Ancess, and Beverly Falk, *Alternative Assessment in Action: Case Studies of Schools and Students* (New York: Teachers College Press, 1995).

28. Ibid.

29. Jacqueline Ancess, *Last Chance School: A Look at Accountability at the Urban Academy*. A case study prepared for the National Center for Restructuring Education, Schools, and Teaching, Teachers College, Columbia University, 1992.

30. Darling-Hammond, Ancess, and Falk, *Alternative Assessment in Action*.

31. The Primary Language Record was developed by the Inner London Education Authority and is widely used in Great Britain to document children's literacy development. It has been adapted for use in California Chapter 1 schools as the California Learning Record, and is also being adapted for use in a growing number of schools in New York City (over fifty at last count). The Victoria (Australia) Literacy Profile is a similar instrument for observing and recording children's development. Other such instruments have been in use for many years. Recently, the High/Scope Educational Research Foundation developed a documentation instrument for early childhood educators.

32. Beverly Falk and Linda Darling-Hammond, *The Primary Language Record at P.S. 261* (New York: National Center for Restructuring Education, Schools, and Teaching, Teachers College, Columbia University, 1993).

33. Ibid., p. 36.

34. Ibid., pp. 31-32.

35. Judith Warren Little, "Norms of Collegiality and Experimentation: Workplace Conditions of School Success," *American Educational Research Journal* 19 (1982): 325-340.

36. Darling-Hammond, Ancess, and Falk, *Alternative Assessment in Action*.

37. Grant Wiggins, "Standards, Not Standardization: Evoking Quality Student Work," *Educational Leadership* 48, no. 5 (1991): 22.

38. Darling-Hammond, Ancess, and Falk, *Alternative Assessment in Action*.

39. Linda Darling-Hammond and Jacqueline Ancess, *Graduation by Portfolio at Central Park East Secondary School* (New York: National Center for Restructuring Education, Schools, and Teaching, Columbia University, forthcoming).

40. See, for example, Jane Andrias, Rhoda Kanevsky, Lynne Strieb, and Cecilia Traugh, *Exploring Values and Standards: Implications for Assessment* (New York: National Center for Restructuring Education, Schools, and Teaching, Teachers College, Columbia University, 1992); Janet Price, Sara Schwabacher, and Ted Chittenden, *The Multiple*

Forms of Evidence Study: Assessing Reading through Student Work Samples, Teacher Observations, and Tests (New York: Fund for New York City Public Education and National Center for Restructuring Education, Schools, and Teaching, Teachers College, Columbia University, 1993); Jon Snyder, Ann Lieberman, Maritza Macdonald, and A. Lin Goodwin, *Makers of Meaning in a Learning-Centered School: A Case Study of Central Park East I Elementary School* (New York: National Center for Restructuring Education, Schools, and Teaching, Teachers College, Columbia University, 1992); Darling-Hammond, Ancess, and Falk, *Alternative Assessment in Action.*

41. Prospect Center, *Prospect Center Documentary Processes* (Bennington, Vt: Prospect Archive and Center for Education and Research, 1986).

42. Rhoda Drucker Kanevsky, "The Descriptive Review of a Child: Teachers Learn about Values," in Andrias et al., *Exploring Values and Standards: Implications for Assessment,* p. 57.

43. Center for Education Statistics, *Digest of Education Statistics 1987* (Washington, D.C.: U.S. Department of Education, 1987).

44. John I. Goodlad, *A Place Called School* (New York: McGraw-Hill, 1984); Theodore Sizer, *Horace's Compromise* (Boston: Houghton Mifflin, 1985); Arthur G. Powell, Eleanor Farrar, and David K. Cohen, *The Shopping Mall High School* (Boston: Houghton Mifflin, 1985).

45. Darling-Hammond, Ancess, and Falk, *Alternative Assessment in Action.*

46. Price, Schwabacher, and Chittenden, *The Multiple Forms of Evidence Study.*

47. New York Council on Curriculum and Assessment, *Building a Learning-Centered Curriculum for Learner-Centered Schools,* Interim Report (Albany: New York State Education Department, 1992).

48. Ibid.

49. Howard Gardner, *The Unschooled Mind* (New York: Basic Books, 1991).

50. Robert Glaser, *Testing and Assessment,* pp. 16, 17.

51. Ibid.

CHAPTER IV

Can Performance-Based Student Assessments Be Psychometrically Sound?

ROBERT L. LINN AND EVA L. BAKER

The bulk of this chapter is devoted to an elaboration of key psychometric concepts that are central to the evaluation of performance-based assessments. The most fundamental and comprehensive of these concepts is validity. Indeed, other traditional concepts such as reliability, generalizability, and comparability as well as the important concept of fairness all require the accumulation of particular types of evidence that contribute to the overall evaluative judgment regarding the validity of uses and interpretations of an assessment.

Because validity depends on the uses and interpretations of assessment results, which are in turn shaped by the assessment purposes, it is important to begin with some consideration of the purposes that are envisioned for performance-based assessments. Therefore, we begin with a brief description of some of the primary reasons for the introduction of performance-based assessment. The characteristics of performance-based measures also are briefly described to provide a context for the discussion of the psychometric issues.

Motivation for Performance-Based Assessments

The rapid growth in demand for increased use of performance-based student assessment is motivated by many considerations. Among the more important reasons often given for moving from the multiple-choice testing format that has dominated standardized testing in the United States for several decades toward greater reliance on performance-based assessment are the beliefs that: (1) assessment tasks should involve activities that are valued in their own right, (2) assessments

Robert L. Linn is Professor of Education and Co-Director of the Center for Research on Evaluation, Standards, and Student Testing in the School of Education, University of Colorado at Boulder. Eva L. Baker is Professor of Education and Co-Director of the Center for Research on Evaluation, Standards, and Student Testing at the University of California at Los Angeles.

should model curriculum reform, (3) assessment activities should contribute to instructional improvement by focusing on instructional targets that are consistent with the goals of instructional activities, (4) assessments should provide a mechanism of staff development, (5) assessments should lead to improved learning by engaging students in meaningful activities that are intrinsically motivating, and (6) assessments should lead to greater and more appropriate accountability. It is no accident that "better measurement" in the traditional sense of higher reliability for a given amount of assessment time is not among the reasons given for wanting to place increased reliance on performance-based assessment.

The movement toward performance-based assessments is not motivated primarily by psychometric considerations. The assessments nonetheless need to be psychometrically sound, especially when they are used to make important decisions about individuals (e.g., certification) or schools (e.g., the allocation of rewards or sanctions). The relative importance of psychometric considerations for any assessment, however, depends on the purposes of the assessment and the uses that are made of the results. Consequently, the application of psychometric principles to performance-based assessments needs to take into account the assessment purposes and uses that are to be made of the results.

Valued activities/authenticity. Proponents of performance-based assessments such as Resnick and Resnick[1] and Wiggins[2] argue that assessments need to involve the direct observation of performance on tasks that are valued in their own right. Such tasks are contrasted with test items that are meant to be useful as indicators of valued "real-world" performances. Writing an explanation of a solution to a practical problem to communicate to a specific audience is an authentic writing task provided the problem is valued by the student, the audience, and in terms of the goals of instruction. On the other hand, answering multiple-choice questions about grammatical errors and punctuation errors in a paragraph that appears on a test would not qualify as an authentic assessment because the student is not demonstrating ability to perform a specific writing task.

As Messick[3] has suggested, the claim that an assessment is authentic is in essence a validity claim. The example of an explanation of the solution to a practical problem has packed in it many qualifications that need to be justified. Providing justification for the claims is the essence of validation and is an issue that is considered in more detail below.

Modeling curriculum reform. The desire for major reform of the curriculum provides a second major motivation for the introduction of performance-based assessments. A widely held belief is that you get what you assess and conversely that you do not get what you do not assess. A major concern about standardized tests is that they drive instruction in undesirable ways by focusing on the accumulation of facts and decontextualized skills.[4] A curriculum that focuses on decomposed bits and pieces presented without context is incompatible with the type of curriculum reform advocated by groups such as the National Council on Education Standards and Testing, the National Education Goals Panel, the New Standards project, and leading professional organizations such as the American Association for the Advancement of Science, the National Council of Teachers of English, and the National Council of Teachers of Mathematics.

Performance-based assessments seem to be more compatible with curriculum reforms that emphasize the identification and solution of real-world problems, reasoning, and higher-order thinking skills. Indeed, performance-based assessments are considered an integral part of curriculum reform.

Instructional improvement. Closely related to the notion that performance-based assessments are an important element of curriculum reform efforts is the idea that the assessments should provide exemplary instructional targets. Unlike standardized tests where teaching to the test may be counterproductive because the tests are intended to be only indicators of the achievement of valued instructional outcomes, performance-based assessments are expected to be indistinguishable from the goals of instruction. Hence, teaching to performance-based assessments is not only considered acceptable according to this view; it is also considered exemplary instructional practice. Indeed, in the case of some conceptions of portfolio assessments—those that include initial problem-solving attempts or drafts by students, feedback from teachers or other students, edits and revisions, and eventually a final product—assessment and instruction are indistinguishable.

Staff development. One of the more frequently cited benefits of performance-based assessments is their role in staff development. Teachers too seldom have an opportunity to interact with other teachers regarding fundamental issues of instructional goals. The involvement of teachers in the development of performance-based assessment and their associated scoring rubrics as well as in the scoring of student performances provides a rare opportunity for the discussion of what is and what should be valued in the curriculum. To the extent that the assessments fulfill the promise of providing desirable instructional targets, they also provide models for instructional activities.

Improved learning. The previously mentioned motivations for a movement toward performance-based assessments are all aspects of the fundamental motivation, that is, improved student learning. There is widespread dissatisfaction with the levels of achievement of the nation's students, and performance-based assessments are seen as powerful means of enhancing achievement. The first annual report of the National Education Goals Panel, for example, strongly stated the conclusion that the nation's students are performing far below what will be needed in the technologically advanced global economy of the future. That conclusion was reiterated in the second annual report of the Goals Panel, which also emphasized the importance of higher standards of achievement and assessments in efforts to achieve the nation's educational goals.[5]

Accountability. For a number of years accountability has been an important reason for the introduction of testing programs. And the demand for accountability continues to be an important part of proposals for new systems of performance-based assessment. The proposed performance-based assessments are thought to be more closely aligned with the most important educational goals and therefore more appropriate than standardized tests, which were the main feature of accountability systems of the past.

Characteristics of Performance-Based Assessments

There are many varieties of performance-based assessments. Indeed, it is easier to say what they are not than to define what they are. They are not fixed-response (e.g., true/false, or multiple-choice) tests where students are presented not only with the question or problem, but with a set of alternative answers from which they are to select the right or best answer. Saying what performance-based assessments are not is hardly a satisfactory definition, however. Hence we will briefly describe some of the characteristics that are most commonly associated with them.

Open-ended tasks. The first characteristic of performance-based assessments is implicit in the statement that they are not fixed-choice. The tasks are open-ended and require the student to construct a response or perform an activity. Of course, an open-ended task could include tasks such as asking students to give the answer to 2 plus 2 or to spell a word. Although constructing the response to such questions is a type of performance, it lacks many of the other features that are generally associated with performance-based assessments.

Higher-order, complex skills. A second characteristic of performance-based assessments is that they are apt to involve complex skills, such as formulating problems, solving problems, reasoning, higher-order thinking, and communication. It should be noted, however, that surface features of a task are no guarantee of the type of thinking that is demanded of a student. A maximization problem that requires considerable reasoning and higher-order thinking for one student, for example, may for another amount to no more than the application of well-memorized rules for finding derivatives and doing routine manipulations.

Extended periods of time for performance. Performance-based assessments often require extended periods of time. In contrast to a standardized test that may allow an average of about a minute per item, a performance-based task may require an hour or even substantially more time possibly extending over several days. The tasks may require the collection and analysis of data as well as the preparation of written or oral presentations of results and conclusions.

Group performance. Performance-based assessments, especially ones that are designed primarily for instructional purposes and are likely to be under the control of individual classroom teachers, are often designed to be performed by groups of students. Working together, students may be asked to formulate hypotheses, design experiments or other means of collecting needed information, analyze data, and prepare reports or demonstrations that any member of the group would be prepared to present or explain.

Student and teacher choice of tasks. In contrast to standardized tests where the same set of items is administered in a uniform fashion to all students, performance-based assessments often allow some degree of latitude in the choice of tasks to be performed. In the free response section of the Advanced Placement Test in Biology, for example, students have an hour and a half to respond to three problems they choose from a set of six, whereas students taking the American History Advanced Placement Test have one hour and forty-five minutes to respond to one required task and to another task that they select from five possibilities.[6]

Judgmental scoring. A possibly obvious characteristic of performance-based assessments is their reliance on human judgment in scoring. The development of scoring guidelines or rubrics and the training
of judges to do the scoring thus become aspects of the assessment that
are of tremendous importance.

Validity: Expanded Criteria and Sources of Evidence

The high expectations associated with the diverse purposes that
performance-based assessments are intended to serve pose substantial
challenges to those attempting to develop the assessments and assure
that they are psychometrically sound. The characteristics of performance-based assessments, especially the long time requirements per
task and the labor-intensive scoring requirements, make these challenges all the greater. In the remaining sections of this chapter we
describe some of the major considerations that need to be addressed in
order to evaluate the degree to which a performance-based assessment
system is psychometrically sound.[7]

The most fundamental psychometric issue is validity. Validity is a
comprehensive concept. It encompasses the accumulation of evidence
regarding many aspects of an assessment and the analysis and weigh-
ing of that evidence together with logical arguments in order to arrive
at an overall evaluative judgment regarding an assessment. As Messick
has indicated, the overall evaluative judgment should be concerned
with both the adequacy and appropriateness of interpretations or
inferences that are made from assessments and the uses or actions that
are based on the results.[8]

While acknowledging the preeminence of validity, the second psychometric consideration that is normally emphasized is reliability.
Investigations of reliability are concerned with the consistency of
results from one version of a measurement to another or from one
component of an assessment to another, and lack of consistency is
attributed to errors of measurement. "The reliability coefficient quan-
tifies reliability by summarizing the consistency (or inconsistency)
among several error-prone measurements."[9]

Reliability is clearly an important consideration especially when
important decisions are based upon the results of a particular assessment. Since reliability can be more readily evaluated and quantified
than validity, however, it has too often been overemphasized while the
more important consideration of validity is given short shrift. Moreover, the approaches used to estimate reliability sometimes ignore the

most important sources of inconsistency. For example, the consistency of one component of an assessment with another may be evaluated whereas the real concern should be with the consistency of one version of the assessment with another version. Or the degree of agreement among raters of a single task may be evaluated while the consistency of performance on different tasks is ignored. For these reasons, we focus on the more generic concept of generalizability, which subsumes the traditional notions of reliability. We shall try to make clear that even the broader concept of generalizability is of interest primarily because it provides a framework for obtaining evidence that contributes to an overall evaluative judgment regarding the validity of an assessment.

There are no simple prescriptions for validation of an assessment. As Cronbach has argued, "[v]alidation speaks to a diverse and potentially critical audience; therefore, the argument must link concepts, evidence, social and personal consequences, and values."[10] A number of key issues that are apt to be critical in validating a performance-based assessment can be identified, however. We distinguish two general categories or sources of evidence or validation criteria that need to be confronted for almost any performance-based assessment system. The first category is concerned with the internal characteristics of the assessment such as the nature of the tasks, the content covered, and the degree to which the assessment measures the intended complex skills rather than unintended ancillary skills. The second general category is concerned with external sources of evidence or validation criteria such as the consequences of the assessment, its fairness, and the generalizability of the results.

INTERNAL VALIDITY CRITERIA

The list of internal validity criteria discussed here is not intended to provide an exhaustive prescription for validation. Rather, the criteria reflect the range of issues that need to be addressed in developing a validity argument.

Content quality. One of the previously mentioned reasons for promoting performance-based assessments is the belief that they can provide improved targets for instruction. Such an aspiration certainly requires that the content of the assessments be consistent with the best current understanding of the subject matter. The tasks and their associated scoring rubrics should foster the development of understanding while minimizing misconceptions. The activities required should be worthy of the time that students devote to them and the time that raters spend scoring them.

Judgments about content quality require systematic efforts to obtain reviews of tasks and scoring rubrics from teachers and other subject-matter experts. The involvement of subject-matter experts in the development of tasks and scoring rubrics can also be a useful means of enhancing the content quality of an assessment.

Curricular importance. If performance-based assessments are to contribute to desired reforms of curriculum and are to provide appropriate targets for instruction, they must involve tasks and performances that are an important part of the curriculum. The assessments need to be closely aligned with the valued curricular goals. An issue of concern here is the tendency for tasks to be selected because of their novelty. It is not sufficient to include a task because it is "interesting."

Content coverage. With standardized tests the issue of content coverage is usually approached as a sampling problem. A content domain is identified and used to create a table of test specifications that might define a cross classification of content categories by processes, and items are constructed to fit the various cells of the table. Two features of performance-based assessments make this traditional approach to content coverage problematic. First, because performance-based tasks often require extended periods of time to complete, relatively few of them can be included in any given assessment. Consequently, the desire to cover a wide domain of content cannot be approached by requiring each student to respond to a large number of tasks.

Second, performance-based tasks may involve multiple processes and integration of a variety of content. Therefore, the tasks do not fit neatly into the cells of a traditional content-by-process matrix. It is this second feature of performance assessments that proponents of performance-based assessment look to as a solution to the problem of covering content. But it is also a feature that makes an analysis of a set of tasks in terms of the full array of curricular goals all the more important. For example, even if each performance-based mathematics task making up an assessment is of the highest quality, the overall assessment could be found wanting if critical mathematical goals such as understanding and using concepts of probability or the ability to represent and solve problems using geometric representations are ignored.

Cognitive complexity. One of the central rationales for performance-based assessments is that they encourage a focus on more complex, higher-order thinking skills. But the cognitive complexity of a task cannot be determined solely by looking at the task. It is possible to memorize an algorithm that is then applied to solve a seemingly complex problem without ever developing an understanding of the concepts involved or the ability to solve problems requiring variations or adaptations of the memorized algorithm.

Evidence that performances require students to reason and engage in real problem-solving activities involves more than displaying tasks that seem interesting. Analyses of student responses, observations of group interactions, and protocol analyses may also be needed.

Linguistic appropriateness. Reading and writing in English are central to some, but not all, instructional goals. It is critical that content-based thinking competencies not be inappropriately swamped by language demands that accompany many performance-based assessments. Linguistic demands that are not central to the goal of the assessment need to be identified and minimized. Communication, for example, is one of the standards emphasized in the curriculum standards developed by the National Council of Teachers of Mathematics (NCTM), but that does not justify exclusive reliance on tasks involving heavy reading and writing demands. Communication can take other forms such as equations, graphs, and geometric diagrams. Moreover, the heavy reliance on language could interfere with the assessment of achievement of other NCTM standards such as problem solving, the development of a number sense and numeration, and the understanding of patterns and functions.[11] The general point is that the linguistic demands should be dictated by the instructional goals that tasks are intended to assess, and evidence should be sought to assure that inappropriate linguistic demands do not interfere with the ability of students to perform a task.

Ancillary skills. Linguistic demands that are not an essential part of the outcomes being assessed are but an example of a more general problem that can undermine the validity of an assessment. Wiley makes an important distinction between "the intent of measurement and the ancillary skills needed to respond correctly to the items."[12] Ancillary skills are a source of invalidity. Speed of response is an example of an ancillary skill on a traditional timed test that is not intended to measure the ability to respond rapidly. Reading may be an ancillary skill on certain science tasks, but it may also be a part of the intent of the measurement.

The identification of ancillary skills must begin with a clear specification of the intent of the measurement. Is writing a part of the instructional goal that is being assessed or is it just a convenient way to collect student responses? Once the intent of measurement is identified then likely ancillary skills can be identified through task analysis, and evidence can be obtained to evaluate the degree to which student performances are influenced by ancillary skills.

Meaningfulness of tasks for students. One of the rationales for performance-based assessments is that they will assure that students are engaged in meaningful educational experiences resulting in greater understanding of the task and stronger motivation for students' performance. Validation requires the evaluation of this expectation. Indices of student engagement with the tasks might be derived from observations and interviews of students.

EXTERNAL VALIDITY CRITERIA

The second major category of validity criteria is labeled "external" to distinguish it from the more internal developmental issues discussed above. The concerns here are with the impact of the assessment (e.g., the degree to which it has the intended consequences and the fairness of the assessment to students with different backgrounds) and with issues regarding the generalizability and comparability of results from different assessments.

Consequences for students and teachers. The primary rationales for performance-based assessments all relate in one way or another to the goal of improved student learning. Hence an evaluation of the impact of the assessments on student learning is a critical aspect of their validation. But an evaluation of the degree to which this intended consequence is realized by a performance-based assessment system, while important, is insufficient by itself.

An adequate validation effort needs to look not only at the intended consequences, but at unintended consequences, particularly unintended negative consequences. The history of testing is replete with examples of good intentions gone awry. Indeed, many arguments in favor of performance-based assessments begin with the premise that the type of standardized testing that has been most heavily relied upon in the past needs to be replaced because it is having unintended negative consequences (e.g., a narrowing of the curriculum and a reinforcement of instructional practices that are inconsistent with current views of learning). Unintended negative consequences should play an equally important role in the validation of performance-based assessments.

The impact of assessments on schools, the curriculum, and the amount of instructional time devoted to different content areas needs to be evaluated. Possible changes in the amount of time spent teaching content areas not included in the assessment and in the performance of students in those areas needs to be documented as part of the validation effort.

Specific uses of assessment are important to all aspects of validation research, but uses and specific actions based on assessment results are particularly critical to investigations of the consequential aspects of validity. Decisions about individual students such as tracking, retention in grade, or assignment to a special instructional program need to be defended. The goal should be the accumulation of evidence that students are more likely to learn and show greater gains in achievement when assigned to a particular program or retained in grade.

Fairness. Fairness is just as critical a consideration in the validation of a performance-based assessment as it is for any other type of assessment. Because of the large between-group differences in educational opportunity, it is unrealistic to expect that simply changing the form of assessment will eliminate differences in performance for minority and majority group students, for males and females, or for groups defined by socio-economic status. Without a fundamental change in distribution of educational opportunities, group differences that are all too familiar on current tests can be expected to continue on a new set of performance-based assessments.

Several difficult questions regarding fairness need to be addressed in the validation of a performance-based assessment. To what degree does the assessment fairly consider the cultural background of the students taking the assessment? The issues considered above regarding linguistic appropriateness and ancillary skills are of particular relevance here. What differences are there in opportunity to learn the complex thinking and problem-solving skills that are the targets of the assessments? Such a question implies that the fairness of the assessment needs to be evaluated in terms of the degree to which it is aligned, not only with possibly different curricula, but with the instructional experiences of students in different settings. Since differential instructional experiences can occur within as well as between classrooms and schools, it is also important to obtain evidence regarding the degree to which students within a school are provided with equitable opportunities to succeed.

Transfer and generalizability. No matter how interesting or highly valued an assessment is in its own right, there is a need to consider the degree to which results are generalizable. Since performance-based assessments require judgmental scoring, there is obviously a need to consider the degree to which results can be generalized across raters. Less than perfect consistency in rating from one judge to another contributes to errors of measurement and will always be the source of some degree of unreliability in performance-based assessment. With care in design of scoring rubrics and the training of raters this source of unreliability can be reduced to reasonable levels, but whatever the level, the degree of generalizability across raters needs to be documented.

Although interrater agreement is an issue that requires careful attention, it is actually the easier part of the problem of generalizability faced in the use of performance-based assessments. A second and more challenging generalizability problem that needs to be addressed concerns the degree to which performance on one task provides the basis for generalizations about performance on other similar tasks. Research in a variety of contexts indicates that there is a considerable degree of task specificity in performance. That is, performance on one task provides a relatively weak basis of generalization to other seemingly similar tasks.[13]

The limited degree of across-task generalizability in performance implies that performance needs to be assessed across several tasks. For a wide variety of performance-based assessments it has been demonstrated that increasing the number of tasks is generally more important than increasing the number of raters.[14] This tendency is illustrated in figure 1 where the score generalizability coefficients for essays written in response to historical documents is plotted as a function of the number of topics and the number of raters. It is obvious that increasing the number of essays that students are required to write does considerably more to enhance generalizability than can be achieved by increasing the number of raters.

Both the amount of time required per task and the level of across-task generalizability may vary across different domains. Consequently, the total amount of time required to achieve a high degree of score generalizability may vary substantially from one subject domain and associated approach to assessment to another. This variability in required time is illustrated in figure 2 where the estimated number of hours of assessment time that would be required to achieve a score

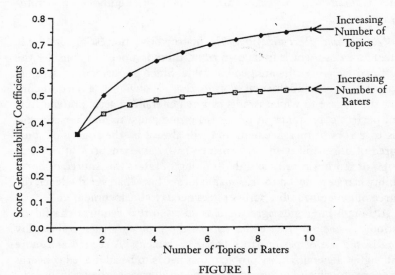

FIGURE 1

Score generalizability of general impression content quality scores of extended history tasks as a function of the number of history topics and the number of raters. Adapted from Robert L. Linn, "Educational Assessment: Expanded Expectations and Challenges," *Educational Evaluation and Policy Analysis 15* (1993): 13. © 1993 by the American Educational Research Association. Adapted by permission of the publisher.

generalizability of .90 is plotted for the free-response sections of twenty-one Advanced Placement tests is displayed. The hours of testing ranges from a low of an hour and fifteen minutes to a high of thirteen hours. Whatever the degree of generalizability across tasks, it needs to be evaluated in arriving at an overall judgment regarding the validity of the interpretations and uses of the assessment results. As the stakes of an assessment increase so too does the need for increased levels of generalizability across both raters and tasks.

Comparability. The tasks used in performance-based assessments are readily remembered because each task may require a substantial amount of time to perform and consequently relatively few of them can be administered to each student. Attempting to track performance over time using the same tasks every year would confound differences in familiarity with the particular tasks from year to year with real changes in the achievement of different cohorts of students. Hence, there is a need to introduce new tasks, but this complicates comparisons by confounding cohort differences with task differences.

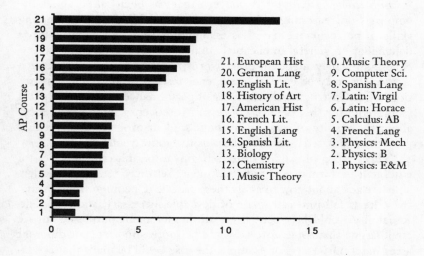

21. European Hist   10. Music Theory
20. German Lang   9. Computer Sci.
19. English Lit.   8. Spanish Lang
18. History of Art   7. Latin: Virgil
17. American Hist   6. Latin: Horace
16. French Lit.   5. Calculus: AB
15. English Lang   4. French Lang
14. Spanish Lit.   3. Physics: Mech
13. Biology   2. Physics: B
12. Chemistry   1. Physics: E&M
11. Music Theory

Hours Testing for Reliability ≥ .9

FIGURE 2

Estimated hours of testing time needed for a generalizability coefficient of .90 or higher on the free-response sections of Advanced Placement Examinations for 21 courses. Adapted from Robert L. Linn, "Educational Assessment: Expanded Expectations and Challenges," *Educational Evaluation and Policy Analysis* 15 (1993): 13. © 1993 by the American Educational Research Association. Adapted by permission of the publisher.

Comparisons may also be desired between schools, districts, or states where different performance-based assessment tasks have been administered. Both the desire for comparisons across time and for comparisons among groups employing different assessment tasks create a demand to find a way of judging the comparability of performances on different tasks.

Equating procedures that are used with standardized tests to make the results on alternate forms of a test comparable are unlikely to be applicable to performance-based assessments because of the stringent requirements that tests being equated measure the same characteristics with equal degrees of precision. Moderation procedures used in some other countries that rely on consensus judgments are more likely to be applicable, but there is little experience with these procedures in this country. Until such techniques have been attempted here it is difficult to know the degree to which they may yield technically and politically acceptable results.

Instructional sensitivity. A concern that has been raised about the emphasis on reasoning, problem solving, and higher-order thinking skills in performance-based assessments is that they may be more dependent on general intellectual ability than on instructional experiences and achievement. In other words, there is a concern that such assessments may be general intelligence tests in disguise. Demonstrations of the instructional sensitivity of performance-based assessments would counter this type of concern. Moreover, accurate inferences about the quality of schools or about student progress demand that performance-based assessment be sensitive to instructional effort.

This lexicon of validity criteria begins to permit critical review of emergent performance-based assessment. Yet there remains considerable latitude about how to apply these criteria. One might suggest that the criteria fall into categories of desirable, necessary, and sufficient. Reliability would be essential for all measurement purposes, but we could argue that some criteria would be more important for different assessment purposes. For example, the case could be made that assessments intended for school accountability must be sensitive to instruction, else their results are of little value in judging the quality of educational programs. In considering the criteria, we have addressed neither the sequence of their technical exploration nor the importance of interpreting findings in the light of specific collateral data, such as opportunity to learn, when drawing appropriate inferences about construct validity and fairness.

Design Issues

It is common to believe that assessments or tests should be prepared and then their goodness should be assessed in short-term empirical studies addressing reliability and validity. Such models have served the measurement community well in the past. Yet current expectations of performance-based assessment are based on the contribution of the assessment itself to change the nature of instructional experiences in the long term. Furthermore, we expect that technical characteristics—such as fairness and criterion-related validity—will depend upon the nature of instruction experienced by students. Traditional, short-term methods to establish technical quality may be inherently less valuable. For example, the use of criterion groups may be impossible because there may be few, if any, students who have had relevant long-term instructional experience. Another option is to defer the study of assessment quality until instruction is naturally in place, a choice whose tautological implications are obvious. Third, we might conduct medium-length instructional experiments (for example, a school year) with various student populations using various performance-based assessments as dependent measures. Unfortunately, the practical inhibitions of this approach are great.

These methodological frustrations could lead to undue attention to reliability. Yet, other, more proactive approaches are available. Instead of delaying our technical look at performance-based assessments, we can take steps at the point of their design to increase the chances that they will exhibit desired characteristics. Design methodologies have increasing currency in the business and industrial communities. Essentially, the idea is to create a product—in this case, a performance-based assessment—so that it exhibits desired characteristics and performances thus meeting internal and external criteria. In automobiles, characteristics might include the feel of the steering or the comfort of the seats. Performance might include frequency of repair or safety. Extending the analogy to performance-based assessment suggests that the defining characteristics of performance-based assessment can be judged before assessments are subjected to costly field trials. For instance, the degree to which a task is open-ended or calls for higher-order thinking can be explicitly reviewed, ideally augmented by some small-sample intensive study of students attempting the task. Internal validity criteria obviously lend themselves to design use. Tasks can be created so that content quality, curricular importance, content coverage, cognitive complexity, and linguistic appropriateness are required attributes of a given task. Specifications describing relevant knowledge, intellectual processes, and language forms can guide the preparation of assessments. Determining the need for ancillary skills will require some empirical demonstration as will the assumption of student motivation and the "meaningfulness" of the task.

Far too often at this relatively early stage tasks are "created" and then rationalized rather than carefully and systematically designed. More interestingly, design processes can influence external validity criteria, that is, how performance-based assessments perform. In the realm of generalizability and transfer, for example, one's definition of the domain to be assessed matters. One could take a broad view, for example, "science problem solving," or conceive of tasks more narrowly as, for example, written explanations of historical texts. This choice influences the required number of tasks to establish generalizability. In a similar fashion, scoring rubrics with common dimensions and standardized rater-trailing procedures will also influence the deeper meaning of generalizability and transfer. Essentially, we desire generalizability that results from instruction rather than from ability levels.

What are the trade-offs? Tight specifications, common detailed scoring rubrics, and operational definitions of domains will likely result in tasks that are more exchangeable, comparable, and amenable to instruction. Yet specification may well mean that students develop relatively limited repertoires. Less completely specified tasks with idiographic scoring rubrics are more likely to assess general ability, and although the tasks may in themselves be teachable, the likelihood of comparability and generalizable performance may well be reduced.

There have been some efforts to design specifications for performance assessments that create common expectations across topics and subject matter boundaries for intellectual processes such as understanding or explanation. Incorporating such definitions and associated scoring criteria in the design of an assessment may benefit the management of instruction in self-contained classrooms and avoid the daunting prospect of teaching multiple and different criteria for every different content area. Notions of comparability, generalizability, and instructional sensitivity become extremely complicated when thematic or interdisciplinary tasks are desired because of the task-specific interactions with the content and contexts of the assessment. Careful design and review of tasks may be able to reduce the numbers of tasks subjected to costly and potentially inefficient empirical analyses. However, the degree to which design attributes are important will vary with assessment purpose.

Current Priorities

Technical quality is an unassailable requirement of performance assessments. There is ambiguity, however, regarding the trade-offs and relative priorities in reaching an overall evaluative judgment regarding the validity of particular performance assessments used for particular purposes. Because performance assessments are emerging phenomena, procedures for assessing their quality are in some disorder. First, there is the tendency to treat all performance assessments, despite daunting differences in design and purpose, as if they were in , need of the same types of technical examination. Second, there is relatively little analysis of the sequence of technical procedures required to render assessments sound for certain uses.

Clarity regarding purposes, intended interpretations, and anticipated uses of performance assessments provides the essential starting place for determining priorities for the evaluation of the technical quality of the assessment. Assessments designed to sample from relatively broad domains (science tasks drawn from different disciplines), for example, can hardly be expected to have the same level of generalizability across tasks as assessments designed with tightly controlled task structures drawn from a narrow domain of content. In both cases the level of generalizability needed, and therefore the number of tasks required, depend heavily on the uses that are to be made of the scores.

Generalizability, while not sufficient, is a major issue for performance-based assessments. Although a high degree of generalizability does not guarantee valid inferences or uses of assessment results, "low levels of generalizability across tasks limit the validity of inferences about performance for a domain and pose serious problems regarding comparability and fairness to individuals who are judged against performance standards based on a small number, and perhaps different set, of tasks."[15] Thus investigations of generalizability across tasks as well as across raters deserve high priority.

In addition to generalizability, there is a clear need to demonstrate the validity of the scores, or better yet, the scoring rubric. Investigations of relationships to external criteria are certainly relevant, but are not sufficient. Much greater attention needs to be placed on research that demonstrates that children can be taught to accomplish the tasks that make up our assessments through experiences provided by schools. Unless assessments are instructionally sensitive they are likely to be useless as measures of school-based learning.

The problem is that we cannot learn enough from the conduct of short-term instructional studies, nor can we wait for results of longer-term instructional programs. We must depend upon studies that provide clues and glimmers about how assessments will work in the future. But until that future arrives, we must continue to operate on faith. The disagreement in the field is on the science-to-faith ratio.

Summary and Conclusions

Performance-based assessments are expected to serve a wide array of purposes. They are expected to be useful in staff development and to lead to improvements in day-to-day instruction and student learning when used by individual classroom teachers. They are also expected to be a powerful educational reform tool and to provide better accountability. An assessment that is judged to have adequate validity when used for one of these purposes may not have adequate validity when used for another purpose.

The judgment of the degree to which an assessment system is psychometrically sound is in essence an evaluation of the degree of validity of the inferences and actions that are based on the assessment results. There are a number of validity claims that are implicit in the interpretations that are proposed for performance-based assessment. Authenticity, the measurement of cognitively complex skills, and the motivating effects of engaging students in performing more meaningful tasks are examples of implicit validity claims that need to be supported by evidence. The expectation that performance-based assessments can contribute to improved learning is one that clearly needs to be validated, but it is even more important to evaluate the degree to which particular uses of assessment results have unintended negative consequences.

Validation is never an easy process. It is made more difficult by the diverse range of uses and interpretations that are likely to be associated with some performance-based assessments. The success of the movement toward performance-based assessments, however, will depend heavily on the level of effort that is put into addressing validity issues such as those discussed in this chapter.

Work on this chapter was partially supported by the Educational Research and Development Center Program cooperative agreement R117G10027 and CFDA catalog number 84.117G as administered by the Office of Educational Research and Improvement, U.S. Department of Education. The findings and opinions expressed in this chapter do not reflect the position or policies of the Office of Educational Research and Improvement or the U.S. Department of Education.

Notes

1. Lauren B. Resnick and Daniel P. Resnick, "Assessing the Thinking Curriculum: New Tools for Educational Reform," in *Changing Assessments: Alternative Views of Aptitude, Achievement, and Instruction*, edited by Bernard R. Gifford and Mary Catherine O'Connor (Boston: Kluwer Academic Publishers, 1992), pp. 37-75.

2. Grant Wiggins, "A True Test: Toward More Authentic and Equitable Assessment," *Phi Delta Kappan* 79 (1989): 703-713.

3. Samuel Messick, "The Interplay of Evidence and Consequences in the Validation of Performance Assessments" (Paper presented at the Annual Meeting of the National Council on Measurement in Education, San Francisco, April, 1992).

4. Resnick and Resnick, "Assessing the Thinking Curriculum."

5. National Education Goals Panel, *The National Education Goals Report, Building a Nation of Learners* (Washington, D.C.: U.S. Government Printing Office, 1991); idem, *The National Education Goals Report, Building a Nation of Learners* (Washington, D.C.: U.S. Government Printing Office, 1992).

6. The College Board, *Technical Manual for the Advanced Placement Program* (New York: The College Board, 1988).

7. For further elaboration of some of the validity criteria discussed here, see Robert L. Linn, Eva L. Baker, and Stephen B. Dunbar, "Complex Performance-Based Assessment: Expectations and Validation Criteria," *Educational Researcher* 20, no. 8

(1991): 15-21, and Eva L. Baker, Harold F. O'Neil, Jr., and Robert L. Linn, "Policy and Validity Prospects for Performance-Based Assessment" (Paper presented at the Annual Meeting of the American Psychological Association, San Francisco, August, 1991).

8. Samuel Messick, "Validity," in *Educational Measurement*, 3rd ed., edited by Robert L. Linn (New York: Macmillan, 1989), pp. 13-103.

9. Leonard S. Feldt and Robert L. Brennan, "Reliability," in *Educational Measurement*, 3rd ed., edited by Robert L. Linn (New York: Macmillan, 1989), p. 105.

10. Lee J. Cronbach, "Five Perspectives on the Validity Argument," in *Test Validity*, edited by Howard Wainer and Henry I. Braun (Hillsdale, N.J.: Erlbaum, 1988), p. 4.

11. National Council of Teachers of Mathematics, *Curriculum and Evaluation Standards for School Mathematics* (Reston, Va.: National Council of Teachers of Mathematics, 1989).

12. David E. Wiley, "Test Validity and Invalidity Reconsidered," in *Improving Inquiry in Social Science: A Volume in Honor of Lee J. Cronbach*, edited by Richard E. Snow and David E. Wiley (Hillsdale, N.J.: Erlbaum, 1991), p. 88.

13. See, for example, Robert L. Linn, "Educational Assessment: Expanded Expectations and Challenges," *Educational Evaluation and Policy Analysis* 15 (1993): 1-16.

14. Eva L. Baker, *The Role of Domain Specifications in Improving the Technical Quality of Performance Assessment*, Technical Report to OERI (Los Angeles: Center for Research on Evaluation, Standards, and Student Testing, University of California, 1992).

15. Linn, "Educational Assessment," pp. 12-13.

CHAPTER V

Coherence, Assessment, and Challenging Content

MARSHALL S. SMITH AND JESSICA LEVIN

Assessment has taken on mythic proportions in education in the United States. Individual teacher-sponsored assessment may be similar in scale for our children when compared to students in other nations. This, however, is not true for testing required by federal, state, and local governments, where demands in the United States are far greater.[1]

This chapter is about assessments for K-12 students required by institutions outside of school—federal, state, and local governments. The standardized tests previously required by Chapter 1 under the 1988 Hawkins-Stafford Amendments[2] and state-required assessments are illustrations. We are not concerned here with the teacher-generated, day-to-day assessments carried out in classrooms as part of the everyday curriculum and pedagogy. One exception is an assessment required by a government that may use the products of testing by individual teachers as part of its assessment (products found in portfolios, for example).

Such assessments often are viewed as having different (and sometimes multiple) purposes. These are (1) providing motivation to students and teachers by recognizing the effects of hard work and good practice; (2) supplying information and feedback for teachers and principals to use to improve their practice; (3) creating capacity building opportunities for teachers and others to engage in learning about their craft by participating, for example, in constructing, administering, and scoring the assessments; and (4) providing independent and valid information for legitimate institutional and individual accountability, including a system of rewards and sanctions that can influence institutional behavior and student opportunities.

Marshall S. Smith is Under Secretary of the U.S. Department of Education. Jessica Levin works in the Office of the Under Secretary, where she is a special assistant to Smith.

This chapter is also about "coherence." Here, the amount of coherence in an educational system, such as a school or district or state, is defined as the degree to which the various policy instruments in the system are aligned to achieve a common goal.[3] For this discussion, the goal we care about is the quality and content of teaching and learning. A district with little coherence might emphasize hands-on science, problem solving in mathematics, and student-initiated projects in social studies; use a basic-skills-only assessment system; sponsor a professional development program for teachers that has little to do with the curriculum; and have a superintendent who is entirely preoccupied with the nuts and bolts of a desegregation order. A more coherent district would have substantial alignment among the curriculum, assessments, professional development, and major resource decisions across the system.

This chapter has two parts. In the first part we explore the relationship between assessments, coherence, and challenging content standards. We examine the role of a coherent system—particularly the alignment of assessment and teaching and learning—in supporting fair and valid assessments that provide the kind of motivation, feedback, capacity building, and accountability described above. We also explore the pivotal role of content standards in achieving—and performance standards in supporting—coherence in a system focused on challenging and complex content. Finally, we demonstrate how a system can be coherent at one level (e.g., the school or district) and lack coherence at another (e.g., state), in which case a state assessment would probably not support the four assessment purposes we have already outlined. In the second part of the chapter we turn to challenges and obstacles—both technical and legal—encountered in reaching the vision spelled out in the first part, particularly in developing high-quality, fair, and valid performance assessments that can be legitimate tools for accountability and supportive of coherent reform.

The Relationship between Assessment, Coherence, and Challenging Content Standards

Our basic argument is that if assessments operate in a coherent system and are aligned with the content (broadly construed) of instruction, they are more likely to be fair and valid and meet the four broad purposes of motivation, feedback, capacity building, and accountability. This means the assessment must measure whether or not the student is achieving the aims of the curriculum. This argument holds regardless of the content and aims of the particular curriculum or pedagogy.

Would, for example, a multiple-choice assessment of fourth grade reading skills motivate either students or teachers whose curriculum was focused on reading and thoughtfully appraising Grimm's fairy tales? Would a writing assessment that prompted creative and relatively free-form responses necessarily provide salient and relevant information to a seventh grade teacher who is focused on teaching grammar, logic, and structure? Would helping to develop a typical standardized test for science be a useful experience for a high school science teacher in a district that is focused on depth and "doing science" in its curriculum? Does it make sense—is it "legitimate"—to hold a student accountable for her success on an assessment if the assessment measures content and strategies that the student did not study? Would it be "legitimate" to hold the school responsible for its students' success on such an assessment?

The answer usually is "no" for these examples. Yet, in the United States most of our assessments are constructed independently of the curriculum of the schools. Think of typical standardized norm-referenced tests or the Scholastic Assessment Test (SAT). How often do we picture these tests as motivating good practice and hard work, as providing effective feedback for teachers, as useful in professional development, and as "legitimate" information for holding students and teachers accountable for their level of work in school?

Consider two examples in which the assessments and the curriculum are relatively coherent. Advanced Placement (AP) examinations are designed to assess the content of a syllabus in the area of the examination—a syllabus that sets out the core topics to be covered and that is used by most AP teachers as their general guide in teaching the AP course. Hard work by students and good teaching are reinforced by student performance on the examinations. Moreover, student performance on an examination in one year provides useful information to the teacher in thinking about her curriculum for the next year. Over the years, the College Board has developed networks and other strategies to engage AP teachers in the development and scoring of the AP examinations. Many AP teachers view these strategies as opportunities for powerful professional development because of the focus on the content and skills of the AP courses and because they create a strong network of professionals who are trying to teach common material. Finally, the AP assessments are seen as legitimate and useful by teachers, students, and colleges. For students, of course, the examinations have moderately high stakes since opportunities to attend the college of their choice and to meet college requirements rest, in part, on their performance.[4]

A second example of coherence demonstrates the force of alignment whether the content involved is advanced or elementary. During the 1970s and early 1980s, a variety of forces came together to reinforce a minimum competencies curriculum in the United States. A back-to-basics movement had replaced Sputnik-driven and challenging curricula for science, "new math," and social studies, and other progressive reforms of the late 1960s. In many states, passing minimum competency tests became a requirement for graduation. Federal and state compensatory education efforts emphasized basic skills in reading and mathematics often at the expense of more challenging material. It is probable that this inadvertent alignment of curriculum and assessment significantly contributed to a substantial increase in the test scores of African-American and Hispanic-American and low-income students. At the same time, the scores of other students stayed roughly the same, or fell slightly, as measured by the National Assessment of Educational Progress (NAEP).[5] Although this second example of coherence did not accomplish all four purposes of assessment that we have outlined, it did satisfy those purposes related to motivation, feedback, and accountability, at least for some students and some teachers.[6]

HOW DO WE CREATE COHERENCE?

These two examples give us some insight into ways of creating coherence. In the first example, the syllabus for the AP courses provides a clear statement of what students should know and be able to do, and assessments are aligned with the syllabus. Moreover, the scoring rubric for the AP examinations establishes meaningful performance standards for determining the level of competence that students have with respect to the material in the syllabus.

In the second example, the alignment was created less by one deliberate policy than by a series of policies at different levels of government, all of which reinforced the same ends. When passage of the minimum competency examinations became a pre-condition for graduation, however, it is safe to assume that the examinations had a strong effect on shaping the course content for students who were in danger of not passing.[7]

The two examples also differ significantly in the nature of the content taught and tested. In AP courses, the content is advanced, generally requiring hard work and new learning by both students and teachers. In the example of the minimum competency test, the content was far less advanced, undoubtedly requiring little new learning by many teachers; moreover, while some students may have needed to work hard to pass the examinations, failure probably had more to do with lack of motivation and support than with the depth or advanced nature of the curriculum.

As we can see in these examples, the process by which coherence can be created appears to depend on the nature and complexity of the content. Where the content is largely facts and skills, as in the example of the minimum competency test, the assessment itself may drive the content of different courses: many teachers, for example, already know how to teach the material; textbook publishers know what to put in their textbooks. But where the content is advanced and complex, some touchstone or guide to the knowledge and skills expected of participating students appears critical to supporting the systemwide changes necessary to create an aligned system geared to the challenging content. An AP syllabus, for example, plays this role by describing the content expected of children enrolled in that AP course, thus enabling changes in curriculum and teaching, materials and training, to support that content.

The reform movement of the 1990s is closer to the AP example than to the minimum competency example. In particular, its fundamental intent is to move schools to engage all students in learning challenging content and skills in preparation for an adult life where the demands of active citizenship and employment will require people who have both basic and advanced knowledge and skills. This will require new learning by teachers, different teaching materials, and new pedagogical strategies, as well as more challenging assessments and thus a clear idea about the content and skill expectations around which these various parts of the system can be focused.

In many of the current ambitious reforms, state and local content standards provide that guide; they define what all students are expected to know and be able to do, around which assessments, materials, instruction, and professional development can then be aligned. Although analogous to the AP syllabus in role, content standards, in fact, must be far more general in form and structure; for while the AP syllabus supports alignment within a single AP course, content standards do so within and across broader systems (i.e., schools, districts, states). Performance standards address the level of understanding and skill expected of students who are proficient or advanced in relation to the content standards. Performance standards also suggest how student competency may be demonstrated. In fact, when well-developed performance standards include many examples of student work and related commentary, they not only can help guide teachers and others in their instructional efforts; they also can provide powerful guidance for the development of curriculum materials and assessments.[8]

The need to provide a clear statement of goals about improved teaching and learning to guide the central aspects of schools has, in fact, led many groups—including the 103rd Congress of the United States, the National Governors' Association, the National Council on Standards and Testing (NCEST), major national business and labor organizations, a large number of states, and most of the professional education associations—to promote the use of state content and performance standards as the starting point for systemic reforms focused on challenging content and skills for all students.[9]

THE NATURE OF THE ALIGNED ASSESSMENTS

We have argued that assessments cannot successfully meet their intended purposes unless they operate in a relatively coherent system, especially one in which the assessment system and the teaching and learning are aligned. We have also argued that challenging content and performance standards provide a critical touchstone around which to forge a coherent system focused on advanced and complex content. Where does student assessment, particularly performance assessment, fit in this picture?

The answer to this question seems to depend on the character of the content and performance standards. Depending on their nature, alignment can arguably be accomplished with a multiple-choice or short-answer assessment, as in the minimum competency example. In that instance, such a measure even could meet most of the purposes that we sketched earlier for assessments, although often with predictably stultifying effect on curriculum and instruction and the character of the school.

We have argued for a different view of the character of the content and performance standards. Our vision is of standards that set challenging goals for students and teachers alike in order to stimulate changes in curriculum and instruction that will enable all children to achieve the standards. In fact, the great strength (but potentially the Achilles heel of this reform movement) is that we are not simply "raising the bar." Instead, we are simultaneously working on changing learning conditions, curriculum, and pedagogy to meet the future needs of youth in an increasingly complex and diverse economic and social system. In this vision, we do not see curriculum and instruction as ending at the classroom door. Schools, like other organizations in the modern world, must change to be effective. Deeper and different knowledge and skills, joint efforts and products of teachers and students, a greater understanding and appreciation of technology, respect and tolerance for diversity and change will be the characteristics of effective schools of the next millennium.

If this is the vision, the typical multiple-choice and short-answer assessments fall far short. After all, assessments aligned with content and performance standards should animate, not inhibit, the rich and ambitious school-based curricula that these standards are intended to inspire. This suggests that the assessment should model the kinds of learning that we expect students to achieve, not merely be a pale shadow of a single dimension of the curriculum, such as breadth of factual knowledge, which may be easily assessed by a multiple-choice test. If we want to know whether students are able to write a strong essay, carry out a scientific experiment, research a historical issue or work with a team on a way to solve an environmental problem, we should ask them to do so on the assessment. These tasks require a performance assessment that asks students to actually perform the tasks and analyses and to demonstrate the understandings expected of them.

In addition to providing critical support for a coherent system focused on challenging content and performance standards, performance assessment could come much closer than other kinds of assessments to meeting the *intent* of the four purposes for assessment that we set out earlier. Performance assessment could reinforce hard work and study by students and teachers because it would be aligned in a broad sense to the spirit as well as the substance of challenging content and performance standards and, therefore, to curricula based on these standards. For the same reasons, it would supply useful feedback to teachers and principals to help them improve their work in the future. It would create potentially exciting educational opportunities for teachers to participate in administering and scoring the assessments of students other than their own and, for a fortunate few, to help in the construction of the assessments. Finally, performance assessments could provide useful and legitimate information for both individual and institutional accountability.

To meet some of these purposes effectively, performance assessments could be administered at more than one point in time. For example, a structured portfolio of student work gathered over a three- or four-year period might constitute an important element of an assessment. This type of performance assessment might be especially useful for providing feedback to teachers, students, and parents. To give the assessment credibility for individual and institutional account-ability, however, the portfolio would need to be independently scored by professionals from outside the school and at least some parts of the performance assessment should be administered independently.

Nonetheless, there are drawbacks to purely performance-based assessments. They are often expensive and time-consuming to admin-ister and score. Under some circumstances, this may limit the number of "performances," thus reducing the opportunity for measurements to be reliable. In these situations, it may be useful to augment a per-formance assessment by appropriate short-answer and multiple-choice items to broaden the coverage and to increase reliability. In fact, it is important to recognize that no single type of assessment can always meet all purposes, in all situations. Nor does it need to. The challenge is to make the best use possible of various assessment strategies in order to meet the diverse criteria of and purposes for the overall assessment.

LEVEL OF COHERENCE

One final and related issue warranting further discussion is the level at which the alignment, particularly of standards and assess-ments, should occur. Understanding this issue, as well as the pitfalls associated with alignment at different levels, is critical to maximizing the benefits of assessments on teaching and learning.

Although states are frequently overlooked as important actors in reform, the nature of the current reforms recommends their having a greater role. There are several reasons for this recommendation. The in-fighting and inconsistent policymaking among different agencies at the state level now provide a specific deterrent to statewide reform. Moreover, of all the actors in an education system, states have the authority and responsibility, and sometimes the resources, to influence all parts of the K-12 system, as well as higher education. Finally, states have the capacity to raise standards not just for some children but for all children across the state.

Not everyone, however, supports state-based alignment. Some continue to underscore the undesirability of creating alignment of goals, assessments, and curriculum at any level other than the school level. Drawing on evidence of the limitations of the state-mandated reforms of the early 1980s and buoyed by the literature on effective schools in the mid-to-late 1980s, they argue that state level coherence is not only unnecessary for effective school reform; it can even stifle reform at the school building level by stamping out local creativity and experimentation, detracting attention from the problems of delivery at the school level, and bolstering centralized schooling structures geared to the status quo.

Michael Fullan cogently presents this position, arguing that policies designed to create centralized, systemic alignment ignore a fundamental reality about school change: that it is nonlinear and dependent on greater subjective coherence in the minds of teachers rather than on an "objective coherence" passed down from on high. In fact, according to Fullan, state-based systemic reform initiatives may actually exacerbate the problems of school-level overload, fragmentation, and incoherence because "what looks like clarity at the top may contribute more clutter at the bottom. . . ." Fullan does not advocate neglecting system work. But he does recommend concentrating on strategies, such as professional networking and school "reculturing" and restructuring, "which are most likely, especially taken together, to change the conditions at the bottom for systemic change to occur on a large scale."[10]

We agree with Fullan on the central importance of professionally oriented and school-level activities. The point we want to emphasize is that a school-by-school approach by itself will probably not be sufficient to support coherent and high-quality reform in the vast majority of our nation's schools. The very nature of the educational policy environment in which most schools operate creates significant obstacles to deep, sustained and widespread school change: schools are barraged with multiple and inconsistent policies, categorical mandates and short-term "magic bullet" approaches to change. At the same time, the existing system generally provides little consistent support for school-initiated reform efforts, particularly around challenging content. In this context, it is not surprising that successful schools and effective practices often remain isolated success stories.[11]

We recognize that a system may be coherent at one level (e.g., a school or district) and lack coherence at another level (e.g., the state). Networks like the Coalition for Essential Schools and the Accelerated Schools Project continually help build pockets of excellence in the midst of an incoherent system. But even achieving that excellence is difficult when there is no systemwide support. Moreover, in this context, a state assessment probably would not provide support for the four purposes examined at the beginning of this chapter. A state assessment that does not reflect the content undergirding the coherence in those schools generally cannot motivate students and teachers to do their best, supply information relevant to schools as they improve their practice, provide relevant professional development opportunities for teachers and other school staff, or support a system of legitimate accountability. On the other hand, we believe that through a clear vision of what children should know and be able to do, coupled with high-quality aligned assessments and supportive state policies, states and districts can better promote and generalize school-level innovation and provide the supports needed to strengthen teaching and learning, not in just a few schools, but in a majority of schools.[12]

To realize these results, system-level coherence must be thoughtfully pursued. Most important, within a clear structure of instructional goals and challenging aligned assessments, states and districts must champion school-level flexibility and choice. If coherence in principle means uniformity or regimentation in practice, then as Fullan predicts, system-level alignment will impede improvement at the local level rather than enhance it.

This last point has far-reaching implications for the development of state standards and assessments. State and district standards should mandate neither a centralized curriculum nor a particular instructional method. Rather, they should set out broad goals and ambitious bodies of knowledge and skills with which students should become familiar and proficient over fairly large blocks of time (i.e., three to four years). State assessments should provide a fair measure of the degree to which students have succeeded in meeting the standards, without creating straitjackets for the schools. One way of preserving schools' independence and innovation is to align the timing of state or district assessments with the time blocks established for the standards, thereby decoupling curriculum in any one specific grade from a specific assessment. Another way is to provide significant choice within an assessment; this can give teachers freedom in choosing curricula that supports the content standards. Whatever the strategy, schools must have the flexibility, responsibility, and ultimate authority to construct the curriculum and instructional strategies best suited to their students and teachers.

This approach to coherence is neither "top-down" nor "bottom-up." It is designed to strengthen and sustain, not detract from, the instructional efforts and decision making of schools. By coordinating long-range instructional goals, materials development, professional development, and assessment, states and districts can foster the conditions under which school-based management, teacher empowerment and professional discretion may be more effective and broadly based. Even parental choice and charter schools may have a better chance of flourishing in this context. First, high-quality state assessments aligned with challenging standards would provide much of the information needed by parents and students to make informed choices; they would also provide some of the data that states need to support a responsible and legitimate form of performance-based accountability. Moreover, central elements of a systemic reform strategy—challenging state standards, a system of high-quality teacher training, and increased professionalism of teachers through networks and increased responsibility—could create a "protective structure" that would help ensure that all schools, whether rich or poor, urban or rural, provide their students with high-quality teaching and learning.[13]

We recognize that striking this kind of balance—particularly ensuring local autonomy within a system of state standards and assessments—will not be an easy task. Neither present roles and responsibilities, nor existing relationships within school systems, support it. But forging a balance of state- or district-level policy coherence and school-level decision making appears critical to fostering the energy and creativity of individual schools, while supporting the conditions necessary for long-term, effective change in the great majority of schools across a state.

Challenges and Possibilities

In the high-quality school system envisioned in the first part of this chapter, challenging content and performance standards provide the touchstone around which state and local policies are aligned. Performance assessment, coupled, where appropriate, with other assessment strategies, reinforce this alignment and mirror the complexity and depth of the content. Alignment between the nature and content of the assessments and the challenging teaching and learning, in turn, enables the assessments to meet far more effectively not just the letter but also the intent of the four purposes of assessments which we described at the beginning of this chapter.

Breaking new ground, let alone reaching this kind of vision, typically requires overcoming a variety of obstacles. We have already mentioned an assortment of these, ranging from the cost and reliability of performance assessments to the challenges of establishing coherent system-level policies that accommodate school-level differences and school-level choice. To conclude, we have selected three areas where the challenges directly influence the implementation of federal programs and state reforms, particularly the assessment and accountability system. In each area, the context is a coherent system in which its principal components—performance assessments, curriculum materials, and professional development—are each aligned with challenging state or district content and performance standards. We note that the challenges described here are only relevant in an effort to align the system around challenging standards and performance assessment. Of course, we would argue that an assessment required by a district or state would serve little useful purpose if it is not designed and administered as part of the kind of coherent reforms described above.

A TECHNICAL OBSTACLE

New requirements in Title I of the Improving America's Schools Act (IASA) illustrate one of the technical challenges. The reauthorized Title I strives to ensure that the challenging standards and high-quality assessments that states develop for all children also are used for Title I purposes. Moreover, Title I provides schools, districts, and states with far greater flexibility than in the past in using all of the IASA funds to support state and local reform efforts and promote comprehensive school change.[14]

In the context of greater flexibility, the need for stronger results-based accountability under Title I was forcefully advocated in Congressional debates by Republicans and Democrats alike. More widely debated during the reauthorization was the extent to which the law should fill in the parameters of this approach. From the outset, requirements for states to identify at least two levels of student achievement defining challenging performance provided a bare-bones framework for an accountability strategy. Individual students were expected to achieve to the standards, and the performances of these students were to be aggregated to provide a measure of institutional performance. Finally, states were asked to define adequate yearly progress of schools and districts toward meeting the state standards. This form of a "value added" approach for institutional accountability seemed fairer than an approach requiring a school to meet an absolute level of performance.

By the time the legislation became law, however, there were far more specifications than these. To assuage concerns that the newly structured Title I program would neglect the needs of its intended beneficiaries, additional specifications were added throughout the

Title I reauthorization discussions. These included requirements that the assessments be administered at some point during three different grade spans and be designed so as to enable the results to be disaggregated within schools, districts, and the state for many different subgroups of children.[15]

Meeting these assessment requirements undoubtedly promises to lead states into uncharted technical territory. Several of these provisions also may make it far more difficult for states to take advantage of innovations in assessments, particularly rich performance assessments. Producing reliable results on performance assessments for many different categories of children, for example, may simply require too many performance tasks, too much time in individual testing, and too much money to be feasible. Matrix sampling—often critical to addressing generalizability of results as well as holding down the costs of performance assessments—does not typically produce individual scores that would be useful for accountability purposes. Moreover, matrix sampling could be hopelessly complicated by the need to aggregate scores on a matrixed test for a variety of different groups within a school, each of which may contain very small numbers of children.

Given the technical challenge of meeting these requirements with innovative assessments, it will be tempting for states and districts to take an easier route to complying at least with the letter of the law: recreating the current Chapter 1 testing situation and perpetuating the use of multiple-choice, standardized tests. After all, such tests can deliver data in many different configurations—for individual children, subgroups of children, aggregated to the school, district, and state level—more easily, cheaply, and quickly than alternative forms of assessments.

Efforts are already underway to address these technical challenges. A mixture of types of assessments might be used, including portfolios and multiple-choice items, as well as performance assessments. A series of workshops at the National Academy of Science is focusing on specific technical challenges in the new Title I, including the development of performance standards and the definition of adequate progress. The Council of Chief State School Officers, as part of its effort to support high quality assessments and standards for students, also has formed a collaborative program to provide technical assistance on assessment development to evaluation directors, Title I coordinators, and other interested members of each state. These and others knowledgeable in assessments also are exploring ways to obtain comparable and reliable individual data from performance assessments, even when matrix sampling is used, to develop and use multiple measures, and to construct various models for defining adequate progress. Over time, these efforts have the potential of enabling states to meet the Title I requirements with innovative and challenging assessments that are technically sound and educationally strong.

"HIGH STAKES" ASSESSMENTS—
EXPLORING FAIR AND EFFECTIVE ACCOUNTABILITY

A strong performance-based approach to accountability recognizes the role of incentives for high performance, as well as the need for a clearly established stage at which substantial corrective actions are taken by actors outside the system to help protect students. Ensuring that education professionals and students are responsible for the results of their efforts also provides a strong foundation for giving schools far greater flexibility and decision-making authority.

Forging a strong and effective accountability system poses several obstacles. The first challenge is to establish the legitimacy of a performance-based accountability strategy that imposes punitive actions on either students or institutions. Much thought and discussion on this question occurred during the legislative debate on Goals 2000: Educate America Act and Title I, and the debate continues today.

One problem is particularly troublesome. To many, it is not legitimate to hold schools accountable if students are not simultaneously held accountable. If students are not accountable, the argument goes, they may not take their schooling seriously, work hard, or have an incentive to perform their best on an assessment, and consequently the quality of their work on an assessment may not reflect the real effectiveness of their teachers.[16] On the other hand, it does not seem fair to hold students accountable for performance on an assessment without first holding schools accountable; for inadequate performance by a student may depend on factors beyond his or her control, such as poor teaching. One can also logically inquire about subjecting either schools or students to "high stakes" assessments if they are not provided the necessary resources and other supports to succeed. But if students cannot be held accountable until their school is held accountable, and no school can be held accountable unless its students are accountable, and neither can be held accountable until schools have the necessary resources to succeed, legitimizing high stakes assessments becomes a very complex endeavor.

Assuming we can legitimize a system with high stakes, another and far more significant challenge emerges: using that system in a way that promotes, rather than detracts from, high-quality teaching and learning.

We have all seen how pressure to get more students to pass an examination or make a certain amount of progress can lead schools to focus on short-term "beat the test" strategies, rather than longer-term meaningful strategies to improve curriculum and instruction. Although the use of high-quality assessments aligned to challenging standards may mitigate the effects of this problem, the problem will persist. Moreover, if high stakes strategies are insensitive to typical trajectories of performance gains in a meaningful change process—e.g., an initial decline in performance during the first several years followed by nonlinear performance gains thereafter—those strategies can create additional disincentives for innovative and comprehensive reform.

Integral to addressing both challenges is the understanding that accountability ultimately depends on administrative strength and perseverance rather than precise quantitative measures, though such measures can be very useful. We suspect, for example, that many superintendents (and other members of large school systems) currently know which principals are ineffective and which schools are having continuous problems. The fact, however, is that for a variety of administrative and sometimes political reasons, there is generally little action taken to remedy such situations. More test scores, different types of assessments, and even available sanctions will make little or no difference unless superintendents are willing to use them. In this context, a philosophical debate about the legitimacy of high stakes, the validity of assessment data, and the availability of appeals processes may merely serve to obfuscate the significant problems that already are recognized and that administrators already have the authority to address.

Moreover, while an externally driven system of rewards for success and penalties for failure is important, its limits must be recognized. Ultimately, its effects are far more blunt and far less enduring than a self-generated and administratively strong professional accountability in which the ultimate goal for all those involved in education is to hold themselves and each other accountable for how well they are helping students learn every day. This type of accountability does not rely on the reporting of data to someone outside the system who then decides what remedial actions to take; its success ultimately depends on those closest to children having the information, authority, and ability—and assuming the responsibility—to intervene on an ongoing basis to improve teaching and learning.

Self-generated accountability mitigates both challenges described above. When teachers and other school staff feel professionally responsible for enabling their students to meet the challenging standards, their primary strategy is not to "beat the test" but to effectively improve teaching and learning and the achievement of each child. Assessments that tell them how well they are doing thus become part and parcel of good classroom and school practice. Information from periodic external student assessments need not be a threat whose legitimacy has to be challenged. In a similar fashion, information from school reviews conducted by professionals from other schools or districts, professional networks, and technical assistance all linked to challenging standards can provide school professionals with the critical tools to help monitor their own performance and improve their schools. They also can provide the content knowledge and training that can further support a sense of professionalism and responsibility.

While to some this discussion may sound overly idealistic, the goal of a mix of responsible administrative behavior and strong professional accountability seems to us to be the right direction to move in order to have real institutional accountability. Assessment results should play an important role here to motivate professional response and to provide useful feedback.

The problem, of course, is that many school systems lack any system of legitimate professional or administrative accountability, particularly those that serve the most needy and vulnerable students. This creates a powerful argument for accountability "by the numbers," which is one reason why the Title I legislation contains a sequence of technical assistance followed by "corrective action" when a school or district fails to make adequate yearly progress. Nonetheless, even if the assessments are valid, such a formula approach as that contained in Title I cannot guarantee that administrators will take the necessary steps to remedy institutional deficiencies and protect students.

Finally, we have not addressed the issue of student accountability. Both Title I and Goals 2000 leave this issue entirely to the discretion of states and districts. Our own view is that ensuring students' and parents' knowledge of a student's performance on a thoughtfully constructed, challenging, and aligned assessment is more than adequate incentive for most students in the elementary grades. In the middle school years, the results of an assessment could also be made public to students and parents and could operate along with other information to provide guidance for student choices in high school, rather than as an absolute barrier. In most instances, this should also be an adequate incentive to overcome the problem posed earlier about which comes first, individual or institutional accountability. Insofar as the individual accountability does not have an absolute consequence, it seems reasonable to argue that both individual and institutional accountability can be phased in almost immediately. Indeed, in the context of using a measure of adequate progress for institutional accountability it may be in the best interests of the school or district to institute it at the very beginning of the reform process when the baseline for students' performance would typically be low.

The situation is somewhat different in high school where individual accountability might entail an absolute consequence such as not graduating, attending college, or obtaining a good job. In such an instance it seems only fair to argue that the institution should be accountable for preparing students for the assessment before the students are held accountable for meeting the standards. In this case, one strategy would be to phase in student accountability after a period of time sufficient for the institution to prepare the students for the assessment.[17] The following discussion explores a variation on this issue.

EQUITY AND EXCELLENCE

Linking the results of assessments to high stakes also creates possible tensions between short-term and long-term coherence. In the legal context of high-stake assessments, short-term incentives to reduce performance gaps may jeopardize longer-term efforts to forge a coherent system geared to challenging standards and assessments.

Understanding this potential tension requires a brief discussion of Title VI of the Civil Rights Act of 1964 and Title IX of the Education Amendments of 1972. Title VI and Title IX provide that the principles of nondiscrimination on the basis of race, national origin, and gender extend to assessments that are used to deprive students of educational benefits or opportunities.[18] Such assessments include, for example, high stakes tests that deny a student a high school diploma or a place in a gifted and talented program.

Under Title VI principles (as under Title IX), a high stakes assessment that has a disparate impact on the basis of race or national origin (e.g., produces a significant statistical gap between the test scores and passing rates of minorities and whites) would not be a Title VI violation in and of itself. But it would be a violation if the district or state cannot demonstrate that the assessment is educationally necessary, which is defined by the courts as being valid for the purposes for which the assessment is being used.[19] Demonstrating validity, in turn, requires showing not only that the assessment measures the skills it purports to measure but also that students have had the opportunity to learn the material on the test.[20]

These principles play a critical role in ensuring that high-stakes assessments are valid, reliable, and fair. But in the short run, the requirements inherent in those laws may create unintended disincentives to the development of challenging new standards and assessments. While the theory of systemic standards-based reform holds that over the longer term disparities in opportunity and achievement between different groups will be reduced, in the short run standards and aligned assessments that are truly challenging could easily create a greater gap in achievement scores between children of the poor and the well-to-do, and between whites and African Americans and Hispanic Americans.[21] Although a significant performance gap alone would not invalidate an assessment under Title VI, it may raise serious questions as to the assessment's validity.

Districts and states can avoid those questions by enhancing the curriculum and creating supports for minority children and the neediest schools and districts so that all students have the opportunity to learn what is on the test. By so doing, they would ensure that the testing concepts of validity and reliability—central to civil rights laws and educationally sound testing practices—are, in fact, in place for all students.

But another possible response would be for states and districts to lower the standards for all children, thereby minimizing the initial gap in test scores that triggers Title VI scrutiny in the first place. In fact, at least in the short run, before many states and districts are sufficiently geared up to teach the new and challenging content, there will be considerable pressures on them to "play it safe." This may involve continuing to set "the bar" low and even maintaining current standardized assessments that do not pose, or at least seem not to pose, the same kinds of validation problems.[22]

This discussion is not meant to suggest that states, districts, and schools should choose between the goals of equity and excellence. A basic premise of standards-based reform, in fact, is that one cannot choose—that equity and excellence in our educational system are flip sides of the same coin. For without excellence there will be no equity, since students will be denied the right to reach their potential and take advantage of opportunities, and without equitable access to quality education, there cannot be excellence systemwide.

But this discussion suggests possible complexities involved in any reform effort committed to full and equitable success for all children, e.g., the time it will take, possible widening of the achievement gap in the short term, the retraining needs of school-level staff. Our continuing efforts to pursue the twin goals of equity and excellence should be guided by a recognition of these tensions, and a resolve to work through them, as a nation.

Summary and Conclusion

In our examination of the relationships among coherence, assessment, and standards, we have made four major arguments. We began by identifying the critical role of coherence in supporting fair and valid assessments that motivate teachers and students to perform at their best, provide critical information for continual feedback as well as legitimate accountability, and offer meaningful capacity-building experiences for educators across school systems. Next, we examined the role of content standards as the starting point for alignment in a system that focuses on challenging content, and the importance of performance assessments in reinforcing that alignment. Finally, we argued that a strategy focused on "top-down" policy coherence and "bottom-up" reform could foster the energy and creativity of individual schools, as well as the conditions necessary for long-term, effective change in the great majority of schools across a state.

Although addressing the challenges we have presented here will facilitate these reforms, it will not ensure their success. These challenges, however, do illustrate the technical complications that will have to be addressed—as well as the time, imagination, and perseverance that will be required—for these reforms to succeed. In light of the increasing support for and attention to challenging content standards and assessments and systemwide reforms, the technical obstacles probably will be resolved. But like any complex and far-reaching reform effort, the question of resolve remains—that is, the strength of our commitment to the long-term health of this nation, and the education and well-being of every child.

NOTES

1. National Commission on Testing and Public Policy, *Reforming Assessment: From Gatekeepers to Gateway to Education* (Chestnut Hill, Mass.: Boston College, 1990).

2. The *August F. Hawkins-Robert T. Stafford Elementary and Secondary School Improvement Amendments of 1988* (P.L. 100-297, 20 U.S.C. §§2711, 2835; 34 CFR §§200.80-.89).

3. Susan H. Fuhrman, ed., *Designing Coherent Education Policy: Improving the System* (San Francisco: Jossey-Bass, 1993).

4. The Pacesetter Program, also supported by the College Board, provides another tangible example of coherence. Pacesetter has been developed by high school teachers and college faculty in three separate content areas to date (mathematics, English, and Spanish) and has as its purpose the attainment by *all* students of clearly articulated rigorous content

in each subject area. To accomplish this, the program focuses on aligning standards, teaching, and assessment together through course outlines, instructional materials, assessments embedded in instruction with scoring rubrics, professional development for teachers, and an end-of-course assessment. See The College Board, *Facts about Pacesetter: An Integrated Program of Standards, Testing, and Assessments* (New York: College Board, 1994).

5. Jennifer A. O'Day and Marshall S. Smith, "Systemic Reform and Educational Opportunity," in *Designing Coherent Policy*, Susan H. Fuhrman, ed. (San Francisco: Jossey-Bass, 1993), pp. 250-312; Marshall S. Smith and Jennifer A. O'Day, "Systemic School Reform," in *The Politics of Curriculum and Testing: The 1990 Yearbook of the Politics of Education Association*, Susan H. Fuhrman and Betty Malen, eds. (Philadelphia: Falmer Press, 1991), pp. 233-267.

6. These examples are not meant to imply that either the AP or the minimum competency experiences are exemplary. They are intended to show the relationship between alignment (coherence) and the purposes of assessment.

7. Lorrie Shephard, "Will National Tests Improve Student Achievement?" *Phi Delta Kappan* 73 (November, 1991): 232-247; Mary Lee Smith, "Put to the Test: The Effects of External Testing on Teachers," *Educational Researcher* 20, no. 5 (1991): 8-11; U.S. Congress, Office of Technology Assessment, *Testing in American Schools: Asking the Right Questions*, OTA-SET-519 (Washington, D.C.: U.S. Government Printing Office, February, 1992).

8. Lauren B. Resnick and Daniel P. Resnick, "Assessing the Thinking Curriculum: New Tools for Educational Reform," in *Changing Assessments: Alternative Views of Aptitude, Achievement, and Instruction*, B. R. Gifford and M. C. O'Connor, eds. (Boston: Kluwer, 1992), pp. 37-75; Daniel P. Resnick and Lauren B. Resnick "Performance Assessments and the Multiple Functions of Education Measurement," in *Implementing Performance Assessments: Promises, Problems, and Challenges*, R. Mitchell and M. Kane, eds. (Hillsdale, N.J.: Erlbaum, in press); Barry McGaw, "Australian Case Study," in *US/OECD Study on Performance Standards in Education Quality, Curriculum Standards, Assessments* (Paris: Organization for Economic Cooperation and Development, 1995).

9. National Council on Education Standards and Testing, *Raising Standards for American Education: A Report to Congress, the Secretary of Education, the National Goals Panel, and the American People* (Washington, D.C.: Author, 1992); National Governors' Association, *From Rhetoric to Action: State Progress in Restructuring the Education System* (Washington, D.C.: National Governors' Association, 1991); *The Goals 2000: Educate America Act* (P.L. 103:227; 20 U.S.C. 5801 et seq.).

10. Michael G. Fullan, "Turning Systemic Thinking on Its Head," (Paper prepared for the U.S. Department of Education, 1994). Our view is that Fullan is definitely right about the importance of school restructuring, reculturation, and professional networking. But we believe that these strategies are not incompatible with a state standards-based strategy, and may be facilitated by it. See also William H. Clune, "The Best Path to Systemic Educational Policy: Standard/Centralized or Differentiated/Decentralized," *Educational Evaluation and Policy Analysis* 15, no. 3 (Fall, 1993): 233-254.

11. Smith and O'Day, "Systemic School Reform."

12. The intellectual argument and rationale for this approach is set out in a number of places. See Smith and O'Day, "Systemic School Reform"; David K. Cohen and James P. Spillane, "Policy and Practice: The Relations between Governance and Instruction," in Gerald Grant, ed., *Review of Research in Education*, no. 18 (Washington, D.C.: American Educational Research Association, 1992), pp. 3-50; Fuhrman, *Designing Coherent Education Policy*; O'Day and Smith, "Systemic Reform and Educational Opportunity."

13. Smith and O'Day, "Systemic School Reform."

14. *Title I of the Elementary and Secondary Education Act of 1965, as amended by the Improving America's School Act of 1994* (IASA) (P.L. 103-382; 20 U.S.C. 6301 et seq.).

Among the new provisions promoting greater flexibility are the following: there is no longer federally mandated Title I testing; states and districts can seek waivers of specific provisions of Title I and the entire IASA; and schools over 50 percent poverty have far greater discretion to combine all of their federal funds in support of comprehensive schoolwide programs.

15. *Title I of the Elementary and Secondary Education Act of 1965, as amended by the Improving America's Schools Act of 1994* (P.L. 103-283; 20 U.S.C. 6311).

16. O'Day and Smith, "Systemic Reform and Educational Opportunity"; "School Reform: A Special Three-part Section on Standards," *American Educator* 18 (Fall, 1994): 12-27.

17. One irony here is that the nation has tolerated a generalized test (the SAT) as a legitimate measure for determining college preparedness although the test has no relationship to the curriculum of most high schools and is relatively insensitive to hard work by students and teachers.

18. *Title VI of the Civil Rights Act of 1964*, 42 U.S.C. 2000d and its implementing regulation at 34 C.F.R. Part 100 provide that "no person in the United States shall, on the grounds of race, color, or national origin, be excluded from participation in, be denied the benefits of, or otherwise be subjected to discrimination under any program or activity that receives Federal funds." *Title IX of the Education Amendments of 1972*, as amended, 20 U.S.C. 1681 et seq., and its implementing regulation at 34 C.F.R., Part 106, prohibits discrimination on the basis of sex in education programs or activities receiving financial assistance from the federal government.

19. See, for example, *Board of Education v. Harris*, 444 U.S. 130, 151 (1979); *United States v. LULAC*, 793 F.2d 636, 649 (5th Cir. 1986); *Branches of NAACP v. State of Georgia*, 775, F.2d 1403, 1417 (11th Cir. 1985); and *Sharif by Salahuddin v. New York*, 709 F. Supp. 345 (S.D.N.Y. 1989).

20. See, for example, *Debra P. v. Turlington*, 730 F.2d 1405 (11th Cir. 1984); *Larry P. v. Riles*, 495 F. Supp. 926 (N.D. Cal. 1979), *aff'd*, 793 F.2d 969 (9th Cir. 1984).

21. O'Day and Smith, "Systemic Reform and Educational Opportunity."

22. Standardized assessments clearly have validity problems of their own for they are infrequently aligned with the material children are taught in school.

Section Two
REALIZATIONS AT THE DISTRICT AND STATE LEVELS

CHAPTER VI

Coherence, Comprehensiveness, and Capacity in Assessment Systems: The Pittsburgh Experience

Paul G. LeMahieu and JoAnne T. Eresh

The classroom is the crucible. It is the place where every idea about the best or most powerful form of education finds its expression. The classroom is the place where every notion that shapes practice—the good as well as the bad, the strong as well as the weak, even the sometimes contradictory and incompatible—is played out in daily instructional routines. The classroom is the place where bad ideas are ultimately and finally revealed for what they are, and where the uneasiness caused by competing ideas, even good ones, manifests itself in the debilitation of the instructional process. This leads at best to wasteful and ineffective practice and at worst to practice that is downright damaging and destructive. In applying this realization to the articulation and implementation of a thoughtful assessment program, one quickly realizes that a primary concern must be for how the elements of that program relate and interact in the classroom. Ideally, all that is introduced will support the practices that are most highly valued; at the very least, it must not distract from or interfere with those practices.

For better than the first hundred years of large-scale testing in America's schools, measurement was treated as an abstract activity separate from curriculum, teaching, and learning. In effect, teachers were

Paul G. LeMahieu is Director of the Delaware Education Research and Development Center at the University of Delaware. He is also a special advisor for research and development at the Delaware Department of Public Instruction. JoAnne T. Eresh is Director of the Language Arts Program in the Pittsburgh (Pennsylvania) Public Schools.

told to pursue their daily course without particular reference (in either content or process) to the tests that would come at the end of the year. Broad survey tests could be employed to provide data enlightening all manners of discourse about education. Almost paradoxically, it was maintained that these tests could be at one and the same time sensitive to the accomplishments of the classroom and yet impartial, even indifferent, to what actually had happened there.

More recently, beginning with the pioneering work of George Madaus and his colleagues,[1] as well as a rich array of research conducted within that tradition,[2] we have come to appreciate that not only are the assessments in use of considerable influence upon classroom practice, but they are sensitive to the particulars of that practice. In short, all of the elements that define the educational experience—curriculum, instruction, environment, and assessment—are inextricably intertwined. The reform of assessment must, of necessity, deal equally with matters of curriculum and pedagogy.

Any effort to modify assessment practice must recognize that teachers are the final arbiters of all practice in the classroom. Teachers determine the nature of the educational experiences of the students that they serve. No effort to influence those experiences can hope to succeed without particular attention to the knowledge, skills, and dispositions of teachers. This attention to the abilities of teachers means that powerful forms of professional development must be initiated to enhance those abilities. In the first instance, the concern might be for the knowledge and skill development that can lead to changed behaviors in pursuit of improved practice. Ultimately, the concern is for the development of understandings and reflective capacities that empower teachers to shape that practice and contribute to our best thinking about it.

As with any effort that is broadly defined, even systemic, there is a need to integrate a diverse set of ideas and consequent practices into an articulate whole. It has to make sense within the classroom, and therefore assessment reform must concern itself with *coherence*, both conceptually and in practice. Next, the reform of assessment practice, particularly at the school district level, must concern itself first with all aspects of the teaching and learning process, not just assessment as an entity apart from the others. Assessment reform, then, must be committed to *comprehensive* planning and action. Finally, in order to make all of the good ideas work as intended and to involve teachers in the development of new and better ones, there is a need to address the abilities, skills, and dispositions of practitioners. Powerful assessment reforms must concern themselves with the *capacities* of teachers, principals, and others who work closely with assessment.

These three attributes—*coherence, comprehensiveness,* and *capacity*—were consciously adopted to guide the efforts of the Pittsburgh Public Schools in modifying the function and use of assessments within its schools. The result was a program of student assessment that gained widespread recognition for its redefinition of assessment as a genuine contributor to the instructional process.[3] As two of the many involved in the reform of assessment in the Pittsburgh Public Schools, we describe here how that improvement was pursued. We begin by summarizing the guiding vision and how it influenced the definition of practice. We then describe the essential elements of an expanded vision of assessment and relate how those elements were developed and introduced. We enumerate the ways that the district sought to increase the capacities of its professionals in the development and use of assessment. Finally, we share insights earned and lessons learned that may benefit others undertaking a similar comprehensive redefinition of assessment as an essential element of educational practice.

Coherence: The Guiding Vision

In the Pittsburgh Public Schools throughout the 1980s, two central ideas guided educational reform generally and the reform of assessment in particular. The first of these came to be known as "the development of a rational culture." The second was the idea that the purpose for assessment was to produce information that could be placed within this rational frame.

The development of a rational culture. This idea refers to conscious efforts on the part of the district's leadership to shift the predominant mode of decision making toward greater use of data and information as the basis for decisions. There are many bases that can serve to explain or justify decisions.[4] Decisions are made for political reasons or for financial ones. They are made in response to social pressures or moral imperatives. Each of these bases for decision making has unique strengths and powers. The appropriateness of each is situational. In Pittsburgh, however, the leadership of the district firmly believed that decisions based on commonly held and publicly discussed information would very often be more appropriate decisions that more of the participants and implementers could understand and invest in. Rational decisions are likely to have fewer political repercussions. In investigating needs and problems, it is possible to shift the focus of discourse from who is responsible to what the situation is and what the circumstances are that define it. It is then possible to move beyond discussion of blame to the planning of responses.

The leadership of the district formally articulated a belief in the benefits of rational decision making.[5] In doing so, they elevated it as a cultural value. Quite simply, the district leadership asserted its conviction that the most valuable resources in the educational system (and the most often overlooked) were the professionals who made it up. If their skills and knowledge could be elevated and a mode of decision making fostered that rendered decisions public and their logic accessible to all, then immense change and improvement would be possible.

Essential to this view of information and data-driven decisions were the concrete actions taken to implement it. The district's leaders in the highest offices modeled this form of decision making.[6] When decisions had to be made, they actively sought the best information to inform them.[7] When positions had to be justified, they clearly indicated that the acceptable form of justification was appropriate and relevant data. Moreover, they insisted that others working with them do the same. The phrase, "research says" was bandied about the system, sometimes in jest. However, it indicated the growing appreciation for rational decision making and an emerging sense of its centrality to the life of the district.

Every bit as important as this articulation of an epistemological perspective was the development of systems to support it.[8] In 1982, the district had established for the first time a Division of Research, Evaluation, and Student Assessment. The district invested considerable resources in the design and implementation of student information systems, including an extensive student assessment system. It elaborated mechanisms for generating, gathering, maintaining, organizing, presenting, and using data and information. The terms and conditions of access were determined and widespread use was promoted.

Ultimately, the district turned to its student assessment system. Data describing student accomplishment, strengths, weaknesses, and needs were considered to be of the utmost importance to a fully elaborated view of educational planning and decision making. This led to the second element in the vision that was guiding the development of the district's assessment system. This second element addressed the basic purposes for student assessment and guided the definition of an assessment system that could comprehensively address them.

The purposes of student assessment. Those directing the district's testing program spoke often of two fundamental, and fundamentally different, purposes for student assessment activities.[9] The first of these are evaluative purposes such as the determination of status or accomplishment, judgments of merit or worth, and certifications of achievement. The focus of the evaluation can range from a certification of individuals to a public accounting of a system's overall performance to evaluations of programs for various groups of students.

The second basic purpose of assessment is to inform the instructional process by providing clinical or diagnostic information. These clinical purposes require deeper and richer descriptions than do evaluative purposes. They involve descriptions of what students can do well and not so well, what instructional needs the student has, and (ideally) how he or she will respond to different kinds of instructional experiences. The focus is exclusively on individuals and the point is to provide descriptions that inform decisions about instruction.

There are certain attributes inherent in evaluative testing. First, it tends to be relatively infrequent, in some cases *ad hoc* or as appropriate to the evaluation being conducted. Even the most regular public accounting tends to be necessary no more often than once yearly. Many perfectly adequate public accounting systems are based on benchmark years resulting in testing that is even much less frequent. Second, it is imposed from without. As such, it is not explicitly and wholly relevant to the goals or instruction of each class into which it is introduced. Third, the scoring or evaluation of students' performance is rarely conducted *in situ*. The results are not available immediately, but rather often take a considerable time to get back to the student and teacher. Fourth, evaluative data tend to be fairly limited in level of detail. It is not necessary to have the same level of detail and richness that is necessary for good clinical assessment. Reduction in detail and aggregation across individuals or groups is often quite appropriate to serve evaluative ends. This observation is all the more true the further away from the classroom one goes in using evaluative data.

In many ways the characteristics of instructionally supportive assessment are in sharp contradistinction to those of evaluative testing.[10] Clinical assessment requires data that are timely in terms of frequency and of speed of return to the point of use. It should also be richly detailed, even highly contextualized, if it is to be useful to teachers. Finally, clinically supportive data must be explicitly relevant to the goals and instructional events of the classroom.

These sharp distinctions led the leadership of the district to conclude that the challenge for a thoughtful assessment system was to recognize the distinction between the two purposes; build a comprehensive system with components that address each purpose; and work hard to manage the balance between the two. Balance here refers to the time, effort, and resources that are dedicated to each purpose. We also use the term to refer to the amount of influence that each purpose is permitted to exert over practice. Many of the most damaging practices engendered by the undue influence of tests derive from "life out of balance" with respect to the relative influence of each type of assessment.

To speak of balance in these terms in Pittsburgh in 1981 (and many other districts even today) was to describe an ideal, not a reality. We had instruments that were evaluative, but we had nothing that could adequately address instructional needs. Balance was quite unachievable. We realized that we needed to move away from a single test that we had once tried to convince ourselves could serve in both capacities and toward a more elaborate assessment system with components that addressed each. We needed to articulate a more comprehensively defined assessment program with elements that had the characteristics that are listed here, as well as others enumerated elsewhere.[11] Only such a comprehensive view of assessment needs and the proper means of addressing them would suffice to build a system that would genuinely serve education in the district and avoid the educational damage that results from "life out of balance."

Comprehensiveness: The Elements of a Useful Assessment System

In 1981, the district set out to develop a comprehensive assessment system that provided information addressing the varied interests of evaluative and clinical applications. While not necessarily wholly satisfied with them, the district had long used commercially produced survey tests of achievement to address public accounting needs. What was needed immediately in order to provide for a comprehensive and balanced assessment program were additional components that could contribute to decisions about instruction.

The first step was the development of a program called "Monitoring Achievement in Pittsburgh" (MAP).[12] MAP was a system of student monitoring through testing between four and six times a year, varying by subject and grade level. Students were tested in mathematics, reading, language arts, composition, and critical thinking. In the first three areas, the tests were brief multiple-choice measures, each taking between ten and fifteen minutes of class time on average. The composition and critical thinking assessments involved lengthy written exercises and were scored using common rubrics throughout the district. All tests were scored centrally and results returned to teachers within seven school days so that they could use them in instructional planning. The point was to create instruments explicitly tied to the instructional goals of the system, assess progress frequently, and return results to teachers in a timely fashion for their information. No evaluative judgments (likewise no reports to support or suggest any such judgments) were ever made using MAP data.

The development process for MAP involved all instructional professionals in the district. Teams of teachers developed objectives by subject and grade level. Their work was then distributed to all others for review and commentary. The reviews were used in subsequent drafts to articulate a scope and sequence of expectation for students and the schools that serve them. Once outcomes were agreed upon, the next concern was for the means of instruction that could most powerfully realize them. In many cases this meant dramatic changes to prevailing practice, and defined a professional development agenda for the district. In addition materials appropriate to both the adopted objectives and the forms of desired instruction had to be identified and either procured or developed. Finally and only after these concerns had been addressed, attention turned to the design of brief tests that could assess student progress relevant to the learning objectives.

Over time, the district outgrew MAP for a number of reasons; what had initially represented a device for elevating the performance of the system came to hinder ongoing improvement. One reason was the nearly exclusive focus of MAP on basic skills. The objectives themselves were very much a product of their times, and as such focused on basics. Moreover, the technology of assessment used was suggestive both of basic skills as outcomes and transmission methods as appropriate means of teaching. As some success was achieved in improving student performance there was a natural desire to increase expectations of the system to address more closely the goals of the "thinking curriculum." Renewed activity was needed to address new goals and to welcome and even support instruction that more actively involved students in their learning. This new effort would be pursued within the framework of the guiding vision and mode of decision making that predominate in the district.

In 1985, the district began to develop the Syllabus Examination Project (SEP). Initially conceived for core academic courses in grades six through twelve, SEP sought to use performance assessments as capstone exercises for academic coursework. Standard examinations were tied to common syllabi constructed for each course. In establishing syllabi, teachers sought to remove much of the demand for broad coverage in the curriculum. Instead of broad coverage, teachers focused upon significant ideas—ideas that could structure the curriculum and sustain deep engagement in the content.

Following closely on SEP was the Arts PROPEL program. It sought to make students' perception, reflection, and production central to learning. Rather than accept transfer approaches to teaching, Arts PROPEL focused on students' work—its production as the central activity in the classroom and its examination as the invitation to discussions about quality. Active engagement of students was pursued. Teachers were engaged in the construction of common understandings of quality in student performance, with the consequence that those understandings elevated the expectations of everyone and encouraged their more equitable application.

Ultimately, SEP and Arts PROPEL initiated the development of portfolios to support assessment that might inform discussions and decisions about instruction. Initially construed primarily as an assessment mechanism, portfolios quickly became much more. The classroom activities that they encourage and the forms of learning that they support suggested the image of a portfolio culture.[13] As defined in the Pittsburgh system, portfolios are not mere archives of student work. Rather, they are opportunities for students to interact with their work as text, reviewing it to discern strengths and weaknesses. This involves students in the discussion about quality and what can serve as evidence of it. They are called on to review their own work critically, determine necessary improvements, and plan and direct a course of personal development to realize that improvement.

Four characteristics of the Pittsburgh assessment program are worth noting. First, while the testing program is its most salient characteristic, developers were as much (or more) concerned with the establishment of instructional goals, the identification of appropriate curriculum and materials, the transformation of instruction in order to ' realize those goals, as well as the generation, analysis, and use of information on student progress to inform teachers' decision making. The assessment system consciously blurred the distinctions among curriculum, instruction, learning, and assessment. Second, these assessments began to promote a form of thought in which decisions about teaching were based upon data on student performance routinely generated and inspected. Third, the system recognized that the attributes of assessment that can profitably inform instruction are different from those traditionally used in schools. While primitive by more current standards, MAP sought to embody those attributes and to serve as an information system for teachers. Over time, other forms of assessment were welcomed into the system as being able to provide even better information and being more transparent within (or seamless with) the educational process. Fourth, the designers of the district's assessment system recognized the great need for professional development in many areas in order for the system to contribute in any way to the improvement of practice.

As these initiatives were being developed to provide for instructionally useful assessments, the district was using commercially produced standardized tests of achievement to address its public accounting requirements. In time, the district undertook to use evidence derived from the portfolio system to report to the public regarding the performance of the school system.[14] Scoring rubrics were developed and shared interpretive frameworks for applying them were constructed by the development team whose members also served as scorers for the district. Scoring procedures and routines for corroborating scores were also developed. An external mechanism for auditing results was crafted to reassure the public that the statements about the district's performance based on portfolios could be trusted as "good faith" accountings of the system. Reassurances of the quality of the evidence produced as well as the political credibility of the external audit team enabled the district to make a viable accounting of its performance. As a consequence, the district was able to supplant the traditional means of public accounting with a form much more resonant with the classroom activities and instruction that it seeks to encourage.

In a very real sense, the development process had come full circle, but the point of origin was dramatically redefined. Initially, evaluative assessments predominated and instructional applications were forced, at best. By the end of the decade the district had built components for its assessment system that addressed clinical needs. It then undertook to see if assessment built first and foremost to serve those within the classroom could be used to speak beyond the classroom to fulfill public reporting requirements. The success we have had in doing so is very encouraging. However, one question persists. Does the use of portfolios for public accounting compromise their integrity in regard to the purposes for which they were developed in the first place? Should that prove to be the case, then the district should reassert its initial vision. A balanced portfolio of assessment with components relevant to both evaluative and instructional purposes must be established to see that all interests can be served and a proper balance of influence maintained. Here (as in many places) too much progress has been made for developers to make the mistake of trying to determine which interests should prevail.

Capacity: Enabling the Professionals Who Make It Work

In 1981, when the district began its development of the MAP program, committees of teachers were recruited for the areas of mathematics, reading, and writing. The makeup of each committee was representative of the district's geographical areas, and in race and gender it was representative of the teaching staff. The MAP Writing Committee was composed of 24 teachers, two representing each grade level from grade 1 through grade 12. In addition, school supervisors in the language arts were a part of the committee. The Richard King Mellon Foundation provided funding for a staff appointment to chair the committee.

The teachers had been recommended by district administrators who regarded them as leaders in the area of language arts/English. The teachers brought with them a variety of experiences in teaching and in the writing of curriculum. It was the first time in the history of the district that teachers had been assembled from across school levels—elementary, middle, and secondary—to work together. Perhaps the first and most important revelation occurred when teachers at the various grade levels were asked to list the end-of-year objectives for their classes. As the grade level teams put up their lists, it became obvious that these teachers were teaching the very same skills year after year.

Such a realization was only the first of many as the committee worked together over the next six years. Mutual respect developed naturally as the primary teachers worked with the high school teachers and as each teacher struggled to define what students at each grade should know (this was before the days of asking what the student should be able to do), and how their knowledge should be assessed.

The committee struggled with major issues in constructing objectives and test items. They grappled with the problems presented by language abilities (for example, creativity and voice) that could not be tested in the multiple-choice format prescribed by the frequent monitoring system. They argued with and learned from each other and assumed responsibility for creating a monitoring system that would determine the course of instruction in the district for a decade.

The teachers worked within a paradigm that was not foreign to their concepts of knowledge acquisition at that time. The direct teaching model promulgated by Madeline Hunter was the designated teaching model for the school district and the delineation of grade level objectives and the creation of monitoring devices that provided timely feedback on those objectives fit smoothly into the picture. The committee members became adept at providing workshops and presentations focusing on the relationships between instructional practices and assessment structures. Numerous courses for increment credit, summer workshops, and on site in-service sessions were devoted to the implementation of the MAP project. Everyone understood that the district's measure was being taken by the performance of its students on the California Achievement Test administered each spring and it was clearly understood as well that the MAP program was designed to provide a way of bringing curriculum in line with the district testing program.

For a time the MAP Writing Program served the purpose of directing attention toward specific objectives, which in turn increased scores on the standardized achievement test in language arts. Inasmuch as it was also the district's intent to support constantly the further development of its teaching staff, the evolution of thinking regarding the way in which the language arts should be taught began to outstrip the MAP program's implicit transmittal theory of learning. As more and more teachers became part of the National Writing Project and investigated reader response theory and whole language concepts, it became apparent that the knowledge acquisition precepts upon which the MAP system had been based were outmoded. The district began to acknowledge that the evolving theory of learning was no longer consistent with multiple-choice and indirect assessments. Since the district had presented a vision of curriculum and instruction aligned with assessment, it had to begin to pay attention to the need for realignment.

In 1985, a team from Project Zero at Harvard University and a team from the Educational Testing Service met with school district representatives in Pittsburgh to discuss possible collaboration in a project supported by the Rockefeller Foundation. The proposal was to explore ways of investigating Howard Gardner's theories of multiple intelligences in the public schools and the possibility of assessing students' abilities in ways that were not patterned on traditional testing instruments.

The district was not quick to accept the offer. A basic precept of MAP was that it was teacher developed and classroom centered. To engage in a project directed "from the outside" and defined and created by outside interests was not consistent with our previous efforts. It was only after numerous conversations that all three parties decided that a mutually beneficial relationship was possible and work was undertaken.

Middle and high school teachers were recruited to work on committees set up to deal with art, music, or writing. These development teams are an example of building capacity in a group of teachers, as well as an example of the fact that good project work arises as much out of an understanding of group process as from the content knowledge shared. If the Arts PROPEL Writing Portfolio can be thought to be successful at all, it is because of the five-year commitment of all parties to the mutual development of an understanding about change and the change process as well as the shared understandings about the technology of portfolio assessment and its concomitant culture.

The Arts PROPEL Writing Committee was carefully structured. Included as teacher representatives were several who had served on the original MAP Writing Committee. The eighteen teachers represented almost half of the twenty-five middle and secondary schools in the district. They were also as balanced in race and gender as the makeup of the language arts district staff permitted. At least half of the members were fellows of the Western Pennsylvania Writing Project, and even those who were not were fully aware of the writing process movement and were implementing such strategies in their classrooms. Additional members of the committee included curriculum specialists at the middle and secondary levels as well as the Director of Writing and Speaking programs. Over the life of the project there was little change in the committee's make up. It was a stable and collegial group that developed a history of fruitful collaboration on various projects. The working committee also included staff from Project Zero and the Educational Testing Service who were commonly referred to as "consultants" but who functioned in a much more integral manner than that term commonly suggests.

The committee typically met for a week in the summer and one day a month during the school year. Teachers were released from classes one Friday per month, and the consultants spent that Friday and the preceding Thursday in Pittsburgh. The calendar for these meetings was constructed at the beginning of each school year and was strictly adhered to. The simple fact that all members committed their time on a regular basis was a very strong indication of the seriousness with which the district and the consultants regarded the work. The teachers clearly understood this commitment which was modeled for them by the committee and they matched it with theirs.

It was not the time commitment alone that provided the foundation for collaboration. It was clear from the very beginning that this committee was a working group, not a group of teachers collected to give their imprimatur to someone else's project. Decisions regarding the direction of the work and the procedures for investigation came from the group. For example, in the decision to explore the genre of poetry as part of the work for the writing committee, all members of the committee clearly felt that their opinions and interests were sought and accommodated. An atmosphere of openness and mutual respect was carefully created and maintained. The planning for this and other issues was often held at the Thursday meetings with the district staff for curriculum and the consultants.

In the first two years of work, the group focused on the teaching of poetic writing, specifically designing procedures for the teaching of the list poem (an instructional approach to poetic form and sensibilities in which something is described by allusion through an evocative listing of its attributes). The consultants would create draft materials between meetings and bring them to the group for reactions and refinement. The teachers would then use the materials in their classrooms and bring to the working group examples of the student work created through the classroom events as well as their own responses to the work. All members were considered authors of the work. The resulting "domain projects" in poetry and later drama are a testimony to the ongoing collaboration of practitioners and researchers. The consultants would search out best practice and bring it to the teachers who would refine or sometimes redesign the practice to make it viable in their classrooms. A strong sense of collaboration was consciously pursued and realized.

During these years of development, the teachers on the committee regularly shared ideas about the emergent portfolio system with their colleagues during in-service sessions throughout the district's middle and secondary schools. In this way, not only did the work of the group spread, but also the group's identity and leadership were strengthened as its teacher members became spokespersons for the work. Results were shared and emerging materials were often adopted by the teachers' colleagues even as the work progressed. Dissemination of the work beyond the district always included committee members. Presentations at national conferences were made by teams of teachers, consultants, and curriculum specialists who progressively became more and more identified with the project. Thus it was in this spirit and context that the group began its joint pursuit of learning how to examine student work. The development team became a "community of learners" in the best possible sense. It was the experience of reading students' writing together that both solidified and tested the group.

A final form of capacity building within the system was the development of a critical view in which the quality of the work was routinely examined. The development of the instructional assessment systems was dominated by conversations designed to address issues of quality in both instructional and assessment terms. Whereas traditionally such conversations typically exclude one or the other viewpoint, in this case both were pursued with equal diligence.

As the system was developed to the operational levels described in this chapter, numerous analyses were conducted, including traditional psychometric examinations of item properties, studies of the consistencies of judgments in performance assessments and portfolio scoring, investigations of potential racial or gender bias in judgments about students' performance, explorations of the consequences of assessments in terms of educational practice. As the development team learned about the quality of evidence produced as well as the consequences of the system, they made appropriate modifications in procedures. The generally gratifying quality of the results did not occur as a matter of happenstance. The results followed from the efforts in development, including routine analysis, feedback, and response, that have been described here.

Reflections

In this chapter, we have argued the importance of an assessment system that is, first and foremost, coherent. Assessment activities that articulate well with classroom activities are essential if distractions from or even interference with best instructional practice are to be avoided. Using the experiences and efforts of the staff of the Pittsburgh Public Schools over the period 1981 to 1993, we have illustrated the ways that a school system can animate its vision of assessment with a comprehensive systemic change effort supported by extensive commitment to building the capacities of professionals in its service. In this final section we reflect on that experience and offer a number of hard-earned insights that may benefit other school systems confronting similar issues.

The first of these reflections concerns the roles, responsibilities, and relationships of those addressing assessment reform. In the Pittsburgh example, the primary responsibility for change and development was vested in curricular divisions. Those staff were concerned, first and foremost, with the integrity of content and the quality of instruction. The assessment specialists in the district were cast in supporting roles, challenging the efforts of their colleagues. The measurement and research staff were not the prime movers of the effort to reform assessment.

This, it seems to us, is the proper conception of these roles. It assures that the curricular and instructional implications of the assessment are of primary concern. It establishes the three areas (curriculum, instruction, and assessment) as inseparable. This configuration of responsibilities also permits the reform to be disseminated throughout the district more readily. The curricular/instructional specialists are better equipped to promote the initiative among teachers, as they are concerned with similar issues. It enables the reform to be advanced properly as a curricular/instructional effort.

In order to succeed, such a distribution of responsibilities requires very special dispositions on the parts of all involved. The assessment staff, for example, must see themselves clearly in a service or supporting role. Their activity is subservient to the primary curricular and instructional focus. They must serve as the "intellectual conscience" of the initiative with respect to assessment matters, challenging the effort toward integrity in those terms. They must remain attentive to the questions posed by their tradition and devise methods of answering those questions that do not constrain the imagination of the reform or compromise the integrity of the content.

Ironically, this perspective is explicit in the traditional view of test development, which requires *a priori* identification of the content and the specification of the measurement domain. The practice (pursued by many school districts) of making the assessment staff primarily responsible for initiating change is misguided in that it imposes the activity upon the classroom *ex machina*. This invites a natural resistance on the part of teachers, and very often enforces the separation of assessment from curriculum and instruction. In most cases where the assessment staff has had primary responsibility for the implementation of the assessment reform, effective and constructive change has not resulted. In our experience, it is possible to have the curriculum staff take the lead and, with the effective collaboration of assessment staff, produce assessments of high quality. It is not likely that high quality curricular and instructional improvements will result if the assessment staff takes the lead.

Our second broad conclusion is that the district's valuing of decisions based on relevant data was instrumental in obtaining necessary commitment to the development of the new assessments and to the promotion of their widespread use. The disposition of the district's leadership (and gradually many others in the system as well) to invoke this form of thinking about decisions created a hunger for high-quality information.

Where traditional tests failed to provide useful information (whether for lack of relevance, lack of sufficient and appropriate detail, or because they were poorly timed) new techniques were needed. However, the development of the necessary underlying form of thought (i.e., an interest in and capacity for rational decision making) had long been nurtured, first through MAP, then SEP and Arts PROPEL, and then our portfolio initiatives. By the time that the most recent innovations were contemplated, a disposition toward rational decision making was fairly well established. The portfolio effort could focus on new strategies for documenting student learning, and attend somewhat less to the dispositions and skills that enable data use.

A successful effort at the reform of assessment must attend to both the disposition to use data as well as the technology that supports it. Professionals who have no disposition toward or routines for using information derived from traditional tests are not going to change just because the assessment technology is changed. The need for better and more relevant information may be the reason that some did not use older tests. In our experience that does not describe many. Most still need to develop the habits and the capacities that support data use. They must learn how to respond to such information in order to change curricular and instructional approaches for groups and, most especially, for individuals. Those many school systems that are focusing on the techniques of assessment without attending to the forms of thought and use that make assessments necessary are not likely to produce powerful or lasting change.

In this chapter, we have argued for a vision of assessment that recognizes its many and varied purposes and explicitly sets out to address each of them. A reluctance to do so has given us a legacy of testing that is one-dimensional and not well equipped to address many needs, most especially those of teachers interested in using test results to inform and tailor their instructional practice. It would be well to keep in mind that, while we have built a very large educational enterprise, the most important thing happening anywhere within it is what happens every day between teachers and students. The rest of us (parents, community members, business leaders; governors, legislators, secretaries of education; publishers, academics and researchers) are best conceived as support for what happens in the classroom.

All of us should be judged by what we are able to contribute, directly in some cases and indirectly in others, to what happens in the classroom. That is not to say that testing and assessment have little to contribute; just the opposite should be true. It is to suggest, however, that the highest possible standard against which to judge the merits of the assessment that we conduct is the extent to which it contributes to what happens in the classroom. We have never used so demanding a standard before; it is time that we started.

NOTES

1. George Madaus, *The Courts, Validity, and Minimum Competency Testing* (Boston: Kluwer-Nijhoff, 1983); George Madaus and John MacNamara, *Public Examinations: A Study of the Irish Leaving Certificate* (Dublin: Educational Research Center, St. Patrick's College, 1970).

2. Robert Floden, Andrew Porter, William Schmidt, Donald Freeman, and John Schwille, *A Policy Capturing Study of Teacher Decisions about Content* (East Lansing, Mich.: Institute for Research on Teaching, Michigan State University, 1979); Andrew Porter, "Factors Affecting Teachers' Decisions about Content" (Paper presented at the Annual Meeting of the American Educational Research Association, Toronto, 1978); Gaea Leinhardt, "Overlap: Testing Whether It Is Taught," in *The Courts, Validity, and Minimum Competency Testing*, edited by George Madaus (Boston: Kluwer-Nijhoff, 1983); Gaea Leinhardt and Andrea M. Seewald, "Overlap: What's Tested, What's Taught?" *Journal of Educational Measurement* 18, no. 2 (1981): 85-96; Paul G. LeMahieu and Gaea Leinhardt, "Overlap: Influencing What's Taught," *Journal of Classroom Interaction* 21, no. 1 (1985): 2-12.

3. *Ladies' Home Journal*, "The Ten Best Educational Ideas of the Decade," 53 (1984): 72, 149; Walt Haney, "Assessment That Supports Instruction," *Educational Leadership* 43, no. 2 (1985): 4-13.

4. Michael Q. Patton, *Utilization-focused Evaluation* (Beverly Hills: Sage, 1978).

5. Richard C. Wallace, Jr., "Data Driven Educational Leadership," *Evaluation Practice* 7, no. 3 (1986): 24-36; Paul G. LeMahieu, Marina A. Piscolish, Judy Johnston, John R. Young, Debra Saltrick, and William E. Bickel, "An Integrated Model of Program Evaluation, Administration, and Policy Development" (Paper presented at the Annual Meeting of the American Educational Research Association, San Francisco, 1989).

6. Pierce Hammond, Paul G. LeMahieu, and Richard C. Wallace, Jr., "Telling the Whole Story: The Educational Program Audit" (Paper presented at the Annual Meeting of the American Educational Research Association, San Francisco, 1989).

7. Paul G. LeMahieu, "An Assessment of the Needs of Secondary Teachers Relevant to Professional Development: A Story of Evaluation Use" (Paper presented at the Annual Meeting of the American Educational Research Association, New Orleans, 1984).

8. William W. Cooley and William E. Bickel, *Decision Oriented Educational Research* (Boston: Kluwer-Nijhoff, 1986); Stanley E. Denton and Paul G. LeMahieu, "Evaluation

Research as an Integral Part of an In-service Staff Development Center," *Evaluation Bulletin* 6, no. 3 (1985): 45-51.

9. Paul G. LeMahieu, "The Effects of a Program of Student Achievement Monitoring through Frequent Testing," *Educational Evaluation and Policy Analysis* 6, no. 2 (1984): 175-187; Paul G. LeMahieu and Richard C. Wallace, Jr., "Establishing the Credibility of Test Results," *Educational Leadership* 43, no. 2 (1985): 60-62; idem, "Up against the Wall: Psychometrics Meets Praxis," *Educational Measurement* 5, no. 1 (1986): 12-17.

10. Nancy S. Cole, "A Realist's Appraisal of the Prospects for Unifying Instruction and Assessment," in *Assessment in the Service of Learning: Proceedings of the 48th ETS Invitational Conference on Measurement* (Princeton, N.J.: Educational Testing Service, 1987); LeMahieu and Wallace, "Up against the Wall."

11. Richard C. Wallace, Jr., *Monitoring Assessment in Pittsburgh: Assumptions and Components* (Pittsburgh, Pa.: Pittsburgh Board of Education, 1982).

12. Ibid.; LeMahieu, "The Effects of a Program of Student Achievement Monitoring through Frequent Testing."

13. Drew H. Gitomer, "Developing a Portfolio Culture that Enables Learners" (Paper presented at the 1989 National Summit Conference on the Arts and Education, John F. Kennedy Center for the Performing Arts, Washington, D.C., 1987).

14. Paul G. LeMahieu, JoAnne T. Eresh, Richard C. Wallace, Jr., "Using Student Portfolios for Public Accounting," *School Administrator* 49, no. 11 (1992): 8-15; Paul G. LeMahieu, Drew Gitomer, JoAnne T. Eresh, "Portfolios in Large Scale Assessment: Difficult but not Impossible," *Educational Measurement: Issues and Practices* 14, no. 3 (1995): 1-11.

CHAPTER VII

Re-writing the Tests: Lessons from the California State Assessment System

BILL HONIG AND FRANCIE ALEXANDER
IN COLLABORATION WITH DENNIE PALMER WOLF

In 1983, early in the move toward linked standards and performance assessment, the state of California established an ambitious agenda for education reform in which new forms of student assessment were to play a central role. Compared to earlier programs of student assessment in the state, the agenda was far-reaching in at least three ways. First, from the outset, the program argued that the major point of an assessment system was to improve student achievement. Second, in a state with an increasingly diverse student population, the program was intent on building evidence that equity and excellence could co-exist, if educators would accept the responsibility for providing a curriculum that provided all students with the requisite opportunities to learn. That curriculum was to produce students who were able to: (1) compete productively in a changing job market, (2) participate effectively in democratic processes, (3) achieve personal fulfillment, and (4) develop ethical values. Third, the system was to provide state educators with data on effective and less successful efforts that would inform future planning and the use of resources.

In this chapter we explore the consequences that ensued from so broad a mission. First, we turn to the early successes of the program. In particular, we will examine California as a case of a largely coherent approach to redesigning student assessment which involved the development of demanding curriculum frameworks (effectively the precursors to contemporary content standards), professional development, and new approaches to the conduct and reporting of data from the assessments. In a second section of the chapter, we turn to the later difficulties encountered by the program. There we will look at what

---

Bill Honig is Professor of Education at San Francisco (Calif.) State University. Francie Alexander is a vice-president at Scholastic Publishers. Dennie Palmer Wolf is co-editor of this volume.

the case of California, along with similar instances, can teach us about the obstacles, and even the temporary defeat, that such wholesale and new programs often encounter. In a final section we look at what the California case has to teach us about designing assessment systems with the capacity to evolve without collapsing.

The Educational Context for California's Assessment Program

In the early 1980s, California schools were in crisis. Test scores had declined and drop-out rates were climbing. Even those students who stayed in schools were undernourished by the school curriculum. Elementary schools focused solely on basic skills. The curricular demands in middle school were effectively level from sixth to eighth grades, despite the critical nature of early adolescence in students' school careers. In high schools there was a cafeteria-style curriculum which allowed some students to select a thin educational diet, barren of such fundamental subjects as mathematics and science, while others pursued advanced course work. In addition, graduation requirements were set at the local level and, as a result, there were tremendous gaps in the quantity and quality of students' educational experiences based on little more than where the students lived. In essence, beyond setting minimum competency standards and complying with regulations, the substance of schooling had been largely neglected. The result was that differences among educational experiences from school to school and from district to district were unacceptably wide.

The first step in the process of renewing the schools was to describe what students should know and be able to do. While California was, and remains, a state with strong investment in local control, the State Board of Education had the authority to make recommendations on courses of study through the mechanism of commissioning and approving curriculum frameworks. Thus, in 1983, the California legislature passed a major school reform bill which authorized the Department of Education to spearhead the development of model curriculum standards for high schools. Simultaneously, the legislation also reestablished state-level graduation requirements which had previously been left to local districts. The resulting standards were designed to send the message that the new graduation requirements were more than prescriptions for seat-time; they were descriptions of what students were expected to learn.

Across the next several years, this activity expanded to include K-8 schools as well. Because there was no legal mandate for school districts to adopt or enforce the recommendations in the curriculum materials, it was imperative that the recommendations become a widely accepted vision for rethinking what students should know and be able to do. Consequently, the California Department of Education developed a broad participatory process in which teachers from kindergarten through college, parents, business people, and other members of the community developed, refined, and ratified the frameworks. This approach to educational reform has been described as reform by leadership, rather than by control. Having initiated the development of the curriculum frameworks as a broadly inclusive effort, in effect the state initiated a broad-based discussion on the substance and conduct of schooling with a wide constituency of educational consumers. The resulting frameworks in core subjects like mathematics and language arts were, in many respects, among the first state-level public documents (as opposed to research and individual practices) that drew from a constructivist approach to curriculum and assessment. Specifically, the various frameworks argued that:

• All students should have access to a "thinking curriculum." According to the frameworks, students are to be actively involved in a curriculum which provides them with the opportunity to build their understandings and to apply what they have learned in real world situations.

• There is a body of knowledge that should be learned by all students. Important content from the subject areas connects students to the political, physical, social, ethical, and aesthetic worlds.

• Less is more. Not all content is created equal; some concepts are more important than others for gaining world knowledge and for developing understanding. These deserve intense attention and supportive forms of assessment.

• All students can achieve at high levels. The curriculum frameworks represented the state's expectations for its students and the interdependence between excellence and equity.

Thus, the resulting frameworks were a sharp departure from the long familiar, and apparently neutral, sets of goals and objectives often published by state departments of education. Instead, they were strongly positioned documents which took pronounced stands in favor of a number of nontraditional views of learning. To be specific, the frameworks both questioned familiar hierarchies and challenged customary definitions of knowledge. For example, the mathematics framework put problem posing and problem solving, rather than calculation and problem answering, at the heart of the curriculum to an extent later critics would consider unwise. Also, the mathematics framework upset at least two long established hierarchies. First, it suggested that the traditional sequence of eight years of arithmetic, followed by algebra I, geometry, algebra II, and calculus forestalled important topics for too long. The mathematical formalization of patterns usually reserved to high school should begin in elementary school. Second, the framework questioned the usual rank ordering of formal and applied mathematics. It suggested that the "messiness" of applied problems was equally as important as the power of formal mathematics. The literature framework also challenged familiar definitions of knowledge. First, it acknowledged that texts included film, video, and illustrations. Second, it replaced established views of reading with contemporary ones. It questioned the role of skills like phonics in ways that later critics found extreme. Instead of sending students to find what was "in" the poem or story, the frameworks stressed readers' individual responses to literature, and allowed for, or even encouraged, the play of emotion, experience, and cultural background. In addition, the literature frameworks emphasized the fictional and imaginative, rather than the public or civic, uses of language, giving play to the private and the subjective, over the public and the agreed upon.

Finally, in an effort to support teachers in their implementation efforts, the frameworks ventured deep into curriculum, including examples and suggestions rather than the bare-bones language of goals and objectives. Consequently, several years later when controversies over the assessment system arose, those in opposition could argue that the frameworks and the assessments based on them legislated values that should be up to local educators, families, and communities, not state departments of education. Thus, one of the great strengths of the frameworks was their forward-looking, active stance—their commitment to taking a clear stand and making change. However, this same commitment eventually became an Achilles' heel. The very lack of neutrality that made the frameworks visionary, also made them appear dangerous to persons who did not share the set of values implied by the frameworks.

The initial response to the curriculum frameworks was largely enthusiastic. They received the endorsement of a number of bodies in California (e.g., teachers' unions and parent-teacher organizations). They also drew attention from outside, essentially establishing a pattern repeated in many other states (e.g., Connecticut, Maryland, Kentucky, New York, Vermont) and eventually at the federal level when the national standards projects were funded as a part of federal school reform initiatives. Not surprisingly, then, the frameworks became the cornerstone not only of curricular reform, but also of professional development and assessment designs.

Also not surprisingly, once the frameworks were public, many educators began to raise questions about the tests the state used to measure student progress. The then current California Assessment Program (CAP) had been launched in the context of post-Sputnik school reforms (1972) and was conservative in many ways. Its items were entirely in the multiple-choice format. In addition, the system was, in large part, designed to answer traditional questions about the performance of the state system as a whole and the relative performance of schools compared to one another. One teacher complained that she felt like Charlie Brown when Lucy held the football in front of him, encouraged him to kick it, and then removed it so that he would fall. Like this individual, many educators were worried that the curriculum recommendations would not be implemented because teachers would have no interest in or motivation for teaching either content or processes that would never be tested.

However, the system did have several innovative features on which to build change. For instance, the CAP system had a longitudinal—or developmental—emphasis. The results were presented on a scale ranging from 100 to 400. This scaling system enabled school districts to measure their progress over time. In addition, schools facing similar types of challenge (e.g., poverty, high numbers of students acquiring English) were compared to one another. Although critiqued for setting differential expectations, this effort to construct bands of similarly challenged schools was in large part intended to help policymakers and school personnel ask how factors like poverty and language background interact with school success. There were also absolute scores so that no one was misled. This deliberate range of ways of reporting school performance was a major effort to see that schools that were making significant progress could get the credit they deserved. In addition, CAP assessments were based on matrix sampling in order to test the large numbers of students in the state at grades 1 (later abandoned), 3, 6, and 12 in reading, writing, and mathematics. In this system, students in one classroom received different forms of a test so that perhaps 300 items for a subject could be tested, even though an individual student completed as few as 30 items. Thus, students could be tested for a shorter period of time, each taking only a portion of the total assessment. At the same time, the scope of the assessment could be ten times as broad as any one individualized test and the results reported at the school level were at least twice as reliable. This approach set several significant elements in place: (1) a focus on the effectiveness of institutions and programs, rather than individual students; (2) the expectation for broad coverage of a field of knowledge; and (3) the simultaneous expectation that state assessment of students' learning could be designed to be administratively elegant as well as economical.[1]

Finally, and not insignificantly, CAP was the first program in which the state assumed the responsibility for developing its own assessments rather than simply buying what was commercially available. Given that essential autonomy, the state was in the position to pursue a second part of its leadership strategy. The California Department of Education began to support processes designed to align both the textbooks and the tests to the envisioned curriculum. This alignment was more easily said than done, because state assessments coexisted with local use of commercially published batteries, creating a hodgepodge of different sources and types of information about student learning. Thus, it became increasingly clear that the state would have to engage in a massive effort to design a more coherent assessment *system*. What emerged was a new type of state assessment system more open than ever before to performance assessment. For the next decade, that program operated with its major goal being to design, administer, and report on students' progress toward mastering the new curricula, using instruments consistent with that vision of teaching and learning. The process was long, complex, and full of lessons about the possibilities and limits of building mutually consistent practices, assessment policies, and instruments.

Even though highly regarded for these innovations, CAP was seriously at odds with the principles and content of the revised curriculum frameworks. Major changes were needed. Most pointedly, it became clear that the variety of testing formats had to be dramatically expanded to support the thinking curriculum portrayed in the frameworks. Thus, the urgent question soon became, "What are the possibilities of including open-ended items, more extended projects, collaborative work, and problems that require equipment and materials such as science experiments in a large-scale testing system?"

In 1983, the omnibus education reform bill provided the occasion for moving CAP from a basic skills test to an assessment of learning in the context of a rich curriculum. Students were to be tested in grades

3, 6, 8, and 12 annually. History-social science and science were added. Significantly, CAP also made the move from curriculum-independent multiple-choice items, to curriculum-based questions as it developed end-of-course examinations for middle and high school levels. The Golden State Examinations (GSE) were developed as challenging end-of-course assessments that, like the Advanced Placement or Regents exams, would provide individual scores so as to recognize outstanding achievement. Equally important, in 1987 CAP began using writing assessments where students drafted and then revised entire pieces in a wide range of genres. This use of direct, rather than indirect, measures of learning was also a significant change in the design and conduct of state level assessments.

These new developments in CAP were designed to maintain the consensus that the frameworks represented. The agreement on what California hoped to accomplish in the area of student assessment was best expressed in a widely circulated "Vision Statement" prepared by the California Department of Education in 1990. (See figure 1.) In concert with the framework themes and this vision of assessment, a new generation of assessments was developed. Samples of these assessments provide the best illustrations of what was envisioned.

WIDENING THE RANGE OF INSTRUMENTS

The assessments that fulfilled this vision moved "beyond the bubble"; they demonstrated that the recognize-and-select formats characteristic of earlier generations of low-demand multiple-choice items need not represent the outer limits of what a state assessment could ask students to demonstrate. For instance, even while preserving the efficiency and reliability of multiple-choice items, it was quite possible to design questions that provoked thought and drew on a number of modalities. (See figure 2 for an example.)

But innovations did not stop at enhancing familiar multiple-choice formats. Consistent with the recommendations of the *Mathematics Framework for California Public Schools*,[2] the new assessments engaged students in complex problem solving that involved more conjecture and reasoning than selecting the correct answer from a short list of possibilities. In so doing, the designers complemented enhanced multiple-choice items with open-ended performance tasks. (See figure 3 for an example.)

Significantly, this work was pushed beyond the boundaries of familiar testing in literacy and mathematics. Subjects such as science

What if

-- students found assessment to be a lively, active exciting experience?

-- they could see clearly what was expected of them and believed that the assessment provided a fair opportunity to show what they had learned?

-- they were challenged to construct responses that conveyed the best of what they had learned--to decide what to present and how to present it-- whether through speech, writing, or performance?

-- they were educated to assess themselves, to become accurate evaluators of the strengths and weaknesses of their own work, and to prescribe for themselves the efforts they must make to improve it--ultimately, the most important form of assessment available to our students?

-- the assessment allowed students to use their own backgrounds and indicated ways of building on their strengths for further learning?

-- their learning were recognized by the school and the community when they had made outstanding progress--regardless of their initial level of achievement?

-- teachers could look at the tests and say, "Now we're talking about a fair assessment of my teaching"?

What if the assessment system is one that

-- focuses on the essence of the student outcomes that I am striving for-- not one that focuses on the peripheral skills or the isolated facts which are easiest to measure?

-- shows they can produce something of value to themselves and to others-- an argument, a report, a plan, an answer or solution; a story, a poem, a drawing, a sculpture, or a performance; that they can conduct an experi- ment, deliver a persuasive oral presentation, participate cooperatively and productively in groups?

-- is accessible to all my students, yet stretches the most capable students as well--not one that measures some mythical minimum competency level?

-- matches the assessment that I use on a day-to-day basis to guide my teaching and that guides my students in their learning--not one that takes an artificial form and then naively expects students to give a natural response in an artificial situation?

-- doesn't take valuable time from the teaching/learning process, but is an integral part of that process?

-- doesn't treat me as a "Dispenser of Facts," providing and prescribing the concepts and the content that students are to know--but rather as a coach and a fellow learner, helping my students to become active learners who are prepared to discover what is important to them now and enthusiastic about learning in the future?

What if the new assessments led parents, taxpayers, legislators, and the business community to exclaim:

-- I can see that the schools are focusing on the important things--that students are achieving levels of academic excellence which truly prepare them for the future.

-- I can see that students are learning what they need to fulfill themselves as individuals, to become concerned and involved citizens and workers who can adapt to the changing demands of our world--creative people who can think and take initiative, who care about what they do, and who can work with others to solve problems.

-- I can see the results in the newspapers which give me the information I need in terms I can understand, which show me the progress our schools are making on assessments that really matter, and where they need my help and support.

FIGURE 1

Vision Statement on Assessment (California Department of Education, 1990).

Which one of the areas in the diagram represents the probability that a basketball player who has a 70 percent probability of making a basket will make two consecutive baskets?

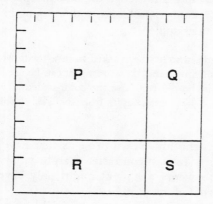

A. Area P   C. Area R
B. Area Q   D. Area S

FIGURE 2

An enhanced multiple-choice mathematics item

Source: *A Sampler of Mathematics Assessments,* California Assessment Program, 1991.

For the figure below, show 1/2 in as many ways as you can. You may draw more figures if necessary. For each way you find, explain how you know you have 1/2

FIGURE 3

An open-ended mathematics item

Source: *A Sampler of Mathematics Assessments,* California Assessment Program, 1991.

and social science and history rapidly became a part of the system. For example, as early as 1990, science assessments appeared that endorsed students demonstrating knowledge of the concepts and processes of science, the ability to solve problems, and engaging in hands-on tasks. The following is an example:

> You are a scientist who has been asked to investigate why a large number of fish are dying in a mountain lake. A test that can be used to determine the health of the lake is the pH test. Use the color-coded chart on the table to determine the pH of the water samples from the lake. (California Assessment Program, 1990).

While not yet the full-blown projects that have emerged more recently, this type of request contrasted sharply with earlier CAP multiple-choice items where a student might only have been asked to select the correct definition of pH.

Similar developments occurred in the field of history-social science. Whereas the traditional social science curriculum was a mile wide and an inch deep, the 1987 social science framework called for depth. Based on that framework, assessments were developed that focused on students' capacity for historical empathy, the analysis of cause and effect, and the manner in which the past events continue to affect contemporary life. For example, a 1991 history assessment included a group assessment task on the reunification of Germany—a task that required three class periods to complete. Students were asked to advise the President of the United States on our country's policy toward reunification. After examining primary documents and incorporating knowledge from their studies, the students generated a memo to the president, participated in a debate on the issue, and wrote an essay defending their chosen position.

Inherent in the development of performance tasks was a move away from systems of machine scoring for percent of items correct to an entirely different system that depended wholly on human readers' informed judgment. Moreover, this new system was criterion-referenced rather than norm-referenced: students' performances were scored using descriptions of different absolute levels of performance, not relative rankings. The literacy assessments that emerged from CAP in the early 1990s provide excellent examples. For instance, in the direct writing assessments mentioned earlier, students were asked to respond to a prompt that represented one of eight types of writing (e.g., autobiographical incident, persuasive essay). To score these performances teachers came together, were trained to use a six-point scale using descriptions of levels of performance and actual samples of student writing, and worked as teams to discuss problematic instances and establish respectable levels of interrater reliability.

DEVELOPING TEACHERS AS DESIGNERS, SCORERS, AND CONSUMERS OF ASSESSMENT

The human and financial capital invested in the development of the new assessment system was substantial during times of economic strain in the state. The effort was particularly expensive if it was compared to the long-established costs of multiple-choice testing. However, California's assessment system was designed to do double duty. Not only did it monitor student performance levels; it also provided considerable opportunities for the professional development that was absolutely necessary if the promise of the frameworks was ever to be translated in common practices. As the state developed its growing crop of performance assessments, teachers became involved in any number of aspects of this work: they served on development committees where prototype tasks were fashioned; they piloted and critiqued early versions of tasks; they acted as readers in local and statewide scoring sessions; and they worked on publicizing and translating the frameworks and associated assessments to parents and the public. This involvement soon began to have ripple effects, such as strengthening teachers' belief in the state's educational reform initiative. After over 50,000 sixth-grade students participated in the 1990 field test of new performance assessment items in science, one teacher wrote:

I can see it (CAP) making our staff more ready to step away from text-driven science instruction and into hands-on, conceptually linked curriculum design. With validation from the California Department of Education, teachers feel more willing to take risks and teach in new ways.

While this kind of professional involvement has now become commonplace in any number of state assessment systems, it is important to remember that until the California Learning Assessment System (CLAS) made it widely possible, such opportunity was tightly restricted to teachers who worked in specialized fields (e.g., music and art) or to the small cadre of professionals working in Advanced Placement or International Baccalaureate programs. With CLAS, the dual powers of strong assessment programs became widely apparent.

THE DEVELOPMENT OF AN OPEN SYSTEM OF ASSESSMENT:
CRITERIA, RUBRICS, AND BENCHMARK PAPERS

Most accounts of the history of performance assessment stress the clearly observable changes in format, the move to criterion referencing, and the reliance on scorers' judgment. But California's system makes clear that there is another, much less often discussed, shift involved. This is the move from a closed to an open system of assessment. When the multiple-choice individual testing of CAP was in place, the assessment system was effectively the exclusive private property of technical developers. The tests were secure and scored entirely by machine. The net result was secrecy: students and educators, as well as the consuming public, were entirely outside looking in. However, with the advent of a system that included performance testing much of this changed. In order for the assessment to model good instruction, it was important that the types of tasks (if not the exact instantiations) become public, that the rubrics be widely understood, and that, in their training, teachers have access to benchmark papers that exemplify each of the six levels of performance.

One result of this more public system was instructional change. This was clearest in the case of writing. For instance, at individual school sites, teachers often used CAP-like prompts (or retired actual prompts) with their students, scored the resulting essays in class, and talked with their students about how to improve their performances. Not surprisingly, a study of teachers and students conducted by the Center for the Study of Writing at the University of California (Berkeley) found that the majority of teachers surveyed (78 percent) indicated that following the advent of CAP assessments and training, they assigned more writing. The main reason they gave for this was the visibility that the state assessment program gave to the nature of valued performances. In a more recent report from the U.S. Department of Education, California students were compared to their counterparts nationally. The state's twelfth graders reported doing more writing than seniors in the rest of the nation. Twenty-seven percent of California's twelfth graders reported writing two or fewer papers in the previous week, compared to 49 percent nationally. And most important, overall progress on the direct writing assessment was reported for California students.

At the same time that the public nature of this new system made it possible to identify and move toward curricular goals, it also opened the system to much broader and franker inspection. Not only the final results, but the tasks and the rubrics were open to public scrutiny. They were developed by groups of educators working in the system, not by the technical staff of publishing companies. They were pilot tested and thus versions of them were circulating in public in their "newborn" state prior to revision. As performance tasks, they required scoring rubrics and benchmark papers that, in essence, broadcast the content and evidential basis of the judgments that underlay the difference not only between scores of 2 and 5, but even between scores of 3 and 4. Because performance testing was in its infancy and because the judgments involved are complex, tasks and rubrics could easily become the targets of active criticism. These discussions and ensuing revisions are fundamental strengths of a performance-based system. However, following a tradition in which troublesome items are removed through techniques like differential item functioning, this open debate struck some critics as evidence of an enduring weakness, not a fundamental flexibility of the system which would allow for refinement over time.

Recent Challenges and Difficulties

The CAP assessment system that California developed was respected and emulated. For instance, the 1989 report of the Government Accounting Standards Board cited CAP and the California School Performance Reports as outstanding examples of comprehensive performance monitoring. Even though there had been significant investment in developing a state-of-the-art system, that system was cost-effective. Its annual budget of $15 million represented less than one tenth of 1 percent of the state's budget for education from kindergarten through grade 12. The California Education Summit in 1989 recommended increasing this amount to 3 percent, so considerable was the respect for the design and effects of the system.

However, trouble brewed on both national and local fronts. The economic boom of the 1980s collapsed. The "culture wars" between conservatives and liberals boiled over from universities and colleges into schools. In California, the governorship passed from a Democrat to a Republican. Beginning in the 1990s, the state assessment system was caught in the cross-fire of conflicting expectations. Based on state legislation passed in 1991, CAP was reformulated as the California Learning Assessment System. Specifically, the legislation passed in 1991 required testing at grade 4 (language arts and mathematics), grade 5 (history-social science and science), grade 8 (all subjects), and grade 10 (all subjects). CLAS was also charged with providing individual scores. Simultaneously, the legislation called for curriculum-embedded tasks (standardized assignments introduced throughout the year to guarantee the kind of teaching and learning demanded by the assessments) and portfolios. As envisioned the portfolios would include not only a longitudinal selection of student work, but also curriculum-embedded performances and the results of end-of-course assessments mandated by the state. Amidst these rising demands, none of the additional financial support that had been recommended was forthcoming.

Nationally, the so-called "culture wars" began to play out in public schools. In California, public discussions about the changes in the curriculum long endorsed by the frameworks heated and boiled over. As much of the discourse arguing for higher standards solidified around mathematics, science, technology, and vocationally relevant learning, much less attention was paid to building coherent positions in the arts and humanities. Tremendous factionalism developed, particularly in the fields of literacy and history. In the elementary schools, there were pitched battles between proponents of whole language and proponents of phonics. In upper grades, there was a growing rift between advocates for teaching children to understand and appreciate the foundations of Western civilization and those who wanted to see world history expand to acknowledge the contributions of Meso-American, Native American, Asian, and African civilizations. At least as fierce were the confrontations between proponents of an honorific version of American history and those advocating a critical version.

Finally, after the first blush of enthusiasm over performance assessment, it was increasingly clear that like all complex technologies, it was not a ready-to-hand panacea. Everything depended on the quality of its design, the way in which it was implemented, and whether teachers had the requisite content knowledge to teach, respond to student work, and act as scorers in thoughtful ways. In addition, it also became increasingly clear that the system had not been born fully formed. Like any system of human judgment—whether in judging competitions in choral singing or in ice skating—it would take resources, training, and a considerable period of development to become valid and reliable. Nevertheless, in the wake of bold initial claims, this second wave of caution and gradualism was interpreted as wavering, even failure. Instead, there were equally bold claims about how unfeasible and unreliable such measurements were.

Thus, by the early 1990s, California's assessment system became the locus of conflicting demands. An ambitious program met financial stringency. A system designed largely as a tool of education reform was charged with increasingly high demands for accountability. The same program that was to assess thinking was also to provide evidence of the mastery of basic skills. In the context of different philosophies of education and political affiliations, the assessment system became a flash point for conflict.

The conflict reached a high pitch by the spring of 1994 when multiple controversies erupted in rapid succession. First, the consensus built for the frameworks eroded; this was most dramatically evident in the humanities assessments. Concerned conservative parents and interest groups stirred controversy by arguing that many of the literature passages featured in the new performance tasks were offensive. Some were marked as being the work of authors like Alice Walker, whose other works offended the plaintiffs. Others, like a story featuring a snowball fight, were singled out as too violent. Still other items were described as too personal, too political, and too vague to be part of a statewide assessment. Among the questions cited were: "Do you think that people today are as strong as their parents and grandparents were?" (4th grade); "Why do you think some teenagers and their parents have trouble communicating?" (8th grade); "Why do you think people can seem to be shy in one setting and outgoing in another?" (10th grade).[3]

The furor over the language arts items ignited a second controversy over the secure nature of what was certainly a publicly funded assessment. Representatives of concerned conservative groups requested to see the questions. The Department of Education, eager to protect the confidentiality of the test, refused, failing to realize that there might be no assessment unless the public was satisfied that its best interests and deepest values were respected. The response was swift and outspoken, as in this letter to the editor in a San Diego paper:

Is the California Department of Education really afraid that CLAS (California Learning Assessment System) questions will leak out to students? Or is it afraid the questions will leak out to parents? Why does the CLAS pre-test ask about the parents' annual income, education level, employment classification and welfare status? What does this have to do with learning assessment?

The state must keep the CLAS test secret. Otherwise, taxpayers who paid millions of dollars for its creation and more millions for its administration might expose the test for what it is—a probe for problems at home and how they relate to academic achievement. Then the "educrats" can say, "See, it's not our fault Johnny can't read, it's yours."

I dare them to make the exam questions public after the testing is over to prove me wrong.[4]

In this climate, a judge in one California jurisdiction ruled that students could opt out of taking the test and questions were eventually made public. Conservative parents proposed a lawsuit which argued that the tests not be given without advance parental consent.[5] However, the broader contention that the tests invade privacy was eventually rejected by the courts.

A third controversy also erupted in the spring of 1994, with the release of the data from the first round of CLAS testing from the spring of 1993. Under considerable political pressure to demonstrate what it could do for the $15 million that the assessment had cost, the Department had piloted, administered, collected, analyzed and released public data on school-level performances. Given its meager resources, the state had developed a plan for sampling the data, but had promised that in no case would fewer than 25 percent of student performances at a site be analyzed. However, when the data were made public, a secondary analysis conducted by the *Los Angeles Times* revealed that these guidelines had been violated in more than a few cases.[6] The newspaper claimed that, while 48.7 percent of the tests had been scored, the analysis found that in 49.8 percent of the cases the assessment did not meet its own guidelines. The resulting press was graphic in its description of how these oversights played out:

At some of the schools, the small numbers of graded tests probably skewed the school's results severely. At one school, where less than 4 percent of the children have learning disabilities, 40 percent of the tests graded were from children with learning disabilities.[7]

Leading organizations like the California School Boards Association and the California Teachers Association withdrew their support from at least the existing version of CLAS. In an effort to sustain support for the controversial assessments, state Senator Gary Hart, the sponsor of the original bill creating CLAS, sponsored amendments in a new bill (SB 1273). Those amendments prohibited questions that probed personal or family values, called for an independent review panel, and required samples from previous tests to be made available to the public. Eventually the legislature approved the Hart bill and sent a budget request for $57.3 million for the California Department of Education to the governor, which included $26 million for state testing (renamed for the third time as the California Comprehensive Testing Program). But in September of 1994, despite the recommendations of his own appointed State Board of Education, the governor vetoed the bill citing several reasons: (1) the projected time-line, which delayed individual scores on performance tasks until 1999 when the Department of Education felt the system would have matured; (2) the need for a greater emphasis on basic skills; and (3) the failure to include more traditional testing formats such as multiple-choice items.[8] In the ensuing months, CLAS was effectively stranded by lack of further funding. The Governor's office was urging the quick design of what was to be the California Comprehensive Testing Program aligned with the corrections noted above. In essence, what was once a broad and reform-minded assessment *system*, with a largely coherent approach to curriculum, instruction, and professional development has been eviscerated. The result is ironic: California, the state that cut the path may soon have an assessment system markedly more conservative than the national legislation that it helped to inspire. For example, the new federal legislation concerning Chapter 1 now calls on schools to have a system of performance assessments in order to monitor the growth and achievement of students participating in its programs. Many California schools that would have depended on the CLAS system for help with performance assessments are now without support in their efforts to meet new Chapter 1 requirements.

Reflections and Lessons

The designers of other state assessment systems, poised to incorporate performance assessment into their work, look at what happened in California and shudder. But is it really a warning to steer clear of large-scale performance assessment? As a state, California has a long history of innovation mixed with retraction. As early as 1978, the state's voters passed Proposition 13, a measure which limited the annual tax rate on property to 1 percent of market value. The measure passed, even though the consequences for municipal services such as libraries and schools were severe. In terms of more contemporary events, the CLAS system was dismantled at a particular historical moment when many conservative groups raised fiscal and moral questions about using public dollars to support programs as unfamiliar as, and as positioned as, the California frameworks and assessments were. In this light, the battle over CLAS is not all that different from what has occurred in the ongoing congressional debates over public television and radio, or the National Endowments. It echoes any number of moves to reassert local and familial control in arenas where government has intervened and sought to regulate the prohibition of school prayer, the use of vouchers to pay for private and parochial schooling, or the effort to repeal busing orders stemming from desegregation cases. California was, in some sense, simply the site of a particularly fierce version of what was a national reaction to public spending and programs. In the same election that returned Governor Pete Wilson to office, there was a referendum for a statewide school voucher program as well as the highly controversial Proposition 187, which denied illegal aliens access to public services, including public schooling and health care. Nonetheless, the recent history of CLAS is not without important lessons which should perhaps be listed among its contributions. These are lessons regarding inclusion and consensus building, public accountability, and the rate of tolerable change.

Inclusion and consensus building. In California, the writing and publication of the curriculum frameworks was the major phase of consensus building. Once they were in place, it was assumed that there was sufficiently widespread agreement on the nature of knowledge, learning, and what should be taught. However, the original frameworks were drafted more than ten years prior to the development of the test items which generated furor in the spring of 1994. Moreover, there is an enormous difference between a visionary document addressed largely to interested educators and the actual items on a statewide test. This is particularly true as the stakes go up and the system heads toward scores for individuals. This points to the enormous need for continuous consensus building.

As a part of this consensus building, the architects of public programs as innovative as the California Learning and Assessment System have to guard against self-enclosed certainty. For instance, the CLAS designers and committees developed a clear and articulate view of literacy as personal meaning-making. It is a view of language use backed up by considerable contemporary theory if not by conclusive research, but it lent CLAS items a very particular stamp. It led to writing that was largely personal and narrative. The assessments were noticeably short of assignments in civic discourse (e.g., letters to the editor, texts of speeches for public meetings) and in functional or applied learning (e.g., instructions, proposals, plans). But the capacity to write as a concerned citizen or an innovative member of the economy is much more highly and widely valued than the ability to critique literature or write a journal. Similarly, the history and social science framework as it was realized in assessments emphasized the interplay of points of view and, at least to critics, a strong sympathy for just some of those points of view. Such a highly positioned stance makes a program vulnerable. It is possible, for instance, to underscore the constructed nature of history and the partial and often conflicting nature of evidence without taking sides. A recent example from a California classroom provides an illustration. The students' final assessment in an elementary school history class was to select and discuss an event for which there are a number of different points of view. To comply with this assignment one student produced an illustrated book where she included the Christian biblical account, Aztec creation myths, and evolutionary theory, giving equal weight to each.[9] In addition to this kind of "equal time" approach, any program entailing significant changes in what is tested (and consequently what is taught) must bring its constituencies steadily and gradually along. Such efforts are evident, for instance, in the later stages of the assessment reform in Kentucky. There, a series of local committees (known as the Prichard committees) work at a local level to build support for the changes introduced by the Kentucky Educational Reform Act.[10] In part, their duty is to find viable local translations of the reform. As one Kentucky teacher explained:

If I talk about children as constructing meaning, or the need for critical and creative thinking, I lose my parents. Not all of them are eager to have children who raise questions or who want to go away when they go to college. Instead, I have to find a local basis for the changes I need to make. So, for instance, when it comes time to talk about portfolios, I don't spend much time on the usual lines about student choice and ownership, or mathematical power. There isn't one of my families that doesn't worry about their kids always wanting new things, or not knowing how to fix or value the things they have. One of them calls it "mall fever." So, I explain that portfolios are about helping kids to learn to take care of things, to work hard at getting something right, for valuing hard work, for repairing things.[11]

Public accountability. As mentioned earlier, one of the dramatic changes introduced in the California effort was that of a much more open system of assessment. Rather than the assessment being entirely the enterprise of test designers, CAP and then CLAS were developed by the California Department of Education, in conjunction with a broad network of teachers who acted as designers, pilot testers, and scorers. However, the relatively open nature of such testing was much less clear or available to the consuming public. Like all prior generations of tests, the CAP and the CLAS items were secure and even in later public reporting only selected items were released. This relatively tight control backfired badly in the spring of 1994 when the Department refused to cooperate with parents and others who raised questions about the too personal and intrusive nature of many of the items used in the humanities tests. In the resulting furor, Senator Hart, a long-time sponsor of the state's innovations in assessment, sought to save the effort by proposing a much more public approach to the tests. Notably, he recommended an internal review committee that would deliberately incorporate the full spectrum of public opinion; an external audit committee, and the public release of a substantial sample of the items following any given year's testing. While all three measures would certainly add to the cost of the assessment, the investment in public knowledge and support is clearly warranted.

Portraying the rate of possible change. CAP and especially CLAS moved very swiftly—perhaps too swiftly. This is true in at least two respects. As discussed above, the initiative was too quick for a broad constituency to understand and endorse the changes. However, it was also too fast for the technology of performance testing to keep pace. Multiple-choice testing has been developed steadily (and with considerable funding) since it was first used on a large scale to sort recruits in World War I. More than three-quarters of a century later, it is a well-oiled technology: it is low-cost, efficient, and highly defensible as objective, reliable, and quantifiable. None of this is yet true of performance-based testing in this country—although it certainly flourishes unchallenged, for example, in the education systems of Australia, New Zealand, and the United Kingdom. In the United States, where teacher judgment, qualitative methods, and criterion-referenced descriptions of performance are foreign and suspect, and where the threat of litigation is enormous, it will take a period of long and steady investment for open-ended testing to mature sufficiently. There will be serious glitches along the way: for instance, low levels of reliability such as those that plagued the early portfolio efforts in Vermont and the sampling errors that made such ugly news in California newspapers in the spring of 1994. This presents an enormous problem since long-term efforts are so clearly vulnerable to changes in political fortunes: what was lauded under earlier California governors, was vigorously opposed by Governor Wilson. Here the recent history in states like Connecticut and Vermont is instructive. In the case of Connecticut, for instance, since the state tests are low-stakes, describing only the performances of districts and the state, it has been possible to pursue a decade-long effort to gradually change the modes of assessment. (See chapter 8, this volume.) Thus, one possible strategy is to bracket the period of highest innovation, standing back from high-stakes testing until there is technical soundness and broad-based community support. Another strategy is the one emerging in Vermont. First of all, the state has made a decision to concentrate its efforts on one major mode of student assessment—portfolios. In so doing, the State Education Department has made a public commitment to move gradually and steadily to a point where those instruments are reliable and valid. Thus, when early reports of low reliability appeared, the effort was not dismantled. The next year's goal became adequate professional development to increase that reliability (See chapter 9, this volume.) The point is that the efforts, both in Connecticut and Vermont, have been presented as steadily evolutionary, not as revolutionary. Any state assessment system undergoing substantial reform has its own battles to fight and defenses to make. Its designers must have vision, but a zealous crusade to change a dominant epistemology radically and quickly may overtax the public tolerance for change.

There have been numerous headlines declaring the crumbling of the ambitious efforts in California. And there is certainly evidence that the CLAS programs, *per se*, are gone. Nevertheless, CAP and CLAS have left any number of valuable legacies to a second generation of efforts at assessment reform. Some of these lessons are the sobering lessons just described. But there are others. One of the most striking is the work initiated by the frameworks. Those documents remain the blueprint for much of the work on content standards carried out in other states and at the federal level. In a period when the burning questions should be "Who has the educational opportunity to meet high standards?" most discussions continue to center on how students must perform. The corresponding question about what schools owe students to help them meet those higher standards finds one of its clearest and fairest statements in the California frameworks. Similarly, the CLAS system provided one of the earliest and most serious visions of the necessity for engaging teachers and building their understanding of assessment. Both CAP and CLAS allowed large numbers of educators to become involved and to use that involvement to build

their understanding of the links between curriculum and assessment.
Where California districts seized these opportunities for learning,
they have put in place systems of their own which carry out assessment and reflection at a community level. Quite possibly the most
important legacy is the still difficult to realize vision of a coherent system of delivery standards, professional development, teaching, and
assessment. When a false report of his demise was printed, Mark
Twain once quipped that the reports of his death "were greatly exag-
gerated." So it is with the work that California initiated.

The account of the development of California's state assessment
system in this chapter stops short with the events of 1994. As such, it
is inevitably incomplete. The elections of 1995 could once again make
a considerable difference in the support and funding of the program.
Similarly, if other large-scale assessment programs based on performance tasks, such as those in Vermont and Kentucky, prove their
long-term viability, the climate of criticism and doubt that eroded support for California's early efforts might shift. It is particularly hard to
call the movement toward more diversified student assessment "over"
in California. Beginning as early as the first curriculum frameworks in
the 1980s, unparalleled attention was paid to building robust educational motivations for new forms of assessment. There was an equally
strong investment in professional development across an entire decade
which yielded a core of teacher-leaders and sympathetic administrators. These investments will be hard to extinguish.

NOTES

1. Francie Alexander, "Accountability and Assessment California Style," in *Education Reform in the 90s*, edited by Chester E. Finn, Jr. and Theodore Rebarber (New
York: Macmillan, 1992).

2. California Department of Education, *Mathematics Framework for California Public Schools* (Sacramento, Calif.: California Department of Education, 1992).

3. J. Wilgoren, "A Look at What's Really There in the CLAS Tests," *Los Angeles
Times*, 18 June 1994.

4. R. Earle, Letter to the Editor, *San Diego Times-Union*, 9 May 1994.

5. *Los Angeles Times*, "A Key Question for Any Test," 7 May 1994.

6. *Los Angeles Times*, "Grading of CLAS Tests Called Skewed," 10 April 1994.

7. Ibid.

8. California Office of Child Development and Education, Press release, 27 September 1994.

9. Dennie Palmer Wolf, observation in Teachers' Historiography Seminar, Oak-
land Public Schools, October, 1993.

10. R. Sexton, "Building Public Support for Educational Assessment Reform: The Case of the Prichard Committees in Kentucky" (Paper presented at the Harvard Summer Institute on Assessment, July 5, 1995).

11. Dennie Palmer Wolf, interview with Kentucky teachers, Louisville, Kentucky, October, 1993.

CHAPTER VIII

Developing Performance-Based Student Assessments: The Connecticut Experience

JOAN BOYKOFF BARON

Two new approaches have been added to those already being used to improve student achievement as growing numbers of policymakers and educators are supporting the development of assessments and accompanying performance standards to bolster the effects of new curriculum and pedagogy. During the past twenty years, state and local educational agencies have been charged with the responsibility for collecting and reporting assessment data. Performance standards are established to answer the question, "How much is good enough?" At the state level, data about students' achievement have been used to inform the educational policies of state boards of education and legislatures as well as to influence the daily practices of state departments of education. For example, funding formulas are adjusted, curriculum priorities are reordered, and professional development activities are mounted. At the school level these same assessment data have been used to improve local school curriculum, instruction, and assessment as committees of teachers and consultants collaborate to develop new curriculum and learning activities in areas in which students do poorly. Assessment data have also been used to guide placement and other instructional decisions for individual students who score below established performance standards and therefore may need remedial assistance. Because of the proliferation of uses and the high stakes currently attached to these data, there is a growing body of evidence that the assessments themselves are beginning to affect students' achievement by influencing, and sometimes even inappropriately narrowing, curriculum and pedagogy.[1] Given their increasing influence, it behooves us to create assessments and scoring systems which model and elicit best practice. This requires that assessment developers be

Joan Boykoff Baron is an education consultant at the Connecticut State Department of Education and Director of Assessment Systems at the Performance Assessment Collaboratives for Education (PACE) at the Harvard Graduate School of Education where she is also a Lecturer in Education.

sensitive to national and state-level debates about the latest curriculum
frameworks and standards available.

Essential Characteristics of Performance-Based Assessments

During the past fifteen years, Connecticut has developed large-
scale performance-based assessments in a wide variety of subject areas.
These areas include: English language arts (1980-1995); art and music
(1980-1981); business and office education (1983-1984); science
(1984-1985 and 1989-1995); foreign language (1986-1987); industrial
arts and technology education (1986-1987), and mathematics (1990-
1995).[2] Our experience has taught us that we should design assessments that increase access, build capacity, and establish coherence for
both teachers and students. We have selected these three characteristics from among many others because of their centrality in improving
students' achievement. In this chapter I will describe the different
ways in which our performance-based assessments in writing, foreign
language, and science were developed, administered, and scored in
both high- and low-stakes testing environments in order to clarify the
conditions under which such assessments can be used to increase
access, capacity, and coherence for teachers and students. I begin by
discussing briefly what we mean by each of these terms.

Access. Access is a direct function of the availability of models of
exemplary tasks and student work. Newer forms of performance-based
assessment can provide teachers with ways of understanding the kinds
of problems and tasks implied by the most current curriculum frameworks. For example, what do curriculum frameworks and standards
documents mean by such phrases as "communicate mathematically,"
"use mathematical reasoning," or "design and carry out scientific
investigations"? Assessments can increase access for both teachers and
students by including (and thereby modeling) strong learning events
designed to help students synthesize and apply the major themes and
"big ideas" represented in a content area. These assessment events can
yield tangible examples of student work for teachers to evaluate
according to well-articulated, often multidimensional, rating criteria.
When teachers are able to discuss a wide range of student performance with their colleagues, they develop a language for describing
the attributes of strong student work. (See chapters by Mills and by
Daro in this volume.) Similar discussions about the qualities of strong
work can then take place in their classrooms, thereby helping students
to understand what a high-quality performance is.

Capacity. We use the term "capacity" to refer to the actual or potential ability to do something. If teachers and students do not have models of new curriculum expectations for competence in given domains, it is difficult for them to realize those expectations. Consequently, capacity building is a direct function of access to models of effective tasks, exemplars of students' work, and a vocabulary for describing high-quality work. Generally, before students can build their capacities, their teachers need to feel efficacious about teaching them. Therefore, when teachers are included in all phases of the assessment cycle—that is, developing and/or refining tasks, implementing and administering them in their classrooms, and then working with their colleagues to describe and rate students' work on some commonly shared criteria— they can develop their own capacities and those of their students.

Coherence. Coherence requires natural or logical connections. It demands consistency and mutual reinforcement among the different parts of a system. If assessments are to be a viable approach for improving students' achievement, the assessments must be consistent with *best practice.* Therefore, wherever possible our assessments have been aligned with the recommendations of the most current curriculum frameworks and standards that have been endorsed by statewide committees of teachers and curriculum experts. Furthermore, we have always been hopeful that strategies used on statewide assessments would gradually be incorporated into the daily practices of teachers. This has meant that the practices used on our statewide assessments, when initially introduced, have been more advanced than the classroom assessment practices of many teachers.

In the early 1980s there was considerable concern among educators nationally about curricular and instructional validity. Because stakes were high on statewide assessments (most of them were minimum competency tests), there was a concern that tests be fair and represent what was present in the schools' curricula as well as what teachers and students were actually doing in their classrooms. Today, there is a widespread recognition that we need to change classroom practices. If assessments are a legitimate part of the repertoire available for implementing these changes, we will have to be concerned with a different kind of validity, namely, the extent to which the new assessments are coherent with best practice and are likely to bring about desirable changes in teaching and learning.

It is for this reason that the stakes associated with an assessment are so important and have such a substantial impact on major elements of the work of designing assessment tasks. Our experience in Connecticut shows that the lower the stakes in effect when an assessment is introduced, the greater the opportunity for the assessment to be coherent with best practice. There are two reasons for this. The first is that it will take a few years for teachers to update their practice. Therefore, the stakes should remain low for several years during which time teachers have opportunities to develop their capacity to teach and assess in ways that are consistent with the new standards. (This principle will be illustrated in the discussion of our foreign language and science assessments later in this chapter.) I will also suggest a more comprehensive assessment system which makes use of an ongoing series of embedded learning events in the classroom and serves to blur traditional distinctions between assessment and curriculum. A second reason for recommending low stakes when introducing an assessment is that when stakes are high (as they are in the case of the writing assessment described in this chapter), assessment developers sometimes have to make some compromises which, if care is not taken, may serve to narrow inappropriately the learning experiences of students.

We often speak of access, capacity, and coherence as if they are separate and independent entities. However, when assessments are designed to elicit best practice, all three are interrelated. Test developers often begin with very abstract notions of best practice. Before designing assessment tasks, they first must develop a more concrete understanding of what best practice looks like in classrooms and how it is manifested in student work. Then task designers can experiment with a variety of approaches to elicit such practice. This is a crucial and often very time-consuming process. In Connecticut, on several occasions we have underestimated the amount of time it takes to produce the initial tasks and scoring prototypes. We have also come to recognize that in situations in which curriculum standards are available but good examples do not yet exist in practice, the edges among access, capacity building, and coherence are blurred. If tangible examples of best practice do not exist, it is not possible to provide access to them. It is also extremely difficult to be coherent with curricular practices and learning events that have not yet been developed. However, on the positive side, our experiences in Connecticut over the past decade have taught us that the very struggle to develop the models necessary for providing access and coherence can itself be capacity building. I will illustrate this phenomenon in the discussion of the development of our foreign language and science assessments. I will also provide an extended example of one of our science tasks in order to illustrate the ways in which we have attempted to increase access, capacity building, and coherence through the development of model assessment tasks and scoring rubrics that were aligned with best practice. We cannot emphasize enough the importance of using significant tasks. They are the primary building blocks of any assessment system and send clear messages to teachers, students, parents, and the entire educational community about what is most important in a content domain.

In the course of developing new assessments, we in Connecticut have worked closely with advisory committees composed mostly of teachers and curriculum experts who have kept abreast of changes in their disciplines. These committees designed the specifications for the assessments, reviewed the assessment tasks, and suggested revisions of the tasks and scoring rubrics. In each assessment we also worked closely with an external contractor who produced our tasks and organized our scoring sessions. Whenever possible, Connecticut teachers were invited to come together at central scoring sites to score students' work. Connecticut teachers were used to score students' papers at regional scoring sessions from 1980 through 1991. In 1992, because of large cost savings we began to send students' papers out of state for scoring.

In our work with these committees, we have learned two important lessons. First, it is often extremely difficult to accommodate some critical elements of best practice in traditional forms of on-demand assessments, even when performance-based assessments are used. The example of a writing assessment provided here will describe some of the compromises that take place in high-stakes testing environments. Second, there are substantial differences in the degree to which teachers have been able to incorporate elements of best practice in their classrooms. The examples of assessing communicative proficiency in four foreign languages (French, German, Italian, and Spanish) and scientific experimentation in four sciences (biology, chemistry, earth science, and physics) will illustrate how assessments can be used as a mechanism to make best practice more accessible to teachers and students who have not yet adopted it. Furthermore, as we study these three cases, the contrast between the high stakes operating in the writing example and the low stakes operating in the foreign language and science examples will help to highlight the significant impact of stakes on designing assessments.

Assessing Writing Ability: A High-Stakes Case

In 1979, in response to the Education Evaluation and Remedial Assistance Act, Connecticut developed what was viewed by our local school districts as a relatively high-stakes assessment. For the first time, every ninth grade student would be tested in English language arts, mathematics, and writing. Schools were expected to use the aggregated scores for instructional improvement and to report each individual student's scores to his or her parents. School personnel were expected to review the achievement of students who scored below a statewide level of expected performance and, where necessary, design appropriate remedial strategies. Even though the stakes for individual students were relatively low, those for school districts were high. It was the first time in the state's history that all the students in a grade level were taking the same test, and politicians and others including realtors would be able to make town-to-town comparisons. Despite the state's discouragement of comparisons based on a single set of test scores, people made them anyway. For example, people moving to Connecticut sometimes choose a particular school district on the basis of its test scores in reading, mathematics, and/or writing.

In 1978, Connecticut teachers let their views be heard through their representatives on the state's Language Arts Advisory Committee. They believed that the only legitimate way to assess writing skills was to have students write an essay. Whereas many editing skills could successfully be assessed on multiple-choice tests, the assessment of students' abilities to express themselves clearly, organize their ideas effectively, and provide adequate supporting details required that they produce a piece of writing.

Because of a concerted statewide effort during the 1970s, most Connecticut elementary and secondary teachers of writing were familiar with the process approach to the teaching of writing and had been using it in their classrooms. Consequently, students wrote numerous drafts of their essays and were encouraged to use a variety of discourse modes (for example, narrative, expository, and persuasive). The teachers' pleas were heeded and Connecticut, like several other states during the late 1970s and early 1980s, included a writing sample on its statewide assessment. Connecticut teachers were also eager to help score the writing tests and many of them returned year after year to participate in large regional scoring sessions where they could view the essays of several hundred students, discuss areas of perceived progress, and talk informally with each other about successful classroom practices.

However, our experience in assessing writing cautions us that the use of performance-based assessment *per se* does not necessarily guarantee coherence with best practice, even when such practices are widespread in classrooms. Because we were operating in a high-stakes testing environment, we faced two difficult issues. The first had to do with the type of writing to be assessed. Ideally, in order to develop a test that would encourage teachers to use a variety of discourse modes in their classrooms each year, we would have liked to test several different modes on the test or, at least, alternate the modes of writing tested from year to year. If we had had available unlimited testing time and scoring resources or if everyone did not have to take the same test, this problem would have been much easier to solve. But since these are luxuries most states do not have in high-stakes assessment programs, we had to make difficult decisions about which types of writing to test and when. Our decision was further complicated by research indicating that the type of discourse affects the quality of student writing.[3] That is, students statewide may write stronger narrative essays than persuasive essays or stronger persuasive essays than expository essays. If states want to report growth in students' writing, they must use parallel forms of the writing test each year.[4] This means that they are safer if they do not switch the discourse modes of their writing samples from year to year. Therefore, the practical problem for assessment designers was how to measure the variety of important types of writing and still be able to use the results to measure growth reliably.

In 1979, our advisory committee recommended that we assess expository writing each fall on our ninth grade test. However, in 1985, when we replaced the ninth grade writing test with our Connecticut Mastery Tests (CMT) in grades 4, 6, and 8, we partially dealt with the discourse-mode restriction problem by incorporating a greater variety of writing genres across these grade levels. Continuing to the present, students write narrative essays in grade 4, expository essays in grade 6, and persuasive essays in grade 8. Ideally, we would have preferred to rotate these genres within each grade level, but their lack of parallelism makes it difficult to do so while still accurately reporting student growth.

A second problem in test design arose because of the importance that had been given to the writing process in Connecticut classrooms for more than a decade and its apparent incompatibility with on-demand single-session testing. In learning to write, students are encouraged to write multiple drafts of a work using feedback from their peers, teacher, and others to make changes. Statewide assessments, largely because of the high stakes associated with them, have always required high levels of test security and have resulted in measuring writing during a single sitting. When it was suggested that students be given the writing topic along with several days to work on it, several groups of critics expressed concerns over issues of equity and ownership. The equity concerns centered on the unequal amounts and quality of help children with different backgrounds, family situations, teachers, and peer groups would receive. The issue of ownership focused on the difficulty of interpreting the authorship of the final products. If students had several days to work on their writing and were encouraged to read each other's work and provide feedback, then *whose work* was being evaluated?[5] The argument, made by several writing experts, that in the world outside of school many people commonly read and revise each other's work proved less compelling than the security needs resulting from the high-stakes accountability demands.

Therefore, since the inception in 1979 of the ninth grade test (required in Connecticut under the Education Evaluation and Remedial Assistance Act [EERA]), we have asked all districts to give our writing tests on a designated day so that all students would be exposed to the topic at approximately the same time. The need to keep the writing topic secure forced us to sacrifice some of the integrity of the writing process and acknowledge that the state was assessing students' "first-draft writing."

We believe that using writing samples instead of multiple-choice tests represented a major step forward in the direct assessment of writing and that its effect on the teaching of writing has been largely positive. Yet, because of the high-stakes assessment climate, we were forced to make compromises which prevented the assessments from more completely modeling best practice. Whereas the EERA and CMT programs stimulated more writing in Connecticut classrooms, the compromises we made to satisfy psychometric needs for parallelism and to be more certain about student ownership may have served to limit the kinds of writing experiences to which students are given access in any given school year. To some extent, we tried to compensate for this within-year specialization by including different discourse modes in different years so that over a six-year period, students would be asked to write in at least three modes. We also hope that despite the fact that we assess only first-draft writing, students continue to benefit from a wide variety of feedback in their classrooms and so produce multiple drafts. Writing teachers believe that the development of multiple drafts through the continued use of the process approach to the teaching of writing should result ultimately in better first drafts as well.

Although this experience sensitized us to the need for assessment models that encouraged the development of multiple drafts, it was not until a decade after EERA that we developed some assessment prototypes that could be embedded in classrooms to provide that encouragement. These will be described later in this chapter when we describe our science performance tasks. As the next two examples illustrate, lowering the stakes makes it considerably easier to model best practice on large-scale assessments.

Assessing Proficiency in Communication in a Foreign Language: A Low-Stakes Case

A very different reality confronted us when we set out to develop our 1986-87 Connecticut Assessment of Educational Progress (CAEP) program in French, German, Italian, and Spanish. At that time, there was a growing consensus among the nation's experts in the teaching of foreign language that the main goal of foreign language programs should be communicative proficiency. However, there was also the recognition that many of the curricula and instructional strategies used by Connecticut teachers did not yet reflect this view. In many classrooms, grammar and literature were still dominant—with speaking, listening, and extended writing given much lower priorities.

In this case, because CAEP had always been a low-stakes assessment program, our advisory committee encouraged us to design a series of performance tasks to represent the most advanced thinking in the field. They wanted to use the assessment as an occasion to create positive models of how curriculum and assessment based on communicative proficiency might eventually look. In addition, they urged us to use the assessment opportunity to provide extensive training by staff from the American Council on the Teaching of Foreign Languages (ACTFL) for fifty Connecticut foreign language teachers in conducting interviews with individual students (from classrooms other than their own) and rating the audiotapes of these interviews on a scale from "Novice" to "Advanced." Furthermore, the advisory committee encouraged us to develop a way to score students' written communication skills and provide the necessary training to several dozen teachers.

The CAEP in foreign language provides an example of how we used a low-stakes statewide assessment successfully to increase access and capacity in a situation in which we were developing coherence with best practice. This was made possible because results of this assessment were reported only at the state level (by the contractor to the State Department of Education and by the Department to the State Board of Education). In this way, no district or school data were reported publicly and districts would be spared any embarrassment stemming from scoring poorly on an assessment that was consciously designed to be out in front of the curriculum. However, at the outset and in order to maximize teachers' exposure to the test, which had a variety of new item formats, we provided a low-cost local option that would enable high schools to test generalizable samples of their students and receive results directly from our test contractor. More than 86 percent of Connecticut's high schools (119 out of 139) chose to participate in the local option, thereby receiving individual and school scores from some 22,000 of the nearly 27,000 students tested. In this way, the assessment enabled large numbers of teachers of students enrolled in the second through the sixth year of foreign language courses to have direct access to models of what language experts meant when they talked about communicative proficiency. They had examples of how newspaper advertisements and restaurant menus could be used to develop reading comprehension skills. They could see how conversations on a number of academic and everyday topics could be used both to develop and assess students' speaking and listening skills. They could read students' letters (to a hypothetical exchange student who would be coming to live with the student for a year) in which vocabulary related to family, home, and school was used and sentences were written in the present, past, and future tenses with varying levels of fluency.

However, this assessment served to remind us that although access to models of changing curriculum is necessary, such models are hardly sufficient for change. There must also be significant attention paid to building teachers' capacity to adopt new practices. Toward this end, wherever possible in all of our assessments throughout the 1980s, we asked Connecticut teachers to administer the tasks in their own classrooms and then invited them to meet in central locations to score the work of Connecticut students other than their own. We believed that administering and scoring tasks were too valuable as professional development activities to relegate to others outside the state.

Because of rigorous standards required by ACTFL, at the end of our training sessions only twenty-six (of the original fifty) teachers were qualified to conduct a total of 454 oral interviews. An additional thirty-seven teachers were able to score the writing samples. This represented only the tip of the capacity-building iceberg. If we are to see changes in every foreign language classroom in the state, we must reach more teachers. Virtually every foreign language teacher must have opportunities to become familiar with the assessment tasks and interview protocols. This means that professional organizations, colleges and universities, state department consultants, and others have significant roles to play. For example, foreign language departments can engage the help of the teachers trained for the CAEP assessment (as well as the dozens of others who fostered many of these communicative proficiency skills in their classrooms well before our assessment) to provide training to the hundreds of teachers who are ready to change but need additional skills. We do not underestimate the magnitude or the importance of the capacity-building strategies required; we recognize that without massive amounts of professional development, we are doomed to maintain the status quo.

The writing and foreign language examples illustrate how well-meaning and sophisticated groups of teachers working with state department consultants are differentially affected by several powerful forces operating within the assessment context. As we and others continue to develop and use performance-based assessments, considerable attention must be paid to both the nature of the stakes and incentives in effect and to the opportunities provided for professional development. Stakes are the largest single determinant of the degree of risk that states can afford to take. If the test scores for individual students, schools, or school districts are reported publicly, then stakes are high and the assessment will have to be very sensitive to psychometrically oriented concerns about accountability. In the writing example, we saw how equity, ownership, and test-security issues took precedence over the development of multiple drafts with peer and teacher feedback and how the need for measuring longitudinal growth of groups of students narrowed the choice of discourse modes. In the case of the foreign language assessments, we saw that despite the increased access provided through the development of models that were coherent with best practice, the lack of widespread professional development for foreign language teachers can severely limit the amount of change that will take place in their classrooms.

In the next example, therefore, I will examine some new possibilities for developing teachers' capacities for change through the use of embedded (that is, classroom-based) assessments. I will also explore some options for dealing with two additional constraints that impact the design of an assessment—its length and the timelines for development.

Developing Performance-Based Assessments in Science and Mathematics for the "Common Core of Learning"

In 1989, education consultants in the Bureau of Evaluation and Student Assessment were charged with the responsibility of developing assessments to determine how well Connecticut students were able to display the attributes, skills, and understandings delineated in the "Common Core of Learning," a document that had been approved by the Connecticut State Board of Education in 1987. This document, which had been publicized widely and had been revised in light of considerable public feedback, represented widespread agreement about the expectations of teachers, administrators, parents, and the larger community for all Connecticut students from kindergarten through twelfth grade.

The "Common Core of Learning" had three sections: Attributes and Attitudes, Skills and Competencies, and Understandings and Applications. Not until one sets out to create curriculum or assessments based on such documents does it become apparent that they do not specify with sufficient clarity exactly what kind of work should be done in a classroom or what level of student work is expected or acceptable. For example, one short statement subsumes all of the science experimentation skills: "As a result of education in grades K-12, each student should be able to identify and design techniques for recognizing and solving problems in science, including the development of hypotheses and the design of experiments to test them—the gathering of data, presenting them in appropriate formats, and drawing inferences based upon the results." Anyone who has been involved in developing statements of mission or of broad curricular goals can appreciate that such statements are only the beginning of change. Transforming the vision into practice requires that teachers have a clear understanding of both the goals of the program and the characteristics of the students who will be attempting to meet them. Thus, the development of assessments and performance standards are helpful in breathing life into documents like the "Common Core of Learning."

Because this was a Department priority rather than a legislative mandate, we did not have choking time constraints on our assessment development activities. We could take several years to pilot different types of assessment tasks. Second, we did not have constraining limitations on test length. Therefore, we could experiment with tasks that took several days of combined in-class and out-of-class time. Third, we had the time to apply for and receive a National Science Foundation grant that enabled us to bring together groups of people to collaborate with Connecticut teachers and curriculum specialists in the development of assessments. These groups included creative teachers, scientists, mathematicians, and assessment specialists who represented state-of-the-art thinking in their fields.

In 1989 we brought to Connecticut eighteen outstanding teachers from six other states where the use of performance-based assessments was being contemplated as part of future statewide assessments. We also brought fifteen teachers from the Coalition of Essential Schools who were committed to developing student exhibitions. We would use the tasks developed in this assessment consortium to determine how well our students had attained the understandings, skills, and attributes delineated in the "Common Core of Learning." More specifically, we expected students to display a variety of attributes, for example, take responsibility for their own learning; demonstrate persistence, dependability, and intellectual curiosity; be motivated; be willing to consider and evaluate alternative viewpoints; and be able to work in a collaborative group to solve problems. We also expected students to display a variety of skills including communicating clearly through speaking and writing, questioning effectively, formulating and solving complex multistep problems, making effective decisions, and synthesizing knowledge from a variety of sources. Specifically, in science we expected students to demonstrate an "understanding and application of the basic principles, concepts, and language of biology, chemistry, physics, earth and space sciences," and in mathematics to "apply mathematical knowledge and skills to solve a broad array of quantitative, spatial, and analytical problems." Although the broad brush strokes were present in the "Common Core of Learning," the details were still needed. Which biology concepts? Which kinds of analytical problems? And how could we assess communication, collaboration, and problem-solving skills concurrently with the attributes and content understandings? It soon became clear that a new kind of test was necessary to accommodate this expanded set of student accomplishments.

Two critical documents released in 1989 greatly facilitated our work—*The Curriculum and Evaluation Standards for School Mathematics*, developed by the National Council of Teachers of Mathematics (NCTM), and *Science for All Americans*, published by the American Association for the Advancement of Science (AAAS).[6] The NCTM document stresses the importance of mathematics as problem solving, communication, connection making, and collaboration and it relates content to these broader purposes. The AAAS document describes the major conceptual understandings that underlie our view of the natural world as well as the appropriate attitudes and dispositions associated with science. Both documents support a view of education as producing active and engaged students who are able to formulate problems, plan investigations, collect and analyze their own data, and communicate their findings orally and in writing. They both envision students who are able to solve problems by themselves and in groups.

Three other resources made possible by our National Science Foundation grant also contributed to our efforts. First, over a four-year period we were able to bring together, in several working groups, close to two hundred of the most talented high school teachers in the country. Second, we had assistance from several very creative practicing mathematicians and scientists who agreed to be part of a national advisory committee to help us make our assessment tasks as rigorous and authentic as possible. Finally, we engaged several educational and social psychologists who helped to inform our task-development efforts with current psychological theory and research findings in the areas of cognition, motivation, learning, and instruction.

Our experiences in the 1980s in developing large-scale assessments like the writing and foreign language assessments described earlier revealed both the possibilities and limitations of using large-scale assessments to improve student achievement. In 1990, we felt ready to extend our performance-based assessments in five important ways that we believed would increase the access of large numbers of teachers and students to assessments that modeled best practice and at the same time would build their capacity. First, we felt ready to supplement our work with on-demand assessment tasks by developing classroom-embedded tasks. This approach encourages teachers to choose which assessment tasks to use and when, thus allowing the assessment tasks to be better integrated with their curriculum. Second, we viewed our assessment tasks as learning events. They are intended to provide students with interesting problems which provide opportunities for them to "pull their learning together," that is, to integrate and synthesize separate bits of knowledge about science and/or mathematics and deepen their understanding of the big ideas in these disciplines. These problem-solving tasks begin to blur the traditional distinctions among curriculum, instruction, and assessment.[7] Two other changes allowed for considerable peer feedback and the development of multiple drafts—two desirable aspects of learning that could not be accommodated in our earlier high-stakes assessment programs. By embedding our assessments in classrooms and allowing them to take place over several days, we were able to make them both more substantial and sustained. By sharing the scoring criteria with students and teachers as a routine part of the assessment, we allowed for a series of important capacity-building conversations about the qualities of strong work to take place among students and teachers. A fifth change was the inclusion of group tasks as well as individual tasks. This decision was motivated by two considerations. First, business and industry as well as the general public recognize that it is important for most people, including scientists and mathematicians, to be able to work as part of a team, as most jobs are accomplished by groups of workers. Second, by making use of group work on assessment tasks, we also build upon Vygotsky's notion of the zone of proximal development (ZPD) since students are likely to reach a higher level of achievement through collaborative efforts earlier than they would through working alone. The ZPD as used by Vygotsky is a dyadic relationship involving a mentor and a learner. In the context of our assessment tasks, we are extending the ZPD to include groups of peers, generally larger than two. The knowledge and skills required to complete the assessment tasks are distributed naturally among the group members who bring these attributes to bear on completing the task and in so doing share their expertise with the other members of the group. We view this peer teaching and learning process as also related to Aronson's *The Jigsaw Classroom* and Perkins's concept of distributed intelligence.[8]

Assessing Problem-Solving Ability in Science: The MapleCopter Task

To see how well students would integrate scientific attributes, skills, and understandings, we developed several problem-solving tasks that require students to both design and carry out experiments. In such a task students do individual work but the task also requires that they work together in small groups to define their own research questions, design appropriate experiments, and support their conclusions with evidence. Each of the problem-solving tasks for the Common Core of Learning Science Assessment has the same format. Each begins with notes to the teacher and student that specify criteria by which students' performance will be judged. When these criteria are known, students can be guided toward expected outcomes and encouraged to monitor their progress during the assessment. The notes to the teacher and students are followed by instructions for each of the three parts of the assessment: Part I, Getting Started by Yourself; Part II, Group Work; and Part III, Finishing by Yourself. Completion of the task generally requires approximately one period of class time for five successive days.

To illustrate the manner in which such a problem-solving task is presented to students as well as the kinds of activities that take place in each of the three parts of the task, I use "The MapleCopter Task" as an example. This task, designed for use in a high school course in general physics, poses the problem "What causes maple seeds to spin as they fall?"

Part I. Getting Started by Yourself. The emphasis in Part I is on having each student access his or her prior knowledge. Individual students are asked to provide information about their knowledge of task-relevant scientific concepts and processes. Each student is asked for an initial impression, an estimate of the solution, and/or a preliminary design for an investigation that will lead to the solution of the posed problem. In the MapleCopter Task, the students are given the following instructions for Part I:

Throw a winged maple seed up in the air or drop it from your hand. Watch it "float" down to the floor. Describe as many aspects of the motion and the physical properties of the seed that are relevant to the motion as you can. You may add a diagram if you wish.

1. Record all the observations that you have made. Do not attempt to explain the seed's motion at this time.

2. After you have finished recording your observations, try to provide an initial explanation of the spinning motion of the seed which integrates your observations with your knowledge of physics.

There are at least four important reasons for asking students to recall and use prior knowledge. First, it helps each student get ready for the group discussion by doing some preliminary thinking about the problem. Second, it increases the likelihood that each group can begin its deliberations with a variety of assumptions and strategies. Third, it makes more obvious what each student understands about the scientific concepts being assessed. These conceptions (or misconceptions) can be used by the group as a springboard for discussion and/or by the teacher to make changes in the curriculum. Fourth, it provides the students with documented records of their early thinking about the task, which can be reflected upon from time to time. Students' work in Part I can be collected and used as a baseline against which to measure individual growth and understanding.

Part II. Group Work. In this second part of the task (by far the longest part) students work together in teams of three or four members to identify, specify, and clarify the problem to be solved, to investigate solutions to the problem, and to prepare a final product in the form of a laboratory report. The instructions to groups in the Maple-Copter task are as follows:

1. Discuss the motion of the winged maple seed with the members of your group. Write down all of the factors that your group thinks might affect the motion of the winged maple seed.

2. Discuss with the members of your group what kind of experiments you can perform to clarify the motion of the spinning seed and the effect of various factors on this motion.

3. Sometimes experimenting with simplified models (or simulations) might help one to understand a more complex phenomenon, such as the motion of the winged maple seed. Use a model, rather than the original seed, to carry out experiments which will clarify different aspects of the spinning motion.

   a. Construct models of the winged maple seed. If after several attempts to improve the seed model, your model still does not work, you may ask the teacher for instructions for building the paper helicopter.

   b. Throw or drop the model and observe its motion.

   c. Design and carry out experiments to test the effect of different variables on the motion of the model.

4. Summarize your group's findings in a final report which includes:

   a. What your group tried to investigate (statement of the problem with clear definitions of dependent and independent variables).

   b. How your group performed its experiments (clear description of experimental procedures).

   c. What your group found (raw and processed data, organized in charts or graphs, as necessary).

   d. What your group concluded (based on experimental findings) and how valid your group thinks these conclusions are. The report should be clear enough to enable the reader to replicate it.

5. Prepare an oral presentation of your group's experiments, findings, and conclusions. Include graphical materials to aid your presentation. Each member of your group should be ready to participate in any part of the presentation. Your teacher will determine the order of presenters at the time of the presentation.

Throughout Part II of the task, interdependence and cooperation are fostered by having members of the group keep records of their discussions, experiments, and findings. In complex tasks, the work can be divided among the members of the group for part of the time. By using a variety of accompanying documentation tools (such as laboratory records, journals, videotapes of discussions) students have frequent opportunities to provide evidence of their deepening understanding of the topic of their investigation.

During the oral group presentations at the conclusion of the group work, students and teachers are expected to ask presenters probing questions about the validity of their design, their results, and their conclusions. The oral presentation is important because it allows students to share ideas with members of groups other than their own, thus creating the opportunity to counterbalance the effects of any differences between the groups. The written report is also seen as important because of the nature of scientific knowledge, a defining characteristic of which is that it has to be submitted to rigorous public scrutiny in order to be accepted by the scientific community.

Part III. Finishing by Yourself. In this part of the assessment, each student is asked to reflect upon the group activity, to analyze and critique another group's report, and to apply knowledge gained through his or her study. Figure 1 shows the instructions given to the students for this final part of the MapleCopter task.

Scoring the MapleCopter Task. "Teacher's Scoring Guides" have been prepared for use in obtaining profiles for individuals on three dimensions: "individual understanding," "collaboration," and "oral presentation." Group scores are obtained for "group experimentation." The scoring guide for "individual understanding" is shown in figure 2, and the scoring guide for "group experimentation" is shown in figure 3. "Collaboration" is addressed by asking each student to complete a series of self-ratings on six groups of traits (group participation, staying on the topic, offering useful ideas, consideration, involving others, and communicating) and then circulate those ratings to each person in the group for his or her review and comments. The "oral presentation" dimension has two aspects: "message" and "style." This dimension can be scored by the teacher, the other students in the class, or both. The five "message" criteria address content and include: organizes presentation effectively; reports and explains clearly; fits his or her presentation into the presentations of the other group members; provides thorough and clear answers to questions, and uses scientific terminology accurately and appropriately. The five criteria that focus on "style" are: uses a voice clear and loud enough for all to hear; maintains eye contact with the audience; uses a conversational tone rather than reading to the audience; uses visual aids that are easily seen and understood; and avoids distracting behaviors.

Exploring the MapleCopter

Part III: Finishing by Yourself

1. Suppose you want to explain the motion of the winged maple seed to your friend. Write an explanation that is clear enough to enable your friend to understand the factors and forces which are involved in the spinning motion of the winged maple seed. Support your explanation with findings from your experiment. Specify the aspects about which you are more certain and those about which you are still unsure.

2. In this activity, you used simplified models to help explain a more complicated phenomenon. Describe several advantages and disadvantages of using a model in the study of the motion of the winged maple seed. Include specific examples from the work of your group.

The following report was written by one group of students working on the MapleCopter task. Read the report and answer the questions that follow.

Group Report

We tested paper helicopters to see if different lengths (3), stiffness (1), and weights (3) will affect the helicopter.

We used:

    1) 3 cm wing length, stiff (4 paper clips)
    2) 6 cm wing length, stiff (4 paper clips)
    3) 10 cm wing length, stiff (4 paper clips)
    4) 6 cm wings flexible (4 paper clips)
    5) 1/2 way cut through 10 cm wings, stiff (4 paper clips)
    6) 3/4 way cut through 10 cm wings, stiff (4 paper clips)
    7) 3 paper clips on 10 cm wings, stiff (3 paper clips)
    8) 5 paper clips on 10 cm wings, stiff (5 paper clips)

Paper Model	Time
1) 3 cm, s	0.49 sec.
2) 6 cm, s	0.66 sec.
3) 10 cm, s	1.29 sec.
4) flexible, 6 cm	0.77 sec.
5) 1/2 cut, s, 10 cm	1.07 sec.
6) 3/4 cut, s, 10 cm	0.97 sec.
7) 3 pc, s, 10 cm	1.15 sec.
8) 5 pc, s, 10 cm	1.21 sec.

Our data confirmed our beliefs that wing length, flexibility, weight, and solidness would affect the helicopter. The results turned out as expected.

---

3. A scientific report is written to share information and to enable others to replicate (repeat) the same experiment. Does this report give you enough information to replicate the experiment? Please write a specific critique to the group in which you describe what is missing or not completely described in the report.

4. The group forgot to make specific conclusions about their study. Based on their data, can you come up with conclusions about any of the variables that were studied by this group? If so, what are your conclusions, what are the data that support them and how valid are these conclusions? Please be specific in your answer.

FIGURE 1

Exploring the MapleCopter, Part III

TEACHER'S SCORING GUIDE

Exploring the MapleCopter Dimension I — Individual Understanding

Student Code: _____ Scorer Code: _____

Date: _____

Part III: Finishing by Yourself

<u>Directions</u>: For each criterion below, circle the letters of the standards for which students have provided sufficient evidence in their written work. Then add the numbers of standards met and circle the corresponding total from 0 to 5 in the columns to the right.

Criteria and Standards	Performance Levels				
	Excell.	Good	Fair	Poor	No Evid.
I.3 Final explanation of motion	4	3	2	1	0
a. Vertical movement due to gravitational force b. Horizontal movement due to different air pressure/ airfoil/unequal "catching the air" c. Tilt due to mass distribution along the wing length d. Spin due to mass distribution along wing width					
I.4 Use of models	4-5	3	2	1	0
Explanation should be based on the following criteria: Advantages a. Materials are cheaper or more readily available/non-destruction of originals b. Easier to control and manipulate variables/ uniformity of models c. Easier to observe and measure variables Disadvantages d. Parameters of model are not the same as the "maplecopter" (i.e. shape, materials, etc.) e. Uncertainty about the generalizability of results from the model to the original					
I.5 Analysis of Report	4	3	2	1	0
a. No description of model (e.g. shape, size) used b. No description of experimental procedure c. Incomplete or fuzzy description of independent variables d. Lack of coherent conclusions					
I.6 Tentative conclusions about:	4-5	3	2	1	0
a. Longer is slower (compare 1,2,3) b. Mass inconclusive (compare 3,7,8) c. Stiffer is faster (compare 2,4) d. Smaller cut is slower (compare 3,5,6) e. Other (e.g. skepticism, insights)					

FIGURE 2

Teacher's Scoring Guide for "Individual Understanding"

This multifaceted assessment provided multidimensional profiles of students' strengths and weaknesses.[9] But it also taught us a great deal about capacity building. Every phase of performance-based assessment (development, implementation, scoring) has the potential to help teachers improve their instruction. However, effective capacity

TEACHER'S SCORING GUIDE

Exploring the MapleCopter   **Dimension II — Group Experimentation**

Student Code: _____   Scorer Code: _____

Date: _____

Part II: Group Experimentation

Directions: For each criterion below, circle the letters of the standards for which students have provided sufficient evidence in their written work. Then add the numbers of standards met and circle the corresponding total from 0 to ≥6 in the columns to the right.

Criteria and Standards	Performance Levels				
	Excell.	Good	Fair	Poor	No Evid.
II.1 Identification of relevant factors	≥6	4-5	2-3	1	0
a. Total mass b. Distribution of mass c. Surface area, length and wing d. Shape and curvature e. Air (currents, pressure, etc.) f. Materials (seed's moisture, veins' structure, etc.) g. Dropping position h. Physical forces					
II.2 Experimental design	4	3	2	1	0
a. Matches the factor to be studied b. Defines independent and dependent variables c. Controls variables, when possible d. Includes description of model used					
II.3 Data collection and presentation	4	3	2	1	0
a. Sufficient repetitions of measurements b. Mathematical treatment of data (averages, etc.) c. Appropriate presentations (labeled charts, appropriate graphs) d. Adequate description of procedures					
II.4 Conclusions	4	3	2	1	0
a. Related to studied problem b. Supported by experimental findings c. Appropriate generalization d. Include discussion of effect of errors					

FIGURE 3

Teacher's Scoring Guide for "Group Experimentation"

building also requires considerable amounts of time for teachers to work together on a regular basis. Therefore, there are many feasibility issues still to be solved. How do teachers best learn to create and present interesting and complex challenges to their students? How can they learn to score their students' work on a set of multidimensional criteria? Will they find the effort required worthwhile? Will they be able to use the assessment tasks as models from which to design others? Will these tasks be viewed as legitimate learning occasions or will they prove to be too cumbersome?

Changes in long-standing practices do not come easily for teachers, students, or parents. Learning any new set of complex skills takes substantial time before one reaches a comfortable threshold. Just as many novices give up tennis before they reach the pleasurable point of being able to carry on a consistent rally, there is a tendency for even highly motivated teachers to give up using performance-based assessments when students complain about assuming responsibility for solving loosely structured and challenging tasks or when teachers see unscored papers containing students' explanations and critiques beginning to pile up. Adequate coaching on fundamentals, sufficient time to practice, and specific and individualized feedback are just as important in developing proficiency in performance-based assessment as they are in tennis or music.

An Optimal System for Student Assessment

High-stakes assessments grab and hold teachers' and students' attention. But because the design of such assessments frequently must make compromises with best practice, the curriculum and pedagogy that result are often less than optimal. On the other hand, low-stakes assessments and the classroom practices they stimulate tend to be more consistent with best practice, but they often fail to capture and hold the attention of busy or tired teachers or well-intentioned but over-committed teachers and students. Therefore capacity building generally falls short of the mark when both high- and low-stakes assessments operate alone.

Over time, we have grown to understand that the optimal assessment system is one that is composed of both high- and low-stakes assessments. In such a system, teachers would be encouraged to choose several embedded tasks from a task bank and work with their colleagues and others to create additional embedded tasks during the course of the school year. Students would keep track of their work in a portfolio-like system that calls upon them to use well-publicized criteria in reflecting continually upon their progress. These embedded tasks would be scored by the students' own teachers. At the beginning and end of the year, students would also take some shorter on-demand tasks similar to the embedded tasks. These on-demand tasks might be scored by both the student's own teacher and another teacher.[10] Several state and national assessment projects are currently exploring different combinations of high- and low-stakes assessments.[11]

The various examples of student assessments examined in this chapter suggest that it is reasonable to expect assessment designers to create systems composed of both embedded and on-demand assessments. Such a system would be marked by as many as possible of the following characteristics:

1. Assessments are coherent with best practice as defined by curriculum experts and outstanding teachers in the state. Low-stakes embedded assessments are more likely to fully accomplish this than are high-stakes, on-demand assessments that often have to make compromises.

2. Assessments are themselves strong learning events or provide access to them. Low-stakes embedded assessments that are represented frequently within a curriculum and possibly incorporated into ongoing portfolio-like systems are more likely to provide this type of access than are high-stakes, on-demand tasks.

3. Assessments help to build teachers' and students' capacities as experts within their discipline as well as in the cross-cutting attributes, skills, and competencies valued across disciplines. Embedded assessments that involve teachers in collaborations in which they develop and implement assessment tasks and describe and rate students' work are more likely to build capacity than are on-demand assessments that occur infrequently and are designed and scored externally.

4. The stakes attached to the assessment are high enough to attract and hold the attention of teachers and students yet do not distort classroom practice. If we want teachers to use low-stakes embedded assessment tasks that are coherent with best practice, we must create incentives to support them. One solution is to develop a high-stakes, on-demand system to parallel the embedded portfolio system. If the on-demand tasks reinforce the same skills and understandings as the embedded tasks, teachers and students will see the embedded tasks as instrumental and will probably persevere in their use. For example, if foreign language teachers were expected to complete from three to five embedded tasks during the school year that would prepare their students for an external on-demand assessment at the end of the year, this greater coherence should also result in greater access and capacity building. Similarly, if science teachers knew that their students would be expected to take an on-demand task that reinforced the skills assessed on the embedded tasks, they would be more inclined to provide several embedded tasks to help their students hone their skills. If the on-demand writing test described at the beginning of this chapter were supported by an embedded assessment system of writing tasks

we would worry less about the narrowing effects of the former. A writing portfolio could be used to ensure experience with different discourse modes and the development of multiple drafts that are central to the use of the writing process.

Advocates of performance-based assessment often claim that such assessments are better suited to enhancing access, capacity, and coherence than are traditional tests. Are performance-based assessment systems robust enough to support these claims? Can they ultimately improve student achievement? We must evaluate these claims within the broader context of school change. We know that excellence in schools cannot be mandated. It requires the joint commitment, encouragement, and support of administrators, teachers, students, parents, and the broader community. We also know that teachers cannot accomplish the work required by performance-based assessment systems alone; they must have the time and opportunity to collaborate with their colleagues. Furthermore, there must be consistency among the many messages sent to teachers from different levels of the system. They cannot be expected to "cover" hundreds of pages of text materials and at the same time provide extended learning and assessment tasks designed to help students apply their knowledge and develop deep understanding. We acknowledge that even though state leadership may be important, all change is ultimately local and will require schools to customize their assessment tasks according to their priorities and their teachers' and students' needs and talents.

Can a performance-based assessment system serve as a viable cornerstone for these educational changes? There is growing evidence that when compared with more traditional forms of assessment, performance-based assessment has a greater likelihood of increasing access and building the capacity of teachers and students by providing models of learning and assessment events that are coherent with the best practices defined in a variety of disciplines. Furthermore, the various stages in the development of performance-based assessments require that teachers grapple with questions related to identifying what is most important in their discipline, defining the characteristics of strong student work, and setting standards for how much is good enough.[12] Teachers' conversations about these issues should also serve to increase the validity of inferences made about students. Consequently, performance-based assessment should be viewed as one viable point of entry for meaningful school reform. If nurtured and supported, such assessment has the strong potential to improve teaching and student achievement. It should not be viewed as a panacea.

The work reported in this chapter is the result of the efforts of many individuals and groups. We gratefully acknowledge their help. The external contractors who assisted the CSDE in developing, coordinating the scoring, and reporting the results of our performance-based Connecticut Assessments of Educational Progress were: Advanced Systems in Measurement and Evaluation (Business and Office Education, English Language Arts and Science); Educational Testing Service and Scholastic Testing Service (Foreign Language); National Evaluation Systems (Art and Music); National Occupational Competency Testing Institute (Drafting, Graphic Arts, and Small Engines). The Psychological Corporation and Measurement, Inc. assisted in the development, scoring, and reporting of the performance-based sections of the Connecticut Mastery Test and the Connecticut Academic Performance Test.

Through a grant from the National Science Foundation (SPA-8954692—Principal Investigator, Joan B. Baron), the Common Core of Learning Assessment Project was able to involve directly close to 200 science and mathematics teachers from Connecticut, Michigan, Minnesota, New York, Texas, Vermont, Wisconsin, the Coalition of Essential Schools, Project RE:Learning, and the Urban Districts' Leadership Consortium of the American Federation of Teachers. Without the cooperation of these teachers and their students, we could not have developed and revised our assessment tasks. We are also grateful to the nearly one hundred project advisors—scientists, science educators, mathematicians, mathematics educators, state education specialists, psychologists, and psychometricians who provided helpful suggestions at key points in the project. The Common Core of Learning Assessment Staff at the Connecticut State Department of Education consisted of Jeffrey Greig, Michal Lomask and Sigmund Abeles in science, and Bonnie Laird Hole, Steven Leinwand, Susan Dixon and Judith Collison in mathematics. Pascal D. Forgione and Douglas A. Rindone directed the project with the assistance of Steven Martin, Amy Shively, and Hannah Kruglanski. Claire Harrison and Bruce Davey provided psychometric expertise and Arlene Morrissey and Martha Szykula furnished clerical assistance.

NOTES

1. Linda Darling-Hammond and Arthur E. Wise, "Beyond Standardization: State Standards and School Assessment," *Elementary School Journal* 85 (1985): 315-336; Linda McNeil, *Contradiction of Control* (New York: Routledge, 1988); Leslie Salmon-Cox, "Teachers and Standardized Achievement Tests: What's Really Happening?" *Phi Delta Kappan* 62 (1981): 631-633; Loretta Shepard, "Why We Need Better Assessment," *Educational Leadership* 46 (1989): 4-9; Mary Lee Smith, "Put to the Test: The Effects of External Testing on Teachers," *Educational Researcher* 20, no. 5 (1981): 10.

2. Many of the assessments are described in Joan Boykoff Baron, "SEA Usage of Alternative Assessment: The Connecticut Experience," in *Proceedings of the Second National Research Symposium on Limited English Proficient Student Issues: Focus on Evaluation and Measurement*, vol. 1 (Washington, D.C.: U.S. Department of Education, Office of Bilingual Education and Minority Language Affairs, 1982) and in Joan Boykoff Baron, ed., *Assessment as an Opportunity to Learn: Connecticut's Common Core of Learning Assessment in Secondary School Science and Mathematics*, Final Report to the National Science Foundation, Grant SPA 8954692 (Hartford: Connecticut State Department of Education, 1993).

3. Joan Baron, Edys Quellmalz and Steven Court, "Alternative Approaches to Measuring Writing" (Paper presented at a joint meeting of the American Educational Research Association and the National Council of Measurement in Education, Chicago, 1985).

4. Frederick M. Lord, *Applications of Item Response Theory to Practical Testing Problems* (Hillsdale, N.J.: Erlbaum, 1980), p. 185.

5. Maryl Gearhart and Joan L. Herman, "Portfolio Assessment: Whose Work Is It? Issues in the Use of Classroom Assignments for Accountability," *Evaluation Comment* (Winter, 1995): 1-16.

6. National Council of Teachers of Mathematics, *Curriculum and Evaluation Standards for School Mathematics* (Reston, Va.: The Council, 1988); American Association for the Advancement of Science, *Science for All Americans: A Project 2061 Report on Literacy Goals in Science, Mathematics, and Technology* (Washington, D.C.: American Association for the Advancement of Science, 1989).

7. Joan Boykoff Baron, "Performance Assessment: Blurring the Edges among Assessment, Curriculum, and Instruction," in *This Year in School Science: Assessment in the Service of Instruction*, edited by A. B. Champagne, B. E. Lovitts, and B. J. Calinger (Washington, D.C.: American Association for the Advancement of Science, 1990), pp. 127-148.

8. Lev S. Vygotsky, *Mind in Society: The Development of Higher Psychological Processes*, translated and edited by Michael Cole, Vera John-Steiner, Sylvia Scribner, and Ellen Souberman (Cambridge, Mass.: Harvard University Press, 1978); Eliot Aronson, Nancy Blaney, Cookie Stephan, Jev Sikes, and Matthew Snapp, *The Jigsaw Classroom* (Beverly Hills, Cal.: Sage, 1978); David Perkins, *Smart Schools: From Training Memories to Educating Minds* (New York: Free Press, 1992).

9. Michal Lomask, Joan Boykoff Baron, and Earl Carlyon, "Performance-based Assessment as a Multiple Mirror: Reflections of Students in Science," *Proceedings of the Third International Seminar on Misconceptions and Educational Strategies in Science and Mathematics* (Ithaca, N.Y.: Cornell University, 1993); Michal Lomask, Joan Boykoff Baron, and Jeffrey Greig, "Assessment of Performance-based Problem Solving," in *Assessment as an Opportunity to Learn*, edited by Joan Boykoff Baron (Hartford: Connecticut State Department of Education, 1993), pp. S30-S38.

10. Dennie Palmer Wolf and Joan Boykoff Baron, "Options Paper: A Realization of a National Performance-Based Assessment System" (Paper prepared for the National Council on Education Testing and Standards, Washington, D.C., October 31, 1991).

11. Vermont and Kentucky are currently using combinations of high and low stakes assessment. (See chapters 9 and 10, this volume.) Other states like Delaware and Massachusetts are moving in that direction. The New Standards project is also using a combination of on-demand and portfolio assessments. (See chapter 12, this volume.)

12. Joan Boykoff Baron, "Strategies for the Development of Effective Performance Exercises," *Applied Measurement in Education* 4 (1991): 305-318.

CHAPTER IX

Statewide Portfolio Assessment: The Vermont Experience

RICHARD P. MILLS

Look for the plastic milk crate as soon as you walk into a fourth or eighth grade classroom in Vermont. That is where they keep the student portfolios. I don't know why teachers decided to store them this way—it is one of many conventions about the Vermont assessment that teachers worked out and shared with one another. In a sense, you need to stand on that milk crate to get the clearest view of student work, the quickest understanding of what goes on in that classroom.

Leafing through a writing portfolio with a student, the visitor can see the result of process writing—the idea webs, outlines, rough drafts, notes from conferences and editing sessions, and final drafts. And in some places, one can still see more traditional drill sheets, too; the revolution in instruction has not reached every classroom. In the mathematics portfolios of most classes, the standards of the National Council of Teachers of Mathematics come to life in pages of alternative solutions to complex problems, and in thoughtful applications of mathematics to explain, communicate, and, after the best answer is found, confront that provoking last question, "So what?" The portfolio shows what counts as good work in that classroom. Portfolios reveal the standards.

Most Vermont fourth graders I've talked to can give a credible explanation of the portfolio. One said, "It's just my work. When I write something, it goes in the folder. And then I look back to see if I am getting better." An eighth grader, speaking with the feigned detachment of new competence, observed that he thought something he had written months earlier was pretty good, but looking back on it more recently, he said "I couldn't believe that I wrote like that."

Inventing ways to provoke that kind of reflection on a wide scale has been at the heart of the Vermont assessment from the beginning.[1] The assessment has always had two purposes: to boost student performance,

Richard P. Mills is President of the University of the State of New York and Commissioner of Education. From 1988 until 1995 he served as Vermont's Commissioner of Education.

and to create the basis for a sensible discussion of that performance. In the fall of 1988, as Vermont's assessment proposal took shape, a chance conversation with a superintendent led to an adaptation of the New England town meeting—School Report Night. "It's not enough," he said, "to have a good assessment. We need a way to get people to talk about the results." Here is what it looked like in Cabot, Vermont, on School Report Night.

With 246 students, Cabot is the smallest K-12 system in Vermont. It is a rural community where most people farm or work at Cabot Creamery. On School Report Night, the whole town crowded into the gym. The school board was introducing its six new education goals to the community, and they were doing it from six booths around the edges of the room. From each booth, a team of board members, students, and teachers explained, with examples, what the goal meant. The backdrop for these rolling seminars on goals was a fiberboard wall that snaked through the middle of the gym from one end to another. On one side of the wall was mathematics and on the other, writing. Hundreds of examples of student work from kindergarten through twelfth grade comprised a kind of schoolwide portfolio. At intervals along the wall were piles of student portfolios. The whole town—parents, teachers, students, and others—was slowly walking along that wall, soaking up the first-ever comprehensive view of the curriculum. And as they walked, they talked about performance.

Cabot invented this device after a previous attempt the year before that I've always remembered as "the dueling math portfolios." At the time, there was an upper and a lower mathematics group in the school. The more advanced students had invented a complex problem and sent it off to the lower group as a challenge. The lower group had solved the problem as a group, tinkered with it, made it even more complex, and then fired it back to their tormentors as a counterchallenge. Spread across the back wall of the gym was the evidence—charts, calculations, graphs, sketches, essays. It was a stunning expression of mathematical power. Many adults in the gym on that occasion had never seen that approach to mathematics, but having seen it, they wanted it for their children.

Getting to sensible discussions about performance takes that kind of imagination. Half a dozen students and their teacher came to see me toward the end of the first year of the assessment to make sure that, as Commissioner of Education in Vermont, I could tell the public what the assessment results really meant. Everyone was remembering what happened at the end of the pilot the year before. Back then, there had been a long press briefing to explain how the portfolios were created and scored, and to report the first results (which were encouraging in writing, but much less so in mathematics) with all the richness of detail that was now possible. But the headline the next day was devastating to teachers: "Math scores don't add up." We could not blame the press or the headline writers. We had a subtle story to tell. And we had not learned how to tell it.

The students said that telling the score was not enough to tell the story. They passed around their mathematics portfolios and talked about examples of work in connection with the seven scoring criteria. They could point to examples of how they met the first criterion for problem-solving, and how attempt after attempt fell short in meeting the criterion dealing with extension, that "So what?" question. What was striking was their ability to reflect on their own work in relation to a set of internalized standards—standards that they shared with many others.

After the first full year of implementation, we have all learned a lot—about standards, about change, about practice, and results. Before sharing those hard-won lessons, it might help to sketch the main features of the Vermont assessment, and how they came to be. But first, a word about perspective: Vermont's portfolio effort is a story about plain hard work—most of it in the classroom. As commissioner, I did a lot of policy work in the beginning, usually with only one colleague, Ross Brewer, but the heavy effort fell on teachers and my colleagues who worked directly with them. Teachers were the design team members, network leaders, trainers, scorers, and ultimately the ones who put the assessment through its paces in the classroom. I could only know of their effort by report. My version of events can never be more than a small part of the story.

The Vermont Assessment in Brief

While the portfolio has attracted the most attention in the Vermont Assessment it is really only a portion of the total effort to measure results. The whole idea was to use multiple measures of performance in writing and mathematics at two grade levels, fourth and eighth, with other subjects and other grades to follow. The three main elements are the portfolio, the "best piece," and the uniform test.

The portfolio is a collection of student work gathered over the course of the year in consultation with the teacher. The portfolio is intended to show the whole range of student work. It contains finished products and rough drafts. In writing, students include a piece of imaginative writing, a writing assignment from some class other than

English or language arts, and a letter to the evaluator on how they selected their best piece. In mathematics, the portfolio is to include complex problems, applications, and investigations.

The best piece is a single work in writing and five to seven in mathematics that the student feels best represent peak performance or work from which he or she learned the most. It was intended to be a deliberate answer to the teacher's question that I always dreaded most: "Is this the very best you can do?" The best piece allows unique talents to shine, and leads the student to confront personal standards of high performance as well as the scoring rubrics established for the assessment program.

The uniform assessment is much more traditional than the other two elements. In writing, we used a writing sample based on a prompt. In mathematics, we used multiple-choice and open-ended problems. The uniform test is there as a kind of safety net, a way to provide usable results as we experiment with less conventional forms of assessments.

Other key elements of the assessment program include the scoring rubrics, the benchmarks, and the professional development of teachers.

The teachers on the design teams developed the scoring rubrics.[2] Figure 1 illustrates how a sample of writing is assessed by noting the level of frequency (extensively, frequently, sometimes, rarely) at which the sample demonstrates attention to each of five criteria for writing (purpose, organization, details, voice or tone, and grammar/usage/mechanics).

In mathematics, the scoring rubrics include four criteria associated with problem solving and three criteria associated with communication. Each of these is assessed at four levels. For example, in problem solving one of the four criteria is "understanding the problem." Four levels of performance related to this criterion are identified: (1) misunderstood the problem *or* didn't understand enough to get started or make progress; (2) understood enough to solve part of the problem or to reach a partial solution; (3) understood the problem, including identifying and using any information minimally required to solve the problem; and (4) identified factors beyond those minimally required to solve the problem *and* applied the factors consistently and correctly. Levels of performance are also defined for the three other criteria related to problem solving.

Similarly, four levels of performance are defined for each of the three criteria associated with communication in mathematics. For example, one of the three criteria in communication is the use of "mathematical language." The four levels of performance related to this criterion are described as follows: (1) used no mathematical language

	Purpose	Organization	Details	Voice or Tone	Grammar/Usage/Mechanics
In assessing, consider...	...how adequately intent and focus are established and maintained (success in this criterion should not depend on the reader's knowledge of the writing assignment: the writing should stand on its own)	...coherence: ...whether ideas or information are in logical sequence or move the piece forward ...whether sentences and images are clearly related to each other (Indenting paragraphs is a matter of Grammar/Usage/Mechanics)	...whether details develop ideas or information ...whether details elaborate or clarify the content of the writing with images, careful explanation, effective dialogue, parenthetical expressions, stage directions, etc.	...whether the writing displays a natural style, appropriate to the narrator ...or whether the tone of the writing is appropriate to its content	...the conventions of writing, including: *Grammar (e.g. sentence structure, syntax) *Usage (e.g. agreement and word choice) *Mechanics (e.g. spelling, capitalization, punctuation)
Ask how consistently, relative to length and complexity...	intent is established and maintained within a given piece of writing	the writing demonstrates coherence	details contribute to development of ideas and information, evoke images or otherwise elaborate or clarify the content of the writing	an appropriate voice or tone is established and maintained	As appropriate to grade level, command of conventions is evident, through correct English or intentional, effective departure from conventions
Extensively	Establishes and maintains a clear purpose and focus.	Organized from beginning to end, logical progression of ideas, fluent and coherent.	Details are pertinent, vivid or explicit and provide ideas/information in depth.	Distinctive personal expression or distinctive tone enhances the writing.	Few or no errors present; or departures from convention appear intentional and are effective.
Frequently	Establishes a purpose and focus.	Organization moves writing forward with few lapses in unity or coherence.	Details develop ideas/information; or details are elaborated.	Establishes personal expression or effective tone.	Some errors or patterns of errors are present.
	Is author's focus clear within the writing? Yes / No	*Does the organization move the writing forward?* Yes / No	*Do details enhance and/or clarify the tone?* Yes / No	*Can you hear the writer? Or, is the tone effective?* Yes / No	*Does writing show grade-appropriate command of G/U/M?* Yes / No
Sometimes	Attempts to establish a purpose; focus of writing is not fully clear.	Lapse(s) in organization affect unity or coherence.	Details lack elaboration, merely listed or unnecessarily repetitious.	Attempts personal expression or appropriate tone.	Numerous errors are apparent and may distract the reader.
Rarely	Purpose and focus not apparent.	Serious errors in organization make writing difficult to follow.	Details are minimal, inappropriate, or random.	Personal expression or appropriate tone not evident.	Errors interfere with understanding.

FIGURE 1

Vermont analytic assessment guide for writing.

Nonscorable: Writing is illegible or incoherent; blank piece of paper submitted; portfolio does not have required minimum contents.

beyond problem statement *or* consistently used inappropriate or inaccurate math language to communicate his/her solution; (2) used appropriate mathematical language to communicate his/her solution; may have some errors in accuracy and lack variety; (3) used mathematical language accurately and appropriately throughout to communicate his/her solution, *and* exhibited variety; (4) used mathematical language accurately and appropriately throughout, exhibited variety, *and* used sophisticated math language to communicate some aspect(s) of his/her solution. Levels of performance are also defined for the two other criteria related to communication in mathematics.

Table 1 summarizes the scoring rubrics by showing the four criteria for problem solving in mathematics and the three criteria for communication in mathematics, together with descriptions of "level four" performance for each criterion.

TABLE 1

CRITERIA AND DESCRIPTIONS OF LEVEL 4 PERFORMANCE IN SCORING RUBRICS
. FOR PROBLEM SOLVING AND COMMUNICATION IN MATHEMATICS

CRITERIA	LEVEL 4 PERFORMANCE
Problem solving	
PS1 Understanding the problem	. . . identified special factors beyond those minimally required to solve the problem and applied the factors consistently and correctly.
PS2 How student solved the problem	. . . approach worked *and* was efficient or sophisticated.
PS3 Why—Decisions along the way	. . . work *clearly exhibits* correct reasoning used in making decisions throughout the problem.
PS4 So what?—Outcomes of activities	. . . solved the problem and made a general rule about the solution *or* extended the solution to a more complicated situation.
Communication	
C1 Mathematical language	. . . used mathematical language accurately and appropriately throughout, exhibited variety, *and* used sophisticated math language to communicate some aspect(s) of his/her solution.
C2 Mathematical representation	. . . used sophisticated mathematical representation(s) accurately to communicate the solution.
C3 Presentation	. . . presentation of solution is clear throughout, well-organized, and detailed.

The level of detail shown in the scoring guides produced a rich picture of student performance. It also made reliable scoring a real challenge because teachers had to keep in mind many shades of performance.

Benchmarks are examples of student work that illustrate one of the levels on a particular scoring criterion. Teachers weighed a great many examples of student writing and mathematics to find pieces that brought the criteria to life.[3] These are central to the training for scoring portfolios, but are also part of the process of showing everyone—teachers, students, parents—what quality looks like.

Professional development proved to be the most powerful and also the most troublesome element. It is the fuel that drives many of the changes associated with assessment. Teachers on the design team devised a training-on-demand concept and promoted it with what looked like a take-out menu.[4] The "menu" listed ten topics in writing and mathematics, and promised to deliver them during school, on week ends, in the evening, wherever. The design team divided the whole state into seventeen networks, each with one or more leaders in the teacher network. To keep the communication intense, the menu listed home and work numbers for those leaders. For those literate in telecommunications, there was a free access number that enabled teachers to get on a computer network to seek help, complain, share solutions, and just exchange ideas.

The power of this professional development as a strategy for instructional improvement is obvious—expert teachers working with other teachers have great credibility. The troublesome aspect also became obvious to us. Since training was so connected to reliability in scoring, it had to be consistent. Because everything about the assessment program was so new, the training had to be continuous. And that crowded into instructional time.

How Vermont Chose This Path

In many ways, our design strategy is one of the most interesting parts of the story. We sought to combine strong state leadership with strong classroom leadership. All our success and failures were public because the whole design process was public from day one. The process was never smooth or easy, but it was a powerful force for instructional change if only because highly visible teachers made most of the design decisions. To be sure, even this level of teacher involvement left many teachers unconvinced. But this was no top-down enterprise.

The need for an assessment had become a topic for policymakers in Vermont during the late 1980s. Vermont was nearly the last, if not *the* last state to create a statewide assessment, and in 1988, it still had no way to measure student performance. As the new Commissioner of Education in March of 1988, I wanted to avoid imposing a reform agenda on a community I did not know. Instead, I traveled the state asking questions and pulling the agenda out of the responses people gave me. I asked: "We spend $600 million on education but can't say what we get for it. Is that OK with you?" Audience after audience demanded a statewide assessment of some kind. But *what* kind?

Shortly before I arrived in Vermont as commissioner, Ross Brewer, who was policy director at the Vermont Department of Education, had arranged to use Maine's standardized test on a sample of Vermont eighth graders, in large measure to get people used to the idea of talking about results.[5] It was a good idea, if only because it revealed how difficult it was going to be for people to have that talk. Publication of those results elicited bickering about reliability, validity, and other psychometric concerns but not talk about performance.

We tried to get to the heart of the matter by going to a hundred citizens with a dozen or so questions. What do you know about the performance of your school and what more do you want to know? What would you do differently if you did know that? What does high performance look like? How do you think we should measure it? Should we compare schools? How? Ross Brewer and I had five dinner meetings with people around the state to get answers to these questions.[6]

We commissioned a telephone survey to ask similar questions of hundreds more, and then published the results in a piece called "Through Citizens' Eyes."[7] People clearly wanted more information about school, but they were much less clear on how it was to be gathered or used.

Late in the summer of 1988, we prepared a short outline of a proposal for a conventional standardized assessment and took that on the road for what we expected would be a last check before we acted. The first public hearing was uneventful and poorly attended. But as the hearings continued, more and more teachers showed up to protest. They did not want to be accountable for results, or so it seemed. It was not until the third hearing that I got the real message. As I listened to the opposition, a teacher observed that it made no sense to promote process writing as an instructional strategy, which Vermont had done for years through the University of Vermont, and then measure writing performance with a multiple-choice test. That comment led to the central tenet of our design: assessment had to be a part of instruction, not apart from it. Assessment had to arise from sound instructional practice. And that meant that teachers would have to participate in all the decisions about the assessment.

We called a halt to the hearings and turned back to the literature on alternative forms of assessment. Condemnation of multiple-choice testing and extravagant claims for "authentic" assessment have become such articles of faith—unexamined articles for all too many—that it is difficult to convey the sense of perplexity and anxiety we felt as we set about reformulating the assessment design. We had heard enough about traditional assessment to see that it could not be the center-piece, but we could find little documented experience with emerging forms of assessment to make them a safe bet either. It was a time of furious reading and checking of fragments with whoever would listen. We learned a great deal from colleagues around the nation who were working along the same path. As we listened, we became convinced that assessment was on the cusp of change everywhere, that no con-sensus had emerged, and that the only sensible strategy for Vermont was to spread the risk by using multiple approaches. An investment counselor would describe this as a "mixed portfolio strategy" (there is that word again), which included some blue chips and some decidedly more risky investments. And that is exactly how we thought about it.

In this heated atmosphere, Ross Brewer and I wrote a short paper that was to become the conceptual framework of the assessment. Rather than have more hearings, we picked three national leaders in assessment with very different perspectives, and one local colleague who had helped us with the Maine experiment, and asked them to tear the design apart and put it back together with us.[8] Over one weekend, it was done. The basic design that we took to the public and the teach-ers emerged from that session. The State Board adopted it and Gover-nor Madelaine Kunin became an enthusiastic supporter.

We established two design teams made up entirely of teachers, gave them our paper on the conceptual design, and asked them to cre-ate the detailed design. What would standards look like? How would we score the portfolio? What were training needs? How would we make the application of standards consistent? It was a huge assign-ment, and while we showered the teams with support in the form of contact with the most thoughtful people we could find around the country, the teachers on those teams had to do the heavy design work, relying primarily on their classroom experience.

At many points, that experience turned probable failure into success. For example, in our first attempt we had been unable to convince the state legislature to invest in the assessment. A year later, the legislature took up the discussion where they had left it. They wanted to know what a portfolio is. Skeptics questioned the ability to compare results among schools, and envisioned huge files of paper. The House Education Committee in the legislature listened and questioned, and I made a great many presentations but little headway. And then, in one inspired afternoon, we held our peace and invited board members, superintendents, principals, and teachers to tell the story. A teacher spoke last, and when she did, she simply put a thin folder on the committee table and said that this was a student portfolio. It represented her student's work. Enabling that student to grow in competence was what she cared about, and she said that she could not imagine a way to teach or assess performance without focusing on that work. So she was going to keep doing it, no matter what the legislature decided. That was our turning point. By the end of the session, the legislature had invested in the pilot program, and would later support the implementation through all its triumphs and difficulties.

The design teams labored on. We abandoned our earlier thoughts on how quickly design issues could be resolved. The teams went to great lengths to include their colleagues around the state. For example, the writing committee produced a thoughtful model of how the whole thing would work, complete with a long list of scoring standards, and then they sent it to all of the more than 2,000 teachers and administrators who would be directly involved.[9] They packed their plan with specifics, and also with questions. And when the answers came back, the committee re-engineered the whole idea.

I would read the almost verbatim minutes from these committee meetings in wonder as they struggled with the issues. How do we prevent people from just ranking the schools on a single statistic? How do we balance the need for accountability with the central purposes of instruction? How fine can the judgments about quality be? How can we use the scoring sessions to break down the fundamental isolation of teaching? Can we combine individual teacher scoring with a regional or statewide moderation system to ensure that each teacher internalized the standards while retaining overall quality control? Why do we have to score the portfolios anyway?

First Lessons, and the Decision to Press Ahead

The pilot program was supposed to be limited to forty schools in a stratified random sample. Not only did the invited sample decide to participate, but also nearly a hundred more schools volunteered. The mathematics team drew several lessons from the pilot year:[10]

•The portfolio provided the "window on mathematics programs" that the designers had hoped for, but teachers would need a lot more support.
•The scoring rubrics needed refinement, but they did work (except where they were not *supposed* to work, that is, with pointless drill sheets).
•The contents of the portfolio needed more definition. There was considerable variation among different schools in what teachers considered portfolio material. Some included sophisticated problems, while others contained only work sheets.
•"Mathematics instruction must change." The team found striking differences in the kind of instruction offered. They concluded that the standards that drive the portfolio demand a mathematics program that stresses problem solving, mathematical communication, and clarity in the use of mathematical language—all of which were features of the National Council of Teachers of Mathematics standards and Vermont's rubric for scoring portfolios.
•And it would take time. The team recommended a statewide training network to begin the extensive support for teachers and students required by the change they envisioned.

The final chapter in the report on the writing pilot carried a title that reflected hope in the midst of all the uncertainty: "Assessing the assessment: 'I've been meaning to tell you. It hasn't been that bad!'"[11] The team found a wide range in the quality of the student work, and in the work of their colleagues: "In some groups of portfolios, the writing was very tightly controlled by the assignment. Thus, the purpose was the teacher's. In other groups, the writing was varied, open, and trusting. These portfolios had a much stronger voice. The students took risks, explored feelings. The gap in the two approaches was significant."

From their conclusions, the mathematics and writing committees devised a number of changes for the following year: more professional development, more teacher networks, earlier information about the scoring criteria, more training for all teachers in the fourth and eighth grades, and more resources to make assessment a part of instruction.

There was little doubt that we would go ahead, but the decision to move from pilot to full-scale operation was in some ways a leap of faith in spite of the thoughtful reports from the pilot effort. We had no increase in funds. The list of needed changes was long. Conversations with superintendents and teachers confirmed the need for those changes. Teacher reaction to the initial press accounts of low student performance demonstrated that we did not know how to talk about results. Yet the momentum was there. The principals were sure that we should take the next step to statewide implementation. Strong leadership in both education committees in the legislature, continuous pressure and support from the State Board ("When will we have statewide results?" was the State Board chair's repeated question), and the general sense that we were on a promised schedule to act were all part of the decision.

Most of the proposed changes were actually accomplished. The most dramatic was the creation of the teacher networks for professional development. An insistent demand for professional development was only the most visible of the changes that assessment had ignited. Vermont was also pursuing opportunities for school restructuring in middle grades, early education, elementary science, and in other areas. We announced a campaign to "Seize the Summer of '92" for professional development, and the schools, higher education, and the professional associations responded powerfully. The assessment training network took shape very quickly and was carried almost entirely by teacher leadership. As the year went on, our "on demand" approach to teacher professional development appeared to be the right step, but it put enormous pressure on the budget. By April of that first full year of operation, the Department found training funds nearly gone, and had to halt all training except for what was needed to prepare for scoring.

Two changes that did not occur to the extent we had hoped were new resources and early delivery of information about training. We did not have enough money. We reallocated what had been funded for development but it worked only up to a point. Major development tasks still remained. Early fall meetings to inform everyone of training dates and other details of the process also worked better for some participants than for others. Most difficult was the fact that we had not used the summer to train all the teachers and administrators who would be involved. Some teachers were still receiving critical information for the first time late in December.

During that first full year, the most commonly heard complaint was about the quality of training, but there were other worries on teachers' minds. I made a habit of inviting myself to faculty meetings whenever a superintendent reported an unusual level of tension. By year's end, I had attended five such faculty meetings. Teachers were concerned about the time demands imposed by the assessment. Training was one such demand, but teachers also had to alter their whole approach to grading as the year came to a close. Some started individual student interviews and turned to substitutes to cover classes for two days or more. The scope of the change was huge. As one teacher said, we had expected them to change assessment, curriculum, and teaching practices all at the same time.

A conversation with fourth grade teachers illustrated the change.[12] Several said they felt that they had cheated their students out of the rest of the curriculum. "I never got to long division," said one. Another thought that problem solving was fine, but fourth graders could not deal with the scoring rubric that pressed for extension beyond the answer. "The kids are just not ready for the 'so what?' part of it." Another observed that she spent too much time on problem solving. "We spent two whole days on one problem!" Others listened in sympathy, but as they listened, the conversation slowly turned. Maybe, they concluded, spending that much time to get something as basic as problem solving right the first time was not a bad idea.

What tormented fourth grade teachers the most was having to manage both writing and mathematics portfolios. The burden for some was crushing, and anecdotes circulated about those who fled the fourth grade classroom for safer berths in fifth grade.

Teachers in the two grades that were part of the assessment reported feeling isolated from colleagues in other grades. They worried that school-by-school reports would target them for low results. And that concern has not gone away.

All the conversations with teachers underscored our obligation to strengthen support, clarify expectations, and improve professional development. It was a powerful exercise in what business calls "listening to the customer." Teachers seemed to support the assessment, even to the point of expressing concern that it might not continue. But they demanded ever greater quality in the efforts of the Department to provide support.

What Have We Learned?

From the outset, the Vermont assessment was developmental. We planned as thoughtfully as we could, listened as teachers gained experience, and modified the assessment as we went. This stance was at once the greatest strength and the greatest source of irritation. In September 1990, when the large-scale pilot began, more than 700 teachers gathered for the kickoff. I told them that we would listen and modify, and it sounded like a sensible approach at the time. But when we did make what we thought was a very modest improvement in the scoring criteria a month later in response to teachers' suggestions, the response from many teachers was very negative because they valued stability while so much else was changing. The incident illustrated the continuing task of balancing stability and continuous improvement.

Development efforts require continuous informal listening and rigorous formal evaluation. The informal listening happened all the time. An individual teacher would write an angry letter and I would call for a talk. A group of superintendents would come to see me to report the frustration of their teachers. In faculty meetings I would recount what I had heard at second hand and ask for confirmation.

The need for formal evaluation was something that Ross Brewer had foreseen and provided for early on. He arranged for the RAND Corporation to conduct this evaluation. Daniel Koretz led the evaluation, which became a comprehensive review of both the effect on instructional practices and the reliability of the results. The RAND reports were to have a powerful effect on the future direction of the assessment.

The first RAND results appeared in two reports in July and December 1992. The July report, which presented findings from interviews and surveys of a large sample of teachers and principals, concentrated on the changes in classroom practice and participants' views on the implementation of the assessment.[13] Koretz examined both the 1990 pilot effort and the statewide implementation of 1991-92. He found that during the pilot year teachers had difficulty with the scoring system. Some kinds of student work did not fit the scoring standards. Scoring required raters to keep many different rating points in mind and this made scoring difficult. There was a great deal of variation in student tasks, and that also complicated scoring.

Data from the 1991-92 statewide implementation expanded on these themes and added many more. Principals reported that the assessment was a burden, but a worthwhile burden. Portfolio assessment was new for almost all the principals, but the support they provided was exceptional. More than 90 percent provided extra help for teachers, most often in the form of released time for scoring or training.[14] Teachers were very enthusiastic about the quality of support they got from principals. Ninety-five percent of fourth grade teachers reported that their principal supported them "adequately" or "very well" in the program.[15]

In more than half of the schools, portfolios had spread beyond the fourth and eighth grades even during the first year. While RAND did not pursue that finding, it may reflect principals' efforts to relieve teachers of the isolation that many felt at being the only ones in the school undergoing such major changes in their work.

Time was one big concern, as it is in any school change. Teachers spent, on average, thirty hours a month on portfolio-related tasks.[16] This time included finding tasks, preparing lessons, helping students manage the materials, and scoring. Another concern was closely related: the adequacy of training and other support. The state had provided a variety of training opportunities, including summer and fall mathematics institutes, training through the networks, and other sessions to prepare teachers for the scoring. Teachers at the two grade levels reported very different reactions to the help we offered.[17] While the *summer* mathematics institute got high marks from fourth grade teachers (93 percent said the sessions prepared them "adequately," "well," or "very well") a third found that preparation received at the *fall* mathematics institute was either poor or very poor. Eighth grade teachers had the reverse reaction—only 13 percent reported the fall institute to be "poor" or "very poor," but 21 percent were critical of the summer institute. Support provided directly to local teachers was highly regarded by eighth grade teachers, but not by the fourth grade teachers.

Whenever I had an informal discussion with teachers, one topic sure to emerge was the difficulty of changing classroom practice so quickly. The RAND results offer a glimpse of how great that change was.[18] Among fourth grade teachers, 82 percent reported spending "somewhat more" or "much more" time on problem solving and 49 percent report spending "somewhat less" or "much less" on computation and algorithms. Forty-eight percent of those teachers said they spent "somewhat more" or "much more" time on patterns and relationships. The eighth grade teacher profile is very similar. One obvious conclusion is that the National Council of Teachers of Mathematics standards were appearing very quickly in classroom practice. These changes suggest one reason for the level of anxiety that many teachers reported and the powerful demand for professional development. But those figures also reveal the profound and positive effect of the portfolio assessment on instruction.

Teachers' reports of positive effects were another indicator of success in the RAND findings. Teachers reported greater enthusiasm for teaching mathematics, improved goals for instruction, closer links between mathematics and other subjects, improved student attitudes, and more student learning.[19] The most frequently reported concern was "not enough time to cover the full math curriculum." Eighty-one percent of fourth grade teachers said that, and 65 percent of the eighth grade teachers agreed. Other big concerns were "students don't know how to solve problems" (45 percent of fourth grade teachers said that was often or always the case) and "low ability students have difficulty with tasks" (60 percent of fourth grade teachers said that happened "often" or "always").

Another issue during the statewide implementation was reliability. Concerns about inconsistencies in training and anticipation of future reporting at the school level generated questions about just how reliable these results would be. The State Board and I openly discussed this issue and shared that discussion with school leaders for months. In the course of that discussion, we pledged that we would not report unreliable results.

The second RAND report answered the questions about reliability. While the reliability of the uniform portions of the assessment were high, the overall reliability of the portfolio results was low.[20] Our plan had been to report state level and supervisory union results in the first year and school level results a year later. RAND studies revealed that while the state level results could be reported with confidence, the supervisory union data could not. (Each of Vermont's 250 school districts is a member of a supervisory union, a middle level administrative unit. There are sixty supervisory unions in the state.)

Koretz suggested several reasons for the low reliability, and offered some thoughtful recommendations for improving reliability in the future. First, the scoring criteria might be unclear or overly complex. A possible solution was to evaluate the criteria and revise or simplify them. A second and probably more important source of low reliability was insufficient or inconsistent training for those scoring portfolios. RAND suggested concentrated training for those teachers who would be scoring during the second year. A third problem might be the lack of standardization of tasks. Early on, the design team had considered how to clarify the kind of work expected in the portfolio, but this third RAND finding would require empirical investigation on efforts to standardize portfolio tasks. The report includes this telling sentence: "Given that the raters are teachers, low reliability suggests that teachers remain uncertain what skills are sought or, at the least, what performances constitute evidence that their students have mastered them."

Reaction to this report in the public and the field was not what I had expected. Superintendents who had earlier expressed great concern over reliability now urged that we not get so obsessed about reliability that we let the portfolio plan falter. Press reaction was positive and pointed out that most educational innovations are dropped at the first sign of trouble and that now was the time to dig in for the long haul on portfolios. Governor Howard Dean praised the project and predicted ultimate success in his "state of the state" message. Teachers seemed to feel that their concerns had been validated. But all of this supportive reaction rested on an unspoken assumption that the state and its many partners would act quickly to resolve the problems. Susan Rigney joined the Department of Education as the new assessment director and immediately led an aggressive response to those problems.

Responding to the Results of the RAND Report

The assessment team immediately confronted the RAND results, reaffirmed the purposes of the assessment, and set out what they had learned.[21] Portfolio assessment was making a difference, but consistent scoring would require changes in the system. It would take time for the scoring to "mature." Teachers had offered many practical solutions for improving both the training and the scoring. The big dilemma they faced was whether to continue training for all teachers or to go for immediate gains in reliability by concentrating limited training funds on a few teachers who would do the scoring.

In the end, they found a balance that reflected the fundamental design of the program. They decided to review the scoring system with both Vermont and national experts to find and eliminate inconsistencies. They redesigned the network training to ensure that all teachers received uniform training and immediate feedback on their performance in scoring. Scoring for second-year state reports would be done during the summer by a team of teachers recruited from among those who demonstrated reliability in the training sessions. That select group would receive additional training as a part of their scoring session.

The team also decided to simplify the mathematics portfolio by eliminating the category of puzzles which had not proved to be a good source of scorable work. Finally, the team agreed to an aggressive reporting schedule that would provide state-, supervisory union-, and student-level results in portfolios and also school-level results for the uniform tests. The school level results in particular will have to be interpreted with great caution. The urge to compare, particularly among school boards, is very strong. But Vermont has many very small schools. No matter what assessment or test is used, scores from schools with fewer than thirty students in a grade will remain unreliable as a measure of the quality of a school program simply because of school size. This is an obvious point for any statistician, but it may elude many people who are hungry for school-level results, and so it must figure prominently in all future discussions of assessment results.

Current Issues

The first two RAND reports were followed by others. In 1994, Brian Stecher and Karen Mitchell examined the mathematics portfolios from the perspective of how well teachers understood the fundamental issue of problem solving.[22] Their findings were disturbing: "teachers did not appear to have an organizing structure when they talked about problem-solving skills." Their work underscored the many positive results of the portfolio approach—positive changes in curriculum and teaching practices, continued teacher enthusiasm for the reforms, and heightened demand for professional development— but they also point to lingering problems. Stecher and Mitchell see a "fundamental conflict between good instruction and good assessment for accountability purposes."[23] That is an issue to watch, but I still think that we were right in the first place: good assessment must be part of instruction, not apart from it.

Another issue concerns how best to make the assessment comprehensive. Assessments in writing and mathematics in two grades are not sufficient. The State Board listened to the many voices demanding more results, and found, not surprisingly, that different audiences had different needs for performance data. While teachers were not much interested in comparing scores among schools, school board members insisted on that information. In late 1994, the State Board concluded these conversations and adopted a three-year plan to expand the assessment into the high school, then to add science, the arts, and social sciences.

The Vermont Institute of Science, Mathematics and Technology developed a high school mathematics assessment, including both portfolio and more traditional components, and at the request of the State Board, turned immediately to the development of a science assessment. The legislature, with strong support from Governor Howard Dean, increased funding for the assessment program to a full $1 million for the first time, which permitted the high school mathematics assessment. These changes were not without difficulty. While the

School Boards Association strongly endorsed these changes, superintendents expressed reservations about the speed of the expansion,
although they too supported the assessment.

By 1995, the Common Core Framework of standards was nearly
complete, and this will exert new pressures for adjustment in the
assessment, particularly as the performance standards appear in final
form at year's end.

One of the biggest problems has been the lack of front line tools to
support training and scoring of the portfolios. While image processing
and computer telecommunications are commonplace in some fields,
teachers still have to gather in person for network training and for the
week-long scoring of the state sample of portfolios. And yet, Vermont
teachers are becoming a "virtual faculty" in the sense that they are
coming to share a common view of the standards, and a common body
of increasingly sophisticated student tasks for the assessments. Lou
Gerstner, Chairman and Chief Executive Officers of IBM, gave the
whole enterprise a huge boost in 1995 when he came to Vermont to
award a $2 million "Reinventing Education" grant to the portfolio
effort. The challenge and opportunity is to create technology tools to
support teachers in the portfolio part of the assessment.

Unexpected Benefits

The many who contributed to the design and implementation of
the Vermont assessment thought hard and "designed in" many of the
successes. But there were other benefits that just happened along the
way. No report would be complete without mentioning some of them.

The Vermont Business Roundtable became an early supporter of
the assessment before the legislature voted the funds for the pilot. On
short notice, they formed a panel to examine the plans in detail and
offer some suggestions. One was to change from a fourth and eleventh
grade pattern to the fourth and eighth on the grounds that the gap
between assessments would be too great, and that eleventh grade
would follow later. We adopted their idea. Then the Roundtable did
something else that created an unusual set of stakes for the assessment.
In a program they called "Performance Counts," they told high school
graduates that they would be looking at transcripts and portfolios as
part of the job interview. To drive that point home, the Roundtable,
and later the Vermont Chamber of Commerce, enlisted nearly 300
Vermont employers. Then they turned to principals and won the support of virtually every high school. The message was clear: "What you

do in school is important. Be prepared to show results when you come for the job interview."

A second opportunity that no one foresaw in the beginning was the proposal to adopt portfolios in teacher preparation. The State Board challenged the presidents of all the Vermont colleges and universities that prepare teachers to develop a results-oriented alternative to the process of approving teacher preparation programs. The prize was substantial deregulation of teacher preparation. The presidents proposed that all candidates seeking teaching credentials would develop professional portfolios, and that institutions seeking approval would present an institutional portfolio to an external review team that would also have access to the portfolios of all the candidates. The State Board accepted the response and a second Vermont portfolio experiment began. Two colleges have completed the site visits under this new process for approving programs, and portfolios are a prominent, and promising, part of it.

Yet another unexpected benefit of the portfolio assessment was the heightened demand for professional development. The assessment came to be only a part of the systemic change in Vermont education which provoked demand for training. But the immediacy, scope, and pace of the portfolio project raised almost insatiable demands. This opened the way for a professional development consortium (which was already forming) to respond to demands for help on school restructuring.

When the National Science Foundation's Statewide Systemic Initiative grant opportunity appeared, a large Vermont team built a collaborative response around the assessment. Vermont won a $9 million grant that suddenly provided the opportunity to expand the assessment into high school, and to create an integrated mathematics, science, and technology assessment. The arts community, which could legitimately claim original ownership of the portfolio idea, began to carefully build support for assessment in the arts. When the Jesse B. Cox Charitable Trust created an opportunity to develop portfolio assessments in the arts, Vermont arts teachers were ready and won a significant grant.

The Wider Context

Assessment is only one element in systemic change. Assessment systems have to match goals, curriculum frameworks, professional development and professional standards, and all the other strategies of systemic change. Many complaints from teachers emerge from a ground-level concern that things just have to fit together better.

During the years when Vermont developed its portfolio assessment, this question of fit was ever before us. It tended to appear most clearly whenever we talked about results and the condition of education. One business leader said after an annual recital of the condition of education, "We know the problem. Let's act." His cry of exasperation became the title of the first version of our strategic plan. Six months later, we presented an elaborated version, still in brief form, in which the focus was on the elements of a change strategy, and the connections among the elements. A year later we prepared still another version called *The Green Mountain Challenge* which defined the vision, goals, strategies, and actions. A year later we gathered all the partners, tore the strategy down, and rebuilt it again. We will repeat that exercise.

A most potent strategy from *The Green Mountain Challenge* for elaborating systemic change and the future of assessment is in the Common Core of Learning. We asked more than 4,000 Vermonters what they think every student should know and be able to do. The strategy of involvement has drawn steadily increasing numbers of educators and other citizens into the effort. The Common Core will then drive curriculum frameworks which will, among other things, answer that old student question: "What's on the test?"

However, many questions remain. For example, our approach to the Common Core of Learning is interdisciplinary. So is our assessment. The writing portfolio includes material from across the curriculum, and impressive mathematics portfolios often seem to contain as much writing and science as mathematics. But how will we proceed when the national pressures in assessment and performance standards are decidedly disciplinary in their direction? And look at the reliability question. We cannot ignore accepted standards of reliability as we experiment with new approaches to assessment. But will psychometricians invent new tools to fit the new assessments?

Many important decisions are before us. How will we combine the many emerging components into a comprehensive assessment system—all grades, the whole curriculum—without overwhelming teachers? Will our new approach to training and scoring boost reliability sufficiently, or are there other strategies? How can we encourage the creation of statistical tools that will support the development of performance and portfolio assessment?

So, where are we on the assessment? Where we have always been— in development. There will be more results, more evaluations, more listening to teachers, and continuous improvement in teaching, learning, and assessment.

NOTES

1. Richard P. Mills and Ross Brewer, *Working Together to Show Results: An Approach to School Accountability for Vermont* (Montpelier: Vermont Department of Education, November 10, 1988).

2. Vermont Department of Education, *Mathematics Problem-Solving Criteria*, revised (Montpelier: Vermont Department of Education, December 22, 1992).

3. Vermont Department of Education, *Grade Eight Benchmarks* (Montpelier: Vermont Department of Education, November, 1991).

4. Vermont Department of Education, *Vermont's Portfolio-Based Assessment Network: Information and Professional Development* (Montpelier: Vermont Department of Education, n.d.).

5. Vermont Department of Education, *The 1988 Vermont Assessment: A Report on the First Pilot Assessment of Vermont Eighth Graders* (Montpelier: Vermont Department of Education, n.d.).

6. Richard P. Mills and Ross Brewer, *Summary of Forums on Statewide Assessment* (Montpelier: Vermont Department of Education, September 12, 1988).

7. Ross Brewer, *Through Citizens' Eyes: Education in Vermont* (Montpelier: Vermont Department of Education, September, 1988).

8. Richard P. Mills and Ross Brewer, *Working Together to Show Results.*

9. Geof Hewitt, "Vermont's Portfolio-Based Writing Assessment Program: A Brief History," *Teachers and Writers*, May-June 1993, p. 2.

10. Vermont Department of Education, *Looking Beyond "The Answer": A Report of Vermont's Mathematics Portfolio Assessment Program, Pilot Year, 1990-91* (Montpelier: Vermont Department of Education, n.d.), p. 43.

11. Vermont Department of Education, "This Is My Best," in *Vermont's Writing Assessment Program, Pilot Year, 1990-91* (Montpelier: Vermont Department of Education, n.d.), p. 13.

12. Interview by the author with teachers and administrators in Lamoille North Supervisory Union, December 3, 1992.

13. Daniel Koretz, Brian M. Stecher, and Edward Deibert, *The Vermont Portfolio Assessment Program: Interim Report on Implementation and Impact, 1991-1992 School Year* (Washington, D.C.: RAND, National Center for Research on Evaluation Standards, and Student Testing, July 31, 1992).

14. Ibid., p. 20.

15. Ibid., p. 35.

16. Ibid., p. 32.

17. Ibid., p. 35.

18. Ibid., p. 36.

19. Ibid., p. 42.

20. Daniel Koretz, Daniel McCaffrey, Stephen Klein, Robert Bell, Brian M. Stecher, *The Reliability of Scores from the 1992 Vermont Portfolio Assessment Program, Interim Report* (Washington, D.C.: RAND Institute of Education and Training, National Center for Research on Evaluation, Standards, and Student Testing, December 4, 1992).

21. Vermont Department of Education, "Vermont Assessment Program, 1992-93," memorandum (Montpelier: Vermont Department of Education, January 1993).

22. Brian M. Stecher and Karen J. Mitchell, *Portfolio-Driven Reform: Vermont Teachers' Understanding of Mathematical Problem Solving and Related Changes in Classroom Practice* (Washington, D.C.: RAND Institute on Education and Training, National Center for Research on Evaluation, Standards, and Student Testing, 1994).

23. Ibid., p. 35.

CHAPTER X

Assessment and Accountability in Kentucky's School Reform

BRIAN GONG AND EDWARD F. REIDY

Kentucky has been noted nationally for its ambitious educational reform launched in 1990. Called one of the most comprehensive and systemic state education reforms, Kentucky's reform embodies school finance, governance, curriculum, school organization, and assessment. It has been especially notable for its very rapid implementation under legislative mandate. Four years of operational experience have been marked by real change and progress. The process of implementation, however, has exposed real tensions, many of which center around an assessment system that is struggling to meet multiple goals. How these tensions are resolved will largely determine the success of the state's efforts to make dramatic improvements in public education.

Kentucky's assessment and accountability system is shaped by several goals that call for: (1) an assessment system that provides accurate and trustworthy data to use in making accountability decisions; (2) an assessment system that not only provides credible measurement information but also contributes to positive changes in schools by modeling good instruction, curriculum, and student performance; and (3) a rapid change to statewide performance standards that are to be implemented locally in curriculum and instruction designed by schools and teachers (a state-mandated goal).

In this chapter we examine how Kentucky is dealing with these three goals. First, we examine the tensions between assessment as measurement and accountability as policy in the context of a push for rapid implementation of performance-based assessment of virtually all enrolled students, including those with moderate to severe learning disabilities. We shall also consider the difficulties of moving from student-based assessment to school-level accountability. Next we will use the work

Brian Gong is a research consultant in the Bureau of Learning Results Services in the Kentucky Department of Education and a member of the faculty of the School of Education, University of Louisville. Edward Reidy is Deputy Commissioner in the Bureau of Learning Results Services in the Kentucky Department of Education.

with writing portfolios to illustrate problems that arise in balancing assessment and instruction, including the need for changes in state-sponsored instruction in scoring and in auditing procedures. Third, to illustrate the movement toward common assessment standards on a state-mandated timeline but with local flexibility and variations in curricular implementations, we will examine Kentucky's efforts to devise a content/assessment framework.

We have experienced different degrees of success in dealing with the multiple goals in those contexts. In balancing assessment with accountability, we achieved a compromise that seemed stable for four years but we have recently seen the need for striking a new balance. In our work on writing portfolios, which illustrates an effort to balance assessment and instructional goals, we have had increasing success thus far. In balancing centralized assessment with local decision making with respect to curriculum, we have found that our solutions need to be strengthened.

Undergirding Kentucky's efforts to implement programs to meet these goals is a concern with transforming educational systems throughout the state. The Kentucky Department of Education must be concerned with equitable, effective, and fair requirements and opportunities for all schools. Three aspects essential to the attainment of our goals are (1) increasing the educational *capacity* of students, teachers, and schools; (2) increasing *access* to necessary resources and information; and (3) fostering *coherence*, especially among programs administered by the state Department of Education and between state and local efforts.

We conclude the chapter by pointing out lessons learned from our experience and by identifying some issues that arise in trying to create viable programs that address multiple and sometimes conflicting goals.

Because the focus of the chapter is on assessment and accountability, we make only brief reference here to the larger context of educational reform in the state. More extensive descriptions and technical treatments of Kentucky's educational reforms are readily available elsewhere.[1]

Mandated Assessment within Systemic Educational Reform

The focus of Kentucky's educational reform is to increase students' learning dramatically. This commitment stems from the 1980s, when the publication of *A Nation at Risk* (1983) thrust into public debate the importance of—and the imperiled condition of—American education. The resolve at the federal and state levels was embodied in an unprecedented education summit meeting called by President George Bush and attended by the governors of all fifty states. That summit resulted in the establishment of ambitious educational goals.[2] While many spoke glowingly of the importance of pursuing "world class standards," Kentucky was unusual in taking concrete steps to hold itself to that vision. Chief among these steps was the establishment of a statewide assessment and accountability system with high-stakes rewards and sanctions based on a school's progress toward very high standards.

Kentucky's assessment and accountability system was not merely the result of participation in the wave of enthusiasm for standards in education. Rather it was a product of a combination of state judicial, legislative, and executive decisions that provided a unique mandate. In 1988, a state circuit court handed down a decision that the state's system of school funding was inequitable. The court went further in this case, which was brought by 66 of the state's 176 school districts, by declaring the whole public school system unconstitutional. The decision was upheld by the Kentucky Supreme Court in 1989.

As recounted by the President of the state Senate and the Speaker of the state House of Representatives, "the Court gave us an unparalleled opportunity to build a common school system that can truly put the Commonwealth first in education. The legislative and executive branches of government jointly formed a Task Force on Education Reform, which worked diligently to provide recommendations to the General Assembly. Those recommendations form the basis of the Kentucky Education Reform Act of 1990." The legislative leaders went on to comment, "The Commonwealth never faced a greater challenge than reforming its educational system and paying for it. For those of us who have long advocated fundamental changes in our schools, the opportunity presented by the Supreme Court was welcomed enthusiastically."[3]

The Kentucky Education Reform Act (KERA) stipulated dramatic changes in school finance, governance, school organization, and assessment. The system for financing education was changed from one based primarily on local property taxes to one where the state provides school districts with a minimum amount of money per student. Funded by the largest tax increase in the state's history, overall public support of schools increased dramatically and the gap in funding between the wealthiest and poorest districts decreased.[4] KERA also mandated establishment of school-based decision-making (SBDM) councils. These councils, made up of the school principal and at least two parents and two teachers, were to have considerable authority over school curriculum, finances, and staffing. Over half of the roughly 1400 schools in the state had established SBDM councils by 1994. Another concern in school governance addressed in KERA was the anti-nepotism provision that closely defined permissible hiring and supervisory relationships. KERA also mandated the establishment of a nongraded, multiage primary unit for what had previously been kindergarten through the third grade. Other important provisions in the Act were (1) funding for extended school services, including tutoring before and after school, and family resource centers to integrate school and social services in high-need communities, and (2) substantial amounts of money for schools to buy computers and other technology aids for curriculum and instruction.

A key provision in these massive changes was the establishment of an assessment and accountability system the purposes of which were to provide (1) assurance that the enlarged public investment in education was "paying off," (2) incentives for schools to improve their performance, and (3) support for positive changes in curriculum, instruction, and school organization.

The legislators who framed KERA felt strongly about the importance of the assessment and accountability system, for the Act stipulated that such a system was to be put in place immediately. (This was done during the 1991-92 school year, just two months after the contract for the development and implementation of the system was awarded.) Moreover, the Act specified the main goals to be assessed, the grade levels to be assessed, the nature of rewards and sanctions, the basis for determining a school's qualifications for reward or sanction. It also required that the assessment would be "primarily performance-based."

Underlying this considerable attention to detail were the assumptions that accountability decisions could be formulated on the basis of assessment results, that assessment and instruction could be integrated, and that the state should be limited to specifying common standards and monitoring schools' achievement of those standards, while schools should be free to pursue those standards in whatever way they chose.

Kentucky's experience thus far with merging assessment and accountability, assessment and instruction, and common standards with local implementation has been marked by changes as implementation proceeded. We begin by considering our experience in trying to align the policy of accountability with the practices in assessment.

Aligning Assessment and Accountability

Assessment consists of the measurement aspects of the testing program. The accountability system consists most saliently of the rewards, assistance, and sanctions given to schools on the basis of their assessment performances. However, policy aspects of the accountability system impact the design of the assessment system. Similarly, operational and technical characteristics of the assessment system have implications for decisions made with respect to accountability.

Four decisions made at the outset of the reform in Kentucky gave rise to tensions between accountability and assessment. One decision was to make the school the unit of accountability, not the student, classroom, district, or state. A second decision was to include virtually all students in the accountability system, and to hold students to common performance standards as much as possible. This was operationalized into one set of standards for students with moderate-to-severe learning disabilities and one set for all other students. A third decision was to base the definition of acceptable school performance on improvement rather than on achievement of an absolute standard. A fourth decision was to require that the assessment system directly support good instructional practice by focusing on major content and by modeling performance-based learning.

Each of these decisions had major implications for assessment. The inclusion of all students in the assessment was hailed by advocates for learning-handicapped students as a signal that schools could not use these students to get additional resources without really expecting them to achieve. On the other hand, the tenet that "all children can learn, and most at high levels" is the statement least supported by teachers and the public (fewer than 50 percent agreed) in a survey dealing with KERA.[5] A common assessment for all students, regardless of their perceived abilities, continues to be a source of debate. In addition, the fact that the assessment system allows a number of accommodations for students (as noted in their Individual Education Plans) such as extensions of time, Braille versions, readers, and scribes raises issues of comparability and construct validity.

The decision to make the school the unit of accountability raised issues of the relationship between school accountability and student accountability. While KERA explicitly steered away from student accountability, observers noted early the potential problems with students' motivation to perform on a test when their results on that test were of no concern to them personally. In fact, almost all schools and districts have taken measures to give students some stake in the state assessment results, such as tying students' grades to performance on the test. However, this continues to be a controversial and potentially troubling issue.

One of the most controversial points of KERA was the provision that based rewards and sanctions on school improvement. In the assessment and accountability system this was operationalized as a change in a school's "accountability index" based upon the relationship between its baseline score and its "improvement goal," both of which are set every two years. The improvement goal is determined by adding to its baseline score 10 percent of the difference between that score and the state's goals for all schools, which is a score of 100. Thus, for a school with a baseline of 30, the improvement goal would be 30 + .10 (100 - 30), or 37. In order to achieve reward status the school would have to surpass a score of 37 by at least one point.

In addition to the measurement difficulties inherent in developing this scheme, some educators have argued for the use of other criteria in addition to progress. For example, the high school with the highest accountability index in the state did not achieve "reward status" because it did not meet its improvement goal, while many schools that did not score as high in an absolute sense received rewards because they made proportionally greater improvement. This attention to relative progress in a standards-based system struck many as running counter to a commonsense definition of a "successful school."

When the assessment and accountability system were at the design stage, many asked whether the system would be equitable, particularly for urban schools serving large numbers of disadvantaged and minority students and for rural schools in traditionally disadvantaged geographical regions. The results of the first Accountability Cycle (1991-1994) indicated that background characteristics of schools were not major factors in determining whether a school achieved a certain level of rewards or assistance. A multiple regression analysis was used to determine the relation of percent of improvement goal obtained by a school to the following five variables: accountability grade (the grade at which assessment was done—grade 4, 8, or 12); initial baseline score in 1992; percentage of minority students in the school; percentage of student receiving free or reduced-price school lunches; and size of school (enrollment at the accountability grade).

The percent of improvement goal obtained by schools throughout the state (and therefore the level of reward and assistance) was not strongly predicted by any of these five variables taken singly or in

combination. The "best fit" multiple regression including the five variables noted above had an R-square of .17. This can be interpreted as
meaning that about 17 percent of the variance in percent of improvement goal obtained could be accounted for by the five variables,
and 83 percent of the variance was due to other factors. In other words,
it appears that "school success," as defined in Kentucky, was attainable
by many schools, including those in traditionally disadvantaged areas.

There was a clearly articulated and coherent relationship between
assessment and accountability when the system was designed. That is,
emphasis was placed on the assessment system, and the accountability
system was viewed as a "given," specified in the law. That relationship
held through the first four years of the system's operation. Recently,
however, there has been a shift in the relationship. Because over $30
million in monetary rewards and assistance was distributed in 1995 on
the basis of schools' performance, the assessment basis underwent
increased scrutiny. The state Department of Education had actual data
for the first time to check the models of assessment and accountability.
In addition, external review groups also conducted studies, using data
provided by the Department of Education.

One such external review, conducted by a panel of six nationally
known measurement experts, was sponsored by the Office of Education Accountability (OEA), an administrative arm of the General
Assembly created as part of KERA to oversee the implementation of
educational programs mandated by the Act. This panel conducted a
detailed review[6] of the measurement aspects of the assessment system
and concluded that "the system is seriously flawed," such that assessment results should not be used for accountability decisions until a
number of concerns were addressed, including improved reliability of
measurement, more credible resetting of performance standards, and
more credible equating methods to relate results from one year to
another. The OEA panel also recommended that portfolios not be
used for high-stakes accountability purposes, in part because analyses
indicated that portfolio scoring was of moderate reliability and biased
toward higher scores.

Responses to the OEA panel's report by the legislative subcommittee that oversees the OEA and by the state Department of Education
clearly showed the tension between assessment and accountability.
The legislative subcommittee passed a resolution indicating its desire
to continue the assessment program but to suspend the accountability
provisions until the recommendations of the OEA panel could be met.
That is, the view seemed to be that instructional improvement was less

a function of accountability than of assessment, although in a resolution approved on June 26, 1995 the subcommittee on accountability spelled out its intent to have both: "Accountability is an essential part of the system."

The Department of Education's response to the recommendation to remove portfolios from consideration in accountability decisions clearly showed the Department's resolution of the tension between assessment and accountability. Department personnel disagreed with the panel's recommendation, noting that the writing portfolios were a relatively small part of the assessment system and that the instructional benefits of including writing portfolios in the accountability system outweighed their shortcomings in measurement.

We think it obvious that striking the "right balance" between assessment and accountability cannot be achieved solely by appeal to logic or evidence. It involves application of judgment based on values and a view of the future—"what will teachers be likely to think and do if . . .?" In this sense, the ongoing discussion about assessment and accountability serves to sharpen our understanding of the various players' positions. We hope that discussion will lead not only to greater coherence in articulation, but also to consensus in action.

Relating Assessment and Instruction

An explicit goal of Kentucky's assessment system is to support instruction by (1) identifying content and skills worth learning, (2) providing standards of performance for students and schools, and (3) providing feedback useful for informing instructional and curricular decisions and modeling rich, appropriate student performances.

The latter characteristic is one that distinguishes authentic or direct assessment from less-direct assessments, such as multiple-choice tests. Kentucky's portfolio assessments go two steps further in integrating assessment and instruction. First, the portfolios are composed entirely of work that arises from the student's classroom experiences; there are no state-mandated topics or set prompts. The student is free to work on the portfolio entries over extended periods of time, theoretically spanning multiple grade levels. The portfolio is composed of pieces (selected by the student with the help of teachers, peers, and others) that reflect the student's closest approximation to the state's performance standards. These standards are made public through distribution of a scoring rubric and annotated student work chosen to show certain important features related to performance levels.

Second, the scoring of the portfolios is done by local teachers and the results are entered as the score of record into the accountability system. Thus, the portfolio represents an integration of instruction and assessment in that teachers are trained, supported, and expected to understand and apply the standards for good writing, not only in instruction but in assessment that has implications for the classroom and beyond.

There has been a question about whether teachers can score reliably enough to admit their scores into an accountability system, especially when their scores may reflect on their own school or another school in their district. Based on our experiences of the first four years, we state with confidence that many teachers are able to apply expert judgment in scoring complex performances, and do so fairly and professionally in a high-stakes accountability system. The questions, rather, are: What conditions and tools foster the rapid and widespread development and application of teachers' evaluative skills? What review measures are necessary to ensure the credibility of the assessment system? How are the teacher's assessment and instructional skills related?

The state Department of Education has conducted a series of eight studies involving over 60,000 portfolios during the past three years.[7] On the basis of these studies we conclude the following:

1. Many schools have made dramatic improvements in both student performance and accuracy in scoring writing portfolios over the past three years. On the average, however, portfolio scores given by local scorers tend to be about one performance level higher than scores given in the monitored scoring sessions sponsored by the Department of Education.

2. Over a three-year period, estimates of statewide scorer reliability, based on the percent of exact agreement between original scores assigned by local teachers and review scorers, has improved from approximately 50 percent agreement to 70 percent.

3. Teacher scorers in state-sponsored scoring sessions regularly achieve interrater reliabilities of 80 percent or greater, based on percent of exact agreement. Agreement between review scorers and prescored quality control portfolios (prescored by the standard-setting group for writing portfolios—the Kentucky Writing Advisory Committee) is regularly 70 percent or higher.

4. It is possible to conduct audits of scores on writing portfolios to certify results both in centralized and "self-audit" conditions. The self-audits have powerful benefits for professional development, instructional change, and institutional acceptance of audit results.

These findings have led to an increased understanding of how assessment and instruction are inexorably intertwined. As the Department

of Education has monitored and redefined training and scoring procedures in an attempt to increase accuracy and demonstrate reliability,
the impact of assessment on instruction has become apparent. Our
recent studies indicate that teachers' understanding of appropriate
instructional practice has a direct link to consistent application of
standards in scoring. Thus, our results link instruction, student performance, and scoring accuracy. Those teachers who understand the
qualities of good writing tend to instruct accordingly and help their
students become better writers, according to Kentucky's standards.
When teachers understand the qualities of appropriate instruction,
they also tend to recognize quality writing during scoring and are better able to apply standards consistently, thus scoring more accurately.

Notably, our experience in two major studies indicates that improvements in student performance and in scoring accuracy can occur
quickly, but must occur simultaneously for either to have substantial
growth. For example, results demonstrate that some audit schools
(schools included in a sample of schools where portfolio scores were
audited by external scorers), which were among the least accurate in
terms of scoring during one year, ranked among the most accurate the
following year. This was accomplished through the schools' engagement in targeted professional development. These same schools also
demonstrated substantially larger increases in student performance
than the average school, again providing evidence of the positive
impact this assessment tool can have on instructional practice. The
evidence gathered thus far suggests that reliability of scoring will continue to improve as teachers grow in their understanding of writing
and Kentucky's writing standards. As reliability of scoring increases, so
will the quality of instruction offered to students.

Studies show that teachers who score a significant number of portfolios in an intensive setting begin to see instructional strengths and
needs reflected in the students' work. This was also the experience in
our "scoring analysis" sessions, where scorers found a number of patterns that reflect instructional approaches, opportunity to perform,
and opportunity to learn. The following patterns were identified:

"Cookie Cutter" Portfolios. These were portfolios from the same
classroom or school that looked virtually the same. All the entries
focused on the same topic and/or prompt, and in many cases were
close to a fill-in-the-blank format. These portfolios demonstrated
minimal student investment and choice and a consistent lack of proficiency in writing.

"High Investment" Portfolios. These were highly individualized and personal portfolios that demonstrated strong student investment and choice. They generally dealt with portfolio requirements in a unique and creative manner and consistently showed proficiency in writing.

"Portfolio Week" Portfolios. These contained pieces that were clearly first drafts. As noted by the dated pages, the pieces were developed quickly and at the last possible date for completion. They demonstrated little investment of time, failure to complete the writing process, and low proficiency in writing.

"Content Deficient" Portfolios. In addition to exemplifying previously noted patterns, these portfolios contained writing pieces generated in content area classes (e.g., science, social studies) for purposes other than those of the writing portfolio. When judged according to the scoring rubric for writing portfolios, these pieces had the effect of decreasing the proficiency in writing demonstrated by the student. This was one of the most frequent problems seen in portfolios across all grade levels. It indicated that, although instruction in writing is becoming more widespread, in content areas other than language arts it is still weak. This may be due to a lack of instructional integration and collaboration between teachers of language arts/English and their colleagues in other content areas.

"Prompt" Portfolios. These portfolios demonstrated a lack of student choice. They contained pieces that were based on teacher-generated prompts that were inappropriate and/or served to limit the students' ability to focus on a relevant purpose and/or audience.

The institution of a "self-audit" was an important development in the Department of Education's search for a solution that would merge assessment with instruction in ways acceptable to schools and to the state. From the beginning, because the portfolios are locally scored, an audit system was included. In accordance with this plan, 105 schools were selected to have their 1992-93 writing portfolio scores audited. Portfolios were collected and sent out of Kentucky to be scored by the assessment contractor hired by the Department of Education. As a result of rescoring in the audit, scores of 99 schools were lowered, most by 50 percent or more.

The ensuing discussion was impassioned, intense, and very public for several weeks. Whether to trust Kentucky teachers or professional scorers from out of state became the essential question for many people, including the legislative committee on education that was drawn into the fray. In the end, the audited schools were offered several options by the Department of Education, including rescoring of the portfolios another time by Kentucky teachers or keeping the original scores assigned by the local teachers. Two thirds of the schools chose to keep the original scores.

The results of rescoring in those schools that chose that option closely matched the results of the audit. In fact, an additional twelve schools requested that their scores be audited, and the results again showed local teachers to be scoring higher, from a moderate to a substantial amount.

In the midst of this highly charged situation, one audit school requested to rescore its own portfolios under whatever supervisory conditions the state wished to establish. "If we did something wrong," one teacher said, "we want to correct it." The Department of Education agreed to conduct a pilot project to develop this self-audit procedure. Quality control checks on scoring included initial qualifying requirements for the scorers identical to those used in the audit rescoring process, double blind scoring of all portfolios, a mandatory discussion session to moderate any differences when scorers did not agree, a random reading of at least 20 percent of each scorer's portfolios by experienced Department of Education staff, and anonymous "anchor" portfolios prescored by the Kentucky Writing Advisory Committee.

In this pilot project the rescoring done by the teachers resulted in scores very close to those assigned in the audit. However, the teachers achieved higher quality control of both accuracy and interrater agreement than that achieved by teachers in our rescoring studies. The result was an almost exuberant confidence among the teachers. They were transformed into advocates of the writing portfolio standards. In addition, they felt they knew what to do instructionally to help their students achieve more. In the two years since the self-audit, several of the teachers and the principal of the pilot school have been called to conduct workshops, not on scoring but on instruction, such as "writing across the curriculum" and articulating writing instruction across the grade levels in the school and district.

The payoff to the Department of Education was that the self-audit procedure was officially adopted as a viable option for conducting audits. Differing from the centralized audits, the self-audit procedure is initiated by a school staff, conducted by the school staff, and focuses not only on getting accurate scores but on professional development of teachers and analysis of the school's instructional program for writing.

The self-audit program satisfies the need for both accurate assessment and insightful instruction.

Kentucky's requirements for writing portfolios were developed from the modern movement toward writing process, student investment in writing, and writing standards that were widespread in the nation before the advent of KERA. However, the requirements of mandated accountability meant that many more teachers had to participate in portfolio scoring than had chosen to up to this point. In addition, the imposition of a common standard also presented challenges for scoring reliably across the state.

We believe that the inclusion of writing portfolios in the assessment has impelled school staffs to become engaged in generating and scoring writing portfolios, which produced instructional benefits that in turn strengthened commitment. That Kentucky has experienced such widespread results with 1300 schools and 5000 scoring teachers is phenomenal. In our view, the improvement in scoring accuracy and reliability over the relatively short time span of three years is also very promising. In the case of writing, the goals of instruction and assessment are closely aligned.

However, surveys in the fourth year reveal some conflict between assessment and instruction in terms of practical constraints. Many teachers report that scoring portfolios takes too much time—an objection that was especially strong in schools or districts that require teachers to leave their classes to attend group scoring sessions. These groups of experienced teachers also report that they have learned to score accurately and so scoring now is less of a learning experience and more of a chore. Some of these teachers desire to explore other types of portfolios—portfolios that are focused on student progress rather than on the final product, and portfolios that demonstrate students' ability to integrate content from various subject matter areas rather than focusing only on writing.

The self-audit is strongly supported by the Department of Education because it not only results in certifiably accurate assessment scores and valuable instructional analysis, but it also directly engages teachers in developing their capacity to understand and apply the writing standards in contexts with which they are most familiar and to which they are deeply committed. The Department of Education and the state and regional writing portfolio staff are prepared to support all schools that wish to engage in a self-audit in the future.

Access to writing portfolio information, to training, and to support continue to be concerns of the Department of Education. While every teacher has nominal access to written materials and the telecast training videos, actual in-depth training varies by trainer and by the availability of trainers in each geographical region. A special concern of the Department of Education was that schools in poorer regions of the state were disproportionately represented in the audit and were identified as schools that consistently scored their writing portfolios much higher than was warranted. A third concern beginning to surface is the disparity between schools that have shown significant movement toward creating school-level changes and those making individual classroom- or team-level changes. Districts that have significant central office staff seem to have disproportionate access to resources needed to make these difficult changes. The Department is committed to investigating these differences and their possible effects, but little has been done to date.

In terms of coherence, it is generally agreed by assessors, teachers, students, and parents that portfolios can exist in both worlds of assessment and instruction. The recent OEA panel report, however, recommended that portfolios not be used for high-stakes assessment because of the level of unreliability and the upward bias in scores. Response from teachers, assessment coordinators, administrators, legislators, and others, however, indicate that the instructional power of portfolios is such that that recommendation should not be accepted, at least for now. Continued monitoring will tell whether the promising improvement that links assessment with instruction through writing portfolios continues, or whether it flattens out or declines.

Assessment and Curriculum

A central philosophical pillar of educational reform in Kentucky is that, while the state should set common standards and hold schools accountable for making progress toward those standards, schools should have maximum freedom to progress toward those standards in ways that they regard as most suited to them. As one statement summarized this view, "It *is* the intent of the KERA that a statewide assessment system be developed which will drive instruction in ways that result in every student's development of particular capacities; it *is not* the intent of the law to prescribe or dictate *how* educators go about achieving these ends."[8]

This position is incorporated into law: the Department of Education is charged with implementing a state assessment but is also prohibited from establishing a state curriculum. The statute gives the responsibility for establishing curriculum to local school councils.

To be useful, learning goals must be stated clearly and meaningfully. Kentucky's goals and standards are written broadly, and particular curriculum content is conceived of as "exemplars and demonstrators" of the goals. For example, one of the expectations in science states: "Students identify and analyze systems and the way their components work together or affect each other." The state's curriculum framework consists of over twenty examples of how the concept of systems may be studied at several grade levels using several instructional approaches.

In working on assessments we have found that it is necessary to have greater specificity than is usually contained in statements of goals, standards, and performance criteria. That specificity is needed in order to arrive at operational definitions, for example, of (1) the content that is valued, (2) the level of abstraction and elaboration expected in students' responses to an assessment task, (3) the context in which knowledge and skills are to be used.

In general, assessments that have this greater specificity have been welcomed by those seeking to implement instruction and curriculum consistent with the goals because they specify expected student performances and anchor performance criteria. For example, an annotated sample of students' responses to an open-ended question relating to systems in a biological science context can define the science content and skills needed to answer the question and illustrate the level of performance associated with a certain standard.

But accountability assessment puts a premium on knowing the specifics of a test. When assessment questions are very contextualized, as they often are, knowledge of the contexts in which questions are embedded can have the effect of narrowing the curriculum. For example, if an assessment question on systems is embedded in a context of fertilizers and ponds, teachers may think that their students need to know about fertilizers and ponds in order to do well on the test. They would then emphasize such a context in their instructional program instead of giving attention to other contexts that could serve the purpose equally well. Similarly, teachers might think that their students, having studied the concept of systems in a biological setting, would be at a disadvantage if an assessment question were embedded in a physical chemistry setting.

This issue recalls the long-standing finding from psychology that learners have difficulty "transferring" knowledge or skills learned in one setting to a quite different setting. This same phenomenon is being studied specifically in terms of the "unreliability" of performance assessments where a student may perform well on one form of an assessment and yet perform poorly on a "parallel" form.

Curriculum and instruction present challenges in Kentucky, too. We have observed that few teachers and schools have the background, expertise, and resources to devise significant curricula. While extensive professional development programs have been conducted on devising performance-based assessments, assessments embedded in instructional units, and integrated units, few teachers have moved beyond idiosyncratic activities and units. The net effect of these efforts has been more to sensitize teachers to the issues and engage them in the revision of instruction and curriculum than to produce a body of high quality curriculum materials useful to others in addition to themselves.

Under KERA, schools are given the responsibility for devising curriculum—selecting the content, organizing it into meaningful chunks and sequences, and articulating parts over a year within a grade level and between grade levels and schools. Many schools have felt, incorrectly, that they need to devise the curriculum *de novo*, without reference to existing curricular structures such as textbooks or previous practice. Unfortunately, most schools and teachers are ill-equipped to deal with curriculum at this level. Most of the tools provided to teachers by the Department of Education focus on developing extended tasks or units, not comprehensive or multiyear curricula.

While schools have been more engaged in devising curricula that they think will reflect the state standards and especially the content standards associated with the assessment, their access to curricular frameworks and other support has been uneven. In particular, larger districts with central office staff that specialize in curriculum and districts that have a specialist in certain areas have been able to develop curriculum frameworks and materials. Unfortunately, few schools and districts in Kentucky have such resources. For example, of the 176 school districts in the state, only two have science curriculum specialists in their central offices. While KERA requires schools and districts to organize into regional consortia to provide pooled resources to address such challenges, the regional consortia have been slow to respond, often exhibiting few additional resources beyond what the most advanced single school or district has to offer.

The Department of Education recognizes that the existing situation stems in part from a lack of conceptual coherence between the goal of locally determined instruction and curriculum and the centrally determined standards, especially as the latter are assessed in the current system. The Department is currently considering several ways to increase schools' ability to produce coherent curriculum where increased student performance will be reflected on the state assessment. For example, in science the Department is developing a curriculum/assessment framework that has a number of useful features. First, it incorporates a much smaller number of topics—the goal is twenty to thirty topics instead of the current 150 per grade level. Identification of this "core" allows for reasonable alignment between the limited number of questions included in the assessment and what can practically be done in schools to the desired instructional depth. Second, it organizes the topics into scientific models rather than in lists of unrelated topics. Third, it incorporates the content framework described above and standards and performance criteria for relating student performance on specific content to specific standards, as well as providing specific student work, instructional examples, and commentary to help educators make sense of the materials.

Another means being investigated is the introduction of more student choice and school choice in the assessment. The Department of Education is investigating ways to include assessment tasks that provide more structure than in portfolios but also significant latitude for students to demonstrate that they understand and can do scientific investigations, for example, in ways other than by responding to open-ended questions or a few one-hour performance tasks.

A third avenue being investigated is fostering exchanges between schools of materials, examples, and human resources such as master teachers who have developed successful curricula. The goal is to tap into solutions and have the Department of Education play a role of disseminator and facilitator rather than originator and monitor.

The Future of Assessment in Kentucky

Assessment will continue to play a key role in educational reform in Kentucky. As it has up to now, assessment will be challenged to be both an operational program and a catalyst for change, whether in accountability, instruction, curriculum, professional development or other areas. The assessment and accountability program will need to meet professional standards while also garnering continued legislative support, educators' commitment, and public acceptance. None of this is guaranteed; none will be easy.

However, Kentucky's experience with an evolving and imperfect system under scrutiny is the very thing that enables hard issues to be raised—in great specificity and with immediate relevance. It also holds the promise of rapid learning and development. For example, in a legislative hearing in July, 1995, the subject was the need for technical improvements in the assessment and accountability system. One legislator noted, "It seems that much of our difficulty stems from having a very high-stakes accountability system. It is difficult to meet the technical requirements of having an assessment system that can support these very high stakes, and it also appears that the accountability has negative effects on the instruction we want. Is there a way to lower the stakes—maintain some accountability, but lower the stakes so it doesn't have these negative effects?" Another legislator said, "What I hear is that there are many things we are asking our test to do—to provide individual scores, to provide [data for] national comparisons, to support school accountability, to provide diagnostic feedback. And what I am hearing is that no test can do all these things." Turning to the other legislators, this speaker continued, "Perhaps it is our job to decide what we want. If we can't have it all, then we need to decide what we really want."

These reconsiderations of how to deal with multiple and sometimes conflicting goals are exactly the strength and challenge of Kentucky's assessment system. We hope that the next four years will bring as much progress—in conceptual clarity and practical results—as has been made in the past four years as we have struggled to bring an operational program out of a legislative mandate.

The conceptualization of Kentucky's current reform in this chapter is our own. We recognize that others may differ from us on many points. However, we trust that all will agree with us that the educational improvement in Kentucky has been due to the efforts of many thousands of students, teachers, administrators, the Department of Education staff, citizens, and others. We acknowledge their dedication and commitment to education and to Kentucky's children—past, present, and future—with deep gratitude.

NOTES

1. For a concise overview, see Legislative Research Commission, *The Kentucky Education Reform Act: A Citizen's Handbook* (Frankfort, Ky.: Legislative Research Commission, 1994). The most comprehensive treatment of the technical aspects of the assessment and accountability system, whose official title is the Kentucky Instructional Results Information System (KIRIS), is given in Kentucky Department of Education, *KIRIS Accountability Cycle 1 Technical Manual* (Frankfort, Ky.: Kentucky Department of Education, July, 1995).

2. U.S. Department of Education, *America 2000* (Washington, D.C.: U.S. Department of Education, 1989).

3. Legislative Research Commission, *The Kentucky Education Reform Act*, "Foreword," p. v. (Statement by John A. "Eck" Rose, President Pro tempore of the Senate and Donald J. Blandford, Speaker of the House of Representatives.)

4. Stephan Goertz and David L. Debertin, "School Finance Reform," in *A Review of Research on the Kentucky Education Reform Act (KERA)*, a Report prepared by the University of Kentucky/University of Louisville Joint Center for the Study of Educational Policy for the Kentucky Institute for Education Research (KIER) (Frankfort, Ky.: Kentucky Institute for Education Research, December 1994).

5. Rona Roberts and Steve Kay. *Kentuckians' Expectations of Children's Learning: The Significance for Reform*, a Report prepared for the Prichard Committee for Academic Excellence and the Partnership of Kentucky School Reform (Lexington, Ky.: Roberts and Kay, Inc., September 1993). The report is available from the Prichard Committee for Academic Excellence, P.O. Box 1658, Lexington, Ky. 40592-9980.

6. OEA KIRIS Review Panel, *Review of the Measurement Quality of the Kentucky Instructional Results Information System*, 1991-1994, a Report commissioned by the Office of Education Accountability (OEA), Legislative Research Commission (Frankfort, Ky.: Office of Education Accountability, June, 1995).

7. These studies, directed by Starr Lewis and Amy Aubrey, have been sponsored by the Department of Education's Kentucky Writing Program.

8. Kentucky State Board for Elementary and Secondary Education and the Kentucky Department of Education, "Request for Proposals to Implement an Interim and Full-scale Assessment Program for the Commonwealth of Kentucky," (Frankfort, Ky.: Kentucky Department of Education, April, 1991), p. 7.

Section Three
POSSIBILITIES AT THE NATIONAL LEVEL

CHAPTER XI

A Vision for the Role of New Assessments in Standards-Based Reform

GOVERNOR ROY ROMER AND JOY FITZGERALD

We live in a time of extraordinary and rapid change. Political systems, geographic boundaries, and new applications of technology are evolving in ways that were unimaginable even a few short years ago. As a nation, and as individuals, we can find enormous opportunity in this change, but only if we have flexibility of mind, high levels of skills, and the understandings and attitudes of lifelong learners.

The first step in becoming "a nation of learners" is to begin nothing short of a revolution in our expectations for students and for our schools. Equity and the nation's changing demographics demand that these higher expectations be held for all students, particularly those who are presently underserved. The engine of this revolution is the recognition that achievement is as much a function of expectation and effort as it is of ability.

A major goal of these higher expectations is to create public demand—informed, sustained, and significant—for systemic reform in our schools. But national and local polls consistently reflect that the most significant barrier to real change is the public's satisfaction with what is being accomplished in their local schools. The only way we can build the requisite public demand for change is to help people realize how far we are falling short of the performance levels needed to secure our future.

Governor Roy Romer is the governor of Colorado. Joy Fitzgerald is in the Office of the Governor of Colorado.

234

Some History: How Did We Arrive Here

With this sense of mission, in September of 1989, President George Bush and the nation's fifty governors met in Charlottesville, Virginia, at a national education summit to debate and adopt six national education goals. The summit participants believed the goals, as naively ambitious as they may sound, accurately reflect the levels of performance that we need to aim for and to achieve. But the real value of the goals is not their precise content. The value is in the ambition of their vision, their scope, their commitment to outcomes, their widespread support, and finally, their linkage to a meaningful accountability process.

In July, 1990, the National Education Goals Panel was created by the administration and the National Governors' Association. The panel was charged with developing an annual report through which the nation and the states could evaluate their progress toward meeting the national educational goals over a ten-year period. It was my privilege to chair the panel during its first year of operations.

From that point of origin, the governors and the administration agreed that the indicators in the annual reports should be outcome oriented. They should not focus on how hard we are trying, nor on the difficulty of the circumstances that confront us, but on whether we are succeeding or failing at what we set out to do: achieve the national educational goals. Second, the indicators should measure our progress against the external criteria of world class standards of performance, not by comparing states or school districts one to another. In the ensuing years, the nation has begun to publish just such tough-minded reports. They offer us the encouraging news that we are making significant progress in changing the conditions that underlie children's learning, such as infant health and immunization. At the same time, the reports portray the sobering news that, at least so far, we are doing little more than holding level on outcomes indicative of student achievement, such as the numbers of African-American and Hispanic students entering and completing college.

In trying to construct a national report that approached the measurement of student achievement in this way, it was quickly apparent that the panel faced two huge gaps in theory, practice, and understanding. First, there was a startling absence of a national consensus about what to measure. We frankly did not know, or did not make public, what the essential skills and knowledge were that made a student competent. Second, the panel was repeatedly informed by the nation's most respected experts that for all the tests being taken in American schools and all the money being devoted to testing, we simply did not have the assessment capacity—the measures that are fair, reliable, and comparable—to provide the desired information about student achievement and progress on the national level.

In the face of these gaps, the Goals Panel had to redefine its mission. Before the panel could provide reliable measurements of progress over the long term, we first needed to agree, as a nation, on what should be measured—what skills and understandings should all students possess, what should all students know and be able to do. We also needed to invest in and broaden our assessment capacity in a way that ensured that the tests used not only accurately measure, but encourage, the development of the kinds of serious skills and deep knowledge that our changing world requires.

In short, we recognized three things. First, we recognized that the assessment systems we had in place—largely standardized, multiple-choice, curriculum-independent assessments—were insufficient for providing either a vision or an effective guidance system for the high standards and more broadly equitable public education we had envisioned. Second, we came to understand that in all probability standards-based reform required a system of national accountability based on highly demanding performance assessments and qualitative scoring against world class criteria. With the support of business, diverse educational experts, as well as practitioners and policymakers, the national movement in favor of standards picked up strong momentum. The National Education Goals Panel created the National Council of Educational Standards and Testing which was charged by Congress to make recommendations regarding the desirability and feasibility of national standards and tests and the policies, structures, and mechanisms needed to put such a system in place. This was our third realization, we had to create a coherent system of changes—not just standards, but also assessments worthy of the standards, ways of engaging teachers and administrators, agreements about what the assessments were to be used for, and productive forms for reporting results. Unless the individual parts meshed, we would not have the momentum we needed to shift from business as usual to standards-based educational reform.

As originally envisioned by the council, the national standards were to be national, not federal; voluntary, not mandatory; dynamic, not static. They should reflect high expectations and provide focus and direction to instruction, not a national curriculum. The council recommended that the new national assessment system should have two components, individual student assessment and large-scale sample assessment, such as the National Assessment of Educational Progress. The system of assessments was to be voluntary and developmental and was to consist of multiple methods of measuring progress, rather than a single test.

The initial work of the panel, the council, and other groups has informed debate among policymakers and educators at the national level about what is meant by standards and the system-changing potential of standards-based reform. In most of the country, however, this debate has not yet been played out at the state or local level. Such a broad-based debate is essential to designing the system that we finally need. As national subject-matter standards have appeared, they have provoked precisely such important discussions of whose history, what literature, which attitudes towards science American students must have. Similarly, since the Congressional elections of the fall of 1994 we have seen an equally lively debate about the role of the federal government in setting and enforcing standards. However these debates unfold, the point is that a never-before-held discussion of the expectations for American students is, at last, occurring. However, to negotiate this debate wisely, we will need the support of the American public. If we pursue the implications of such a system seriously, the familiar face of American education will change significantly. For instance, in this new system, what is variable is how long it takes a particular individual to learn the material to a high standard. What is fixed is the knowledge and skills all students must possess. In education, we presently organize much of the system the opposite way. Time is fixed (length of classes, semesters, school year) and what different students learn in the allotted time is variable.

The Role and Responsibilities of Assessment Systems in Attaining this Vision

If this kind of high standards education is our destination, then strong performance-based assessments are compasses that can help us judge our progress in the direction of that destination. These assessments must be linked to and developed in conjunction with the standards. Since teachers teach to the test, we need to develop assessments that are worthy of being the object of teaching and that accurately reflect the skills and knowledge we want students to possess. Equally important, a good assessment tool can facilitate the process of refining the standards on an ongoing basis.

But there are very clear challenges in developing a national assessment system linked to standards. At the present time, one of the most problematic issues is that of equity. There is ongoing and passionate debate about whether it is fair to set high standards and then begin to apply assessments when not all youngsters have had the opportunity to encounter an educational experience that gives them the tools to reach the standards. Many conclude that a national system of assessments should not proceed until there are assurances that educational delivery systems are fair and equitable.

It is possible, however, to understand and support the concerns underlying this argument, but disagree with the conclusion. One of the most inequitable things we can do to any group of youngsters is not to tell them the truth about the skills and knowledge they will need in order to lead productive lives and to have choices. The greatest inequity of all is never to confront a generation with a true assessment of what their condition is relative to what the world will demand of them. In the interests of protecting them from a sense of failure, we do them a grave disservice in the long run. Think of the analogy of a CAT scan. When a person is not feeling well and enters the hospital for tests, the patient wants and needs information about his condition. He wants to know what good health is, how his condition compares to that definition, and finally, what he needs to do to close the gap. A well designed and equitable assessment system fulfills a similar purpose. Standards articulate what educational health is. Assessments should be able to tell individual students and their parents where they stand relative to that mark and provide them with information about how to begin to close the gap.

An equally important issue is that of using the standards and linked assessments, not as ends in themselves, but as tools to build the capacity of our schools to educate large numbers of students well. The real reform potential lies in applying these tools to teacher development, instruction, curriculum, and the policy environment to change the nature of what is going on in classrooms. Standards and assessment are the slices of bread holding the sandwich of educational reform together. But the meat of the sandwich is the delivery system—the quality of teaching, the access to technology and laboratories, the depth and challenge of the curriculum. Standards-based reform, of the kind modeled in strong assessment systems, offers the best hope of ensuring that our entire system is ratcheted up to higher levels of performance and that it serves all our nation's children. The future demands no less. Our children deserve no less.

CHAPTER XII

Standards and Portfolio Assessment

PHILIP DARO

The purpose of this chapter is to pose issues and suggest possible approaches to portfolio scoring based on standards. Many of these issues have existed for a long time in the two most important traditional assessments: report card grades and norm-referenced tests. The habit of the system has been to leave grading standards and practices to individual teachers, without any frame of reference in the professional community. Standards for normed tests are relative to average performance, not to curricular expectations.

There is a world of possibilities between these two old habits. The use of standards in assessments of portfolios can fill the chasm between report cards and normed tests. The impact on grading practices and the use of normed tests remains to be seen. Figure 1 illustrates the place of standards-based portfolio assessment in the overall assessment picture.

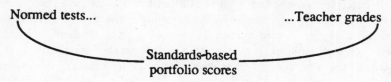

FIGURE 1

The place of portfolios in assessment

New Standards (NS), a joint program of the National Center on Education and the Economy and the Learning Research and Development Center at the University of Pittsburgh, can be thought of as establishing a more broadly responsible and supportive context for the assessment of student accomplishments.* Teachers, students, and the

Philip Daro is Director of Assessment Development for New Standards. He is also associated with the University of California at Berkeley.

*Co-directors of New Standards are Lauren B. Resnick, director of the Learning Research and Development Center at the University of Pittsburgh, and Marc S. Tucker, president of the National Center on Education and the Economy. The program has

public will be linked through national standards and an accountable process for assessing the cumulative accomplishments of students against the standards. Large numbers of teachers will participate in standard setting and scoring. How can this be done across the variety of states, schools, teachers, and students?

Many of the questions discussed in this chapter are resolved differently for different purposes of assessment. Yet too much can be made of differences in purpose or uses of assessments; it is convenient for us assessment designers to say that we intend our instruments to be used in certain limited ways, and we deplore the misuse of the instruments for purposes for which they were not intended. It can be unprofessional, and perhaps unethical, to assume this posture if our intended use has low value in the marketplace and the unintended uses we deplore have very high value and there is no alternative product for this highly valued misuse. If the de facto situation is that the primary use to which the clients put our assessment produces is what we call misuse, there is a serious misunderstanding driving the marketplace, if not a misrepresentation. Making inferences about individual students with respect to curricular opportunities is the most common misuse of tests not based on the curriculum and not designed for individual high-stakes use.

What assessment instruments have been designed and validated for determining whether a given student has met expected standards in mathematics, for example? This certainly is the widely understood purpose of report card grades. How does a given student's achievement in mathematics, as shown by the grade on the report card, compare to the achievement of other students in the country? The score on a norm-referenced test is certainly believed to answer that question. How does achievement in mathematics as evaluated on the report card relate to achievement as measured by the norm-referenced test? What are the standards?

For all practical purposes, any scrutable assessment of individual students will have heavy consequences for at least some students in at least some schools, even if it "only" influences the student's and parents' estimation of the student's worth and potential as a student. Therefore, we have to design for this use, even when it is not part of our system. Likewise for assessments of teachers and schools. In other words, in addressing the issues below, assessment designers have to

attracted partners—states and local school districts—that were already far along in designing and administering a new generation of assessments based on performance rather than on multiple-choice tests.

anticipate consequences beyond our intentions, and, within reason, take responsibility for the validity of such consequences. In this sense, all assessments that create information about individual students are high stakes; information has impact.

What to Assess

What are we trying to assess? A common view of normed tests is that they assess mental traits that are otherwise invisible. They assess something inside the head of the student. How do we know what is really being assessed? Is it really what is valued? How does it relate to curricular expectations? Can we hold the student, teacher, and school accountable for the score? These are fundamental questions about validity.

Report card grades are commonly thought to assess how well the students did what the teacher asked: so many points for homework, so many for participation in class, and so many for examinations. Certainly, the validity of a report card grade with respect to the individual teacher's curriculum is fairly direct. But what is the validity of teachers' grades with respect to national, state, or professional expectations of curriculum? What is the consequence of the variation in standards from teacher to teacher, school to school, and state to state?

Using national curricular standards to assess students' portfolios holds much promise for bringing standards into the regular discourse between student and teacher, among teachers, and between educators and the public. This promise has prompted widespread work in the development of portfolio assessment.

Much of the early work has concentrated on the portfolio culture in the classroom. Great enthusiasm flows from teachers and students about the power of portfolios to focus student effort and reflection on their own learning and accomplishments. There can be little doubt of the utility of portfolios in instruction, at least for some teachers who have tried them. But it does not necessarily follow that it will be practical to bring national standards into the focus of self-assessing students and their teachers. Clearly, such an effort will influence and draw upon the traditional investment of time, credibility, and funds in report card grades and normed tests. While my view is that the trade-offs are well worth it, it is not the purpose of this chapter to make those arguments. Rather the purpose here is to examine the issues facing any effort to use standards to score portfolios. These begin, perhaps, with the question: What should we score?

Should we score entries, exhibits of several entries, dimensions, aspects of performance, traits, or some combination of these? How does what we score relate to performance standards based on curriculum standards? How does what we score relate to what we prompt? What will our scores communicate to students and teachers? If teachers emulated our scoring in their report-card grading systems, would our scoring schemes serve them well?

Much of the discussion among experts in assessment contrasts holistic scoring with dimensional scoring. For scoring cumulative accomplishments, I believe this discussion can be restructured so that a synthesis of the insights precious to each point of view can be achieved, and a more powerful and useful system devised. Each type of scoring solves a different problem by making different trade-offs.

Holistic Scores

As used to score single performances, *holistic* scoring respects the wholeness and interconnectedness of the performance by refusing to impose any a priori analytic structure on the structure created by the student in performance. The holistic scorer is asked to judge how well the performance accomplished the purpose set in the prompt. Of course, the purpose that animates and steers the student in performance is constructed as an interpretation of the prompt. There will typically be many reasonable variants of performer's purpose, and therefore, the purpose is only set in the prompt in a hopeful way. In ordinary course work, a student has numerous checks and debugging opportunities to make sure he or she understands the assignment. Course work, compared to noninteractive examinations, is far less prone to assessment error because of misalignment of the student's purpose with the scoring scheme. Such variance in performer purpose raises a number of problems. First, by reasonable interpretation, a student can make a task more or less difficult. A second problem is to account for the variation in anchor papers and rubrics. The design and crafting of prompts can help mitigate these problems but cannot eliminate them. The attempt to mitigate them often creates other problems, such as denaturing the task, preempting the opportunity to perform by too much leading. Grappling with the effective communication of purpose is a key to the craft of designing performance tasks. It requires many iterations of student trials.

The scorer uses anchor exemplars and a criterion (rubric) that together express the prompted purpose as a scoring standard. The anchors show the variety and range of performances. This holistic judgment allows for great variety in how a student approaches the accomplishment of the purpose. In particular, it allows for the student to respond in *whatever dimensionality he or she chooses*.

For example, in assessing how well students can formulate simple mathematical models of realistic situations, students must create their own structures and variables. This is central to what we want to assess. Some may use geometric thinking, others will create functional relationships, while still others will overpower the situation with the cunning use of arithmetic, expressing generalizations in practical recipes or procedures. While these approaches differ in their mathematics, they all accomplish the set purpose, and can be scored with a common holistic rubric. This works well for the strategic standards set by the National Council of Teachers of Mathematics (NCTM) in its first four standards. But it leaves work to be done in assessing specific goals relating to mathematics concepts.

There has been considerable success in scoring writing and open-ended mathematics tasks using task-specific rubrics and anchors. Most experienced scorers and teachers I have talked to doubt that a general rubric would work very well. Task-specific rubrics can deal with the purpose of the task in very direct, easily interpreted ways. Knowledge from pilot testing can be used directly in the construction of the rubric.

Many do think, however, that genre-specific rubrics might work for different prompts within well understood genres. This has more immediate use in writing than in other subjects, although promising exploration of these ideas is underway in mathematics. If genre-specific rubrics can be made to work, then teachers or curriculum leaders can select their own prompts within genres, even in a national system like New Standards.

Holistic scoring of portfolios can be based on the holistic scores of each entry in the portfolio. One advantage of this approach is that we know most about how to do this kind of scoring reliably. Also, the scores are directly applied to an object (the piece of work) that is real to the student, teacher, and public. On the other hand, the set of scores for the set of objects lacks much meaning of its own beyond *how well the student has done what he or she has been asked to do*. Notice that this is approximately the same meaning as a report card grade. It may be possible to give considerable meaning to score sets of this kind by also scoring what the student has been *asked* to do against curriculum standards—an "opportunity to perform score."

Another approach is to score holistically across entries in the portfolio. Kentucky is using this approach. A similar approach has been piloted on a small scale in California. When scoring across entries, the possibility arises for *setting a purpose for the selection of tasks*; the purpose of the selection is greater than the sum of purposes of the individual tasks. This purpose can be communicated directly to the student and teacher making the selection. In this case, it functions as a higher-order prompt for the portfolio as a whole. When this is done, students and teachers are often asked to comment reflectively on the selection vis à vis its purpose. The criteria used by the student in making the selection should parallel the criteria for scoring and the curriculum standards. Kentucky has made a deliberately transparent attempt to do this.

It may be useful to distinguish true holistic scoring that emphasizes the integrity of the performance and seeks to judge it on its own terms from *fused multidimensional* scoring. The Kentucky approach to cross selection scoring uses an *a priori* multidimensional schema based on curriculum standards. Scorers are asked to make one overall judgment of how the portfolio entries as a whole meet the multidimensional standard as a whole. In some ways this multidimensional fusion lacks the directness of true holistic scoring. On the other hand, it assesses balance in the curriculum more explicitly.

Holistic scoring relies heavily on the entries themselves to link the scores to the curriculum standards. The scores connect to the curriculum through the entries' connection to the curriculum. This raises the question, Who is responsible for the range and balance of tasks: student, teacher, school, partner, National Standards, professional community, developers of instructional materials, others? The answer will surely involve all these people in some way. These issues will be taken up later in this chapter. It is noted here, however, that holistic scoring depends more than other scoring methods on a satisfactory answer to this question, since the selection of tasks is such a central part of the definition of the performance standard. For this reason, holistic scoring may require more standardization of entries than other methods.

Every argument I have heard or thought of against this conclusion that holistic scoring leads to more standardization has been one of the following three kinds:

1. External standards-based assessment should not impose on the reality of teacher choices and therefore all arguments that go back to standards are invalid.

2. The link to national standards is rhetorical anyway, so it is not as important as the integrity of the teacher-student relationship to their own circumstances. Only they can decide what is right for them. Therefore it is all right for the link to standards to be very general.

3. Types of tasks can be partially standardized without standardizing the tasks themselves.

Arguments 1 and 2 are not available to New Standards, whatever their merits. Argument 3 has possibilities, especially in a system that includes an on-demand examination to complement portfolios. Kentucky is trying this.

Some public explanation of how the portfolios relate to performance standards rooted in the curriculum standards will be needed. It will be easy to provide vivid examples, but difficult to explain the breadth and detail of what is systematically assessed.

Dimensional Scores

Dimensions (or aspects of performance) derived rationally from the curriculum standards can be formulated so scorers can evaluate how well a performance exhibits power in a particular dimension. For example, Vermont is interested in how well students generalize and make connections to other mathematics beyond the solution to a problem. (See the NCTM Standards, especially number 4.) They score a dimension referred to as the "so what" dimension. To score high, a performance must go beyond the solution; it must also make a valid generalization. This is true for all entries. Other dimensions used in Vermont relate to use of mathematical language, approaches to problems, and other curricular goals originating in the NCTM standards. As with holistic scoring, dimensional scoring can be applied to individual entries or across entries to the selection as a whole.

A weakness of dimensional scoring is the necessity for assuming we know the dimensionality of the performance. The move toward more realistic curricula and pedagogies calls for more realistic assessments. Much more than with artificial performance, the dimensionality of realistic performance varies interactively among individual students by context, by task, by interpretive assumptions of the student, and by personal factors (just as reality does). The same scoring dimensions applied to performances of widely varied dimensionality will produce measurement errors that correlate highly with the dimensionality of the performance. This may be unfair in gross ways to individuals or classes of individuals, if there are consequences to individuals or classes of individuals.

One strategy for addressing this weakness also adds an important strength. That strategy is to *teach students the dimensions used for scoring* prior to the performance. To the extent they learn to self-assess in the desired dimensions, their performance will be in the dimensions used in scoring. To the extent that the dimensions are central curricular insights, learning to use them will be of central curricular value. Thus, dimensional scoring with a strong self-assessment component amplifies the curricular influence of the assessment. Teachers in Vermont and Oregon are enthusiastic about the effects of teaching dimensional self-assessment to their students as early as fourth grade.

How well the central values of the curriculum can be expressed as scoring dimensions for use in self-assessment is an intellectual and empirical question on which the soundness of this approach depends. Criteria like "so what" really communicate a piece of work, a generalization in this case. Other criteria are more like the advice given to the sprinter, "run faster." While running faster certainly sums up the ultimate performance dimension, it is uninformative to the sprinter and lacks utility for self-assessment. "Work on your mechanics" is barely any better. For the self-assessment argument to hold as a rationale for dimensional scoring, the dimensions have to inform students of how they might improve performance.

The "so what" type of criterion does this because it denotes an ingredient that can be added by the student; criteria that look at the quality are more elusive for the student. This question may be answered differently in different areas of curriculum. Expressing curricular values as a small set of dimensions risks encouraging simpleminded versions of curriculum that invest too much in a few tricks that have large payoffs in the simple dimensionality of the scoring scheme. Holistic scoring represents curriculum as "tasks like these, exemplars of tasks." The meaning of "like these" is left to the various interpreters, including the student. Dimensional scoring provides a framework for interpreting the tasks in a general way, giving some definition to "like these."

Scoring Collections

Figure 2 frames possibilities for scoring a collection of student entries. The columns represent individual entries, while the rows represent aspects of performance (dimensions). The corner represents an overall score with many possible relationships to rows and columns. Aspect scores compare evidence from an exhibit of performances to criteria based on national standards: How well do the exhibits evidence problem-solving power? How well do they demonstrate the power to use multiple representations effectively?

	Entry #1	Entry #2	Entry	Entry	Entry ...#n	
Aspect A						Aspect A Score
Aspect B		Critique and Self Analysis				Aspect B Score
Aspect C			Critique and Self Analysis			Aspect C Score
Aspect ...				Critique and Self Analysis		Aspect Score
Aspect ...						Aspect Score
.	Holistic Score	Holistic Score	Holistic Score	Holistic Score	Holistic Score	Corner Score

FIGURE 2

Framework for scoring a collection of student entries.

It is possible to obtain row scores directly by having judges evaluate the collection as a whole. One suggestion for this procedure is to train judges to search for evidence like a detective, finding it wherever it happens to be located. A student could get a high Aspect B score for an impressive body of evidence distributed throughout the selections or concentrated in just one selection even though other selections lacked evidence.

Alternatively, row scores can be obtained by scoring each entry on Aspect B, and then aggregating across the row in some fashion. The disadvantage of this kind of procedure is that it enforces a stereotyped dimensionality on all entries. Unless the entries were intentionally all of the same genre (expository prose, for example), this would likely be reflected in an unwanted monotony and narrowness in the curriculum, no matter how cleverly the Aspects were formulated. The Aspects will have a broader, more satisfying meaning in rhetoric than they will in practice. The practical meanings are inevitably more mechanical and banal.

One way around this difficulty is to use a balanced list of aspects from which different subsets would be applied to different tasks. The procedures for deciding which aspects to apply to which selections raises interesting possibilities. The designers of a particular task could be asked, as part of the design, to articulate the aspects which apply. Teachers, students, and scorers would all be using the same scorecard as they played their respective roles. Yet even with a balanced list of aspects, this promotion of the scorecard to the foreground will tend to narrow the curriculum. How long would the list of aspects have to be to avoid this effect on the curriculum? As long as the NCTM standards, perhaps?

A variant of the selected aspects approach is to let the chips fall where they may; ask the judges to select aspects to apply to an entry on the basis of the evidence before them (the actual student performance). To be fair, this approach would probably have to use a "positive evidence" method. An aspect would only be triggered for application by the positive presence of evidence. The lack of evidence would not contribute to a selection score. In this variant, some determination would probably have to be made about how to interpret the lack of evidence for Aspect B, for example, across an entire row. The burden can be placed on the student and teacher to submit a balance of entries that supplies ample evidence of all aspects. With the burden of evidence so assigned, the lack of evidence across a row can be interpreted fairly as evidence of lack in performance.

Column scores can be obtained directly through holistic scoring of each entry. *Holistic scores* compare performance on an entry to the purposes of the assignment. The question is, How well did the student accomplish what he or she was asked to accomplish? This corresponds to teacher grades and report cards.

Whatever aspects relate to an entry are expressed in the prompt and criteria for holistic scoring. The holistic score can be supplemented by a small number of additional scores for aspects (often called traits, in this context). These scored aspects can be drawn from the balanced list based on the genre of the selection, or be specific to the entry.

Column scores can be obtained by aggregation of scores for each aspect applied to the entry. This amounts to an analytic procedure. It requires a great deal of presumption regarding how the aspects relate to a particular student's performance.

Cells might have no generalizable interpretation (no generalizable score) across columns, rows, or students. The relationship between an individual cell and its row, or aspect, is very unstable because for any particular selection the importance of the aspect varies widely from student to student depending on the strategy used to accomplish the task. The dimensionality of the selection is determined to an important extent by the student. The relationship between a cell and its column will be unstable because students will rely on different aspects of mathematical power for the same task. This is without even worrying about the differences among selections across students. For an individual student, however, the cells have meaning as revision tools during instruction.

The variation in dimensionality from performance to performance (inclusive of all possible dimensionalities) is too much a matter of performer choice for any performance to be realistic enough to qualify as realistic. Anything we can do to eliminate choices eliminates the possibilities for assessing the students' power to make effective choices. We are left with the anemic domain of the assessors' predetermined choices; we can only assess how well the student can guess our choices.

This partly explains why cell scores may not generalize well even within student across task. The same student may very legitimately choose different dimensionalities of response for tasks that appear to the assessors to be very similar. Indeed, students may be motivated to do so by the assessment situation itself.

Nonetheless, cells are useful analytic categories for student self-assessment and teacher critiques during instruction. For these purposes, the systematic consideration of each aspect for each piece of work raises useful issues that could lead to learning how to produce higher quality work. To raise issues for consideration is one thing; to decide fate is another. Cellular analysis is a questionable procedure for high-stakes assessments.

GENRE

Using figure 2 as the conceptual base, higher-order concepts can be used to organize assessment designs. Three of the most promising are genres, exhibits, and syndromes.

Entries (the columns) can be assigned to genres of similar selections. In writing, this has been a common and useful practice: persuasive essay, autobiographical sketch, expository essay, poem, story, descriptive report, and so forth. In California, a taxonomy of writing genres is explicit as the basis for the writing sample assessment. The taxonomy is much broader than the genres traditionally taught. A direct consequence has been the opening up of the writing curriculum to include more genres.

In mathematics, the variety in kinds of work in traditional programs is radically narrow. NCTM and others have called for a serious broadening in the kinds of assignments given to students. It may be possible to express this curricular goal as a balance of genre, although this is not yet clear. Other subjects will probably be easier than mathematics, but not as natural as writing.

Genres, or something like them, can solve a number of problems. Each genre could have genre-specific standards that derive from the purposes of the genre. The persuasive essay, for example, has persuasion as its central purpose. These purposes transcend particular prompts within the genre. There are four related advantages to this:

1. Students can learn how to perform in a genre, transferring across performances within genres; they can get better at working in a particular genre. Genre-specific assessment criteria can be powerful self-assessment tools. Students can learn from performances on different prompts within a genre. For example, students can study performances of other students on other tasks that exemplify the genre, as preparation for work on a new prompt in this genre. By developing a sense of genre, students also acquire the values of good performance in a genre.

2. Scorers can learn to score a genre. Rubrics can be constructed for a particular genre. This does not preclude task-specific rubrics within genres; indeed, it provides a common framework for constructing task-specific rubrics. A genre score can be derived from holistic task scores within a genre.

3. Genre-specific rubrics can be used by external assessment systems like New Standards, thereby allowing local variation in specific prompts within genres. This is especially important if we want to assess a considerable amount of curriculum; the alternative to local flexibility would intrude on too much instructional time.

4. In assessing cumulative accomplishments, some requirements can be made for each genre, for example, "include a selection that belongs to the genre *applied research report*" (defined elsewhere); the rubric for assessing *applied research reports* is provided along with exemplars at

several levels of performance. Suggestions and sources of suggestions for *applied research report* assignments are also given.

Most genres can be defined in ways that make sense across grade spans. Standards for performance in a genre can be independent of grade level or can be specific to grade level. If we want to build in standards for the use of mathematical representations in *applied research reports*, we would probably want to tailor them to grade level expectations.

In figure 3 the scheme presented in figure 2 has been augmented to show where genres fit in. Each genre can have associated with it a characteristic subset of dimensions, or aspects, that are particularly valued for that genre. Students can be taught these as in the Vermont example. The variation in dimensionality from response to response for a student within a genre will probably be much less if the students understand the genre.

	Genre I		Genre II			
	Selection #1	Selection #2	Selection	Selection..	Selection ...#n	
Aspect A						Aspect A Score
Aspect B		Critique and Self Analysis				Aspect B Score
Aspect C			Critique and Self Analysis			Aspect C Score
	Holistic Score		Holistic Score			Corner Score
	Genre I		Genre II			

FIGURE 3
Framework for scoring a collection of student
selections in different genres.

By varying dimensions from genre to genre, the effect of dimensional scoring on the curriculum can be greatly mitigated. "So what" from Vermont works well in the problem genre that Vermont has used, but different dimensions would work better for pure investigations. It is also possible to give more specific and meaningful definition and exemplification of a dimension for the limited range of work within a genre than across all sorts of work. There is no reason why the same dimension cannot be defined and exemplified differently in two or more different genres. For example, a dimension might be "mathematical reasoning" from the NCTM standards. In an *applied research report* the reasoning would be embedded in the application, and the constituents of argumentation would mix realistic issues with mathematical structures. In a *pure investigation* the reasoning would adhere more closely to the standards for an abstract proof. Yet, both are expressions of a common dimension: mathematical reasoning as defined in the curricular goals.

The question of how the use of a higher-order category like "genre" affects dimensional scoring needs further investigation. It seems likely, however, that a meaningful organization of genres that captures important curricular issues of breadth (across genres) while allowing for more attention to depth (within a genre) can only help stabilize the dimensionalities of performance. This will greatly improve prospects for generalizability.

EXHIBITS, ENTRIES, AND STANDARDS

The portfolio can be made more manageable and concrete for the student and for scoring if it is broken down into a small number of exhibits. An exhibit is a collection of entries put together by the student to demonstrate accomplishment of a standard or group of standards. Instructions to students on the preparation of exhibits can carry the substance of the standards in a very concrete way. Exhibits can have a clear purpose and audience.

The straightforward instructions to students for making exhibits alleviate the need for the scoring rubrics to communicate all the substance. Scoring rubrics do not communicate very well outside a scoring session; they are too abstract, with a peculiar purpose and audience.

Some exhibits consist of single entries (a major investigation); some will be a structured set of entries (for example, an exhibit of writing consisting of a set of entries of different genres, or in mathematics a set of five entries exhibiting problem solving); some will be an assemblage of parts for a common purpose (for example, a reading exhibit).

An exhibit for writing may consist of a specified set of entries (in specified genres of writing), each of which is scored as an entry according to a rubric for that genre of writing. An exhibit of problem solving could have five entries scored as a set on several dimensions (for example, on approach, analysis of the situation, formulation, execution, conclusion, generalization, communication).

An exhibit such as the reading exhibit may be scored holistically for several dimensions or aspects. In such a case, the student would include an introduction to the exhibit that addresses the dimensions across the various parts of the whole exhibit. For example, the parts could include some listing of books read with comments on some of them and an introduction that addresses range, depth, and so forth, and a piece of writing in response to literature.

PROFILES

Turning now to the rows, it is possible to construct higher-order patterns connecting dimensions or aspects. Many have suggested the use of "profiles" across aspects as interpretive devices. The intent is to preserve information and add to the utility of the assessment. Such suggestions often evoke images of diagnostic profiles. But a profile merely presents the dimensional scores as a set. The interpretive process, whether employing some form of cluster analysis or not, imposes a post hoc theoretical pattern on observed data. This can be useful, but we should not settle for it. If the theoretical patterns appear to have merit, let us put them to empirical test.

A priori patterns across assessment profiles might better be called *syndromes* than *profiles*. This term correctly suggests our obligation to connect the patterns to a consequential response.

The dimensions relate to the particular construction by a student of a response, a construction involving choices as well as knowledge and, for example, mathematical power. If students are well informed about the dimensionality by which the response will be judged, then it is fair to let the score depend on the choices. The choices become part of what is assessed and part of the curriculum. If not, it is not fair.

The dimensions also relate to the curriculum. We are assessing performance in a curriculum. Creating dimensions that express the values of a curriculum is necessary; otherwise students and teachers are led away from the curriculum toward what counts. The eternal question, "Is it going to be on the test?" exemplifies how this connection operates in report card grading. What craft and technical "know how" do teachers employ to express their own curricular values in their report-card grading schemes? How do these compare with their colleagues and national or local standards?

Since the dimensions can be standard and somewhat independent of particular tasks, especially if genre dependencies are established, the scoring can be to a standard that is not undermined by weak assignments. It would not be fair to students to give them low scores on a dimension on which they had no opportunity to perform (because of weak assignments). But it is very much to the point to give the program (classroom or school) a low score on dimensions where their students performed poorly for whatever reason.

Syndromes can be used to characterize how actual curricula in practice compare to standards-based curricula. For example, the NCTM standards make an explicit comparison identifying the shifts in emphasis from the traditional curriculum to the standards-based curriculum. From this, a traditional "syndrome" can be defined and looked for in the score patterns of schools to identify curricular opportunities to learn.

SCORING A PORTFOLIO: AN EXAMPLE

At New Standards we are field testing a hybrid of genre-specific holistic scoring and aspect scoring of portfolios. The hybrid seeks to strike a practical balance of trade-offs while emulating good curriculum in the assessment. The key design feature is structuring the portfolio into exhibits. Each exhibit is associated with a subset of the standards in the standards-based system.

The student will write exhibit introductions based on his or her self-assessment to guide the scorer to the best evidence. This is an example of how students are expected to play a responsible role in the assessment beyond being an object of assessment. Realistically, this is analogous to situations where an adult is applying for a job or standing for promotion: the adults are expected to assemble and present their best case.

Figure 4 shows how a portfolio based on New Standards will be structured in the field trial version.

Since specific directions are written for each exhibit, the portfolio is structured more than many teachers expect. It is no longer an open selection from the population of all course work. In earlier versions we maximized flexibility and breadth which resulted in maximizing generality, abstraction, and vagueness of rubrics.

By settling on a basic exhibit structure we are trading some flexibility for simplicity and concreteness of instructions. The instructions for exhibits can be straightforward. The voice is "Here is how to put together Exhibit I. . . . We, the (distant) audience of teachers from around the country, will be looking for x, y, and z."

The exhibits themselves have an explicit purpose and audience. They are wholes worthy of holistic interpretation. The instructions

I. **Exhibit of Mathematical Concepts**

Four entries, one in each area of mathematics. In each area, the student selects a single concept and exhibits the following evidence of understanding: (a) use of the concept in a realistic problem, and (b) explain concept to another student or show multiple representations of the concept. Taken together, these two parts must deploy the major representations of the concept such as numerical table, graph, diagram, formula, verbal, and chart.

Each entry is scored on conceptual understanding as explained in the instructions for the exhibit plus a scant rubric.

A.	Number	0-5
B.	Geometry	0-5
C.	Functions	0-5
D.	Data	0-5

II. **Exhibit of Problem Solving, Reasoning, and Communication**

Five entries scored on two dimensions. By means of an entry slip, a student can refer the scoring to an entry in another exhibit. It is possible to score these as a set rather than scoring each entry separately.

A.	Problem Solving and Mathematical Reasoning	0-5
B.	Communication	0-5

III. **Exhibit of Skills**

An Exhibit Introduction prepared by the student refers scoring to entries in other exhibits, probably in a simple matrix of major skills by entry. This is supplemented by the inclusion of two tests or quizzes that show deployment of selected skills in an on-demand setting.

IV. **Exhibit of Putting Mathematics to Work**

This exhibit consists of two projects. Each project will get its own score. The score will be based on the exhibit instructions and published genre-specific rubrics. These rubrics will be available to the students and teachers in advance. In their exhibit introductions, students will explain how they view their own project against the standards of the genre rubric that best fits their work. It may even be possible for a student and teacher to propose a new rubric for a new genre. The two projects are selected by the student from two groups of possible genres of projects:

Group A:
° Study with inference from data
° Decision-making report (management and planning)
° Other

Group B:
° Formulating a mathematical model of physical behavior
° Design a physical structure that achieves design objectives
° Pure mathematical investigation with justified conclusions

Each of the five genres has its own genre-specific rubric built on the genre-specific purposes, methods, and generalizations.

Group A Project	0-5
Group B Project	0-5

FIGURE 4

A mathematics portfolio based on New Standards as
structured in its field trial version

for the exhibits function as genuine prompts. This seems far less mysterious than relying on one big complicated prompt for a wide open portfolio governed mysteriously by standards that glitter too generally across all the entries.

Exhibits simplify the relationship between standards and entries by narrowing down the possibilities. Instructions for each exhibit establish a concrete basis for assembling a small body of work for the purpose of showing accomplishment with respect to specified standards to an audience of teachers (and the public) from around the country.

Opportunity to Perform

There are, of course, many factors contributing to a student's opportunity to learn. Some are more direct than others. Among the most direct and specific are those that can be appraised in portfolios of student work at classroom and school levels. A classroom sample, or school sample, of portfolios can be appraised from this standpoint.

The selection of entries as a representation of the curriculum—the range, type, and depth of assignments students are being taught to accomplish—reflects the students' opportunity to learn in a direct way. This direct evidence does not tell the whole story, but it can contribute a necessary piece of the puzzle in the actual work of students. It is possible to obtain an opportunity-to-perform profile from portfolio scoring.

First, an appraiser can readily determine the breadth of assignments included in the portfolios. Are the genres that the curriculum calls for well represented in each student's portfolio? Are some groups of students working in a good balance of genres, while other groups are working in a constricted set (low-order skills, for example)? What is the pattern of performance across dimensions? Is one or another syndrome of ill-balanced curriculum in evidence for all or some groups of students?

Such appraisals can probably be made for programs quite readily and reliably. Indeed, these judgments have proved to be easier than the judgments about students. Their performances are contingent upon opportunity to perform. When, as in a portfolio, performance is embedded in the curriculum over a substantial time sample, then opportunity to perform converges on opportunity to learn. Students with narrow opportunities to perform can still score well on tasks they did perform, but their scores on dimensions or aspects will be low. Scores on some genres are also likely to be low, since some genres are probably going to be missing or superficially represented.

The interpretation created in reporting such results must, in fairness to the students, make clear that the students did well what they were asked to do. What they were asked to do, however, lacked balance in specific ways and therefore scores for some dimensions and genres are low. The consequences of the assessments can be more validly aimed in this way. It is one thing if students do not do well what they have been asked; it is another if they have not been asked to do it. Whoever manages the curricular priorities is responsible for the balance of genres and dimensions.

The quality of instruction that prepares students for their assignments is another matter. The distribution of selections across genres, and the fullness of their dimensionality can be appraised somewhat independently of the quality of performance. But the distribution of performance scores must be considered in order to support any inferences about the quality of instruction. These are dangerous inferences. Many persons in addition to the student are responsible for the quality of performances.

Difficulty

A closely related issue is the difficulty of the challenge inherent in the selections. Variation in the difficulty of the challenge from student to student, class to class, and school to school can cast doubt on the fairness of comparing scores. One problem here is the multidimensional nature of "difficulty." Some sources of difficulty are valid (they are what we want to measure) while others are invalid. If some dimensions of difficulty are valid but overrepresented across tasks in assessment, we can get weighting bias. For example, the "reading" challenge of word problems in mathematics can exceed the mathematical difficulty. Across a set of problems where the mathematics ranges over the scope of the curriculum but the reading is consistently difficult, we may not be measuring much mathematics but instead a narrow type of reading. This produces especially undesirable biases when some students find the reading transparent and therefore can exhibit their knowledge of mathematics, while other students find the reading opaque and cannot exhibit their mathematical knowledge.

A second concern arises from interaction effects between some dimensions of difficulty and student characteristics other than what we are trying to measure, for example, interaction of cultural or socioeconomic background with the contexts of performance. Interactions of personality or temperament with the circumstances of performance constitute another troublesome matter. Students react differently to high-pressure timed tests, for example. If we are trying to measure mathematics learning, a pervasive time effect can overwhelm the domain of primary interest differentially among students. It can penalize thoughtful workers and reward people good at shooting from the hip.

It would be convenient to employ normative methods for determining difficulty; but I do not think the inferences that can be drawn from normatively established scales of difficulty have consequential validity in the situations for which external assessors are primarily responsible: accountability, formative and summative evaluations. Normative methods inherently confound the loci of responsibility and consequence by ignoring the *differences in cause* of task difficulty.

Effects due to student abilities are confounded with student effort, and these with opportunity to learn, and these with every other input variable for which someone should be responsible. Normative methods, in general, have ill effects on systemic and consequential validity. Both validities are grounded in responsibilities. Who is responsible for causing the condition being assessed, and what are they going to do about the assessed condition in consequence?

Normative methods, by confounding causes (of difficulty, for example), insulate those with the power to cause from attribution, and thus from responsibility. Under these circumstances, the negative consequences tend to settle to the lowest academic levels: the student and his or her "background" (Can we disown our backgrounds? Should we? What is that part of me that is not related to my background?) Positive consequences tend to be shared by all levels. We need methods that distinguish opportunity and accomplishment from background and ability. Assessments heavily influenced by components for which no one can be responsible have little legitimate use as accountability tools at any level. Intentionally or not, such instruments have the effect of covering up responsibility and breeding a quasi-factual basis for fatalistic attitudes toward the effects of education. This is a sad irony, given that a deep purpose of education is precisely to overcome the hopeless fatalism of stagnant social orders of inherited opportunities.

Is the source of difficulty the quantity or quality of opportunity to learn? Is it inherent in what is being assessed (understanding of a difficult concept)? Is it inherent in the design of the task (difficult problem but requiring ordinary mathematics)? Is it cultural interference between the background of the student and the background of the task? Is it in the circumstances surrounding the performance (easy task but not enough time)? By confounding these and other sources of difficulty, normative methods invalidate distinctions needed to identify responsibility and take action to improve future performance. We certainly need to distinguish opportunity to learn from conceptual difficulty, for example.

Such distinctions are particularly critical for students, teachers, and local leaders trying to bring about improvements. Assessments that cover up these distinctions can and often do bolster existing beliefs and prejudices about who and what is responsible. We need assessments that highlight the causes of performance that can be influenced by the student, teacher, curriculum, school structure, or community.

Problems relating to difficulty can be lessened by communicating the appropriate level and character of the challenge to the students and those making the assignments. One way to do this is through standard tasks, or standard exemplars of tasks along with commentary. It would be even better, along with standard exemplars, to set up a system whereby students can query a reliable authority on assessing challenge difficulty regarding a task of interest. Such feedback can have a strong moderating effect on the volatility of standards in the system.

Clearly, the best resource to develop into such an authoritative feedback system is the community of teachers and students. If they can give reliable feedback to each other across classes and schools and states, the comparability problems arising from student and teacher selection of entries are much less. Even when they make bad selections, it is, to a great extent, their right and responsibility.

Students and teachers need a *curricular* basis for evaluating difficulty. We need tools for the appraisal of challenge that allow for situations where most students succeed at something appraised to be very difficult (per the curriculum), and also where most students fail at something very easy, but rarely taught.

Everyday reasoning recognizes this common situation: It is difficult to run five miles, but everyone in our school worked hard all year and everyone did it. It is easy to pick up wrappers and other litter, but the kids in this school just don't care and hardly anyone does it; the hallways are a mess every afternoon. In the case of running five miles, the students worked for and achieved a standard. In the littering case, the school operates on low standards.

Grades and Report Cards

The United States has long had high-stakes assessment for individual students' grades and report cards. A student's future opportunities are profoundly affected by report cards, even in the primary grades. The validity of these assessments for their consequences to the students has never been properly evaluated. Worse, serious efforts to improve the validity and reliability of such assessments are rare and local. The professional community has taken little responsibility for the technical quality of the practice of its members in this fateful area. Individual teachers have had nowhere to turn for guidance and standards; they have been left on their own.

From a systems standpoint, grades are of almost no use above the individual level for assessing performance at classroom, school, or higher levels. Even if the problems of comparability could be solved, a system that delegates everything to individuals who have a direct interest in the outcomes would have no credibility. Past practice delegates virtually everything to individual teachers: setting standards, scoring procedures, designing assessment instruments, scoring performances, due process, complaints, proctoring, auditing, and recording. The interaction between new assessment systems and grading practices has the potential to alter profoundly the role of the professional community in its relationships with the public.

Developments in holistic scoring, especially widespread teacher participation in moderated scoring sessions, can have a revolutionary impact on the quality of assessment for grades and report cards. Since grades and report cards are the operational expression of the value system of the teacher and school, reforms can directly transform the value system, and with it the culture.

If standards are to have any real consequence, it will have to be through the engagement of teachers in a professional community holding each other to a mutually accountable standard. They can only hold each other to standards they understand in terms of their own students' work. Thus, deliberating upon their students' work with colleagues in open but moderated scoring discussions will be needed to make standards a reality for teachers and thereby for students.

CHAPTER XIII

The Evolution of College Entrance Examinations

DONALD M. STEWART AND MICHAEL JOHANEK

Over the last 150 years, one of the hallmarks of American education has been the testing of increasingly large groups of people through processes of growing sophistication made possible by continuing advances in the technology of information processing. Much of this testing has been largely external to the instructional process, driven by the interests of policymakers and governments, especially vis-à-vis grades K-12, and has served various ends. A report of the Office of Technology Assessment to Congress, exploring the general history of educational testing in the United States, noted that:

- Since their first administration 150 years ago, tests have been used to assess student learning, hold schools accountable, and allocate educational opportunities to students.
- Continuous advances in design, innovation, and scoring technologies have helped make group-administered testing of large numbers of students more efficient, more reliable, and less expensive.
- Standardized tests, including college admissions tests, were perceived as instruments of school reform, and as a prod for student learning.
- Although generally viewed as instruments of fairness and scientific rigor, some educators believe that admissions tests may have exceeded the limits of their design, and more important, no longer reflect either the best thinking about how the mind works or the evolving normative goals for the inclusion of all students in the educational process.[1]

One of the dynamic changes currently occurring is that educators are trying to reclaim and reshape educational assessment, including admissions testing, to serve purposes of teaching and learning as well as monitoring and accountability. One outcome of the change in the way tests are viewed is that "performance-based" or so-called "authentic" assessment—examined in various ways by other authors in this

Donald M. Stewart is President of the College Board. Michael Johanek is a Research Associate and Special Advisor to the President at the College Board.

volume—is being proposed as the basis for a new wave of admissions testing. Performance-based tests may include writing samples, extended constructed response items, portfolios of student work, exhibitions, simulations, and interviews as means of supplementing traditional testing methods. The College Board's efforts along these lines, evident in its evolving Pacesetter initiative described below, illustrate the promise that performance assessment offers in the pursuit of educational reform. Future technological breakthroughs offer further exciting opportunities, and their possible directions for admissions testing are outlined in this chapter as well.

But innovations in assessment formats, as even their most fervent advocates will testify, do not in themselves answer the more fundamental questions of the ends of education, of the normative values we wish these assessments to serve. Whatever system of assessment we use, it will reflect the fact that education is not random. It is animated by desired processes and it proceeds toward defined ends and values. One such fundamental value of the College Board, as evident in its EQUITY 2000 initiative described in this chapter, was expressed by a distinguished director (and philosopher) of college admissions, B. Alden Thresher some twenty-five years ago: "To a much greater degree than anyone realized, talent is not something stumbled upon and found here and there; it is an artifact . . . [and] it can be produced."[2] An underlying supposition of this chapter is that talent can be produced, *all* children *can* learn, irrespective of their backgrounds, socioeconomic situations, race, or gender. As a result, the primary goal of education, which testing must support, is educational equity for all students, the right of every student to receive the same high quality education that previously has been reserved for only the top quarter of the population.

In order for that to happen, we must confront the wider set of forces that shape both the design and the uses of assessment instruments. It is here that history can offer us some limited though critical counsel, to which we will turn later in this chapter. We may be well advised to hear the optimism of a past reformer of testing, Professor Edward L. Thorndike of Teachers College, Columbia University, writing in 1923 in the 21st Yearbook of the National Society for the Study of Education. After dismissing concerns that the new science of educational measurement would simply encourage students to work for grades and hinder good teaching, Thorndike addressed a final concern:

It will be said that . . . the finer consequences for the spirit of man will be lost in proportion as we try to measure them, and that the university will become a

scholarship factory, turning out lawyers and doctors guaranteed to give satisfaction, but devoid of culture. . . . [T]he fear is groundless, based on a radically
false psychology. . . . Of science and measurement in education as elsewhere,
we may safely accept the direct and practical benefits with no risk to idealism.[3]

We are not sure we share such optimism today. The broad experience of the College Board with the many facets of the transition from
high school to postsecondary schooling provides it with both the
enthusiasm to pursue the promise of performance assessment and the
larger realization that any component of reform must directly address
the wider context that will likely shape the values it ends up serving.

In this chapter we first examine the current state of the art of testing in light of the call for educational reform and then examine new
initiatives being taken at the Board through an integration of assessment and teaching. Second, we peek into the future where technology
provides startling possibilities for assessment to enhance individual
learning and personal productivity. Finally, the essay addresses the
counsel of the Board's own history and lays out several of the key
themes that have dominated the last century of admissions testing in
the United States.

The Current State of the Art

For the past five years, some political thinkers have noted that
what civil rights began at mid-century, economic forces will attempt
to complete as we enter the 21st century, namely, the full educational
preparation, and economic "mainstreaming," of members of all ethnic
and racial groups. In addition to being the right thing to do morally,
in their view, it is also unquestionably the necessary thing to do if we
are to have a society that can sustain a high quality of life for all and
remain competitive in the world economy.

Moreover, the agendas of the Clinton administration, of several
governors, and of some policymakers have called for voluntary,
national educational standards with the integration of policies and programs around those standards. Within this context, the use of assessment will take on multiple purposes: to help inform instruction, to
provide data on the success of schools and systems, and to refine the
delivery of education in order to help all students meet those goals. As
part of this effort, the battle will be joined between (a) those teachers,
administrators, and others who feel constrained by tests that do not
help them reach educational goals directly and (b) other educators and

leading educational measurement experts who emphasize that quality standardized tests are useful tools in gauging the strength, weakness, and progress of American students.

The College Board has been involved in this debate for well over a decade. A long-term decline in the average SAT scores, which began in the 1960s and was recognized and studied in the 1970s by the Wirtz Commission,[4] was also cited by the U.S. Secretary of Education, Terrell Bell, in his 1983 report as one of several indictors that we had become (as the report was entitled) *A Nation At Risk*.[5] (Unfortunately, the neglect of educational and social needs generally can be seen in the gyrations of the economy as well as in disastrous social upheavals from Los Angeles to Crown Heights.) From one point of view, the comparability of the SAT over time—the possibility of comparing levels of learned, precollegiate verbal and mathematical abilities among a key group of students over different years—has provided moderation of the sad practice of grade inflation in high school and has given an indication of the decline in the level of preparation of students for college. It is significant that in the mushrooming of "developmental courses," much of American higher education today resembles the community college sector of two decades ago.

We must, however, go beyond mere measurement of our changing levels of ability, and devise programs to improve them. Also in the early 1980s, as part of its groundbreaking work in determining, through national consensus among educators, what students need to know and be able to do in order to go to college, the College Board canvassed business leaders about their requirements for entry-level workers. They, in turn, told the College Board that the basic precollegiate skills are also those needed for entry directly into the workforce. (This work culminated in the *Academic Preparation for College Series*, a set of six booklets describing the knowledge and skills needed by all college entrants in the basic academic subjects.) As jobs have become more sophisticated, the ability to think independently, work collaboratively, and communicate effectively, as well as the achievement of collegiate levels in mathematics and verbal abilities, is becoming widely recognized as requisite for entering the twenty-first century workforce as well as postsecondary education.

The consequence of this is that an educational system based on tracking by presumed ability levels in the early grades, followed by the filtering out of the top third of the students for postsecondary study, must give way to a new philosophy. This new philosophy, this new normative view, of what we want education to do, asserts that all students have ability, all students have the right to a quality education, assessment must inform and support instruction, and college entrance examinations must both reflect and reinforce this new philosophy. Therefore, voluntary national education standards must be defined and appropriate assessment instruments identified or developed to measure the progress of students and schools in meeting these standards.

New Initiatives by the College Board

Had the College Board developed new forms of assessment in the 1980s to match the work done in the *Academic Preparation for College Series*, the nation would have had a good jump on the kind of assessment now being called for. Responding to social and political change, as well as to the specific mandate of its trustees, the Board in the 1990s is moving to answer these needs. Current cognitive theory and curriculum reform are built on the view that learning is constructive and interpretive and that learning increases when knowledge is reconfigured and facts and skills are interpreted in relevant contexts. As a result, assessment is changing to reflect how students think, perform, and learn from instruction.

These developments in cognitive theory and curriculum reform illustrate that our understanding of how people think is fundamental to education and to assessment. Responsive to these changes, the new College Board initiatives comprise the revising of the SAT to reflect curricular trends and to include "performance-based" elements; expanding the use of Advanced Placement courses and assessment to enrich the high school experience among poor and minority students; and the creation of three major programs of precollegiate preparation and assessment—the "new" SAT, EQUITY 2000, and Pacesetter. These programs, starting as early as the middle schools, are designed to end the pernicious practice of tracking and to promote significant and systemic school reform, in order to insure that all students are ready for college whether they choose to continue their studies immediately after high school or enter the workforce directly. It is impossible to understand the Board's larger philosophy about the transition from high school to college, and thus the role and evolution of entrance examinations, without taking these new programs into consideration.

THE REVISED SAT

The "new" SAT, introduced in 1993/94, reflects technical and philosophical changes as well as what students experience in today's classrooms. SAT-I: Reasoning Tests requires the familiar three hours of testing time, with some significant changes. In the verbal section, antonyms no longer appear. In their place are more reading passages that reflect both what colleges expect of students and current instructional theory, focusing on the student's ability to read critically. Thus, approximately half of the questions are based on longer, more engaging passages to be read and include a pair of passages on the same or related topics, one of which opposes, supports, or in some way complements the point of view of the other. Even with vocabulary questions, the emphasis is on testing students' verbal reasoning skills and knowledge in context.

Similarly, on the mathematics sections of the SAT-I Reasoning Test the focus is on problem-solving skills important for success in college, and there is an increased emphasis on a student's ability to apply concepts and interpret data. In addition, for the first time, there are questions that require students to supply their own answers instead of selecting one from multiple-choice alternatives, and students are advised to bring a calculator.

The SAT II: Subject Tests, still known as the Achievement Tests, reflect important new directions and give students an opportunity to show their academic strengths in a wide variety of subject areas including writing, literature, foreign languages, history, mathematics, and sciences. New tests in Japanese and Chinese include a listening component. A Korean Achievement Test is also being created. Tests with listening components, including new offerings in French, Spanish, and German, are administered in secondary schools, not in test centers. Although not officially launched until 1994, some changes were introduced earlier and the introduction of new elements in the SAT II test will continue throughout the decade.

The new Writing Test includes a direct writing sample and questions that require recognition of the conventions of standard written English, as well as effective and logical expression. Among the advantages of the test are:

• an essay providing a direct measure of writing ability while not assuming any specific subject-matter knowledge;

• revision-in-context passages that present a context larger than a discrete sentence and therefore permit questions on logic, coherence, and organization which are similar to common in-class exercises in which students revise their own essays; and

• usage questions requiring students to recognize errors, and sentence-correction questions requiring recognition of errors and selection of the correct rephrasings.

It should be noted that, despite the inclusion of the word "aptitude" in its original name, experience over the last seven decades has shown that scores on the SAT reflect learned abilities rather than some inborn, immutable level of intelligence. Accordingly, the SAT is now called the Scholastic Assessment Test. This confirms Thresher's opinion that "talent can be produced" and that student abilities are a function of work done by the individual. Interestingly, as several observers have noted, schooling also appears to raise general developed cognitive ability as measured by tests of what was thought to be an inherent quality (intelligence) as well as by so-called aptitude tests. Thanks in part to the rise in educational attainment throughout the United States, the average IQ has been rising for much of the twentieth century, a phenomenon found in other nations across the globe.

Similarly, there is a strong relationship between academic preparation and achievement on the one hand and mean SAT scores on the other. Over the past decade, the College Board has reported a consistent pattern: the more years of academic study and the higher the grades and rank-in-class achieved, the higher the SAT score. In 1994, for example, students who reported taking physics in high school had average SAT verbal scores of 463 and average mathematics scores of 538, considerably *above* the national average for each. (Students who took calculus in high school had the highest average in mathematics, 598, *and* the highest SAT verbal average, 501.) By contrast, students who had taken mathematics courses other than those in the traditional college preparatory sequence had SAT scores 23 points *lower* than the national average on the verbal section and 31 points lower on the mathematics section. This clearly contradicts the assertion of some critics that the SAT is unrelated to course work and thus is an unfair or inappropriate measure of student abilities. On the contrary, the clear statistical evidence is that the more and better courses students take, the better, on average, they are likely to do on the SAT as well. (Since, by and large, certain minority students are still being tracked out of academic courses in the early grades, it is not surprising that as a group, many minorities do not do as well on the SAT. The issue is one of "savage" lack of equity in schooling, not discrimination by the test against one minority group or another.)

Admissions testing is just one step in a continuum of awareness, learning, and preparation that begins well before entrance to college. If all students are to reach new high standards at graduation from high school, efforts toward higher standards of preparation in earlier years (middle school and early high school) will also be required. The College Board has been concerned about the extent to which mathematics has become a filter of students in the nation's high schools. Those who take algebra and geometry have the option not only of higher mathematics, but of academically rigorous fields of study in college preparatory courses across the curriculum which are closed to students who do not take those key math courses. Thus, we started a project called EQUITY 2000.

EQUITY 2000

EQUITY 2000 is a national school reform initiative designed to achieve the following ambitious goal: By the end of the twentieth century, minority and disadvantaged students will enroll in and complete college at the same rate as majority students.

Three elements underlie this initiative. First, the program ensures that *every student* in the participating school districts completes algebra and geometry, the "gatekeeper" courses that are prerequisites to preparation for college. Experience and research indicate that students who enroll in college preparatory mathematics courses are likely to enroll in college preparatory courses in all subjects. According to a study by Pelavin and Kane, high school students who took one year or more of algebra were two to three and a half times as likely to attend college as students who did not take algebra.[6] Students taking geometry and algebra are between three and five times as likely to attend college as those who have not taken either.

Second, EQUITY 2000 involves teachers, parents, counselors, principals, and others in the educational community to create an ethic of educational excellence within entire school districts.

Third, the program uses a variety of activities to enrich students' academic experiences, particularly in mathematics, and to build aspirations toward a college degree.

The program represents the College Board's commitment to districtwide (K-12) systemic change in school districts, and is being implemented in fourteen districts through six EQUITY 2000 sites around the country. The model includes the elimination of tracking—a policy that leads too many students to an academic dead end—and also includes rethinking the way to handle heterogeneous mathematics classes. With students having widely varying backgrounds and experiences in mathematics, heterogeneous classes require that teachers approach mathematics instruction in a manner that enables every student to achieve his or her fullest potential.

EQUITY 2000, for the first time, executes a full complement of precollege initiatives within entire school districts so as to reach every student. Four major components comprise the EQUITY program: in-service training for teachers and administrators; academic enrichment for students; parental and family involvement; and community involvement and support.

In-service training for teachers and administrators. Teachers, counselors, and principals are all crucial to changing educators' expectations of students' success. At summer and academic year institutes, mathematics teachers strengthen their knowledge of mathematics and enhance their ability to teach effectively in heterogeneous classes. Guidance counselors focus on strategies for building students' aspirations to pursue a college degree, including advising students to enroll in college preparatory classes, involving parents in students' academic development, and disseminating information about college options and costs to *all* students. Principals focus on creating a wholly supportive academic environment in their schools for all students, including the creation of teacher-counselor teams that meet the needs of individual students. Far exceeding our expectations, more than 2400 teachers, counselors, and principals participated in the 1994 summer institutes and workshops.

Academic enrichment for students. Because academic tracking has been so pervasive and has denied the opportunity of algebra and geometry to so many students, schools have an obligation to offer them academic enrichment activities to ensure that they participate in the courses on a "level playing field." These activities, aimed at raising both skills and expectations, include:

• Summer Scholars Programs. Taught by teams consisting of a college or university professor and a master teacher from the local school system, these programs are designed to support regular academic course work every day for five weeks during the summer;

• Saturday Academies. Six Saturday sessions are similarly team taught and give attention to skill-building across many disciplines; parents accompany their sons and daughters to class and work with them on specific academic exercises;

• Academic Enrichment Laboratories. Capitalizing on the impact those nearest to the students' age group can have, these laboratories use college and university students as role models for middle and high school students.

Parental and family involvement. Family involvement is critical. Two specific activities in EQUITY 2000 are (a) family mathematics workshops and other activities in which parents participate jointly with their sons and daughters in academic work and college planning; and (b) Career/Resource Centers at each school, through which information on college and career options is disseminated.

Community involvement and support. Each site has established formal partnerships with institutions of higher education and with community organizations to support and participate in EQUITY 2000 program activities, such as the team teaching at all Saturday Academies held on local college/university campuses.

The summer institutes and follow-up workshops for mathematics teachers do not occur in isolation; a serious commitment to both equity and excellence would not allow it. Rather, they are key components of a comprehensive educational reform initiative that includes a variety of interventions leading to districtwide (K-12) systemic reform. The program is being thoroughly evaluated by an independent research group, and the College Board intends to disseminate the model broadly to school districts across the country using its vast network of resources.

PACESETTER COURSES

From the creation of the SAT in 1926, which made it possible to identify a significantly larger pool of qualified candidates for college, to the subsequent use of the SAT to attract a considerably larger number of minority students to higher education, to EQUITY 2000, whose goal is to put all students on a full academic track, the College Board has contributed to an increased democratization of education in America. In this same spirit, another new effort of the College Board—the Pacesetter courses—is directed at helping schools implement higher standards by providing new course syllabi and assessments for high school courses in key subject areas, through which teachers can learn to teach to higher standards as well. These courses are being designed so that schools that wish to raise their standards will have course materials, assistance with preparation of teachers, and assessments to help them achieve that goal. In most cases, Pacesetter courses will embody the top level of the high school curriculum. By contrast, Advanced Placement courses, for which Pacesetter will prepare students, are essentially college-level courses given in high school to those students ready to take them.

Based on high standards, Pacesetter initiatives take as their starting point the development of detailed substantive course frameworks each of which specifies the structure and content of what should be taught and learned in a key course of study. Pacesetter will offer professional development activities so that teachers will be able effectively to instruct all students, as well as activities in the classroom that allow students to translate concepts into hands-on situations, and teachers to evaluate students' skills and understanding, thereby informing instruction. There will also be end-of-course assessments to measure student attainment of course objectives.

Pacesetter courses in mathematics, English, and Spanish are currently in field tests; subsequently we intend to complete development of world history and science courses. Each of these Pacesetter courses is being developed through task forces in collaboration with the major national discipline associations—the National Council of Teachers of Mathematics and the Mathematical Association of America; the National Council of Teachers of English; the American Council of Learned Societies and the National Council for the Social Studies; the National Science Teachers Association, and the American Council on the Teaching of Foreign Languages.

As we move forward with the process of educational reform, we must keep in mind the distinction between assessment for instructional purposes as opposed to accountability purposes. Pacesetter draws on two kinds of assessment: classroom (formative) and end-of-course (summative). Assessment of both kinds will include performance-based tasks, essays, projects, case histories, portfolios, and multiple-choice questions. The assessments embedded in instruction will be used for a variety of purposes—to help students and teachers evaluate the students' progress and to plan future instruction; to evaluate activities that occur over time, such as projects and portfolios; and to strengthen the teachers' role as an effective and supportive facilitator and mentor.

By contrast with the in-course formative assessments, the Pacesetter Culminating (or summative) Assessments provide a key input to an overall certification that student learning has met the high standards of the Pacesetter course. The overall purpose of these end-of-course assessments is to evaluate students in terms of public standards, and validate student accomplishments. In addition, they will evaluate both classes and schools in terms of their having achieved standards, provide information to school districts on progress in instructional approaches, and finally, provide employers and colleges with a range of information about students that may be useful for decision-making purposes.

More specifically, we envision each of the Pacesetter Culminating Assessments as being two to three hours in length and including the following (or more) types of activities:

• a complex task for which students prepare themselves in advance to demonstrate their abilities to apply concepts and skills to real-world problems;

• an extended task which includes a number of short-answer questions, problems, or subtasks to draw the student toward a larger task; and

• an integrative task which requires the student to integrate ideas and concepts learned in the course and provide a brief reflection on the integrating process.

Thus the Culminating Assessment would call for (1) application or evaluation in the context of a prepared task; (2) analysis, problem solving, or problem construction in the context of a guided task; and (3) integrating and reflecting on a task that requires a student to draw freely on course content and his or her own strengths and interests. This assessment might include multiple-choice and short-answer questions needed for the purposes of standardization and comparability.

EQUITY 2000 and Pacesetter represent a push-pull strategy. In EQUITY 2000, we are helping schools to "push" students, particularly minority and poor students, into more demanding preparation for high school and college. With Pacesetter we are providing a concrete pull toward a goal of high standards of achievement for all students. We believe these two efforts together can be a major start in helping schools implement higher standards in programs where no student is left behind.

As exciting as these innovations are, we must remain circumspect. After studying initiatives like the alternative assessment system being pioneered in Vermont, a growing number of researchers are sounding cautious about the use and the cost of performance-based assessment. The nature of the tasks, inequalities surrounding the opportunity to learn the requisite skills, and the unreliability of scoring procedures all appear to present potential for disadvantaging minority students and offer serious challenges. Recent Rand Corporation reports found that the reliabilities of the portfolio and performance-based assessment among Vermont fourth and eighth graders in both mathematics and writing were quite low, although positive with regard to the professional development of teachers.[7] Researchers in other situations have found problems with regard to mathematics in insuring reliable scores caused, in part, by the prohibitively large number of tasks a student needs to perform in order to get reliable estimates of his or her performance. It is, of course, wonderful to believe that we have a new system that will solve all our old chronic problems. But it would be foolish to embrace what, in fact, is not yet fully substantiated. As researchers Dunbar, Koretz, and Hoover put it: "Quality control in terms of both evidence and consequences of (performance assessments) is not a question of faith, but an empirical matter when measurement is intended to inform public policy."[8] Decisions, therefore, about the kinds of assessment to use in the future might be based not only on an accurate analysis of current forms of assessment, but also on a complete and well-documented evaluation of the proposed options.

The initiatives described above have been inspired by new cognitive theories and are being developed using current technologies in testing. Yet, perhaps the greatest potential for creating assessments that truly empower students and support the process of learning will come from future advances in technology and psychometrics.

Technological Advances in Assessment: A Challenge to the Future of Assessment

As we look to the year 2000, we find ourselves on the verge of a revolution in educational testing and assessment. A number of forces, some societal and others technological, are the engines of change, compelling us to look carefully at how and why we test in our schools and colleges.

Currently in its embryonic state, new test theory promises to influence and shape the practice of educational assessment and make possible a host of new educational measurements. In addition to continuing to capitalize on the advantages of multiple-choice-type items, future assessments will include, among other things, extended responses constructed by students, portfolios, and simulations of scientific experiments and modeling. As is true of well-constructed multiple-choice questions, these new kinds of assessment will require higher-order problem solving and critical reasoning. Therefore, college entrance testing programs, such as the SAT, undoubtedly will continue to undergo dramatic redesign in the twenty-first century.

The revolution in the cognitive sciences beginning in the 1950s and 1960s, for example, has brought us a new view of learning. No longer do we view students as passive learners and teachers as "talking heads." Today's notions include the learner as an information processor, the teacher as a facilitator of learning and not merely an expert dispenser of facts and prescriptions. Technologies emerging from the field of artificial intelligence are now beginning to adopt many of the advances in cognitive theory. Not only are we witnessing the development of computer systems that "understand" spoken language, programs that mimic "experts" and "novices" in particular fields or specialty areas but also systems that "learn" from experience and data. Many believe that in the not too distant future testing will permit us to assess not only traditional forms of knowledge, such as the acquisition of facts and analytic abilities, but the very nature of the learner's "mental models," i.e., how he or she views a complex system of concepts and rules. More important, these new assessments will help us design and deliver instruction that serves to correct the inaccuracies and incongruities in those mental models. Although we must be vigilant that new technologies do not exacerbate the differences in opportunities that exist currently among different groups in our society, smarter testing technologies, assessments that adapt to the examinee and provide enriched diagnostic information, will offer the opportunity to tap new dimensions of developed ability. This new assessment paradigm, one that includes intelligent testing technologies, will foster a fundamental change in the nature and uses of educational tests and assessments.

New forms of assessment, such as adaptive testing, portfolios, and other types of performance assessment, will continue to be developed to measure both individual achievement and the effectiveness of local educational reforms. Currently, many states and school districts are placing an increased emphasis on performance assessment as a means of supplementing their traditional testing programs. As students, teachers, parents, and educators gain more familiarity with these methods, and as the test theory and psychometric methods needed to ensure quality and fairness are advanced and developed, this trend in educational assessment will continue to develop if issues of cost and feasibility can be resolved.

The most likely development is the powerful combination of advances in computer technology with respect both to hardware and software, and progress in test theory, that will lead to a widespread increase in the availability of different kinds of tests. Just as increasing access to higher education since World War II accomplished a democratization in education, these new tests will accomplish a democratization of assessment. Changes of this sort will place the information derived from educational assessments more directly into the hands of students, teachers, administrators, and policymakers, and enhance the instructional relevance and desirability of individually administered tests. Current projects to increase the uses of computer technology, including the development and construction of powerful national, and ultimately global, computer networks, as well as an abundance of more powerful and affordable personal computers suggest that computer-based testing products and related services will grow exponentially in the next decade and beyond.

With its long history of sensitivity to the needs of test takers and test users, the College Board is moving actively in the direction of increasing the role of computer-based technology in its testing programs. These new directions and initiatives are captured by the Board's project tentatively called *Transition 2000*. Our blueprint for future assessment will move beyond paper and pencil tests and operate on a common or linked delivery system. Much like the electronic databases commonly used today, students and their families will be able to create, maintain, and access computer-based academic portfolios which will include transcripts, applications, and assessment information. Ease of access and encrypted file transfer will make transmission of all or parts of a student's academic record to colleges, universities, and other institutions of higher education easier for both students and school administrators. The burdensome paperwork, long delays, and the attendant uncertainty of applying to college will be a thing of the past.

The range of potential enhancements in the assessment include:

• the use of adaptive testing to reduce students' frustration with too easy or too difficult tests;

• the widespread use of performance-based assessments, like portfolios, simulations, and extended response formats;

• closer links between measures of reasoning ability and academic achievement;

• the introduction of new measures of affect and of cognitive abilities (motivation, practical intelligence, and learning abilities);

• an increase in the diagnostic information available to students, parents, and teachers to aid in guidance and instruction.

The long-range success of the *Transition 2000* project depends on finding effective ways to deliver these new services to all students. Thus, we will be exploring the role that can be played by high schools, community-based computer centers, colleges, and private businesses.

There is no doubt that in the future microcomputing technologies will permeate the school environment. As already envisioned and piloted by producers of hardware and software, master classrooms complete with multimedia tech-desks and liquid crystal displays will become the teaching tools of a new generation of teachers and the learning environments of our grandchildren. Students will take notes using electronic organizers, personal computer assistants, and other forms of microchip "techno-tools," many of which have yet to be designed.

Intelligent assessments like the SAT will include multimedia presentations, brilliant color palettes, lively animation, and 3-D graphics that will bring simulations and other forms of dynamic, interactive testing to life and help make assessment more authentic. Test formats that include choosing from among an array of options using pull-down menus and windows, conceptually similar to multiple-choice tests of today, will be used to gauge academic abilities accurately and fairly. After taking the next generation of "smart" tests and using the electronically linked guidance software, students and adults will have a clear idea about levels of achievement and what they need to do to gain admission to college and to succeed there. Testing in a high-tech educational setting will be radically different from what we have in American schools now. In the future, the SAT may well be available on demand at the local high school's computer laboratory or at a learning center or public library.

In sum, the "black box" of testing technology, formerly controlled by remote "experts," will be opened for full participation and extended use. As a result, democratization of assessment can be expected to expand well beyond its current scope. Drop-in, on-demand testing will be the norm everywhere. With test scores in hand and detailed information about their proficiencies in specific skills and academic subjects, students will leave the testing situation with the intellectual capital of self-knowledge. They will be armed with the information to make meaningful choices in the near term, choices that will help secure access to higher education in the future.

Tests and other educational assessments—heretofore only seen and appreciated by a handful of scientists and educators—will be seen as fair, user friendly educational tools, an array of powerful instruments for self-transformation and educational change.

Lessons from a Century of Testing

The latter part of the twentieth century is witnessing an explosive growth in testing in an effort both to stimulate educational reform and to capture its successes. With the current emphasis on national education standards and the advent of widespread computer-based testing, the evolution of educational assessment will undoubtedly continue well into the next century.

For many—students, teachers, and parents, as well as testmakers and psychometricians—this ongoing evolution is a welcome development based as it is on advances in cognitive theory and psychometrics. In the future, we can expect to know more about how humans learn and what schools can do to foster learning. To keep pace, the science of educational measurement will push test design and construction into new and, we hope, more productive directions. So-called "smart" computerized testing technologies may help further the ongoing democratization of the educational process.

Over its 93-year history, the College Board has worked with countless changes in testing. From this experience, it may be useful to ask how assessment changes have fit into the wider web of forces in which schools are embedded. A glance backward may help us to move forward, and to do so with a refined view of the complex forces shaping educational outcomes, including those forces shaping the ends served by assessments.

The College Entrance Examination Board was brought into being on the campus of Columbia University in 1900 under the tutelage of Harvard president Charles Eliot and with the leadership of Columbia's president-to-be, Nicholas Murray Butler. The goal was to resolve what was then called "educational anarchy" caused by the fact that each postsecondary institution had its own admission procedures at a time when the number of public high school graduates had more than quadrupled over the previous two decades. A common examination, cogently advocated by President Eliot as early as 1890, was the solution agreed upon by the small group of forward-looking representatives of schools and colleges who founded the Board. Originally, this examination was a series of what we would today call performance-based tests. The "College Boards," as they soon came to be called, were subject-matter essays which students wrote in "blue books." The problem was that this approach assumed a specific curriculum which only a few elite preparatory schools followed. After World War I, during which a multiple-choice, general abilities model of testing Army recruits was developed, the College Board devised a new admissions test, the SAT, using a new multiple-choice format. Far more curriculum-neutral than the original College Boards, it allowed colleges to identify qualified students from high schools all across the nation no matter what the specific nature of the curriculum might be. In so doing, it greatly served the democratization of higher education based on academic merit by making it possible to identify qualified students from secondary institutions that were remote from, and unknown to, the top tier of colleges and universities.

The historical context of testing over the last century provides important insights into factors beyond the classroom doors that have influenced—and may yet influence—the evolution of testing and the aims it serves. At least four sets of factors have significantly shaped the design and implementation of testing:

- national security interests and the demands of wartime;
- changes in psychological theory and in the testing industry's technology;
- changes in organizational theory and practice in business;
- developments that have affected the "politics of knowledge."

External forces continue to influence how we think about testing, and must be addressed if testing innovations are to serve the goals of equity and excellence that we desire.

National security interests. Curious as it may seem at first blush, throughout this century national security interests and the demands of wartime have spurred waves of innovations in assessment. With the goal of sorting top talent for the common defense, large-scale, systematic testing of individual aptitudes and achievement levels first occurred in the United States under the pressure of World War I, with the famous Alpha-Beta tests administered to over a million recruits. This effort gave a tremendous boost to measurement psychologists, and while the test results did not inspire much enthusiasm within the Army, a corps of several hundred psychologists saw the possibilities for wider use. After the war, they promoted more systematic and more "scientific" tests, finding a receptive audience among educators. By 1920, some 200 colleges and universities were administering Army Alpha tests or similar instruments, especially for purposes of college admissions. To develop what became the SAT the College Board in 1924 chose a group of psychologists, including many like Robert Yerkes and Carl Brigham, who had played key roles in developing the Army tests. Two years later, over 8,000 students took the first SAT. While the enthusiasm for mental testing often overran the technical capacities of those early tests, and while much skepticism arose during the testing boom of the 1920s, the use of standardized testing took significant root in schools across the United States.

World War II provided another key boost in testing. The Air Force developed a whole series of special batteries for pilots, radio operators, range finders, and other military specialists. For more generalized ability testing, the Office of Strategic Services (OSS), the precursor of the CIA, developed a performance testing program for selecting spies that later inspired assessment methods for business executives.

World War II also forced retrenchment in school testing; the demands of the war were cited as the chief reason for dropping the essay-type exams the Board had offered for forty-one years. Owing to the need to provide more efficiently for the personnel needs of the armed forces, colleges sought to start first-year courses during the summer, requiring a faster turnaround time for reporting examination results than the essay format would allow. Wartime economies also encouraged cuts in the costs of the examinations. The multiple-choice SAT, along with the recently developed multiple-choice Achievement Tests, then became the norm for subsequent decades.

The Cold War, especially after the Korean War, provided its own impetus for better assessment techniques. In an era keen on human resource management, Henry Chauncey, president of Educational Testing Service, his friend James Conant, and others left little doubt that improved school testing and guidance formed the core of an efficient process for identifying the more accomplished students that was critical to the national interest. The number of students taking the SAT grew dramatically during this period, rising tenfold between 1951 and 1961. The Educational Testing Service (ETS), it should be noted, was founded in 1947 by the College Board, the Carnegie Foundation, and the American Council on Education in order to handle the increasingly complex and psychometrically technical aspects of preparing the SAT and the Achievement Tests and to oversee their actual administration. Over the past three and a half decades, ETS and the College Board have worked closely together with regard to the SAT and to other testing and financial aid programs as well.

In the post-Cold War era, uncertain as it currently is in geopolitical terms, we are told that the battlegrounds will be economic, and the shock troops will be well-trained workers. For the United States to prevail in an "economic conflict," all our human resources must be fully tapped. Whereas Sputnik fueled reforms in mathematics and science to compete against the Soviet Union, international economic competition inspired a new wave of reform, with generals marching forth from the business community, announcing that if we are to maintain economic security, we must improve our ability to develop all talents and assess them accordingly.

Advances in psychology and testing technology. More obvious forces influencing the evolution of testing are ongoing advances in psychological theory and in the testing industry's technology. Psychologists' work on intelligence and cognition theories has continuously informed changes in testing—from Galton's studies of heredity, to Binet's "mental level," to Thorndike's "connectionism" and scales, to Spearman and "factor analysis," to Cattell's fluid and crystallized intelligences, and to the more recent work in cognitive psychology by researchers such as McClelland, Resnick, Hunt, Sternberg, and Gardner. More recent advances in understanding cognitive functions have encouraged educators to develop assessments for these processes and to abandon the pedagogical assumptions of outdated learning theories. Assessment and instruction must reflect new understandings of how we process information and how we construct meaning.

Advances in testing technology inspired by the pressures of national security as well as by changes in psychological and psychometric theories have facilitated an ever larger number of test-takers and established a vast testing industry. Industry suppliers and educational psychologists frequently have cooperated in implementing testing innovations. For example, in 1928, the expense of hand scoring early tests prompted Columbia psychologist Ben Wood to urge ten corporations to develop a scoring machine. A response from Thomas Watson of IBM led to a lifelong association between Wood and Watson. An IBM tabulator later reduced the per-test scoring cost of the *Strong Vocational Interest Blank* from $5 to 40 cents, encouraging wider usage of the test. Recent advances in multimedia computer technology promise to facilitate broadened assessment methods, with the eager support of the computer industry.

Changes in business organization. Another influence on the development of education and testing has been the change in management theory and business organization, which has often reverberated through the administration of schools. In particular, shifting notions of productivity and efficiency have been used to justify the aims and uses of testing. Sensitive to their relatively low status in communities and faced with considerable managerial challenges, school administrators eagerly borrowed both ideology and terminology from the business community.

This appears to be a recurrent theme in schools from the scientific efficiency days of Frederick Taylor to the more recent PPBS (program planning and budgeting system) enthusiasm, to "flatter organizations," or the current total quality management (TQM) drive. The current emphasis on testing the *process* of schooling—consistent with the wide interest in quality management principles—clearly reflects business management's continuing influence. The uses of testing have been affected by this historical relationship for better and worse. Valuable assessment innovations born of dreams of efficiency have often fallen prey to our desire to sort human lives based on perceptions of their probable destinies, or to subordinate schooling's democratic promise to other, less enabling, economic interests.

The politics of knowledge. Finally, the past century has seen a number of developments in testing that have been affected by what has been called "the politics of knowledge." This phrase, coined by Ellen Condliffe Lagemann, refers to a set of questions including: What knowledge is authoritative? Who determines this? How does one gain access to this group? And how do the "experts" communicate with the non-experts? Part of the appeal of recent proposals for new forms of assessment has been their claim to facilitate wider educational reform. But if so, we then must ask, How will we produce authoritative knowledge about new kinds of assessment, and how will this affect the roles of both institutions and individual practitioners? Innovations such as performance assessment imply changes in how authoritative knowledge about testing is produced and distributed, and these changes need to be discussed and debated. Moreover, the challenge of maintaining standards in more variegated testing formats forces into consideration substantial changes in the politics of knowledge with regard to assessment, which need to be addressed directly and explicitly.

A brief historical comparison from the early years of the SAT may be illustrative. When the SAT was undergoing initial refinements and debate in the early 1920s, the original College Boards, the subject-matter essay tests, were still being given for purposes of admission. At the same time, a group of thirty "progressive schools" under the aegis of the Progressive Education Association began its Eight Year Study of student success in college as it related to admission testing procedures. On one level, these three simultaneous admissions approaches—the still-fledgling SAT, the traditional "boards," and the arrangements of a set of progressive schools with various colleges—represented three different assessment systems. On another level, each approach reflected a distinct politics of knowledge, that is, they reflected different answers to the questions of what knowledge was authoritative and who determined this knowledge. The original "boards" were largely created and graded by university professors, with a few high school teachers assisting, and were meant to assess student achievement in subject areas determined by the colleges. A group of progressive schools developed their own means of assessing student performance based on their own vision of education in which high school teachers carried out evaluations and submitted them to colleges that had agreed to participate. The SAT, developed to assess "aptitude," was both created and evaluated by teams of university-trained psychometricians. The choice of which assessment model to use involved implications far beyond the technical pluses and minuses of the specific testing techniques employed. It was based, rather, on which group mounted the best claim to "authoritative knowledge." The subsequent triumph of the SAT had to do not only with its utility and practicality, but also with how these issues related to the politics of knowledge were sorted out. Similar to the rise of the other professions in the United States around the beginning of the twentieth century, testing expertise was also seen as residing not primarily among teachers either at the secondary or postsecondary level, but rather among a central core of university-trained professionals, including psychometricians, who were acknowledged as possessing authentic knowledge of educational measurement. Thus, it was their right and responsibility to devise educational programs and instruments of assessment.

Narrower institutional politics may have also played a role. As late as the mid-1950s, College Board membership included 172 colleges and 24 associations but no high schools. Only during the late 1970s was a rough parity between schools and colleges established, a parity that became more evident in the late 1980s, when community colleges began to find a place within the Board as well. It is only natural that a university-dominated College Board would emphasize the predictive roles of testing over its potential to inform instruction.

Today, we see a shift in point of view. Current Board efforts to enhance assessment's instructional role, as in Pacesetter and the new SAT initiatives, reflect the Board's more balanced school-college membership and more collaborative organization. Not surprisingly, the Board has developed a new mission statement committing it to "educational excellence for all students . . . through the ongoing collaboration of schools, colleges, educational systems and organizations." The implications of this commitment for student preparation and assessment are far reaching.

Brief as it is, this historical reflection should help inform current debates about assessment. Any innovation in assessment must take into account the social, cultural, and institutional factors that will influence its implementation. If we value equity, we must face directly how these contextual forces are likely to affect the equitable distribution of educational outcomes. We must realize that any change in a factor so central as testing is not neutral with regard to purposes and ultimate aims. Technical adjustments to the assessment system do not answer the questions about why we are assessing what we are assessing, or who is determining the ends of testing. The premises from which a particular assessment develops may not be the purposes for which it is employed. Testing reforms in the past have not only been shaped by their designer's intentions; they have also been shaped by perceived national goals, economic interests, and institutional constituencies. Therefore, to assume that performance assessment in and of itself will spur the kinds of far-reaching changes in schooling that many claim for it is to ignore crucial lessons from our history as well as recent experience in practice.

Over the last century, we have seen the influence of a variety of exogenous factors such as national security interests and organizational changes in business on the aims and implementation of testing. Prudence urges us to consider such factors in the present and future as we evaluate the impact of proposed changes in assessment on the goals we hold for our children's education. It is in this spirit that the College Board eagerly pursues the promise of performance assessment in its Pacesetter and Transition 2000 initiative, while insisting through EQUITY 2000 on addressing the contexts that will shape the ends assessment serves.

Conclusion

The College Board's experience in addressing the admissions process—what Alden Thresher called the "great sorting"—reinforces the imperative that we must continue to confront the contextual and historical factors that have directly influenced testing. While the College Board's initial years concentrated on its subject-matter essay tests ("The College Boards") and later on the multiple-choice based SAT, in the post-World War II years the Board's involvement has expanded to include financial aid, academic enrichment, equity, and public policy initiatives all in the service of improving the transition from high school to college. The Board's current work with detracking through the Equity 2000 and Pacesetter projects illustrates the need to address the entire schooling system in the effort to enable all students to succeed. If we are truly serious about such goals as equitable educational outcomes, we must work together in addressing the social and educational factors, including test innovations, in the reality of today's environment.

Continuing immigration, the growing disparity in the distribution of wealth, international economic competition, and the search for a new international order echo worries expressed a century ago in a very different world. At that time, many people also called for the dramatic restructuring of schooling as the twentieth century approached. In 1894, the Committee of Ten attempted to indicate, among other goals, "the best methods of instruction" and "the best methods of testing the pupils' attainments therein."[9]

While the Committee's report received a great deal of attention at the time, its direct influence on schools appears to have declined dramatically by the early 1900s for a number of reasons worth recalling. One critique claims that the report "dodged the key educational questions" and "failed to deal with the crucial issues that affected the schools and would continue to affect them for decades."[10] These issues included the political control over schools, the changing student demographics, ethnic tensions, wide variations in school resources, racial discrimination, and the financial constraints on schools. The failure to address these wider contextual issues of schools may have guaranteed the report's early obsolescence. In the same way, unless educational reform today addresses the full range of issues, whatever solutions we propose will be obsolete as well.

If future generations are to judge us favorably on issues of equity and excellence, then we must confront the wider contextual issues that will shape educational outcomes of all youth. What we are confronting is a very difficult dialectic: the desire for education based on high standards and the equally strong need for equality of education for all. An overly stringent pull toward equality can result in a tragic tumbling of all to distressingly low levels of achievement. On the other hand, we know only too well that exclusive emphasis on high standards can result in devastatingly unequal opportunities for education because of tracking and other discriminatory practices.

In addition, we must decide to what degree assessments will serve instruction as opposed to selection or accountability. Can instruments designed for administrative purposes be adapted to pedagogical ones? What do we need to know as we follow the apparent trend toward more standards-driven and curriculum-based tests and away from the measurement of general reasoning skills? Can you tap cognitive skills more effectively via content-based tests? How will these changes interact with efforts toward national standards? And how will these changes be influenced by current national economic goals, varied business interests, the "politics of knowledge," and simple struggles over institutional "turf?"

No single innovation, whether in testing or in standard setting, will spawn the reforms equity demands, nor answer for us what purposes we have chosen for schooling. However, without a doubt, we must try to ensure that the future instruments for admission testing include the best of both multiple-choice and performance-based assessments. These new instruments must reflect high standards that can be meaningfully equated, draw heavily on new theories of cognition and new technologies, and be financially affordable. Only in this way can we be certain that *all* students in America really do have the same educational opportunity. Yet it is clear that we need to use different assessments for different purposes. Tests for purposes of accountability ought to be sample-based, as in the National Assessment of Educational Progress (NAEP), while tests for improved instruction can be designed for individual students and classrooms (for example, portfolios). Admissions tests or high-stakes tests for graduation can be complementary to both, but distinguished by high validity, reliability, and fairness. In short, admissions tests need predictive power.

Finally, equity and excellence demand a renewed collaborative effort among educational institutions across all levels, moving beyond simply greater inclusion of our national diversity and toward reimagining a wider public participation in education's purposes. Only then can we be sure our excellence will be equitable and our equity excellent. Equity, by way of rich and sustained collaboration among the members of the educational community, may be our only guarantee of excellence. As Jane Addams observed over ninety years ago:

We have learned to say that the good must be extended to all of society before it can be held secure by any one person or any one class; but we have not yet learned to add to that statement, that unless all men and all classes contributed to a good, we cannot even be sure that it is worth having.[11]

We wish to express our deepest appreciation to Alan Heaps for his support and outstanding collaboration throughout this project. Special thanks also go to Howard Everson and James Lichtenberg.

Notes

1. U.S. Congress, Office of Technology Assessment, *Testing in American Schools: Asking the Right Questions*, OTA-SET 519 (Washington, D.C.: U.S. Government Printing Office, 1992), p. 103.

2. B. Alden Thresher, "Frozen Assumptions in Admissions," in *College Admissions Policies for the 1970s*, edited by C. Vroman et al. Papers delivered at the colloquium on college admissions policies, Interlochen, Mich. (New York: College Entrance Examination Board, 1978), p. 11.

3. Edward L. Thorndike, "Measurement in Education," in *Intelligence Tests and Their Uses*, Twenty-first Yearbook of the National Society for the Study of Education, edited by Guy M. Whipple (Bloomington, Ill.: Public School Publishing Company, 1923), p. 9.

4. Advisory Panel on the Scholastic Aptitude Test Score Decline, *On Further Examination: Report of the Advisory Panel on the Scholastic Aptitude Test Score Decline* (New York: College Entrance Examination Board, 1977).

5. National Commission on Excellence in Education, *A Nation at Risk: The Imperative for Educational Reform* (Washington, D.C.: U.S. Department of Education, 1983).

6. Sol H. Pelavin and Michael Kane, *Changing the Odds: Factors Increasing Access to College* (New York: College Entrance Examination Board, 1990).

7. Daniel Koretz et al., *Can Portfolios Assess Student Performance and Influence Instruction? The 1991-92 Vermont Experience*, RP-259 (Santa Monica, Cal.: RAND, 1992); idem, *Interim Report: The Reliability of Vermont Portfolio Scores in the 1992-93 School Year*, RP-260 (Santa Monica, Cal.: RAND, 1994).

8. Stephen B. Dunbar, Daniel M. Koretz, and H. D. Hoover, "Quality Control in the Development and Use of Performance Assessments," *Applied Measurement in Education* 4, no. 4 (1991): 301.

9. National Education Association, *Report of the Committee of Ten on Secondary School Studies* (New York: American Book Company, 1894), p. 33.

10. Theodore Sizer, *Secondary Schools at the Turn of the Century* (New Haven, Conn.: Yale University Press, 1964), p. 144.

11. Ellen Condliffe Lagemann, ed., *Jane Addams on Education* (New York: Teachers College Press, 1985), p. 119.

CHAPTER XIV

The Evolution of the National Assessment of Educational Progress: Coherence with Best Practice

EDWARD H. HAERTEL AND INA V. S. MULLIS

From its inception in the late 1960s, the National Assessment of Educational Progress (NAEP) has been innovative. The scorable elements of NAEP assessments were initially referred to as "exercises" rather than items, in part because NAEP has always included tasks and activities that looked quite unlike typical objective test items, but also as a reflection of its measurement philosophy, in which NAEP is not seen as a test. Its goal has always been to show what children actually know or can do, not just to rank them relative to one another. Each assessment question or exercise is included because it represents some significant learning outcome, because it is important in its own right, not just for its contribution to a total score. Consistent with this philosophy, the designers of NAEP questions and tasks have adapted or invented a wide variety of exercise formats to measure the broadest possible range of learning outcomes, free from the usual test design criterion that, other things being equal, each item should have the highest possible correlation with the total score or with some external criterion to maximize reliability or criterion-related validity.

Alternatives to objective paper-and-pencil testing figure prominently in current proposals for educational reform. It is widely held that overreliance on multiple-choice and similar item formats has led to curricula and instructional methods that encourage learning isolated bits of information and mechanically applying isolated skills, at the expense of more complex reasoning and meaningful problem solving. The solution proposed by advocates of assessment reform is to create tests that we would want teachers to teach to. High-stakes tests, those that have significant consequences for schools, teachers, and students,

Edward H. Haertel is Professor of Education, School of Education, Stanford University. Ina V. S. Mullis is Research Professor in the School of Education at Boston College, where she is affiliated with the Center for the Study of Testing, Evaluation, and Educational Policy.

should comprise assessment activities that are also models of good instructional activities.

Thus, it is natural to turn to NAEP for ideas and examples of questions and performance tasks that could encourage teaching to more meaningful learning outcomes. In this chapter, we describe hands-on activities from NAEP assessments in various content areas, activities which we believe could serve as useful models for instructional activities, for the assessment activities individual teachers use in support of their own instruction, or perhaps for large-scale high-stakes assessment programs. However, these different contexts and purposes are not interchangeable. Before describing some NAEP performance tasks, we briefly consider some differences between the various contexts and purposes for which these tasks were created and for which they might be used.

Classroom Testing, High-Stakes Testing, and NAEP

A major distinction can be drawn between *classroom tests*, those which teachers create or choose for their own instructional purposes, and *externally mandated tests*, those controlled by some authority beyond the classroom and generally used to evaluate students, teachers, or schools. When significant rewards or sanctions are attached to the performance of students, schools, districts, or states, these are referred to as "high-stakes" tests. The categories of classroom versus externally mandated testing are essentially what Linn referred to as testing for instructional versus accountability purposes, what Cole called assessment for instruction versus assessment for measurement, and what Nitko referred to as internal versus external assessment.[1] Tests in these two categories can be quite dissimilar. They are designed to satisfy different criteria and are used for different purposes.

External tests must be carefully standardized so that scores earned in different times and places have the same meaning. They must be reliable enough to produce trustworthy results for individual students or at least for schools. In general, such tests have tried to minimize both student testing time and scoring costs. Because they are given at about the same time in classrooms with varying curricula, external tests cannot be closely tied to the immediately antecedent classroom activities. Instead, they tend to measure the cumulative effects of instruction over a year or more. The tests created by major publishers tend to cover material that is common to most school districts' curricula, avoiding idiosyncratic content in order to appeal to as broad a market as possible.

Classroom tests face quite different requirements. Standardization and reliability are relatively unimportant. The scores are used to evaluate the levels of attainment of individual students or to compare students within a single classroom, and the teacher can interpret them in the context of rich information about students' individual backgrounds and their performance on other tasks. Classroom assessments can employ a broader range of formats, including projects, written themes, speeches, or demonstrations. These kinds of assessments would take too long to administer and score in the context of most current large-scale testing programs. Perhaps most important, classroom tests are intimately connected to curriculum and instruction. A teacher's unit test generally covers just what has been taught in the days and weeks preceding.

Clearly, the context in which NAEP questions and performance tasks are used is more like that of externally mandated tests than classroom tests, but there are perhaps enough differences to place NAEP in a class by itself. The administrations of NAEP assessments are carefully standardized and except by chance cannot be closely related to the immediately preceding classroom instruction, but with the partial exception of the NAEP Trial State Assessments (TSAs), NAEP is not externally mandated and it is not high-stakes. No immediate consequences can ensue from an individual student's good or poor performance because the anonymity of participating students and schools is assured. Apart from the TSAs, NAEP scores are not even reported for geographic regions smaller than several states combined and never for districts or schools. Moreover, schools randomly chosen for NAEP testing may refuse to participate, although historically NAEP has enjoyed very high rates of cooperation.

In addition, NAEP exercises have used a broader range of formats and covered more content than any other assessment of comparable scope. Single tasks may take a half hour or longer to administer, and performance exercises of different kinds have been a part of NAEP almost since it began. National assessments have been conducted in art, music, and U.S. history as well as in the more heavily tested subjects, and the design of each exercise pool has begun with an exceptionally broad framework setting forth the learning objectives to be assessed, with no pressure to exclude material not everyone may have been exposed to. Moreover, once questions and performance tasks are developed, even those that do not correlate highly with some total score are retained unless they are technically flawed. Finally, although resources are always limited, NAEP has fielded many performance tasks that might be judged too expensive for most large-scale assessments. Not only has NAEP been well funded, but with matrix sampling, a given exercise is administered to only a fraction of the examinee sample, usually about 2,000 examinees nationwide. Thus, high costs for scoring substantial performance components are tolerable. In summary, NAEP assessments cannot be related to the immediately preceding instruction the way classroom tests can, but they are more innovative and more comprehensive than most externally mandated tests.

These differences among classroom testing, external high-stakes testing, and NAEP suggest two cautions in looking to NAEP exercises to guide assessment reform. First, NAEP exercises may be unsuitable for other large-scale testing programs because they are too expensive, because they do not correlate sufficiently well with some total score, or because the knowledge, skills, or dispositions they assess are outside the scope of other testing programs. The curricular goals and objectives that have guided the development of NAEP exercises will almost certainly not match those of any other assessment program exactly. Sound test design must begin with a conception of what is to be measured, not with a collection of assessment tasks.

Second, NAEP exercises are not likely to be good models for classroom instruction without some modification. Designers of performance assessment tasks often begin with a hands-on instructional activity, but the final product must be standardized, reliably scorable, and self-contained in the sense that nothing need be assumed about classroom activities in the days or weeks preceding the test administration. Whole-class discussion, cooperative learning, and other instructional features that complicate scoring or detract from the comparability of different students' scores can be problematic. Moreover, directly appropriating *any* assessment task as an instructional activity will change its meaning. In particular, testing higher-order thinking requires that there be something unfamiliar, something novel, about the assessment task—a requirement for transfer of learning from a familiar to an unfamiliar context. Simply teaching students to perform an assessment task will often fail to promote the abilities the task was designed to measure.

If these cautions are borne in mind, much may be learned from the rich history of performance assessment in NAEP. No NAEP exercises as they stand should be unthinkingly appropriated for either assessment or instructional purposes, but the formats and materials created for NAEP can serve as a rich source of inspiration for meaningful teaching and testing. In the remainder of this chapter, we describe some of the performance exercises used in NAEP assessments of art and music, writing, reading, mathematics, science, history, and geography.

NAEP Performance Assessments in Art and Music

Art and music are natural areas in which to use performance testing, and they were among the first in which NAEP made substantial use of performance-based exercise formats. A national assessment of musical achievement was conducted in 1972-73, and national assessments in art were conducted in 1974-75 and again in 1978-79. Each of these assessments included multiple-choice objective questions as well as performance tasks. In the 1990s, NAEP began working toward an even more ambitious arts assessment, including dance, music, theater, and visual arts.[2]

The performance tasks included in the art assessments conducted in the 1970s asked students at ages 9, 13, and 17 to produce pencil drawings intended to assess abilities such as fluent expression of visual ideas (e.g., sketching a design for a piece of art), production of works fulfilling intrinsic demands of space or shape (e.g., sketching a design for a friend's bedroom wall given a drawing of the wall which included a door), production of works with a particular mood or feeling (e.g., drawing an angry person), production of works with meaning based on the use of established or novel symbols (e.g., drawing a person running, showing motion), or production of works containing various visual conceptions (e.g., drawing four people seated one on each side of a table, as seen from the other end of the room). As with all NAEP assessments, a matrix-sampling design was used, so each individual student was presented only a fraction of the exercises. Some drawing tasks were used at all three grade levels and others were used only for the older students. In addition to the performance exercises, all students also answered questions about their experience with art in and out of school, their attitudes and values about art, and their knowledge of art history. The total testing time for each student was forty-five minutes, and the time limits for the various drawing tasks ranged from approximately five to nine minutes.[3]

Some lessons for contemporary performance testing may be taken from the NAEP experience with the art assessments. First, significant compromises were required in going from the bold, expansive set of measurement objectives and associated exercises favored by art educators to the more limited set of exercises actually administered. For the first art assessment, budgetary changes in 1973 forced the elimination of exercises that were to be individually administered, of exercises using media other than ordinary lead pencils and writing paper (e.g., paints, different papers, scissors, and models), and of stimulus materials using full color rather than black-and-white reproductions of works of art. The assessment actually fielded was certainly a landmark in art assessment in the United States, but fell far short of the original vision of its creators.[4] Second, the exercises could be scored reliably, but scoring was more costly and time-consuming than anticipated. Again due in part to budget limitations, the first report on the data collected in 1973-74 did not appear until 1977. High inter-rater reliabilities were reported for scoring elements of students' drawings,[5] and from the examples published in relevant NAEP reports, the scoring did seem to capture both global differences in the quality of students' drawings and differences with respect to the particular aspects each rating scale was designed to assess. It should be noted, however, that experience in a variety of content areas has shown that even though individual exercises may be scored reliably, students' patterns of performance across a variety of different exercises are often uneven and correlations among exercises are often low.[6] Because of the matrix-sampling design used in these early NAEP assessments, it would be very difficult to estimate the correlations among most pairs of performance tasks. For this reason, the critical question of how many performance tasks of this kind would be required to develop a reliable score for an individual student cannot be answered from the information provided. (Note, however, that the analyses presented in the NAEP reports are entirely adequate and appropriate for addressing most of the questions these assessments were designed to answer, which focused on different populations' performance patterns for separate exercises requiring different drawing skills. If these exercises were used in different contexts or for different purposes, then additional technical requirements would have to be addressed.)

In addition to 9-, 13-, and 17-year-olds, the music assessment also included a sample of young adults from 26 to 35 years of age. The performance portion of the assessment consisted of fifteen exercises, although again, no one individual responded to more than a few. All performance tasks were individually administered. Stimulus materials were played on an audio recorder and respondents' performances were audiotaped on a second recorder for later scoring. The tasks included singing familiar songs (for example, "America" either solo or along with a prerecorded choral group), repeating unfamiliar musical material (rhythmic or harmonic patterns of several bars), improvising (rhythmic accompaniment to jazz using bongo drums, sung melodic completion to a four-bar musical phrase, sung harmonic accompaniment to a four-bar phrase), performing from notation (both sight singing and instrumental or vocal performance of a short musical phrase), and performing a prepared piece (requested of all respondents who stated that they played a musical instrument).[7]

The music assessment may also hold some lessons for the development of new performance assessments. First, the results of the music performance tasks are much easier to describe, understand, and evaluate than are scores on typical objective tests. Criterion-referenced interpretations of tasks like singing "America" or repeating a given four-bar melodic pattern in three-quarter time need not rely on any esoteric standard-setting procedure. Reading the scoring criteria and the tables showing the proportions of performances at different proficiency levels is sufficient to get a good picture of the musical ability of the assessed groups. This is an advantage of well-designed performance tasks and activities that should carry over to other content areas. Second, performance was surprisingly poor. For example, only 2 percent of 9-year-olds, 4 percent of 13-year-olds, 7 percent of 17-year-olds and 9 percent of adults could sing a brief melodic line acceptably after hearing it once (no musical notation was provided for this exercise). One has to feel for the "eleven graduate students in music [who] scored the thousands of responses."[8] When new forms of assessment are introduced in any content area, performance is likely to be surprisingly poor until curriculum and instruction become aligned to them. Finally, the music assessment highlights a contrast between convergent and divergent production tasks. Most of the musical performance tasks, namely singing a familiar song, repeating unfamiliar musical material, and performing from notation, were *convergent*—they had a single correct answer. The remainder, namely improvising and performing a prepared piece, were *divergent*—the number of correct responses was virtually unlimited. Not surprisingly, scoring criteria were considerably more technical and more complex for divergent than for convergent exercises. Most of the content areas and purposes for performance testing today would seem to call for divergent exercises, but there may be some temptation to substitute convergent activities. Not only will they be easier to score, but it is also easier to teach students to follow a recipe or carry out a rehearsed performance than to respond in an original way to a problematic situation.

NAEP Performance Assessments in Writing

As in many state testing programs, NAEP has since its inception assessed students' writing using single-sitting assigned-topic exercises. Inasmuch as a brief essay written in response to an assigned prompt is a direct sample of the criterion performance (writing), assessments of this kind are performance tasks, by far the most pervasive kind of performance exercise used in external testing programs to date. Unfortunately, however, this type of writing assignment does not require students to consult with others, write and revise successive drafts, consult reference sources, or use other writing process strategies increasingly viewed as critical to skilled writing performance. Thus, beginning with a pilot study in 1990 and continuing with a more extensive data collection in 1992, NAEP has sought to extend the range of writing abilities examined. In addition to the kinds of writing prompts used in earlier years, NAEP has collected samples of the regular writing assignments completed by fourth and eighth grade students in their own classrooms.

In the 1990 Portfolio Study, nationally representative samples of about 2,000 students at each of grades 4 and 8 were asked, in collaboration with their teachers, to choose and submit one piece of writing that they considered representative of their best efforts.[9] Partly because of design constraints that precluded notifying the selected students and their teachers far enough in advance, the response rate was only a little over 50 percent, and so the samples of papers received could not be considered nationally representative. In 1992, procedures were changed so that students and teachers were notified in the fall that they would be included in the portfolio study the following spring, and the response rate exceeded 90 percent. For the 1992 data collection, students were to select three pieces of writing from their Language Arts or English class, giving special attention to writing developed using the process strategies referred to earlier. Students were also asked to write a letter explaining their selections, and teachers were asked to complete a questionnaire describing the processes that led to the students' work, time spent, strategies used, and other information.[10]

Despite the low return rate, the 1990 data provided rich information about the kinds of writing assignments fourth and eighth grade students were engaging in, including genres, audiences, types of writing activities, lengths of assignments, and processes and resources used. More than half of the papers at each grade level were classified as *informative* (51 percent at grade 4 and 59 percent at grade 8) and most of the remaining papers were classified as *narrative* (36 percent at grade 4 and 30 percent at grade 8). Persuasive writing, poems, letters, research reports, and skill sheets each accounted for 7 percent or fewer of the papers received.[11] Separate six-level scoring rubrics were developed for the narrative, informative, and persuasive pieces, and inter-rater reliabilities from .76 to .89 were attained for the different types of writing within grade levels. The "percent of adjacent agreement" (percent of papers classified at the same or adjacent levels by the two raters) ranged from 96 percent to 100 percent.[12] Thus, individual assignments could be scored quite accurately. However, the scores assigned to the portfolio pieces bore little relation to the scores the same students earned when they responded to the NAEP assigned prompts. Gentile reports the findings of a study using all of the students who submitted an informative piece and who also responded to an informative NAEP prompt. Scores were recorded into low (1, 2, or 3 for school-based writing; 1 or 2 for NAEP prompt) versus high (4, 5, or 6 for school-based writing; 3 or 4 for NAEP prompt) and phi coefficients were calculated for the resulting four-fold table. These correlations were .16 for fourth grade students and .06 for eighth graders. Once more, the message is clear: individual performance tasks can be scored accurately, but patterns of performance are likely to be highly variable from task to task.

One might hope that the explanation for these low correlations lies in the different abilities entailed in school-based versus NAEP writing, but even if somewhat different abilities are involved, one would expect those abilities to be rather highly intercorrelated. The correlations may also be low because the quality of the school-based writing depends heavily on teachers' instructional practices as well as students' abilities. Even though, over time, students exposed to better instruction should become better writers, the quality of the writing in response to NAEP prompts would reflect individual differences in the abilities students had developed over years of schooling, and not the quality of the classroom assignments they had been given. The 1992 data are much more informative, because it is possible to examine intercorrelations among different portfolio pieces as well as their correlations with scores on the NAEP writing sample.[13] Even if high intraclass correlations are obtained among portfolio entries, however, it will be important to examine the possibility that they are a function of variation among teachers as well as among students.

NAEP Performance Assessments in Reading

NAEP long ago moved beyond exclusive reliance on brief text passages and multiple-choice questions to measure reading comprehension. Since the early 1980s, reading assessments have included questions requiring written responses of moderate length, and in recent years the maximum length of reading passages has increased substantially. In addition, the 1992 National Assessment in reading featured several new kinds of performance exercises. These included exercises for eighth and twelfth grade students in the area of *reading to perform a task* as well as one special study in which a subsample of fourth grade students were interviewed individually (the Integrated Reading Performance Record, or IRPR) and another special study in which subsamples of eighth and twelfth grade students selected a story from a *NAEP Reader*, read it, and answered a series of questions. Reading to perform a task, the IRPR, and the NAEP Reader studies are described below.

The NAEP frameworks are developed for each content area through a consensus planning process involving curriculum and content specialists, educators, and policymakers. They specify the characteristics of each NAEP exercise pool, including both the objectives to be measured and the kinds of exercise formats to be used. Reading to perform a task is one of the three domains included in the framework for the 1992 National Assessment in reading, along with reading for literary experience and reading to be informed. Reading to perform a task involves reading schedules, directions, maps, forms, applications, or other instructions or reference materials with the intent of applying the information obtained, rather than simply understanding it.[14] In this part of the assessment, students work with separate documents—actual forms, brochures, schedules, catalogs, or miscellaneous "how-to" materials—and use them both to answer questions and to complete associated tasks. In addition to the usual questions about the interrater reliability of scoring for exercises of this kind and about the consistency of students' scores across exercises, these NAEP performance tasks should help to show whether distinct abilities are called for when students must actually fill in a form or carry out a task, as opposed to providing written answers to written questions. It could well be that students are in fact better at actually doing things than writing about them.

The Integrated Reading Performance Record (IRPR) was administered to about 2,000 fourth graders who also participated in the main 1992 reading assessment. These students were interviewed individually to assess their oral reading fluency and to collect information about their reading habits and the reading instruction they had received. During the main reading assessment, these students had all been asked to read one particular passage and provide written responses to some questions about it. As part of the interview, they were given the same story to review and then asked to answer the same questions orally. This should provide information about the extent to which measurements of reading comprehension that rely on students' written responses are influenced by their unwillingness or inability to provide extended written responses.

The NAEP Readers for grade 8 and for grade 12 are paperback anthologies, each containing seven stories of about 1,000 words each that have appeared in authentic young adult publications. The selections feature different cultures, sources, authors, and genres from mysteries to romance. Students are given fifty minutes to select a story, read it, and then answer a series of twelve questions about which story they chose and why, their reaction to it, and some questions about plot, character, theme, setting, and any personal relevance of the story to themselves. There are several ways in which allowing students to choose a story may reduce reliability. Student choice makes the overall task less standardized, introducing a random element. The stories may not be equally difficult, or the questions asked may not be equally applicable to all of them. The option of making comparisons only among students who chose the same story is unappealing because in principle it only permits generalization to the theoretically uninteresting population of students who meet the definition of the original sampling frame and who also, given the specific NAEP Reader, would select that particular story from among the seven provided. On the other hand, the NAEP Reader provides an opportunity for students to demonstrate selection skills and strategies of interest and importance in their own right, and could increase validity by improving students' motivation to read and respond. Students may feel more ownership and engagement in a literary experience over which they have greater control.

NAEP Performance Assessments in Mathematics

NAEP mathematics assessments have been incorporating more hands-on materials and activities with each assessment. Calculators were first provided in 1990 (four-function at grade 4 and scientific at grades 8 and 12), as were combination protractor-rulers. Also, a set of estimation exercises was included in the 1990 assessment, for which the administration was paced by audiotape to discourage students from defeating the purpose of the exercises by calculating exact answers. In addition to these features, the 1992 National Assessment in mathematics also incorporated some longer problem-solving tasks for which students were asked to explain their reasoning. A number of other constructed-response questions asked for explanations or for students to complete tables or various bar graphs or pictographs. For 1996, even more constructed response questions will be included, comprising about half the exercises and about two thirds of the total test administration time. Additional manipulables will also be incorporated, including spinners used in connection with exercises on probability. In a special study of students who are taking algebra (eighth grade) or who have had algebra III or beyond (twelfth grade), students will be encouraged to bring their own calculators, including graphing calculators. Otherwise, NAEP will supply a scientific calculator.

NAEP's extended response questions in mathematics, even those that do not use manipulables, are quite unlike traditional textbook problems. There are always several acceptable approaches to figuring out the correct answer, but these rarely include any of the routinized procedures likely to have been taught in mathematics classes. Students are often instructed specifically to draw a diagram showing the relation of specified elements of the problem. Whether or not a diagram is required, they are told:

This question requires you to show your work and explain your reasoning. You may use drawings, words, and numbers in your explanation. Your answer should be clear enough so that another person could read it and understand your thinking. It is important that you show *all* your work.

The evolution of the NAEP mathematics assessments over the past five years has been strongly influenced by the curriculum and evaluation standards published in 1989 by the National Council of Teachers of Mathematics (NCTM).[15] The NCTM standards include communication about mathematics as a valued learning outcome, support the use of calculators, and emphasize students' ability to notice mathematical patterns, reason mathematically, and explain their reasoning. All these features are reflected in the NAEP mathematics objectives and in the NAEP exercises. Nonetheless, in mathematics as in all content areas, the context, purposes, and resource constraints of the National Assessment limit the kinds of problems that can be included. Group work, extended investigations of mathematical problems over a period of days or weeks, and investigations in which the goal itself may be initially ill-defined are more difficult and time consuming to administer and have not been incorporated into NAEP as yet.

If one imagines a continuum from traditional textbook-driven mathematics teaching at one pole to the ideal set forth in the NCTM standards at the other, then it appears from responses to background questions included in NAEP itself, as well as other sources of evidence, that the NAEP questions and problem-solving tasks are somewhat closer to the NCTM ideal than is contemporary mathematics teaching in most classrooms.[16] In that sense, NAEP is currently leading instruction. If present classroom teaching and testing came to resemble NAEP more closely, many mathematics educators might see that as a move in the right direction. But if exercises like those now used in NAEP were to supplant the NCTM ideal, then before too long the assessment might be seen as impeding progress toward best practice. So long as NAEP is not a high-stakes test, the objectives and the exercise pools in mathematics and other content areas should continue to evolve, reflecting the best thinking of content specialists and continuing to lead toward better instruction. The experience of many testing programs suggests that if NAEP were to become a tool for accountability (high stakes), then pressures would probably arise to keep the exercise pool stable from year to year so that teachers would know what to expect and how to prepare their students,[17] and the assessment would be unlikely to remain at the cutting edge.

NAEP Performance Assessments in Science

Throughout the years, National Assessments in science have made limited use of hands-on activities, but 1996 will bring the first science assessment in which every participating student at all three grade levels will be asked to conduct a hands-on investigation. Under NAEP's matrix-sampled design, each student will take just one of several tasks used at the appropriate grade level. At grades 8 and 12, the examination time for at least some students will be extended from sixty minutes to ninety minutes to give them more time to plan and conduct their investigations and then report their findings.

"Scientific Investigation" is one of three broad process categories in the 1996 NAEP science framework, together with conceptual understanding and practical reasoning. Each of these areas is to be applied to content in the areas of earth, physical, and life sciences. Where possible, exercises are to integrate content from different areas, and some exercises will also deal with the nature of science or with the themes of models, systems, or patterns of change. The 1996 science framework calls for roughly 45 percent of testing time for fourth grade students and 30 percent for eighth and twelfth grade students to be devoted to scientific investigations, and sets high expectations for what these exercises are to cover. "Appropriate to their age and grade level, students should be able to *acquire* new information, *plan* appropriate investigations, *use* a variety of scientific tools, and *communicate* the results of their investigations."[18] The science framework also discusses the shortcomings of most contemporary hands-on science activities:

The following is typical of a performance exercise that is counterproductive: The exercise requires a student to identify several unknown substances by means of indicators; but the student is given minutely detailed directions for performing each step in the process of identification. Unfortunately, even if the answers are correct, the only inference to be drawn is that the student can follow written instructions. A test item formulated with such detailed step-by-step directions reduces to zero the science understanding needed for problem solving.[19]

The committee goes on to call for exercises in which students are free to determine the details of their experimental procedures, and in which problems are "placed in new contexts, applied to new situations, or have new elements introduced."[20] NAEP science investigations are largely successful in meeting these challenges. Each student assessed receives a self-contained disposable kit including everything required, even a bottle of water, if necessary. After the assessment, the participating schools may keep any materials they wish to (for example, magnets or stop watches) and the remaining materials are collected and recycled in an environmentally responsible way. Even at the fourth grade level, students must decide for themselves exactly how to use the equipment provided to carry out their investigation. A typical fourth-grade investigation gives detailed, step-by-step directions for using a strip of chemical test paper to determine the presence of a substance in a solution, but then asks students to solve a relevant problem without the benefit of any further detailed directions. A similar exercise at the eighth grade level might involve two different kinds of chemical tests that must be used in conjunction to solve a more complex problem. At the twelfth grade level, three or more tests or procedures might be involved, and the introductory instructions would be much less specific. As with other content areas, the best science teaching probably incorporates some kinds of problems and activities that are not feasible in the context of NAEP testing, including investigations over a longer period of time, group work, using more sophisticated equipment, or requiring students to formulate and research problems on their own. Nonetheless, the NAEP exercises probably go well beyond the kind of science instruction found in most classrooms.

NAEP Performance Assessments in History and Geography

In assessments of history and geography, separate materials and actual source documents are essential. The framework for geography discusses the various tools students should be able to use, primarily different kinds of maps, globes, atlases, and various computer-based resources for retrieving, analyzing, and displaying information.[21] Of these, different kinds of maps and sections of atlases were used in the 1994 National Assessment of geography. In history, hands-on activities will employ not only source documents, but also artifacts and materials through which students can understand and analyze the experiences of people in different times and places. Present plans call for the history assessment at the fourth and eighth grades to include an activity in which students work together in groups of five, each taking a different perspective on a common experience.

These most recent hands-on activities within NAEP highlight the importance of having topics, materials, formats, and even purposes for hands-on or performance-based assessment be specific to particular content areas. Across all school subjects, however, there have been rewards for asking what students might make or do to inform a broader array of intended learning outcomes. Answers have been embodied in a great diversity of assessments, but all of them measure knowledge and skills that would be difficult or impossible to test in more conventional ways; all of them, compared to traditional objective tests, seem more engaging to students; and all of them are more consonant with classroom practices promoting higher-order thinking.

Conclusion

The theme of this volume and the title of this chapter refer to "coherence with best practice." As this review has shown, there are fundamental limits to the coherence of *any* external testing program with the entire range of best practices in the classroom. The NAEP frameworks, especially in recent years, are clearly leading practice, extending the range of exercise types and formats ever used on such a scale, and pointing the way toward the kinds of instruction envisioned by leading content experts and curriculum specialists. At the same time, problems and projects that require more than an hour (or at most an hour and a half), that involve group work, or that require students to identify and use references or other resources on their own have yet to be incorporated to any significant extent. The 1992 writing portfolio may point the direction for assessments that can transcend even these limitations.[22] One could readily imagine assessment portfolios in mathematics, science, and other subjects, but as shown by the 1990 portfolio pilot study, the technical obstacles are formidable.

There is a tension in NAEP, especially evident in recent years, between assessing the achievement of learning objectives sought today and those set forth in frameworks and policy documents like the NCTM *Curriculum and Evaluation Standards for School Mathematics*, *Science for All Americans*, or *Becoming a Nation of Readers*.[23] As noted several times, students often do quite poorly on the more innovative NAEP activities. Measuring what they actually know and can do requires exercises that look more like the ones they are accustomed to seeing. Thus, if NAEP is to fulfill its statutory mandate to measure and chart the academic achievement of the nation's young people, it will probably always include some exercises that seem quite conventional, perhaps even outmoded. As it encompasses present practice and approaches best practice, NAEP points a direction, but it can only approach the ideal. Still, it should continue to evolve, staying ahead of current practice and pointing the way toward future developments in curriculum and instruction, as well as in assessment.

NOTES

1. Robert L. Linn, "Current Perspectives and Future Directions," in *Educational Measurement*, 3rd ed., edited by Robert L. Linn (New York: American Council on Education/Macmillan, 1989), pp. 1-10; Nancy S. Cole, "A Realist's Appraisal of the Prospects for Unifying Instruction and Assessment," in Educational Testing Service, *Assessment in the Service of Learning, Proceedings of the 1987 ETS Invitational Conference* (Princeton, N.J.: Educational Testing Service, 1988), pp. 103-117; A. J. Nitko, "Designing Tests That Are Integrated with Instruction," in *Educational Measurement*, 3rd ed., edited by Robert L. Linn, pp. 447-474.

2. The College Board, *Arts Education Assessment and Exercise Specifications*, Prepublication Edition, approved by the National Assessment Governing Board, March 5, 1994 (New York: The College Board, 1994).

3. National Assessment of Educational Progress (NAEP), *Design and Drawing Skills: Selected Results from the First National Assessment of Art*, Report no. 06-A-01 (Washington, D.C.: U.S. Government Printing Office, 1977); idem, *Art and Young Americans, 1974-79: Results from the Second National Art Assessment*, Report no. 10-A-01 (Washington, D.C.: U.S. Government Printing Office, 1981).

4. National Assessment of Educational Progress, *Design and Drawing Skills*, pp. 1-2.

5. National Assessment of Educational Progress, *Art and Young Americans*, 1974-79, pp. xiv-xv.

6. Stephen B. Dunbar, D. M. Koretz, and H. D. Hoover, "Quality Control in the Development and Use of Performance Assessments," *Applied Measurement in Education* 4 (1991): 28-303; Robert L. Linn, Eva L. Baker, and Stephen B. Dunbar, "Complex, Performance-based Assessment: Expectations and Validation Criteria," *Educational Researcher* 20, no. 8 (1991): 15-21; George F. Madaus, "The Influence of Testing on the Curriculum," in *Critical Issues in Curriculum*, edited by Laurel N. Tanner, Eighty-seventh Yearbook of the National Society for the Study of Education, Part 1 (Chicago: University of Chicago Press, 1988), pp. 83-121; Richard J. Shavelson, Gail P. Baxter, and Jerry Pine, "Performance Assessments: Political Rhetoric and Measurement Reality," *Educational Researcher* 21, no. 4 (1992): 22-27.

7. F. W. Rivas, *The First National Assessment of Musical Performance*, Report no. 03-MU-01 (Denver, Col.: Education Commission of the States, 1974).

8. Ibid., p. 1.

9. Claudia Gentile, *Exploring New Methods for Collecting Students' School-based Writing: NAEP's 1990 Portfolio Study* (Washington, D.C.: U.S. Government Printing Office, 1992), p. 5.

10. Claudia Gentile, personal communication, 10 December 1992.

11. Gentile, *Exploring New Methods for Collecting Students' School-based Writing*, p. 9.

12. Ibid., p. 24.

13. Arthur N. Applebee, Judith A. Langer, Ina V. S. Mullis, Andrew S. Latham, and Claudia A. Gentile, *NAEP 1992 Writing Report Card*, Report no. 23-W01 (Washington, D.C.: Office of Educational Research and Improvement, U.S. Department of Education, June 1994).

14. NAEP Reading Consensus Project, *Reading Framework for the 1992 National Assessment of Educational Progress* (Washington, D.C.: U.S. Government Printing Office, 1992), pp. 11-12.

15. National Council of Teachers of Mathematics (NCTM), Commission on Standards for School Mathematics, *Curriculum and Evaluation Standards for School Mathematics* (Reston, Va.: The Council, 1989).

16. Thomas A. Romberg and Thomas P. Carpenter, "Research on Teaching and Learning Mathematics: Two Disciplines of Scientific Inquiry," in *Handbook of Research on Teaching*, 3rd ed., edited by Merlin C. Wittrock (New York: Macmillan, 1986), pp. 850-873.

17. Madaus, "The Influence of Testing on the Curriculum."

18. NAEP Science Consensus Project, *Science Framework for the 1996 National Assessment of Educational Progress* (Washington, D.C.: U.S. Government Printing Office, forthcoming), p. 20. Emphasis in original.

19. Ibid., p. 31.

20. Ibid.

21. NAEP Geography Consensus Project. *Geography Framework for the 1994 National Assessment of Educational Progress* (Washington, D.C.: U.S. Government Printing Office, nd).

22. Claudia A. Gentile, James Martin-Rehrman, and John H. Kennedy, *Windows into the Classroom: NAEP's Writing Portfolio Study*, Report No. 23-FR-06 (Washington, D.C.: Office of Educational Research and Improvement, U.S. Department of Education, January, 1995).

23. National Council of Teachers of Mathematics, *Curriculum and Evaluation Standards for School Mathematics*; American Association for the Advancement of Science (AAAS), *Science for All Americans: A Project 2061 Report on Literacy Goals in Science, Mathematics, and Technology* (Washington, D.C.: AAAS, 1989); Richard C. Anderson, E. Hiebert, J. Scott, and I. A. G. Wilkinson, *Becoming a Nation of Readers: The Report of the Commission on Reading* (Champaign, Ill.: Center for the Study of Reading, 1985).

Questions for Further Study

Since its founding in 1901, the Society has had as one of its purposes the encouragement of the "study of education." Its publications are intended to provide a background as well as a stimulus for such study.

To give further emphasis to this purpose, the Board of Directors has requested editors of the two volumes of the 95th Yearbook to prepare some questions that individuals and study groups can use to guide further inquiry into issues raised by the books. Accordingly, the editors of this volume have suggested the following questions which they hope will encourage readers to probe more deeply into the important problems with which this volume deals.

1. All assessment systems are rooted in a particular view of intelligence. Is it fixed versus changeable, unidimensional versus multidimensional, linked versus unlinked to other characteristics like gender or ethnicity? What does your school community believe about intelligence? How do the assessments used in your schools reflect your community's conception of intelligence?

2. What would it mean for an assessment system truly to serve the ends of equity and excellence? How can assessments become a force in reducing the achievement gaps between groups? In establishing and maintaining high expectations for all students? In creating assessments that are consistent with best practices that are not as yet widespread? In providing feedback to schools to improve practice?

3. What do you regard as the essential features of curriculum-embedded assessments, i.e., assessments that are integral parts of learning units? What do you see as the essential features of on-demand assessments such as end-of-unit tests, standardized tests? How could each of these forms of assessment be used to help students improve their performance? To help teachers improve their curriculum and instruction? To help parents work with their children? To help the larger community understand how well their schools are succeeding?

What kinds of data would allow a school to check on the extent to which its assessment system was having the desired effects for each of these stakeholders?

4. What kinds of scoring systems and resulting scores are most useful for (1) students, teachers, and parents to help students improve

their work? (2) states and national testing programs to meet account-ability demands? Do you see ways in which scoring procedures could potentially serve both sets of needs.

5. How can the psychometric demands of validity and reliability be used productively by schools and states to improve their assess-ments and scoring systems. For instance, how can interrater agree-ment be used to clarify the goals of the assessment and communicate them to students, teachers, parents, and the broader community?

6. There is currently a serious discontinuity between most forms of high-stakes assessment (e.g., those used for decisions about college entrance and merit scholarship awards) and what are currently pro-posed by educational researchers and practitioners as the most pro-ductive forms of student assessment. How can we reconcile the demands for efficiency and low cost that are typically a part of high-stakes, large-scale assessment and the highest return on student learn-ing and instructional improvement that ensues from some of the newer forms of assessment?

7. If your state legislature wanted to promote greater accountabil-ity by implementing a high-stakes student assessment program within two years, what advice related to the advantages and disadvantages of high-stakes testing would you give to the legislators, particularly with respect to promoting "best practice" and concerns for equity?

8. What is the proper role of public debate in the development of new forms of assessment and standard setting? What strategies could be used to involve the public in the assessment process?

Name Index

Subject Index

Accelerated Schools Project, 112

Access, as characteristic of performance-based assessments, 167

Accountability: obstacles to establishing systems for, 117-20; school vs. student responsibility for, 119-20; self-generated vs. externally driven systems for, 118-19

Advanced Placement examinations, 106-8

Alpha Beta tests, during World War I, 278

American Association for the Advancement of Science, 86, 178

American Council on Education, 279

American Council of Teachers of Foreign Language (ACTFL), 174

A Nation at Risk, 5, 216, 274

Art, NAEP performance assessments in, 291-92

Assessment: conflicting purposes of, 263-64; critique of traditional approaches to, 32-34, 52; examples of new instruments for, 149, 151-53, 180-86; forces impacting development of, 274-80; growing interest in reform of, 54-56; importance attached to, in current educational reform, 35-36; relationship of, to curriculum and pedagogy, 126, 228-31; use of, to support learner-centered accountability, 58-59; "vision statement" regarding, in California, 149, 151

Assessment and accountability, Kentucky system of: external review of, 221-22; goals of, 213; origin of, 217; portfolios in relation to assessment in, 222; relationship of assessment to curriculum in, 228-231; studies of, 220-21; tension created in, by early decisions regarding accountability, 219-20

Assessment systems, strategies for improvement of, 67-68

Assessments, misuse of, 240

Authentic assessments: development of, as strategy for professional development and for restructuring, 61-74; Glaser's criteria for design and use of, 78-79; nature of, 54; policy considerations in use of, 75-76; potentials of, 52-53; use of, to support curriculum and teaching, 56. *See* Performance-based assessment.

Brown vs. Board of Education, 1, 5

California Assessment Program (CAP): changes needed in, 148; developments in, after 1983, 148-49; essential features of, 147-48; open system for assessment developed in, 154-55; replacement of, by California Learning Assessment System (CLAS), 155; teacher participation in development of, 153

California Learning Assessment System (CLAS): conflicts regarding, 157-59; establishment of, 155; lessons from recent history of, 160-64

Capacity, as characteristic of performance-based assessments, 168

Cardinal Principles of Secondary Education (NEA), 4

Center for Collaborative Education, 68, 75

Central Park East Secondary School (New York City), 61-63, 68, 70, 71-72, 74

Civil Rights Act (1964), Title VI of, 120-21

Coalition of Essential Schools, 26, 56, 68, 74, 112, 178

Coherence, as characteristic of performance-based assessments, 168

Coherence, in educational systems: content and performance standards as guides in creation of, 108-9; differing views on role of states in establishment of, 111-13; examples of, between assessments and curriculum, 106-7; factors involved in creation of, 107-8; nature of, 105; need for balance between state and local efforts to achieve, 114; need for flexibility for schools in planning for, 113; obstacles to achievement of, 114-22

College Board: Academic Preparation for College Series of, 264; changes made by, in the "new" Scholastic Assessment Test, 265-68; college admissions tests of ("the College Boards"), 277, 282; Equity 2000 project of, 268-70; establishment of, 277; expanding activity of, 283-84; membership of, 282; Pacesetter courses of, 270-72; Transition 2000, project of, 275-76

311

INFORMATION ABOUT MEMBERSHIP IN THE SOCIETY

Membership in the National Society for the Study of Education is open to all individuals who desire to receive its publications. Membership dues for 1996 are $30. All members receive both volumes of the current Yearbook.

For calendar year 1996 reduced dues are available for retired NSSE members and for full-time graduate students *in their first year of membership*. These reduced dues are $25.

Membership in the Society is for the calendar year. Dues are payable on or before January 1 of each year.

New members are required to pay an entrance fee of $1 in addition to the annual dues for the year in which they join.

Members of the Society include professors, researchers, graduate students, and administrators in colleges and universities; teachers, supervisors, curriculum specialists, and administrators in elementary and secondary schools; and a considerable number of persons not formally connected with educational institutions.

All members participate in the election of the Society's six-member Board of Directors, which is responsible for managing the affairs of the Society, including the authorization of volumes to appear in the series of Yearbooks. All members whose dues are paid for the current year are eligible for election to the Board of Directors.

Each year the Society arranges for meetings to be held in conjunction with the annual conferences of one or more of the major national educational organizations. All members are urged to attend these sessions at which the volumes of the current Yearbook are presented and critiqued. Members are also encouraged to submit proposals for future Yearbooks.

Members receive a 33 percent discount when purchasing past Yearbooks that are still in print from the Society's distributor, the University of Chicago Press.

Further information about the Society may be secured by writing to the Secretary-Treasurer, NSSE, 5835 Kimbark Avenue, Chicago, Illinois 60637.

RECENT PUBLICATIONS OF THE NATIONAL SOCIETY FOR THE STUDY OF EDUCATION

1. The Yearbooks

Ninety-fourth Yearbook (1995)
 Part 1. *Creating New Educational Communities.* Jeannie Oakes and Karen Hunter Quartz, editors. Cloth.
 Part 2. *Changing Populations/Changing Schools.* Erwin Flaxman and A. Harry Passow, editors. Cloth.

Ninety-third Yearbook (1994)
 Part 1. *Teacher Research and Educational Reform.* Sandra Hollingsworth and Hugh Sockett, editors. Cloth.
 Part 2. *Bloom's Taxonomy: A Forty-year Retrospective.* Lorin W. Anderson and Lauren A. Sosniak, editors. Cloth.

Ninety-second Yearbook (1993)
 Part 1. *Gender and Education.* Sari Knopp Biklen and Diane Pollard, editors. Cloth.
 Part 2. *Bilingual Education: Politics, Practice, and Research.* M. Beatriz Arias and Ursula Casanova, editors. Cloth.

Ninety-first Yearbook (1992)
 Part 1. *The Changing Contexts of Teaching.* Ann Lieberman, editor. Cloth.
 Part 2. *The Arts, Education, and Aesthetic Knowing.* Bennett Reimer and Ralph A. Smith, editors. Cloth.

Ninetieth Yearbook (1991)
 Part 1. *The Care and Education of America's Young Children: Obstacles and Opportunities.* Sharon L. Kagan, editor. Cloth.
 Part 2. *Evaluation and Education: At Quarter Century.* Milbrey W. McLaughlin and D. C. Phillips, editors. Paper.

Eighty-ninth Yearbook (1990)
 Part 1. *Textbooks and Schooling in the United States.* David L. Elliott and Arthur Woodward, editors. Cloth.
 Part 2. *Educational Leadership and Changing Contexts of Families, Communities, and Schools.* Brad Mitchell and Luvern L. Cunningham, editors. Paper.

Eighty-eighth Yearbook (1989)
 Part 1. *From Socrates to Software: The Teacher as Text and the Text as Teacher.* Philip W. Jackson and Sophie Haroutunian-Gordon, editors. Cloth.
 Part 2. *Schooling and Disability.* Douglas Biklen, Dianne Ferguson, and Alison Ford, editors. Cloth.

Eighty-seventh Yearbook (1988)
 Part 1. *Critical Issues in Curriculum.* Laurel N. Tanner, editor. Cloth.
 Part 2. *Cultural Literacy and the Idea of General Education.* Ian Westbury and Alan C. Purves, editors. Cloth.

Eighty-sixth Yearbook (1987)

Part 1. *The Ecology of School Renewal.* John I. Goodlad, editor. Paper.
Part 2. *Society as Educator in an Age of Transition.* Kenneth D. Benne and Steven Tozer, editors. Cloth.

Eighty-fifth Yearbook (1986)

Part 1. *Microcomputers and Education.* Jack A. Culbertson and Luvern L. Cunningham, editors. Cloth.
Part 2. *The Teaching of Writing.* Anthony R. Petrosky and David Bartholomae, editors. Paper.

Eighty-fourth Yearbook (1985)

Part 1. *Education in School and Nonschool Settings.* Mario D. Fantini and Robert Sinclair, editors. Cloth.
Part 2. *Learning and Teaching the Ways of Knowing.* Elliot Eisner, editor. Paper.

Eighty-third Yearbook (1984)

Part 1. *Becoming Readers in a Complex Society.* Alan C. Purves and Olive S. Niles, editors. Cloth.
Part 2. *The Humanities in Precollegiate Education.* Benjamin Ladner, editor. Paper.

Eighty-second Yearbook (1983)

Part 1. *Individual Differences and the Common Curriculum.* Gary D Fenstermacher and John I. Goodlad, editors. Paper.

Eighty-first Yearbook (1982)

Part 1. *Policy Making in Education.* Ann Lieberman and Milbrey W. McLaughlin, editors. Cloth.
Part 2. *Education and Work.* Harry F. Silberman, editor. Cloth.

Eightieth Yearbook (1981)

Part 1. *Philosophy and Education.* Jonas P. Soltis, editor. Cloth.
Part 2. *The Social Studies.* Howard D. Mehlinger and O. L. Davis, Jr., editors. Cloth.

Seventy-ninth Yearbook (1980)

Part 1. *Toward Adolescence: The Middle School Years.* Mauritz Johnson, editor. Paper.

Seventy-eighth Yearbook (1979)

Part 1. *The Gifted and the Talented: Their Education and Development.* A. Harry Passow, editor. Paper.
Part 2. *Classroom Management.* Daniel L. Duke, editor. Paper.

The above titles in the Society's Yearbook series may be ordered from the University of Chicago Press, Book Order Department, 11030 Langley Ave., Chicago, IL 60628. For a list of earlier titles in the yearbook series still available, write to the Secretary, NSSE, 5835 Kimbark Ave., Chicago, IL 60637.

2. The Series on Contemporary Educational Issues

This series has been discontinued.

The following volumes in the series may be ordered from the McCutchan Publishing Corporation, P.O. Box 774, Berkeley, CA 94702-0774. Phone: 510-841-8616; Fax: 510-841-7787.

Academic Work and Educational Excellence: Raising Student Productivity (1986). Edited by Tommy M. Tomlinson and Herbert J. Walberg.

Adapting Instruction to Student Differences (1985). Edited by Margaret C. Wang and Herbert J. Walberg.

Choice in Education (1990). Edited by William Lowe Boyd and Herbert J. Walberg.

Colleges of Education: Perspectives on Their Future (1985). Edited by Charles W. Case and William A. Matthes.

Contributing to Educational Change: Perspectives on Research and Practice (1988). Edited by Philip W. Jackson.

Educational Leadership and School Culture (1993). Edited by Marshall Sashkin and Herbert J. Walberg.

Effective School Leadership: Policy and Prospects (1987). Edited by John J. Lane and Herbert J. Walberg.

Effective Teaching: Current Research (1991). Edited by Hersholt C. Waxman and Herbert J. Walberg.

Improving Educational Standards and Productivity: The Research Basis for Policy (1982). Edited by Herbert J. Walberg.

Moral Development and Character Education (1989). Edited by Larry P. Nucci.

Motivating Students to Learn: Overcoming Barriers to High Achievement (1993). Edited by Tommy M. Tomlinson.

Radical Proposals for Educational Change (1994). Edited by Chester E. Finn, Jr. and Herbert J. Walberg.

Reaching Marginal Students: A Prime Concern for School Renewal (1987). Edited by Robert L. Sinclair and Ward Ghory.

Research on Teaching: Concepts, Findings, and Implications (1979). Edited by Penelope L. Peterson and Herbert J. Walberg.

Restructuring the Schools: Problems and Prospects (1992). Edited by John J. Lane and Edgar G. Epps.

Rethinking Policy for At-risk Students (1994). Edited by Kenneth K. Wong and Margaret C. Wang.

School Boards: Changing Local Control (1992). Edited by Patricia F. First and Herbert J. Walberg.

The two final volumes in this series were:

Improving Science Education (1995). Edited by Barry J. Fraser and Herbert J. Walberg.

Ferment in Education: A Look Abroad (1995). Edited by John J. Lane.

These two volumes may be ordered from the Book Order Department, University of Chicago Press, 11030 S. Langley Ave., Chicago, IL 60628. Phone: 312-669-2215; Fax: 312-660-2235.

DATE DUE